REBIRTH OF THE BLACKFEET NATION,
1912–1954

Rebirth of the Blackfeet Nation, 1912-1954

PAUL C. ROSIER

UNIVERSITY OF NEBRASKA PRESS

LINCOLN AND LONDON

First Nebraska paperback printing: 2004

Library of Congress Cataloging-in-Publication Data
Rosier, Paul C.
Rebirth of the Blackfeet Nation, 1912–1954 / Paul C. Rosier.
   p.   cm.
Includes bibliographical references and index.
ISBN 0-8032-3941-6 (cloth : alk. paper)
1. Blackfeet Indians—History.   2. Blackfeet Indian
Reservation (Mont.)—History.   I. Title.
E99.S54 R67   2001
978.6'52004973—dc21   00-061590

ISBN 978-0-8032-9004-4 (paper : alk. paper)

For Debra

CONTENTS

ILLUSTRATIONS

ACKNOWLEDGMENTS

I want to thank a large and diverse group of people who assisted me in the preparation of this book. The following library and archival staff facilitated my research efforts: Margaret Becket of the University of Rochester's Rush Rhees Library, historian Anna Bullshoe and cultural resource director Joyce Spoonhunter of the Blackfeet Community College, Richard Fusick of the National Archives in Washington DC, George Miles of Yale University's Beinecke Rare Book and Manuscript Library, and the staff of the Philadelphia Free Library's Government Documents collection; the interlibrary loan staff of the Free Library, Montana Historical Society, and Princeton University's Firestone Library proved efficient in obtaining important microfilm for me. Fellowships from the University of Rochester's College of Arts and Sciences and the Department of History enabled me to examine the Felix S. Cohen Papers at Yale University, tribal archives on the Blackfeet Reservation, and Bureau of Indian Affairs records at the National Archives. A Princeton University Visiting Library Fellowship enabled me to examine the Archives of the Association on American Indian Affairs in Princeton's Seeley G. Mudd Manuscript Library. I want to thank Ben Primer and Dan Linke of the Mudd Library and Alfred Bush of the Firestone Library for their assistance. The staff of the University of Nebraska Press steered the manuscript through the various stages of the publication process in a professional, timely, and friendly manner. In addition I want to thank Professor Donald Lee Fixico and an anonymous reader for the supportive comments and thoughtful suggestions they offered during the review stage. I appreciate the collective efforts of those involved in the project.

Blackfeet citizens Anna Bullshoe, Joyce Spoonhunter, Elouise Cobell, Vicky Santana, and Lorraine Owens shared their time and their invaluable perspective on Blackfeet history in stimulating interviews, as did Earl Old Person and Walter Wetzel, past chairmen of the Blackfeet

Tribal Business Council. I hope they appreciate this work as much as I appreciate their contributions to it. I want to especially thank Ms. Owens, the daughter of tribal leader Joseph Brown, for providing me with family documents and with photographs of tribal members and her father. Vicky Santana in particular shared with me her insights into Blackfeet political culture.

The late John Ewers graciously shared his firsthand knowledge of the Blackfeet, providing me with encouragement and support for my research agenda. He read drafts of early chapters and, despite his illness, offered timely feedback. I am very grateful to William Farr, professor of history at the University of Montana, who read early chapters and contributed photographs from his fine collection. William Fenton shared his personal observations of Blackfeet political life. Howard Gaare twice allowed me to take him back nearly fifty years to his tenure as an auditor of Blackfeet tribal finances, adding to my understanding of the tribe's financial operations. Participants of the 1997 Princeton University Graduate Paper Conference offered helpful feedback on a paper presented on the evolution of Blackfeet full-bloods' protest movement. Michael Walzer of the Institute for Advanced Study took time to discuss with me the peculiarities of American Indian democratic citizenship.

I offer special thanks to two friends, both of whom understood personally the joys and travails of writing a book. Dr. Henry J. Schwarz, professor of cultural studies at Georgetown University and a cultural historian of Bengal, shared with me during numerous lunches of korma, pho, and General Gau's chicken his views on postcolonial Bengali nationalism and the parallels with the Blackfeet's campaign of self-determination. Dr. Kevin Mattson, research director at Rutgers's Walt Whitman Center for Culture and Democracy, read drafts of chapters 5 and 6, offering keen insight into the issues of democratic decision-making.

Jarold Ramsey, Robert Westbrook, and Mary Young of the University of Rochester offered criticism and support of an early version of this work. Jerry's understanding of Native American culture helped me to consider different angles of investigation. Robb helped me to understand the nature of participatory democracy and the possible dimensions of the Blackfeet's sense of obligation to the cultural and political construct of the "tribe." Mary inspired me with her own balanced work on Native Americans. She has shaped my understanding of Indian-white relations as well as the fundamentals of good historical writing. Mary, Robb, Celia Applegate, Dan Borus, Ted Brown, Alice Conklin, Christopher Lasch, and Stewart Weaver all helped to make me a better historian. Their accessibility and their intelligence made my tenure at Rochester a productive one. Their fellowship made it an especially enjoyable one.

Portions of this book have been previously published. An earlier version of chapter 2 appeared as "'The Old System Is No Success': The Blackfeet Nation's Decision to Adopt the Indian Reorganization Act" in *American Indian Culture and Research Journal* 23, no. 1 (May 1999) and is published here by permission of the American Indian Studies Center, UCLA. © Regents of the University of California. Parts of chapters 5 and 6 were included in "The Real Indians Who Constitute the Real Tribe: Class, Ethnicity, and IRA Politics on the Blackfeet Reservation" in *Journal of American Ethnic History* (summer 1999).

Members of my family deserve recognition for seeing me through graduate school and assisting with the preparation of the book manuscript. My father, the late James Rosier, professor of English at the University of Pennsylvania, was my role model of the committed and compassionate academic. My mother, Kay Rosier, deserves special thanks for providing editing, babysitting, and encouragement. My two boys, Maxwell and Casey, made writing both a challenge and a joy, giving me time to reflect while goo-gooing, and time to write during their admittedly timely naps. And finally, my wife Debra offered unconditional support throughout the various stages of research and writing, putting up with my extended research trips and late night expeditions in search of clarity and misplaced commas. Without such support, the writing of this book would not have been a labor of love.

ABBREVIATIONS

BIA	Bureau of Indian Affairs
BIWA	Blackfeet Indian Welfare Association
BRCE	Blackfeet Repayment Cattle Enterprise
BTBC	Blackfeet Tribal Business Council
CCC-ID	Civilian Conservation Corps–Indian Division
CRP	Cattle Repayment Program
FYIP	Five Year Industrial Program
IRA	Indian Reorganization Act
NCAI	National Congress of American Indians
OIA	Office of Indian Affairs
PFLA	Piegan Farming and Livestock Association
RCF	Revolving Credit Fund
TMIP	Two Medicine Irrigation Project

REBIRTH OF THE BLACKFEET NATION,
1912–1954

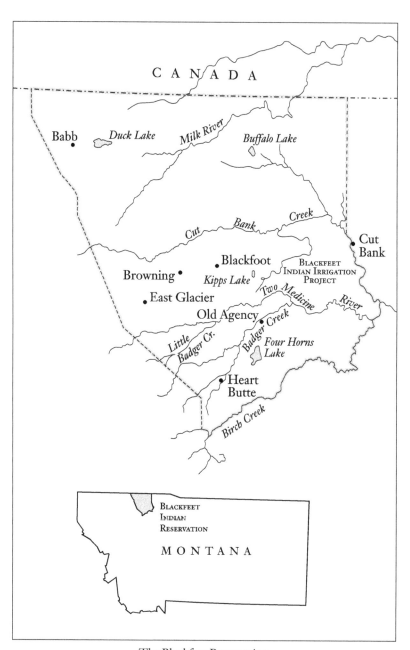

The Blackfeet Reservation

INTRODUCTION

We have every reason to believe that our tribe will develop into a self-supporting condition, if the natural resources upon this reservation are developed. – Robert Hamilton, Blackfeet leader, 1916

There is also need for a working reconciliation of the conflicts between traditional customs of [full-bloods] and the needs of modern living—a solution which should preserve their cultural integrity on the one hand, and hasten progress toward self-support on the other. – Freal McBride, Blackfeet Agency superintendent, 1943

"Termination," Philleo Nash writes, "is a bad word, a bad name, and an evil thought."[1] Earl Old Person, the long-standing chairman of the Blackfeet Nation, told attendees of the 1966 annual conference of the National Congress of American Indians that "in our Indian language the only translation for termination is to 'wipe out' or 'kill off.' We have no Indian words for termination. And there should be no English word for termination as it is applied to modern day terms regarding the relationship of the U.S. Government and the American Indian."[2] The idea of termination and even the word itself elicited similar responses among American Indians during the 1950s and 1960s and continues to do so today. I do not believe it is necessary to revise our understanding of how congressional subcommittees used the white ideology of termination and its legislative progeny as a cudgel to beat upon Indian sovereignty and create the animus that Old Person and Nash convey in such visceral terms. It is worthwhile, however, to consider termination from a new vantage point, specifically, to examine how Indian notions of "self-support" crystallized into Indian-initiated campaigns for the termination of government supervision that had failed for decades to provide Indian communities with coordinated economic programs appropriate to their cultural and climatological contexts. Termination also means the end of "Federal overlordship," as Harold Ickes, former secretary of the interior, called the government's control of Indian economic and political decision-making, and it represented the last stage of the Indian New Deal. Commissioner of Indian Affairs John Collier, the architect of the Indian New Deal, emphasized in his vision of a new Indian America the creation of self-governing Indian communities that eventually were to be given "complete supervision over [their] internal affairs."[3] I do not disagree with either Philleo Nash or Earl Old Person. Lost in the fallout of the termination era, however, is a recognition of the political and economic progress certain Indian nations had made and were striving to make to meet this goal of self-support. In a sense, termination rendered the notion of self-determination (its vernacular cousin) an anomaly in the 1940s and 1950s.

One of the general weaknesses of twentieth-century Native American historiography, and of Indian New Deal historiography in particular, is its failure to establish links between key periods of policy activity. Most studies of the Indian New Deal and of the Indian Reorganization Act (IRA) end with the resignation of John Collier in 1945.[4] Although this terminal point does provide a worthwhile framework in which to evaluate key New Deal economic programs such as the Revolving Credit Fund (RCF) and livestock distribution programs, it covers a period of less than ten years, given that most tribes did not begin to receive RCF monies until 1937. It also precludes a proper investigation of the IRA's political legacy on most reservations; the IRA to this day governs intratribal relations for many Indians. In addition, this framework fails to explore the impact of an important provision in eighty tribal charters of incorporation—the right to call for elections to terminate the supervisory powers of the secretary of the interior. As Donald Parman writes, "[p]erhaps the Indian New Deal defies generalization but must be studied reservation by reservation and even program by program."[5] This book is a modest attempt to bridge the gap that exists between studies of the Indian New Deal and the termination eras. It extends analysis of IRA political provisions and economic programs from 1945 to 1954, the high point of congressional efforts to terminate Indians' trust status and federal supervision of their economic and political relations.

This book is a political economic study of the Blackfeet Nation of northwestern Montana.[6] It is a tribal study and thus limited in scope. But good general histories depend upon good tribal histories—E Pluribus Unum—and most studies of tribes in the twentieth century have been of those that elected to reject the IRA.[7] Good case studies should help define more sharply the features of dominant government policies and Indians' cultural perception of and political response to those policies. This study examines the cultural attitudes, economic pressures, and social forces affecting the interrelations between a nascent sovereign entity called the Blackfeet Nation and the historically coercive Bureau of Indian Affairs (BIA), and it illuminates the problems that leaders of both groups faced as Indians struggled to define themselves politically and socially in the twentieth century. This book also tracks the evolution of the Blackfeet Tribal Business Council (BTBC) and its successes and failures on the reservation and in Washington in representing the tribe's efforts to construct a viable political economy. In 1928, after nearly fifteen years of intense factionalism, the BTBC emerged as the de facto political body of the Blackfeet. The BTBC had adopted a constitution and by-laws in 1922, but the BIA granted little authority to either the council or its constitution. The BTBC served as a formal pressure group that campaigned principally for higher grazing rates and increased federal support of its oil leasing program until the IRA invested it with real economic and political powers.

Indians entered the political mainstream in 1934, participating, in one sense, in a civil rights campaign to secure greater political and economic freedoms. This book is, on one level, a study of the evolution of the Blackfeet's efforts to "develop into a self-supporting condition," which the IRA facilitated by providing the tools of sovereignty and administration necessary for the successful operation of any political economy; it is as much about the *idea* of self-support, or self-termination, as it is about the actual development of Blackfeet institutions designed to implement it. It is not a study of the congressional termination movement of the 1950s; termination in that sense was a nonevent on the Blackfeet Reservation, though it certainly was not a nonissue. This book is, rather, a study of Blackfeet efforts to reorganize relations with the federal government on their terms and to construct an American community of their

own design. Accordingly, I place more emphasis on the Blackfeet's responses to federal policies than on federal policy itself, and more on intratribal relations than on Indian-white governmental relations.

The judgment of most historians is that the IRA, and the Indian New Deal
in general, failed to solve the problems of Indian America largely because
it was the product of white bureaucrats.[8] I do not suggest that this interpretation is entirely incorrect, only that the impact of the IRA on Native
American communities was too varied to justify sweeping statements
that deny Indians the acuity and the agency to adopt the legislation and
use intelligently its various provisions for political and economic change.
The case of the Blackfeet revises this prevailing notion of Indian passiv-
ity and white imposition; the decision-making process was more inter-
active than it was coercive. Certainly some Indians saw the IRA as the
panacea it could never be. Most Blackfeet considered the IRA to be a
flawed but flexible instrument for change during a time when such instruments were hard to find in northwestern Montana; the alternative of
stasis and continued white supervision held little appeal. During a 1944
hearing on the IRA, BTBC leader Richard Grant asked the congressmen
trying to repeal it, "Have you anything in mind that you are going to
present that will be better than [the IRA]?" The committee chairman answered, "I do not believe that anybody had thought through on the
matter and has figured out something to take its place."[9] After ten years,
congressional critics of the IRA could not answer Grant's question. Historians as well have yet to provide an answer. Although tribes such as the
Arapaho prospered without the IRA, the Blackfeet and other tribes that
lacked the Arapahos' stabilizing age-grade social system both embraced
the legislation and enjoyed economic and political progress by doing
so.[10] The IRA did not fail on the Blackfeet Reservation, even as it did fail
to achieve the goals promised and promoted by John Collier and his administration.[11] Indeed, the high standards that historians have applied to
the promise of the Collier era perpetuate an incomplete and somewhat
biased evaluation of its successes. The poverty that the 1928 Meriam Report chronicled in such painful detail clung tightly to the Blackfeet Nation, and to other Indian communities, as did the colonizing forces and
minions that helped to create it in the first place.[12] There would be no
quick fix for such poverty, especially in the inhospitable climate of the
Blackfeet Reservation.[13]

Part I examines the impetus of the Blackfeet Nation's decision to adopt the IRA and attempts to answer the first of two major questions: Why, given the historical and historiographical opposition to the IRA, did 83 percent of the Blackfeet electorate voting on October 27, 1934, brave winter weather to support it? My essential argument is that Collier's vision and the legislative form it took in the IRA mirrored the Blackfeet Nation's own ideas for reform, a mixture of wants and needs and assumptions about its past and its future that had formed during two decades of government supervision. The IRA's political and economic systems offered to the Blackfeet both political continuity and increased economic opportunity. In addition, I contend that the Blackfeet's active participation in the IRA debate influenced the outcome of the bill by helping important policy makers—such as John Collier and Sen. Burton Wheeler, who, as chairman of the powerful Senate Indian Affairs Committee, was both the act's cosponsor *and* its most vocal critic—understand the viability and desirability of its key provisions. The Blackfeet thus played a prominent role in the IRA debate as Collier's vision evolved into policy.

Part 2 attempts to answer a second major question: In what ways did the Blackfeet use the IRA and associated Indian New Deal policies to improve the reservation political economy and facilitate the self-termination of federal supervision? The average income for Blackfeet Reservation families in 1950 was $2,639, one of the highest averages among reservation groups and twice the Blackfeet figure in 1943.[14] This figure ($2,639) both demonstrates the IRA's success and masks the program's failure to ameliorate a great economic inequality that mirrored that of American society at large; wealthy Blackfeet ranchers and oil lessees lived in the reservation's exurbs while the tribe's poor huddled in the capital's "slums." At the same time, I argue, government and tribal credit programs facilitated the creation of an inchoate Blackfeet middle class by providing livestock, farm, and rehabilitation loans to Indians hungry for economic development. By 1950, 603 individual Blackfeet and four cooperatives had borrowed more than $1 million from the Revolving Credit Fund at affordable interest rates, paid back the money to a high degree, and prospered to an extent greater than was possible without such access to credit, the lifeblood of any business or individual enterprise.[15] The Indian New Deal and the IRA both expanded economic horizons and exacerbated political divisions on the reservation. Opposition to the IRA came mainly from full-blood Blackfeet, whose political power had declined due to demographic circumstances that in 1940 favored mixed-bloods by a ratio of five to one. While some younger full-bloods took advantage of IRA and tribal economic programs, an inability or a disinclination to change their ways impelled full-bloods to undertake a campaign to repeal the IRA and abolish the BTBC. Many full-blood elders misinterpreted the act's provisions or ascribed to it powers not codified in the Blackfeet's IRA constitution and charter. Charles Reevis, a leader of the full-blood group, told members of Congress in 1944 that "each year we just cannot understand [the IRA]. I want to get rid of [the IRA]"; he called it "a nuisance."[16] Full-bloods and other Blackfeet dissidents did have legitimate complaints about the IRA and the BTBC. The council's authority to expend tribal revenues under IRA provisions enlarged its role in the tribal economy, with mixed results; council members practiced favoritism, extravagance, poor judgment, and, in some cases, outright corruption. In addition, pressure from both mixed-bloods and full-bloods for per capita payments created political instability and retarded long-term investment, limiting the council's effectiveness as a vehicle for economic development. Members of the "minority group" ultimately mobilized politically to address the weaknesses of the BTBC and the structural flaws of the IRA constitution and charter of incorporation that the council exploited to maintain its power, exercising their right to challenge the council's efforts to terminate the supervisory powers of the Interior Department and to force the council to improve its accountability to Blackfeet voters. This study, then, is an examination of the Blackfeet's experience with democracy.

Joane Nagel writes in *American Indian Ethnic Renewal* that "American Indian identities and communities—tribal and supratribal—are constantly changing and evolving, responding to external threats and challenges as well as to incentives and opportunities."[17] A principal theme of this study focuses on the diplomatic efforts of Blackfeet politicians to harness IRA-based political reforms in their campaign for self-determination, to forge an Indian political identity by asserting their right to govern, associating with supratribal organizations, and staging spirited resistance to "external threats" posed by antidemocratic state intervention. A parallel theme concentrates on the degree to which leaders of the Blackfeet minority group, a *subtribal* group, responded to the *internal* threats of diminished group identity and economic marginalization by using the IRA's democratic tools to resist the attenuation of their social influence, challenge inequitable income distribution patterns, and fashion a syncretic Blackfeet political culture based on both traditional consensus-oriented decision-making and modern democratic decision-making, which rests upon the notion of majority rule. These two themes of the Blackfeet experience—self-determination and intratribal democratic reform—illustrate both the extent of Indian pursuit of sovereignty during the Indian New Deal and the limits of such pursuit.

The underlying theme of this work is the clash between the centripetal dynamics of Indian cultural life and the centrifugal dynamics of white economic life, what I call the agonistic tension between the tribal ideal and the assimilated ideal. Recent studies of the evolving nature of modern Indian political economies aid in understanding the Blackfeet's attempts to construct a political economy based upon cultural and economic conditions specific to their institutional environment. These studies evaluate the role of Indian political institutions as engines of economic development as well as the impact of both informal and formal "rules of the game" on the success and failure of that development. While focusing on the tension between informal and formal institutions, within reservations and between federal and tribal governments, these studies also consider the role of "individual sovereignty" in developing tribal economies, both that of the "egocentric individual who maximizes wealth" and that of the responsible tribal leader.[18] My review of the Blackfeet political economy emphasizes the institutional mechanisms of self-government, the impact of self-aggrandizing individuals, and the *culture* of the political economy—the historical, climatological, and social forces that influenced its development. The Blackfeet Nation was forced by changing demographic and economic conditions to consider the meaning and the value of its cultural heritage while debating its future in a representative democracy and market economy. The Blackfeet's efforts to fashion a modus vivendi, to balance the cultural dictates of long-standing customs and the logic of American democracy and twentieth-century agricultural capitalism, created a fluid political economic system and a protean demos and thus new considerations of ethnicity, class, and race that altered traditional conceptions of Indian identity and tribal obligation.

My examination of this theme of cultural disjunction benefits from the work of contemporary democratic theorists, in particular from Michael Walzer's discussion of political community. Democracy, Walzer contends, is "essentially a reflective system, mirroring the prevailing and emerging distribution of social goods. Democratic decision making will be shaped by the cultural conceptions that determine or underwrite the new monopolies."[19] The cultural conceptions governing the Blackfeet's post-IRA politics and the search for "distributive justice" contributed to an evolving discussion of the tribe's social community—who were the "real Indians" and what constituted the "real tribe"—on the reservation and in Washington. In the process of formalizing their opposition to the IRA and to a revolving group of political elites whom they believed had monopolized tribal decision-making and natural resource development, Blackfeet full-bloods forced tribal members and the Office of Indian Affairs (OIA) to reconsider their respective definitions of "Indian" and "tribe."

Native American factionalism in the twentieth century "usually pitted full-bloods against mixed-bloods and traditionalists against progressives."[20] Blackfeet factionalism followed these lines until the late 1930s, when issues of class, ethnicity, and race intersected. Demographic disadvantages both hardened the views of the full-blood minority group and forced it to expand its appeal to those Blackfeet less interested in the cultural dimensions of their dissent than in their shared angst about economic dislocation in a dynamic postwar market economy and the unstable climate of northwestern Montana. During the Indian New Deal, government officials and social scientists began to view Indian social groups as protean rather than composed strictly on the basis of blood quantum. Felix Cohen, an assistant solicitor in the Department of the Interior, argued that a group "referred to as 'full-blood' in reservation politics actually contains many mixed bloods. The lines of division are social and not simply biological."[21] Ethnohistorian John Ewers in 1944 included in the Blackfeet full-blood group "the great majority of those of a high degree of Indian Blood."[22] Blackfeet were either "Indian-oriented" or "White-oriented," to use anthropologist Malcolm McFee's sensible (though somewhat restrictive) dichotomy.[23] Race entered the Blackfeet political vocabulary when "social" full-bloods decried the presence of "white Indians"—white-oriented Blackfeet of low blood quantum—in tribal political and economic affairs.

The advent of successful oil leasing in the late 1930s engendered an incipient class consciousness that undermined cultural conceptions of Blackfeet ethnic identities. The IRA created new mechanisms for the distribution of tribal assets—specifically, revenue earned from the sale of tribal oil leases—and in the process created the need for new social and political mechanisms to sustain the tribal membership as a "family," as full-blood elders called the tribe. Pressure from marginalized Blackfeet, usually but not always Indian-oriented, forced the tribe to consider the social welfare needs of its poorer class and thus alter prevailing distribution patterns that typically favored economic programs for younger mixed-bloods and "white Indians." The story of the Blackfeet Nation during the first half of the twentieth century is its search for the ways and means of becoming self-supporting and self-determining and of its concomitant effort to reconstitute its political community to achieve that condition and "sustain [its] membership" as both a tribe in the nineteenth-century cultural sense and a municipal corporation in the twentieth-century political sense.[24]

It is difficult if not impossible for a white historian to provide an authentic Indian voice or perspective.[25] This study is *one* possible interpretation of the history of the Blackfeet Nation during its formative stages of modern political and economic development. It illustrates the internal as well as the external problems that the Blackfeet—and other Indian communities—faced in the twentieth century and provides a foundation for further inquiry of the Blackfeet's struggle for self-determination. Where appropriate, the Blackfeet speak for themselves. Their voices emerge from public meetings, the minutes of council sessions, congressional testimony, personal letters, petitions of protest, and newspaper editorials. In addition, past and current tribal leaders contributed their stories and their perspectives on Blackfeet political life in a series of interviews.[26] The book is, in the final analysis, the story of the Blackfeet finding their own voice, as citizens of a sovereign nation and as members of social groups that embraced both traditional and syncretic conceptions of Indian identity.

PART I

1912–1934

1. "THE OLD SYSTEM IS NO SUCCESS"

The Formation of the Modern Blackfeet
Reservation, 1912–1929

> If the condition of the Blackfeet Indians at this time is
> to be taken as an index of the character of trusteeship
> which the Government imposes upon other Indians,
> the work has been a failure. The spectacle is a de-
> pressing one and calls not only for immediate relief but
> for an entire and permanent change in the manner of
> handling their affairs. – Harry Lane, U.S. senator from
> Oregon, 1914

> The blame lies with the governmental supervision.
> – Robert Hamilton, Blackfeet leader, 1916

Glacier National Park, like much of northwestern Montana, used to be
Blackfeet Nation territory. A series of military defeats in the 1860s and
1870s led to a series of political defeats at the treaty table that left the
tribe with a land base of 1.5 million acres from which its people could try
to wrest a living. Blackfeet leaders ceded large chunks of the tribe's land
because their people were desperate for food, clothing, and cattle, which
Mountain Chief called the "second buffalo." Land cessions in 1887 and
1896 opened to settlement several million acres from which white immigrants could covet their Indian neighbors' remaining land. The land that
became Glacier National Park in 1910 had been a magnet for white prospectors who were convinced that its hills glittered with gold. They were
wrong, as it turned out. But the by-product of such greed was additional
pressure for Blackfeet land and the continued buildup of colonialism's
human infrastructure: traders, land speculators, missionaries, and government agents. The white invasion of the late nineteenth century produced a high rate of intermarriage between white men and full-blood
women—the likely result of the fur trade, gold fever, and the Great
Northern Railroad arriving in the wake of the tribe's "starvation winter"

of 1883–84. That disastrous winter killed nearly one of every four Black-feet and precipitated one of the most rapid demographic declines of full-blood Indians on the Great Plains. In 1885 only 18 mixed-bloods lived among roughly 2,000 full-bloods. In 1914, 1,189 full-bloods lived among 1,452 mixed-bloods.[1]

Scores of federal allotting agents began swarming like locusts through Indian country in 1887 after Congress passed the General Allotment Act. Their mission was to remake the physical domain and cultural character of the American Indian in the image of the yeoman farmer, who at that time happened to be waging an insurgency against the forces of industrial and agricultural capitalism.[2] Allotment came rel-atively late to the Blackfeet Nation. Pressure from a critical mass of new settlers and the slow bureaucratic progress of allotment policy imple-mentation finally reaching Montana prompted Congress to pass the act of March 1, 1907, which sanctioned the allotment of the reservation and the sale of the remaining land.[3] One of the most debilitating aspects of the 1887 act was the provision that allowed Congress to direct tribes to sell their "surplus" land to white homesteaders. Both the Office of Indian Affairs (OIA) and the Department of the Interior opposed the Act of 1907, principally because it did not protect the tribe's investment in irrigated surplus land located in the eastern Seville district; one OIA official called the act "an injustice to the Indians of the Blackfeet Reservation."[4] If the 156,000 acres designated as surplus had been sold as the act dictated, white homesteaders would have settled on land irrigated at tribal expense for a fraction of its estimated value.

The mandated sale of the 156,000 so-called surplus acres divided the tribe throughout the 1910s. Between 1913 and 1916, the critical years of early political development, open conflict between two factions was evi-dent both on the reservation and during congressional hearings held to determine the fate of the Blackfeet land base. Class politics and attendant conceptions of land use emerged as the tribe debated the best way to utilize the reservation's resources, from which it hoped to become self-supporting. A predominantly mixed-blood group pushing the dissolu-tion of the tribal estate waged a bitter struggle with a group intent on keeping the reservation intact for the benefit of the tribe. Both groups jockeyed for political legitimacy on the reservation and in Washington, hoping to assume leadership of a community of Indians facing an uncer-tain future in the post-allotment age.

Factionalism was not a new phenomenon. But the emergence of a large mixed-blood population, the advent of natural resource development, and the attendant promise of wealth created new forms of stress, as the tribe—a cultural institution and a mechanism of social control—faced internal and external forces of coercive assimilation intent on attenuating its power to act politically.

The Blackfeet's intense factional struggle precipitated a February 1914 hearing by the Joint Commission of the Congress on reservation conditions and the administration of Blackfeet agency superintendent Arthur E. McFatridge. The hearing and the investigations that followed revealed a tribe facing class, ethnic, and racial divisions; hungry full-bloods clashed with prosperous mixed-bloods and local whites over the future of the reservation and its resources. They also exposed a crisis of political authority on the reservation. Leaders of both factions claimed that they were the legitimate representatives of Blackfeet citizens.[5] The star witness of the hearing was Robert J. Hamilton Sr., a mixed-blood graduate of Carlisle Indian School. Hamilton, married to a full-blood woman, had worked as an agency interpreter before initiating a campaign to give the tribe a voice in the management of its political and economic affairs. He emerged during the hearing as the leader of a predominantly full-blood faction eager to expose agency corruption and anxious about protecting the tribe's land base. In the process, Hamilton earned the enmity of wealthy stockowners—white and both mixed-blood and full-blood—intent on expanding their domination of the reservation economy.

Hamilton testified that Superintendent McFatridge and his associates were trying to discredit him in the hope that Congress would ignore his story of agency corruption and class warfare. He asserted that McFatridge harassed and arrested Indians willing to testify against him and tried to prevent "independent" Indians like himself from traveling to the hearing. His litany of complaints against McFatridge included showing favoritism to white bootleggers, lessees, and merchants. Exhibiting numerous letters from aggrieved Blackfeet to support his claims, Hamilton contended that the tribe's guardian agent "is more certain to collect from the Indians than he is to collect from the white men who are trespassers. In fact, it looks as though the white man, in many instances, was the beneficiary of the reservation rather than the Indian."[6] He also testified that dozens of Blackfeet of all ages, mostly full-bloods, were dying of starvation or disease from lack of nourishment. Many of the wealthier full-bloods were selling their cattle and horses to help feed their starving neighbors, as the custom of the "give-away" dictated, leaving themselves with little sustenance during the harsh winters. Trachoma and tuberculosis, combined with insufficient rations, were killing both young and old full-bloods, particularly in the Heart Butte and Old Agency districts, where most of the tribe's full-bloods lived in cramped, poorly ventilated quarters; most mixed-bloods and whites lived east of Browning or in the town itself.[7]

Hamilton also voiced his opposition to the proposed sale of surplus land, which lay roughly twenty-five miles east of Browning in the Seville district; the district included an experimental farm and land irrigated at tribal expense, though few Blackfeet used the irrigated plots. Since 1913, Hamilton and the tribal members he represented had been actively campaigning against the sale, which he argued was sought mostly by McFatridge and a group of opportunistic Blackfeet allied with white ranchers and merchants. Hamilton introduced a petition signed by "a majority of the members of the Blackfeet Indian Tribe" that contended that "various chambers of commerce and commercial bodies of certain towns near the reservation have, and are bringing pressure to bear on the department, as well as the Montana delegation in Washington, to open the Blackfeet Reservation to settlement at as early a date as possible."[8]

Petitioners rightly complained that the Act of 1907 had been imposed upon the Blackfeet Tribe rather than produced through treaty or diplomatic negotiations. They also asserted that tribal lands were better suited for grazing than for homesteading or farming, and thus the sale of land for settlement would lure unknowing citizens recruited by "selfish" railroad corporations.[9] The petition requested that the surplus lands remain in tribal possession for ten years, during which time the value of the land would rise enough to allow the tribe to reimburse the government for irrigation projects undertaken by the Bureau of Reclamation.[10] The petitioners were not seeking to repeal the allotment of the reservation; indeed, they asked for the "early approval of our allotments." They did, however, "insist that our consent be first obtained before any lands are again arbitrarily taken from us."[11] If the Blackfeet were again to sell valuable sections of their reservation, then Hamilton's faction wanted the sale to be on its terms. Hamilton in particular understood that the intense interest in the land indicated that its value would increase dramatically over the following ten years. He argued both that the surplus land should be "held intact" for livestock cultivation to benefit the tribe and "the State," and that the land contained deposits of coal, oil, and other minerals that belonged to the Blackfeet Tribe of Indians.[12]

Hamilton's opponents were successful stock raisers principally concerned with the related activities of undermining Hamilton's credibility and lobbying for the sale of the surplus land; Hamilton described Malcolm Clark, Charles Buck, and James Perrine, members of the Browning Stock Growers' Association, as part of "the favored class enjoying privileges not enjoyed by other members of the tribe."[13] The document Clark submitted to the Joint Commission of the Congress to justify his presence in Washington reveals a great deal about the "McFatridge faction" (as Hamilton called it) and its agenda. The document stated that during a February 1914 meeting organized by McFatridge, tribal members unanimously supported the land sale and elected a delegation to "confer with a committee selected by the various commercial associations and the chambers of commerce in the towns near the reservation, and, if authorized, to visit Washington for the purpose of taking this matter up in the interest of the tribe."[14] McFatridge falsely stated that most full-bloods supported the mixed-blood delegation.[15] With the exception of Wolf Tail and a small group of successful full-blood ranchers, the majority of the full-blood population of the reservation stood firmly behind Robert Hamilton. Besides exposing the power vacuum that existed on the reservation and the protean nature of tribal authority, the document reveals the degree and the methods of collusion between mixed-bloods and whites. It leaves one with the distinct impression that Clark and his associates were lobbying for the "various commercial associations and the chambers of commerce" that supported the "opening to settlement" of 156,000 acres of prime Blackfeet real estate. Clark submitted five letters from such associations, all of which supported the "vote" of the McFatridge faction; their similar content and style suggests an organized campaign. Several of them opined that it would be "tragic" to open the "entire" reservation to settlement, offering instead that the opening of just the eastern part of the reservation would, as the Valier Commercial Club put it, "best further the interest of the Blackfeet." Their gesture to limit the acreage opened to settlement looked magnanimous compared to those of some white organizations that wanted every available Blackfeet acre sold to settlers.[16]

The Joint Commission of Congress became aware that Clark, Buck, and Perrine were major stockowners who had little regard for most Blackfeet and even most whites. Exhibiting the kind of class consciousness that marked his testimony, Clark expressed his faction's concern that the land sale would attract "poverty-stricken white people," telling members of the commission: "You know what a country is that is full of that class of people."[17] Clark admitted that the 156,000 acres contained the "best of our reservation." Commission members expressed surprise that Clark and his associates were willing to sell such good land, much of it irrigated at tribal expense. Clark explained that they hoped to purchase cattle for the tribe with the sale's proceeds, asserting that stock raising was the panacea for the tribe's problems. James Perrine also earned the commission's enmity by defending McFatridge's conduct and for suggesting that the government buy cattle with the monies and "give the competent Indian his share" while establishing a "communal herd" for those "not competent," implying that full-bloods would not get an allotment of cattle but would somehow profit from a tribal herd.

It is instructive to point out that Buck and Perrine were one-quarter Blackfeet and were two of the three largest stockowners on the reservation. Buck owned more than one thousand head of cattle, or more than 10 percent of the reservation's cattle; Perrine owned the majority of the sheep. Sen. Charles E. Townsend asked Clark, "You and two or three other gentlemen who have been very successful out there . . . would get the larger part of the benefit, would you not, under those circumstances?" Clark maintained that he and his supporters believed that their plan was best for "the Indians."[18] Commission members heard the testimony of Robert Hamilton and that of a wealthy elite and found the testimony of the former more compelling than that of the latter; they did not accept Clark's argument that their "minds [had] been poisoned" by Hamilton's testimony.

Hamilton's concern for the full-bloods' welfare and the tribe's future, buttressed by dozens of affidavits and letters in support of his mission, and the self-interest of Clark, Perrine, and Buck, confirmed in their testimony and in their choice of supporting documents, prompted investigations of reservation conditions in late 1914 by Sen. Harry Lane of Oregon and E. B. Linnen, the oIA's chief inspector.[19] Lane reported to the Joint Commission to Investigate Indian Affairs that "[i]t is well authenticated and can be established beyond a question of doubt to any fairminded person that starvation is the primary though indirect cause of many deaths among [full-bloods]." Some full-bloods told Lane that they were being starved as a way to force them to sell their allotments to mixed-bloods and whites. Lane found evidence that "thrifty part-blood

Indians were defrauding the full-blood Indians in many ways, such as underpaying them for use of their allotments, infringing upon the community lands, etc."[20] Full-bloods, Lane discovered, had no effective way to communicate their plight. Most of those he met could not speak or understand English, and their children were being denied adequate education to remedy this linguistic gap. Lane did manage to allow new voices to be heard when he tried to determine the "disposition" of the tribe to sell more land. He asked the roughly three hundred Blackfeet gathered to discuss the land sale who among them supported it. Lane counted eight supporters. The surplus land was, Lane contended, "the most valuable . . . and could be made the basis for the self-support of many of the Blackfeet Indians for a long time to come if properly and wisely managed with that sole object in view." Lane, highlighting the central issue of Blackfeet surplus lands, argued that "because [the Blackfeet] do not use them their nonuse is used as an argument to secure the consent of Congress to sell them to white people."[21]

Lane concluded from his survey of the reservation that "the affairs of large numbers, if not nearly all, of the full bloods and their children are left at the mercy of the more shrewd half bloods or the whites, or both acting in conjunction, with results that are deplorable. They are . . . deprived of any remedy for their relief and have been left to rot through the incompetence or willful neglect of those in charge of them and their affairs."[22] Robert Hamilton could not have offered harsher criticism. Lane also confirmed Hamilton's contention that McFatridge and his allies intimidated potential witnesses from talking with visiting investigators such as himself; Lane had to warn police not to interfere with the official business of the U.S. Congress. "Right foxy and well able to care for themselves are the gentry who are responsible for the gross mismanagement of the Blackfeet and other Indians," he wrote.[23] Lane's report thus vindicated Robert Hamilton, who had taken on the thankless task of exposing the abuses of the Blackfeet agency and its alliance with a clique of "foxy" mixed-bloods and whites.

Linnen came to a different conclusion after interviewing five prosperous mixed-bloods (including Charles Buck and Malcolm Clark) and six of the most successful white traders and ranchers in the region. In an obvious attempt to smear Hamilton, each interviewee accused him of horse theft, attempted rape, or failure to pay debts, and thus Linnen concluded that "Robert Hamilton is not worthy of serious consideration or belief."[24] But the congressional commission refused to accept this judgment. Chairman Joe T. Robinson ended the February 11, 1915, session by ordering the deletion of the section of Linnen's report "relating to Robert Hamilton's personal conduct." Hamilton had told the commission, Robinson said, "a story of suffering on the part of these Indians that was almost indescribable. A number of others appeared at the same time and disputed his statements; they said that the Indians were in good condition. A year has gone by and those conditions have continued practically until the present time."[25] The commission did not care to consider Hamilton's "alleged personal misconduct," partly because it was irrelevant to the nature of the hearings and partly because the parties making the charges against Hamilton had no credibility with members of the commission. Senator Lane ended the hearing with a dramatic reading of a letter sent by a Blackfeet agency physician, who wrote in part: "These Blackfeet Indians consist of two kinds—rich half blood and poor full bloods. There is only a handful of the rich or well-to-do men, while the main body of these people are poor. Let us get it right—many are slowly starving. . . . These poor fellows are trying to make Congress understand their condition."[26] Hamilton, with Lane's support, had certainly gotten Congress's attention. As a result, he emerged from the hearings with his credibility in Washington intact and the legitimacy of his political leadership among many of the Blackfeet assured.

In 1915 Robert Hamilton became the leading voice of Blackfeet full-bloods and the leading enemy of the prosperous clique of predominantly mixed-blooded ranchers and white traders who supported the land sale to expand their private domains and increase the scope of their markets through white settlement. Leaders of this faction lost their credibility in Congress and their chief ally McFatridge, who was fired by Commissioner of Indian Affairs Cato Sells on Linnen's recommendation.[27] Battle lines and class lines were sharply drawn as a result of the public testimony of faction leaders. This entrenched factionalization exposed the reservation's inchoate political structure and its lack of mechanisms by which these competing groups could engage in debate and dialogue about the future of the tribal estate as a political community rather than as a collection of self-interested individuals with varying degrees of loyalty to the *idea* of tribe and Indianness.

Hamilton's performance in Congress had solidified his influence with full-bloods as well as with those mixed-bloods disinclined to support the agenda of a small number of wealthy stockowners; most full-bloods

viewed McFatridge's dismissal as an example of Robert Hamilton's ability to represent the tribe's voiceless members.[28] Issues of class, ethnicity,
and race intersected to define the internecine struggle between assimilated and tribal ideals of economic organization. Fifty of the fifty-six
owners of more than one hundred head of stock on the reservation were
either mixed-blood or white. Although the pending land sale clearly divided the tribe along ethnic and racial lines, the principal cause of dissension stemmed largely from a class division of stockowners and non-
stockowners. Roughly 2 percent of the tribe owned more than 85 percent
of the livestock, according to Thomas Ferris, a livestock supervisor.[29]
Wolf Tail, the full-blooded former president of the tribe's General
Council and the owner of perhaps the largest horse herd on the reservation, offered his support to the faction that sought the sale of land as a way
to expand its control of the stock industry. Buck, the faction's leader, was
"one of the most successful mixed bloods," according to new superintendent Charles Ellis.[30] Buck's success breeding Black Angus cattle inspired
additional cattle purchases on the reservation, a development that he no
doubt encouraged. He also owed the tribal treasury $579.17 in grazing
taxes, which were levied against Indians owning more than one hundred
head of livestock. Ferris argued that the grazing tax "is in the interest of
the full-bloods who have practically nothing and will hit some of our
lighter brothers a little hard, but it is a case of bread for the full-blood
or gasoline for the breed and white man."[31] The grazing tax was both a
source of contention for large stockowners and a source of revenue
for the tribe. Here again, conflict arose over the meaning of obligation to
the *tribe*. The grazing tax was thus of particular concern to those who had
some wealth; the Blackfeet "give-away" tradition dictated that they
share that wealth with those less fortunate or successful. With such customs and their attendant function of social control attenuated by a declining full-blood demographic presence on the reservation, Hamilton
sought to use the newly formed Blackfeet Tribal Business Council (BTBC)
to counter the stockowners' further aggrandizement of economic power
and influence at the tribe's expense. On December 13, 1915, the BTBC
elected to reject the proposed sale of surplus land by a vote of eight to one,
a decision that triggered a new round of politicization and conflict.[32]

The BTBC formed during a meeting of the General Council held on
September 16 and 17, 1915, replacing the Tribal Business Committee,
which in 1913 comprised two full-bloods and three mixed-bloods, including James Perrine and Richard Sanderville. Hamilton became the de

facto leader of the Blackfeet Nation when he was elected BTBC president.[33] Several Blackfeet immediately protested his presence on the council. In a letter to the secretary of the interior, Richard Sanderville called the new council a "one man council controlled by Hamilton who is the worst enemy these people ever had."[34] Sanderville and Charles Buck, another aggrieved protestant, believed that Hamilton had gained control of the business council improperly, profited from enlarging the tribal rolls, and intended to use the council to prevent the sale of surplus land. Ellis defended the election process, reporting to Sells that though "there is no doubt that the faction to which Hamilton belongs and which he largely controls, dominates the council and controls tribal matters in general," he did not believe that Hamilton used "underhand methods" to gain access to and control of the business council. He also noted to Sells that his survey of tribal members showed little support for the surplus land sale.[35] Hamilton defended himself in a letter to Sells, explaining that agency regulations complicated the process of tribal enrollment and that he alone was willing and able to facilitate that process at no charge or for fees considerably less than those charged by white lawyers; he performed this service because Blackfeet were "disgusted and discouraged" by agency inaction.[36] For many Blackfeet, Hamilton was their superintendent.

Representatives of both the Hamilton and Buck factions traveled to Washington to lobby Congress as it considered S. B. 793—introduced by Thomas Walsh, a U.S. senator from Montana—which would have amended the Act of 1907 by authorizing the sale of Blackfeet surplus lands. BTBC members, who did not trust Walsh, reaffirmed their opposition to the land sale and elected Hamilton, Curley Bear, Bird Rattler, Wolf Plume, and Oliver Sanderville to travel to Washington to fight Walsh's amendment.[37] Commissioner Sells subsequently sanctioned the election of three delegates to present an opposing view. Sells assiduously pressed for the sale of surplus Indian land as a faithful implementation of allotment laws, and his support of the mixed-blood faction was consistent with that agenda; Sells had told his agency superintendents in 1914, "I hold it to be an economic and social crime, in this age and under modern conditions, to permit thousands of acres of fertile land belonging to the Indians and capable of great industrial development to lie in unproductive idleness."[38] During the "Meeting of Those Opposed to Hamilton Delegation," mixed-blood leaders argued that a full-blood should be included in the delegation to demonstrate that "mixed bloods as well as full-blood are represented"—more of a ploy to mitigate the effects of Hamilton's predominantly full-blood delegation than a true expression of the faction's social composition.[39] Malcolm Clark, Richard Sanderville, and Mountain Chief (a Christian full-blood and a former vice president of the General Council) were elected to the delegation; John Galbraith and Charles Devereaux, two of the tribe's wealthiest mixed-bloods, were permitted to accompany the delegation at their own expense.

Walsh was most interested in protecting the interests of Blackfeet mixed-bloods and his white constituency. He had demonstrated his lack of interest in the details of Blackfeet destitution during a Senate hearing held two months earlier. During a discussion of the dilapidated nature of Blackfeet housing, Walsh steered the discussion toward the land sale, depicting it as the best way to generate the monies needed to improve reservation conditions. He also tried to convince his colleagues that his interest in the matter did not extend to Montana's white citizenry. In a rambling speech, Walsh told the committee, "I have no interest or concern in the projects of opening this eastern end of the reservation. There is no demand for it whatever from the white citizens of Montana of any consequence." The issue, he continued, was "of no particular interest or concern to the white people of Montana. It is a matter of no particular concern to me. . . . I am quite indifferent, except for the interest I have in the Indians."[40] Walsh had little or no interest in helping the Blackfeet, with the exception of acculturated mixed-bloods like Buck and Charles Simon, who later asked Walsh to help him take control of the BTBC. "If this is done," Simon baldly stated, "it will get R. J. Hamilton out of the way. Our former agent Ellis was instructed to do this, but was in sympathy with Hamilton and never acted on it."[41] During this hearing, Senator Lane and Sen. Carroll Page of Vermont contested Walsh's claim that the Blackfeet as a tribe would benefit from the land sale. Lane argued that land values were rising so rapidly in Oregon that it made sense for the Blackfeet to hold the land until it brought a higher price per acre. Walsh did admit that "the land values are going up in [Montana], and the immigration in the last couple of years has been very large." He also agreed with Sen. Paul Husting of Wisconsin that leasing of Blackfeet lands would be a good idea. "There is always a big demand for every acre there is there," he told the Wisconsin senator.[42] Walsh neglected to argue these points two months later, during the hearing on S.B. 793—the Walsh Bill. He also opposed taking a cap off appraised acreage prices, which would have opened the lands to the highest bidder, stating that it was a matter of public policy to keep the bidding within the reach of people who were not wealthy. Senator Page pointed out that the rich would still be able to enter a lottery drawing and argued that Walsh's policy thus discriminated against the Blackfeet without guaranteeing that poor homesteaders would get a chance to settle on surplus lands. He asked Walsh, "Is there any reason now why the Indians should not be permitted to realize as much for their lands there? He is poor; he is needy; he is starving. Why should not that property be conserved for his benefit and sold to the man who will pay the most into the Indian treasury?" Walsh could only repeat his specious argument that the sale represented sound public policy.[43]

The debate during the April 1916 hearing on the Walsh Bill and Interior's version of it centered on this issue of long-term economic progress versus short-term needs. Senator Lane argued for the retention of Blackfeet lands so that the tribe could generate income from leasing while retaining the option of selling it when land prices rose. Senator Page supported Lane's view, asking, "are we not acting for 10 or 20 years when we ought to look forward 50 or 100 years to the time when these Indians will want these lands, and let them be rented to piece them along, with the hope that some time they will become farmers?"[44] The Blackfeet, however, were in a financial bind. They were carrying a $1 million debt load generated by the unwanted and unwarranted irrigation projects forced on them by the Bureau of Reclamation. Because of the tribe's debt, its lack of consistent employment opportunities, and its unwillingness to make extensive use of arable land, the short-term strategy to alleviate poverty and expand a viable livestock industry—supported by a powerful triumvirate comprising the Indian Office, the Montana congressional delegation, and a coalition of Blackfeet and their white allies—seemed destined to prevail.

Malcolm Clark, who two years earlier had opposed the immigration of a class of "poverty-stricken white people" to reservation lands, addressed the committee and repeated his contention that the sale of the land would put Blackfeet families "on the road to wealth" by creating a fund for cattle purchases. At the time, Clark admitted, only about twenty full-blood households were supporting themselves from their cattle herds. Clark was overly optimistic when he claimed that a tribal herd purchased from the proceeds of the land sale would make the Blackfeet "almost assuredly self-supporting within a few years." The proceeds, according to Clark, would provide four head per person, or twenty per average family. But it would take roughly one hundred head of cattle to "make them self-supporting," he said. Nevertheless, he argued that leasing the land would only give the Blackfeet "time to starve to death" as they waited for leasing revenues to reach the point of sale revenues.[45] Clark's proposition was a tenuous one, given the harsh Blackfeet winters, the propensity of full-bloods to kill their cattle for food during those winter months, and the "gentry's" record of exploiting full-bloods under such circumstances. As Inspector Linnen put it, "when the Government has issued cattle to these Blackfeet Indians, the majority of same quite speedily passed into the hands of certain educated half and quarter bloods, who have gotten rich by taking advantage of their full blood brothers."[46]

In contrast to Clark's one-dimensional and one-sided proposal for economic development, Hamilton offered the committee a comprehensive plan that combined Indian land tenure and the leasing of what *the tribe* considered to be surplus land to white agricultural and industrial interests. Hamilton had said in 1914 that whites derived more benefit from the reservation than the Blackfeet did. His agenda was to reverse this condition: to make the Blackfeet the "beneficiary of the reservation." The Blackfeet have been suffering, he said, "while the lands lie idle. . . . Lands have been sought by persons willing to pay for the use of them. The development of mines, the development of beet raising, and grazing would give many Indians employment who cannot now get anything to do." These developers, Hamilton said, were waiting for Congress to resolve the surplus land question before investing in reservation resources. The Blackfeet were ready to work. "The blame lies with the governmental supervision," he said.[47] Hamilton gave the committee a brief history lesson on Blackfeet culture, and in the process he attempted to define which Blackfeet groups the legislation should benefit. Change was occurring too rapidly for most Blackfeet, he said; they needed time to make the transition from communal to individual ownership. Hamilton explained that Blackfeet full-bloods

> are of the old Indian system. They only know of property as held in the Indian custom, the family property held by the wife and mother, and the lands in common by the tribe. The change to the modern idea of civilized property ownership, titles, mortgages, loans, taxes, sales, leases, and foreclosures, are not known to them and cannot be taught to them in a few days, weeks, or months of an allotment period wherein the change is made. The change as to them should be a matter of development. . . . As soon as the realization is ac-

quired of the value of agricultural effort, and of cattle raising, the individual ambition will assert itself and there will be many who will make a start on their own account.

Hamilton argued that Congress could ensure the tribe's future by preserving the reservation's boundaries, facilitating the development of its natural resources, and encouraging the creation of community farming efforts so that the tribe could retain "the only property we have on the face of the earth" for "the coming generation."[48]

Hamilton eloquently stated his position, citing numerous legal decisions and the U.S. Constitution to buttress his argument. Hamilton was more persuasive than Malcolm Clark, providing both a logical plan for reservation development and an impelling argument for the protection of the tribe's full-bloods. But he was fighting a strong opponent in Thomas Walsh, who succeeded in undermining Hamilton's claim to represent the tribe's interests by questioning the legitimacy of Blackfeet political organization. The OIA may not have felt compelled to adopt the BTBC's recommendations, but officials appeared to recognize its right to act as a political unit serving the interests of the Blackfeet people; the reservation superintendent usually requested council meetings, attended them, and submitted the transcripts to the commissioner. Walsh, despite Hamilton's protests, described the political process as chaotic and lacking authority.

> I do not know of any council on the Blackfeet Indian Reservation that is authorized to do anything or speak for anybody. . . . The Government . . . is the guardian of the Indians because they are assumed to be incompetent to handle their own affairs. Now, it is a very proper thing for us to try to ascertain what their views about these matters are, but so far as being guided or governed by it is concerned, it is contrary to the theory upon which we act at all, and I do not think any good purpose would be subserved in taking the views of the individual Indians on the reservation touching this question.[49]

Even if Walsh had recognized the legitimacy of Blackfeet political councils, he would not have been influenced by them because he believed that most Indians were "incompetent"—especially those who disagreed with his legislation. Indian consent, for men like Walsh, did not figure into the legislative calculus. Assistant Commissioner Edgar B. Meritt failed to utter a word in defense of the putative Blackfeet democracy. Walsh and Meritt had no interest hearing any argument that treated the Blackfeet

Tribe as a political entity. The Senate debate, for all practical purposes, had concluded.

Although Congress had again ignored the matter of tribal consent, the Senate and the Department of the Interior did recognize the tribe's ownership of its mineral resources. Walsh eventually favored Interior's version of his bill, which granted the tribe control of its oil, gas, and coal reserves, including any found on the surplus land. Hamilton and Walsh thus reached common ground on an important aspect of the legislation. The two Blackfeet factions also reached common ground on most aspects of the department's bill. Buck's faction had requested the protection of tribal mineral rights as well, though only Hamilton assiduously pressed the issue in the hearings and in tribal petitions. Both sides agreed that a ban on liquor should extend to new homesites and townsites within Blackfeet territory and that newborn children also should receive allotments. The sale of surplus lands remained the sole issue dividing the tribe. When the hearings resumed on April 15, Hamilton conceded defeat. After reiterating the Blackfeet's widespread opposition to the sale of any tribal land, he explained that "in consideration of the need of our people and the appropriation of $750,000 to be immediately available for cattle and relief, together with the protection and privileges provided by the department bill . . . we have concluded it will be better for the tribe to accept said bill."[50] The Blackfeet tribe, the Senate, and the Department of the Interior thus reached a joint agreement on the matter of Blackfeet land allotment. The acrimonious debate that had dominated tribal affairs for three years appeared to have concluded when the modified Walsh Bill passed the Senate on July 19, 1916. But its House counterpart, the Evans Bill (H.R. 14732), did not pass. Representatives agreed only to a $150,000 appropriation and rejected the provision that extended allotments to newborn children.[51] Hamilton refused to accept the 1916 House revisions and resumed his campaign to get an acceptable bill passed.

Congress finally resolved the matter three years later when it passed the Act of June 30, 1919. The legislation included many of the recommendations contained in the 1916 Interior Department compromise bill, but it did not mandate the sale of the surplus land.[52] As a result, enrolled Blackfeet received an additional eighty-acre allotment. Although the land could no longer be used for economic development in toto, the tribe retained the land and the mineral rights to the reservation. After a long struggle against an "iron triangle" of interests, to use Theodore

Lowi's phrase, Robert Hamilton's persistent campaign to preserve the territorial integrity of the Blackfeet Reservation and to protect the interests of its Indian denizens succeeded.

After the 1916 Senate hearings ended in April, the BTBC, emboldened by the pending legislation that promised the protection of the tribe's mineral rights, began to press an agenda for economic development that it hoped would make the Blackfeet Tribe self-supporting. During its May 20 meeting, attended by roughly one hundred Blackfeet, the council discussed for the first time leasing tribal lands to oil companies. Hamilton had received two proposals, one from Standard Oil and one from E. B. Cockrell of Baltimore. Cockrell warned that he would not conduct business with the council until Congress consented to such leasing. The council sent to the Senate a "Memorial and Petition" asking it to "expedite the early developements [sic] of the gas, oil, and all mineral resources within the said Blackfeet Reservation," complaining that it lacked "adequate authority" to negotiate the kind of leases requested by Standard Oil and Cockrell.[53] Hamilton attempted to secure that authority shortly after the meeting by outlining to Secretary of the Interior Franklin K. Lane his vision for Blackfeet natural resource development. He told Lane that because most Blackfeet "are now approaching the active stage of transition from a tribal or communal state to one of individual ownership of a part of the common property and the assumption of full citizenship, we also realize that the stage of civilization we are about to assume requires all our business to go through a certain judicial permeability. . . . We have every reason to believe that our tribe will develope [sic] into a self-supporting condition, if the natural resources upon this reservation, are developed."[54] Hamilton requested special legislation allowing the Blackfeet to secure legal counsel to support the tribe's plan for development that would "accrue millions of dollars to our tribe." Hamilton wanted to develop tribal oil reserves but intended initially to supply a blanket lease to a company like Standard Oil. He asked the OIA for permission to lease more than forty-eight hundred acres, the limit specified in department regulations. E. B. Meritt simply explained to Hamilton that regulations prohibited such leases.[55] The council received neither the authority to hire an attorney nor dispensation to sign a blanket lease. The OIA seemed satisfied that mining regulations passed in 1891 adequately served the Blackfeet Tribe's interests. Regardless of whether a blanket lease would have advanced the Blackfeet's interests, the OIA's perfunctory dismissal of Hamilton's requests for aid served to underline the disjunction between the Blackfeet's interest in oil leasing and the distant bureau's lack of it.

Tribal dissension did not disappear after the joint agreement of 1916. Hamilton's aggressive campaign to develop the tribe's mineral resources prompted the Buck faction to initiate a new campaign to attack his authority and his agenda. Charles Simon wrote several letters to Sells asking if the OIA intended to endorse Hamilton's plan, fearing that a blanket lease would jeopardize the sale of the surplus acreage. Simon concluded one letter by writing, "You, Yourself [*sic*] know that if oil in a commercial quantity should be found on our reservation that their [*sic*] is not influence enough in your city to prevent the opening of our Reservation to exploitation by the large Corporations."[56]

Simon and other mixed-bloods opposed to Hamilton feared that large corporations would not only exploit the tribe but would become an economic presence on the reservation. The Buck faction objected to any outside influences entering the reservation—be it congressional investigators, OIA supervisors, or corporate interests—because they might challenge *its* "exploitation" of the tribal economy. Simon organized a campaign to secure the OIA's authorization for a new council election. Leaders of the Buck faction sent to Sells a petition, signed by eighty-two mixed-bloods and eighteen full-bloods, that claimed that the existing BTBC comprised "extremely biased and incapable" men who "should be replaced at this time."[57] The petitioners were hoping to exploit the frustrations of the Indian Office, which Hamilton had been criticizing since 1913. Clark later told Sells, "I must state that the sooner Mr. Hamilton is eliminated from or is curtailed in his domination over the Tribal council, the sooner your office will rid itself of the opposition which has embarrassed it of late. Also, the sooner you replace Mr. Ellis with a man of some backbone, the better your office will controll [*sic*] the Blackfeet."[58] Ellis responded by telling Sells that he was sorry to report that "the factional fight began again, and at present is as bad as ever. In my opinion, no matter how many gatherings we have for the purpose of electing tribal council, the losing faction will impugn the motives and honesty of the election." All the elections, he claimed, were widely advertised and fairly managed.[59]

Although the OIA declined to order a new election, the smear campaign waged against Ellis resulted in his replacement in the spring of 1917, which demonstrated the OIA's support of the Buck faction and its assimilationist agenda of individual economic enterprise. The Hamilton faction and the business council it controlled ran into OIA restrictions, disinterest, and a pervasive prejudice against tribal economic autonomy. Hamilton intended that tribal members would gradually assume the responsibilities of reservation management. The political environment seemed conducive to such an agenda. Sells had written in his 1917 "Declaration of Policy in the Administration of Indian Affairs" that the "time has come for discontinuing guardianship of all competent Indians and giving even closer attention to the incompetent that they may more speedily achieve competency." The new policy, Sells wrote, "[means] reduced appropriations by the Government and more self-respect and independence for the Indian. It means the ultimate absorption of the Indian race into the body politic of the Nation."[60] Hamilton, Curley Bear, and Joseph Grant explained to Sells in April 1918 that "it is the desire of the Blackfeet tribe of Indians to progress as rapidly as possible in the matter of acquiring the habits of industry and thrift and the adoption of the habits of civilized life." The council sought permission to develop a tribal commissary because licensed traders charged high prices and refused to extend credit; an Indian commissary would have enabled Blackfeet to buy goods at cost. The dictum—which could be viewed as their "Declaration of Policy"—was also very general, representing a statement of confidence in the tribe's leadership. The council members told Sells that the BTBC believed

> that there is sufficient business ability among the Indians on this reservation to make this enterprise a safe and successful one. Many of the Indians are carrying on business enterprises of considerable financial magnitude and are notably successful. The Business Council understands it to be the policy of the Indian Office to bring the Indians out of the state of tutelage and induce them to come to a state of self-reliance, as soon as practicable, and this plan of establishing a Commissary will, in the judgment of the Business Council, be a safe and helpful step in that direction. The Patents in trust and in fee are being issued and the Indians recognize they are rapidly approaching the time when they will be thrown on their own resources and this move will be a forward one in that direction.[61]

Assistant Commissioner Meritt kindly responded to the council's rather impressive request for limited tribal autonomy four months later by explaining that the commissary plan was "entirely impracticable and not in conformity with the present policy of the Service, which has in view the gradual absorption of the Indians in the citizenship of the country on the same *individual* [emphasis added] basis as the whites, and the transaction of business along similar lines."[62]

It was one thing to expect the Indian Office to agree to wholesale changes in oil and gas leasing regulations, but it was another to oppose a hearing to determine the viability of managing an economic concession that was integral to daily reservation life. BIA field supervisor Fred Baker had sanctioned a similar plan five years earlier. Because reservation traders overcharged Blackfeet customers who had few retail options, Baker recommended that the government use Blackfeet funds to organize an Indian cooperative store, arguing that the plan was neither "impracticable" nor "socialistic" because it would use Indian money and simply extended "to the Indian Service the methods employed in progressive white communities.... The savings to the Indians would be enormous."[63] An assistant chief of the education division supported Baker's plan, adding that "after the stores were properly started they should be turned over to the Indian.... Eventually the Office could withdraw its supervision over such establishment, and the plan would be not only desirable from the standpoint of dollars and cents but would give the Indians considerable experience in merchandizing [sic] and in the handling of their own affairs."[64] The response from the OIA then, as in 1918, was that it would not become involved in such an enterprise because it would "counteract" its efforts to make the Indian "self-reliant."[65]

Meritt's argument was specious, for what was more "white" or more American than starting a business? It reflected the OIA's bias against *tribal* economic organizations. The acculturated Blackfeet whom the OIA had supported in the 1910s wanted to liquidate both the reservation as a formal zone of economic development and the tribe as an empowered political manager of that development. These Blackfeet and their government backers opposed the tribe's efforts to manage the economic organization of community-owned natural resources because it distributed widely both the control of and the revenue generated from those resources. The OIA seemed particularly opposed to granting Robert Hamilton any management of tribal affairs, even though he had been declared a "competent Indian." Competency, it seems, extended only to those Indians willing and able to sell land to whites and to those acculturated Indians who shared the OIA's contempt of all things tribal and its celebration of white individualism.

By the end of the 1910s the allotment of the Blackfeet Reservation had been completed, but the debate on the best ways and means to utilize the remaining tribal land continued. Robert Hamilton had advanced the tribe's rights, but at the same time his success in resisting the assimilationist pressures from within the tribe and from the OIA had a negative impact on Blackfeet-white relations. Hamilton and his supporters won several battles with his wealthy opponents and helped to defeat the OIA-sponsored land sale, but this success seemed only to embolden the OIA to resist granting his faction any more autonomy or authority than was officially necessary. The OIA had little interest in protecting the tribal entity; its officials consistently supported the agenda of the acculturated mixed-bloods throughout the 1910s. The OIA and the BTBC were thus operating on different schedules and had different agendas for making the Blackfeet self-reliant. Neither party believed that such a condition would occur within a few years, but they differed over how best to achieve it through the exercise of tribal politics and the development of the reservation's natural resources. Hamilton understood better than anyone that any plan for economic progress had to consider the increasing class stratification and cultural disjunction that had developed during the battle over surplus land. The agenda pursued by Hamilton and his full-blood supporters protected the notion of tribe as a way to mitigate incipient class conflict and ensure that a political body truly representative of tribal interests could manage that economic progress by evenly distributing the return from its development of natural resources. The tribe's future depended upon the successful development of those resources, and it was endangered by the exploitative forces of acquisitive mixed- and full-blood Blackfeet who had demonstrated their disregard for this notion of tribe. The Blackfeet Tribe, for men like Charles Buck, Wolf Tail, and James Perrine, was simply a vehicle through which the gentry could maximize its control of local resources. The question for the Blackfeet people in the coming decade, then, was whether or not the government that dominated its affairs would give Hamilton and the business council sufficient opportunity to construct a political economy that was predicated on the cultural and geographical realities of Blackfeet life rather than the pedagogy of its guardian.

Oil and Agriculture Don't Mix:
The Rise and Fall of the Campbell Regime

Conflict between Blackfeet mixed-bloods and full-bloods widened during the 1920s as the mixed-bloods' population expanded rapidly and as they began to dominate the BTBC, the de facto political body of the Black-feet Tribe. While full-bloods became the target of administrative attempts to institutionalize farming as their path to economic salvation, mixed-bloods worked to develop the tribe's putative oil reserves, expand their livestock operations, and engage in other business enterprises. Different conceptions of land use thus emerged during the decade, precipitating a new intratribal battle that ultimately focused attention on the federal government's supervision of the tribe's financial, human, and natural resources.

Robert Hamilton's inclusion of full-bloods in the political process and his attempt to provide a bicultural agenda in recognition of their social disadvantages faced resistance from within the various full-blood communities as well as from acculturated mixed-bloods. Some full-blood leaders had become increasingly alarmed by the evolving composition of the business council despite Hamilton's solicitude, reflecting a perception of their increasing political and economic marginalization and the attenuation of Blackfeet culture in the face of demographic and assimilationist pressures. James White Calf and Bird Rattler wrote Commissioner Sells in March 1919 to complain that full-bloods had become alienated from tribal decision-making. The letter is quoted at length because it provides a good example of the full-bloods' concerns.

> Conditions upon our reservation are changing with great rapidity. . . . We therefore wish to call to your attention the status of our tribal council. We realize that this body does not carry much weight but such influence as it may have should be exerted on behalf of the interests and rights of the wards and full-blood Indians. Since patents have been issued many of our councilmen are now or may be citizens of the United States. Citizens interests and Indians interests are not allways [sic] paralel [sic], so we do not consider it fair that citizens hold seats in our tribal council. We therefore respectfully request that power be given the Council to disqualify all citizens from being or becoming councilmen and that the council be empowered to unseat citizen members and elect in their stead members of the tribe who are wards of the Government.[66]

Assistant Commissioner Edgar Meritt informed them that an Indian did not lose the right to participate in tribal activities after gaining citizenship, explaining that "while [the Indian's] interests are perhaps not identical with those of non-citizen Indians, at the same time they are often such as to entitle him to representation in tribal councils if he so desires. Tribal councils are frequently benefited by having in their make-up a number of citizen Indians of good business judgment and progressive ideas, and while their views may not always coincide with those of non-citizen councilmen, it is believed that in the main their participation in tribal affairs is helpful to the tribe as a whole than otherwise."[67] He told White Calf and Bird Rattler that they had nothing to fear from citizen council members. But Meritt and others in the Indian Office would soon react with similar alarm to the BTBC when it began to campaign for the abolition of the Bureau of Indian Affairs and the termination of its local administrator, Frank C. Campbell. The OIA had set the tone for diplomatic relations with its summary rejection of the council's "good business judgment and progressive ideas" for starting an oil leasing program and a tribal commissary. The OIA's own views did not appear to coincide with those of the council, and especially with those of its chairman, Robert Hamilton, who persisted in protecting the idea of a tribal economy. By the end of the 1920s the OIA would find its own influence challenged by both mixed-bloods *and* full-bloods, as well as their new allies in the U.S. Congress.

Frank Campbell, an imposing red-headed figure of six feet, two inches, assumed the superintendency of the Blackfeet Reservation in March 1921. Campbell had worked for the BIA since 1890, serving as superintendent of the Fort Peck Indian School, allotting agent at the Poplar Reservation, and livestock supervisor on the Blackfeet Reservation. He also had been the Blackfeet superintendent for an eight-month period during the revolving door years of 1917 to 1919, when four different administrators managed Blackfeet affairs. The drought conditions that prevailed in Montana in the summer of 1919 and the harsh winter that followed erased much of the Blackfeet economic progress generated during the war years of 1917 and 1918, decimating the Blackfeet livestock industry and forcing the fire sale of a small tribal herd purchased in 1915.[68] The collapse of the livestock industry and a promising crop of Blackfeet wheat farms produced both a form of class leveling and an alarming expansion of the ration rolls; roughly two-thirds of the population depended on government rations during the winter of 1920–21.[69] The Blackfeet thus had little confidence in the office of the superintendent in 1921. Campbell himself considered the reservation to be bankrupt as a result of his predecessors' policies and the vicissitudes of Montana winters, and he initiated an energetic campaign to revive tribal fortunes using his Five Year

Industrial Program (FYIP) as the vehicle of reform. Despite decades of government inattention and Blackfeet resistance to farming programs, Campbell resuscitated the idea of institutionalized farming to solve the tribe's problems of cultural and financial bankruptcy, a proposition that had been regarded by most superintendents as a lost cause and by most Blackfeet as a means to open the best land to white ranchers.

Campbell began his term by visiting, with the agency physician, nearly every family on the reservation. By itself, this time-consuming affair connected him to the full-bloods who lived in the Heart Butte and Old Agency districts, those most physically and politically alienated from the developing center of power in Browning. He recommended that full-bloods organize into cooperative associations that could pool resources for the purchase of farm machinery and seed. The organizing principle of the FYIP, Campbell wrote, was the need to "awaken the Indian to his own condition and to the fact that the time has come when he can no longer rely upon the government to gratuitously support him in idleness."[70] The FYIP emphasized the cultivation of small gardens and plots of wheat, the construction of a flour mill and a sawmill, and sheep grazing. Its institutional framework comprised twenty-nine chapters of the Piegan Farming and Livestock Association (PFLA); each chapter elected a president, vice president, and secretary to help manage its operations. The object of the program, as full-bloods wrote in their charter, was to create a sense of pride in the Blackfeet Reservation that would put it "first among reservations in a united effort towards—Good Homes, Good Citizenship, Self-support and Loyalty."[71] For full-bloods, increasingly shut out of tribal policy-making, the program represented a comprehensive approach to community living, an opportunity for each cooperative organization to manage its domestic affairs, and evidence that the government had not abrogated its responsibility and promise to make them productive Indian citizens. Full-bloods enthusiastically embraced Campbell's program of small-scale farming, as most were neither able to expand livestock herds due to lack of capital and climate nor content to live on meager government rations.

Commissioner of Indian Affairs Charles Burke wrote in a 1922 OIA bulletin that "without making any invidious comparisons, I may say that no tribe of Indians in the United States has made better progress during the past two years than the Blackfeet."[72] The OIA used the FYIP as a model for other superintendents to adopt, ultimately making it the centerpiece of its agricultural policy. Burke told Campbell that "[y]our program and ideas have not been confined to the Blackfeet Reservation alone, but have furnished an inspiration that we are endeavoring to have adopted upon all of the reservations under the supervision of the Indian Bureau."[73] In September 1924 Campbell held a conference in Browning to introduce the FYIP to superintendents of neighboring reservations; fourteen superintendents and two Indian agents from Canada attended the conference.[74] During the conference the Blackfeet were told that "this Five-Year Program was the coming popular activity among all our Indian people and that any Indian who refused to take part in it was making a mistake and that hereafter they would regard any Indian who complained about the Five-Year Program and refused to take part in it as unworthy of their friendship and support."[75] The FYIP represented a delayed implementation of the cultural component of the 1887 General Allotment Act on the Blackfeet Reservation and others like it in the western United States. The coercive pressure exerted on Indians to conform to the program reflects the tenacity with which white reformers clung to the Dawes model of Indian citizenship as a panacea for all tribal problems.

Campbell's assiduous campaigning for his "industrial" program, which increasingly took him to other reservations as part of the OIA's campaign to implement it service-wide, alienated influential mixed-bloods who had little interest or confidence in subsistence farming. Mixed-bloods supported Campbell's policy of helping full-bloods through small-scale farming only until it became clear that Campbell was both indifferent to their own long-range goals and incapable of furthering them. Campbell's organization of full-bloods thus resulted in a polarized reservation: mixed-bloods and the business council they controlled against the full-bloods of the PFLA.[76]

The reservation split into two camps in 1925, as it had in the mid-1910s over the sale of surplus land. Many of Hamilton's full-blood supporters abandoned him when the council began to call for Campbell's removal. Prominent among Hamilton's new detractors was Curley Bear, who had lobbied with Hamilton against the sale of surplus land. Curley Bear became a leader of the PFLA and served on its Resolutions Committee, which resolved in March 1925 to continue the program for another five-year term. PFLA officers thanked Campbell for "helping the Blackfeet Indians to become the most progressive tribe in the United States."[77] They defended Campbell by arguing that in contrast to previous superintendents who had shown little interest in the full-bloods' condition, Campbell was approachable and committed to helping them. Several officers, however, sought assurances that there would be non-farm labor available to help them support their families and sustain the program; most crops had failed during the summer drought. Full-bloods viewed Campbell's agricultural program as a major step toward a self-supporting condition but insufficient to provide long-term stability. Found a Gun argued that there "is nothing better than farming, but we don't expect to make enough money to put in the bank."[78] Despite tangible improvements in the spiritual ecology and agricultural economy of full-blood communities, many FYIP participants thought security remained out of reach. Mixed-bloods also wanted to put money in the bank and viewed Campbell's forceful campaigning for the FYIP on and off the reservation as neglect of more traditional sources of income such as stock raising. The entrepreneurs of the tribe wanted to expand the reservation economy to include the creation of cash surpluses or profits; they were interested in more than just survival. Frustrated by white stockowners' continual trespass on allotted and tribal lands and the lack of progress in oil development, the BTBC initiated a campaign to remove Campbell from the reservation. The PFLA Resolutions Committee in turn declared that "it would be a calamity now to transfer Mr. Campbell to other fields of work while we are in the midst of a complete reconstruction of our social and economic structure; that we consider the past five years more or less as the formative period of this reconstruction."[79] The Blackfeet were divided between pro-administration and anti-administration forces, not between supporters and detractors of the FYIP. Campbell's program was simply the lightning rod for political action.

The Hamilton faction, supported by Montana state senator Frank J. McCabe, a longtime resident of Browning and the owner of several Blackfeet fee patents, attacked the efficacy of the Campbell superintendency in advance of the January 1926 council elections. That the Hamiltonians easily won the election by securing ten of the thirteen council seats did not surprise Campbell, who had told Burke that "the full bloods are only a small voting strength of the reservation and if Robert Hamilton and Senator McCabe can succeed in keeping them divided, which they are always able to do, they can swing enough of the full blood vote to carry the election."[80] "Professional politicians" like Hamilton and McCabe usually prevailed on a reservation that lacked a dynamic political culture, Campbell noted, though the presence of professional politicians actually signaled that a modern political culture was emerging on the Blackfeet reservation.

Campbell's leadership was on trial during the BTBC meeting of February 25, 1926. McCabe, at Hamilton's invitation, addressed the gathering first. Although he told the crowd that it was foolish to consider "the abolishing of the Indian Department," as some mixed-bloods had demanded, he did ask them to question Campbell's commitment to reservation development. "You never had any Council meetings last year and no business was transacted and the work was neglected. Mr. Campbell never took any interest in your affairs," he said.[81] Hamilton and other attendees criticized Campbell for visiting another reservation on behalf of the FYIP instead of attending the meeting to discuss grazing fees, which the council wanted raised from ten cents per acre to twenty cents. James White Calf, a full-blood from the Starr School community in the Browning district, asked the crowd, "Where is he? . . . If Mr. Campbell is going to go away and take those kinds of trips, he might just as well resign his position as Superintendent. . . . The work is neglected here at this reservation. Mr. Campbell has never assisted the tribe in the re-adjustment of these leases and the people have asked for them for a long time."[82] Rides at the Door, another full-blood from the Browning district, complained that Campbell "is circulating these reports that we are prosperous . . . and I believe that he is misquoting the Indians." Campbell was doing little about developing reservation resources such as rangeland, timber, and oil, he said, and as a result "whenever any of us find out that the Agent is not doing what is right we should get together and ask for his removal."[83]

In pursuing with great zeal the expansion of his industrial program Campbell neglected other areas of the reservation that mixed-bloods and some full-bloods—particularly those not affiliated with the FYIP in the Heart Butte and Old Agency districts—wanted developed. Campbell's critics opposed the FYIP not because it made full-bloods into farmers but because his publicity campaign transformed all Blackfeet into prosperous Indians and thus prevented or delayed genuine economic reform. For Hamilton, the issue related as much to matters of sovereign pride and political process as it did to publicity and prosperity. He argued that the 1924 Citizenship Bill had changed the nature of Indian-white relations: "The Indian is equal before the law, and the money used to operate this Agency is reimbursable money and it comes out of the pockets of each member of this tribe to keep up this Agency. . . . The Indian is no longer to be dominated, he stands on the equal footing as a white man and he has every right to criticize any employee of the Government or State, and I say the sooner the Indians assert themselves the better off they will be."[84]

Eight of the ten council members present asserted themselves by voting to remove Campbell from office, a measure that had no official standing but served to formalize the differences between the two factions.

Full-bloods who had opposed the Citizenship Bill or the idea of full-fledged citizenship did not favor the prospect of indigenous administration and saw Campbell and the OIA, despite their failings, as a buffer between themselves and a governing council increasingly populated by mixed-bloods. Split Ears told the council during the February 26 meeting that it had no authority to call for Campbell's removal because "we of us that still remain Indians do not say so." The Blackfeet, he said, need "a guardian and overseer at all times. . . . If we kick him out we will have to pick out one from the people here."[85] Chapter officers reaffirmed their support for Campbell by planning a counterattack to remove the offending council members from power. Mixed-blood councilman Richard Sanderville, an ardent ally of full-blood interests and a long-standing critic of Hamilton, reported to Campbell after the meeting that "Curley Bear and Chapter Officers all in war path against the present council, those that voted for your discharge as Superintendent."[86]

Despite sharing this animus against the BTBC, full-bloods saw fit to maintain contact with the council in hopes of reforming it, and thus refused, it appears, to accept the physical and political segregation that Campbell encouraged. Campbell later told Burke that he did not support the chapter officers' plan to "supersede the Business Council," explaining that "[i]t was my plan from the very starting of the Industrial Program to keep the same [chapter officers] out of reservation politics and it would be a decided mistake in my judgment to have the Industrial organization participate to that extent in tribal matters."[87] Campbell had decided to control the BTBC by refusing to "recognize any [council] meeting or business transaction" unless he approved it, and he reassured Burke that he would see to it that "a different kind of a Council" would emerge from the next election. Campbell suggested to Burke that the legality of the Hamilton council could be "very consistently dis-regarded or not approved by the OIA," a view that reveals the effect of the growing power struggle on Campbell's ability to act on the reservation.[88]

In order to protest Campbell's attempts to undermine the BTBC's authority and his use of "propaganda" about the FYIP's benefits, Hamilton persuaded the OIA to investigate Campbell's administration.[89] One investigator concluded that "as a promoter of the five year program [Campbell] gives full value to the government" but expressed "doubt that he does in any other way."[90] Campbell did promote the FYIP's value beyond its actual level of success—either to further his career or because it served his evangelical purpose of expanding a program he believed would ultimately raise full-bloods above the poverty line—yet he should get credit for politicizing the full-blood communities, organizing them into workable economic units, and facilitating cultural unity. He clearly failed, however, to serve the burgeoning mixed-blood community and to provide the tribe as a whole with comprehensive economic development. And he was principally responsible for creating the political tension on the reservation by insulating his program and its leaders from a legitimate exercise of tribal decision-making, creating in effect two distinct political communities that were bound to adopt different agendas. Campbell's neglect of the BTBC's program of oil leasing, the one unifying force on the reservation in the 1920s, exacerbated the split and prevented meaningful dialogue between groups divided more by geography than by blood and more by personal struggles than by genuine political differences.

In March 1926, Assistant Commissioner Forrest Stone asked the OIA to answer a couple of basic but important questions: "Just what is the status of the Tribal Business Council?" Could the BTBC act as an "administrative branch" or as an "advisory body"?[91] Six weeks later, the OIA responded that it had no obligation to respond to any resolutions passed by the business council. The OIA would act only "if it desires to do so."[92] The OIA had already answered the questions by both ignoring the business council's request for latitude in oil leasing and failing to honor its obligation to prosecute the terms of leases it did approve. The OIA used its power to apply antiquated mining and leasing regulations to the wildcat territory of northwestern Montana. By maintaining a reactive role it rendered the Blackfeet Reservation a difficult place to conduct a difficult business and thus angered full-bloods and mixed-bloods alike who considered the oil that government and business representatives believed lay under Mother Earth as the tribe's best hope for an economic future.

The development of the gasoline-powered automobile and the Great Northern Railroad's conversion to oil burners in 1910 stimulated great interest in Montana crude oil prospecting. Immigrants traveling the Bozeman trail in 1864 noted the presence of oil, but it was not until 1915 that wildcatters found evidence of commercial quantities in Montana. The Ohio Oil Company struck oil in southern Montana, but the field produced only small quantities. Other discoveries of promising fields, including one on the Crow Reservation, fueled an "oil excitement" in the state in 1921. The discovery of the Kevin-Sunburst field, which lay east of the Blackfeet Reservation, had much to do with the keen interest in Blackfeet resources in the early 1920s; by the early 1930s the Kevin-Sunburst field and the Cut Bank field, which bordered the Blackfeet Reservation, were the largest producing oil fields in the state.[93] The Blackfeet sought to take advantage of this oil excitement in part because the postwar failure of the livestock industry and the collapse in wheat prices had destabilized the reservation economy. Hamilton had been pressuring the OIA since 1916 to liberalize the council's authority to facilitate oil leasing, and by 1920, with most Blackfeet in dire straits, tribal leaders had become restless. The OIA had not approved a single tribal oil lease, and thus no money from oil sales had been pumped into the Blackfeet treasury. The tribe, the constellation of factions and interest groups that occupied the Blackfeet Reservation, was especially eager to develop oil resources that had yielded, in sharp contrast to those of the oil-producing Indian nations of Oklahoma, no revenue.

Oil leasing thus dominated BTBC deliberations. H. L. Lambert, representing eastern oil and gas interests, proposed in January 1921 that the council give him a monopoly on mineral development of the tribe's 553,032 unallotted acres for a period of ten years. Lambert's presence created both excitement and urgency on a reservation in need of good news. The BTBC met on January 8 to discuss Lambert's blanket lease proposal. Lambert emphasized to council members and others in attendance his financial wherewithal to develop the tribe's natural resources, his personal commitment to the Blackfeet people, and his vision of making them as rich as Oklahoma Indians. "You might become one of the rich nations of the United States or of the world as the Oklahoma Indians of today have done," he began, citing the unusually high per capita income of the Osage Indians to illustrate his point. Lambert argued that he was the tribe's best hope for comprehensive natural resource development. If the Blackfeet signed his proposed lease, then he would "deliver the goods," the goods in his context being the Packards driven by Oklahoma Indians. If not, then he would leave and "never return."[94]

Frustrated by the lack of any progress in natural resource development, the false promises of previous developers, and the OIA's tight control of the leasing process, tribal leaders supported the idea of giving control of the reservation's putative reserves to one developer, especially one promising to make the Blackfeet the Osages of the northern Plains. Both mixed-bloods and full-bloods supported Lambert's proposition. Full-bloods seemed unified in their support of large-scale development; Curley Bear supported Lambert's proposal, as did Rides at the Door, who complained that the tribal lands "have been lying idle for all these years." Lambert's project, Rides at the Door said, would "bring joy" to every Blackfeet and make them rich.[95] Mixed-bloods shared the excitement but expressed concern that Lambert could turn out to be yet another speculator who would hold the land for the ten-year term only to sublease it to other developers; the land speculator, after all, was not a breed unknown in the American West. An executive committee, comprising five mixed-bloods and four full-bloods, discussed the lease terms for more than four hours during an evening meeting on January 8. Committee members expressed a sense of urgency for economic development. Curley Bear spoke of "destitute circumstances," calling the lease the tribe's "only salvation."[96] Louis S. Irvin, the tribe's legal adviser and its former allotting agent, cautioned against signing a lease simply because the tribe was desperate to develop its resources and chastised Lambert for creating the impression that he was the Blackfeet's savior. The original lease allowed Lambert to hold the land for a period of ten years, during which time the tribe could fine him only two thousand dollars per year for not drilling. Irvin insisted that Lambert make concessions, telling the committee, "I see no reason why business transacted with Indians should be any more lax than business transacted with white men." Irvin believed that it was foolish to "tie up the field" for one man without a guarantee that he fully intended to develop it; he then asked Lambert to offer a lease that would "preclude the idea of his using this for simply a speculative venture."[97]

During its January 10 executive session the BTBC agreed, by a vote of seven to one with one abstention, to accept Lambert's lease terms. During a well-attended BTBC meeting of January 10 Irvin told the gathering that he was not surprised that the "faint glimmering shadow of money would appeal to everyone on the reservation," but he warned that "you are at the brink of doing a thing that you will regret as long as you live." Lambert refuted Irvin's charges of bribery and in turn called him a "silver-tongued orator." He ended his pitch by again saying that he hoped to "make you Indians as well off as the Osage tribe."[98] After the white businessman and the white lawyer had wrestled for the tribe's trust, the Blackfeet gathered in assembly voted fifty-five to one in favor of the lease.[99] Blackfeet council members ignored Irvin's legitimate con-

cerns to accept a lease they knew was flawed. Conditions on the reservation in early 1921 were bleak, however, and Lambert carried with him
the imprimatur of the commissioner of Indian Affairs. Above all, most
members believed that Lambert intended to drill for oil. The promise of
wealth during difficult times forces people to make concessions, but it
was also the case that the BTBC felt compelled to act for the tribe, which
had given the council every indication that it wanted the lease; the council made a concerted effort to facilitate "the development and progress of
the reservation," as one cautious mixed-blood had described the tribe's
basic goal.

The time and energy spent discussing the lease came to naught when
the OIA again informed the council that department regulations prohibited leases of more than forty-eight hundred acres.[100] The superintendent, prominent members of the tribe, and white business leaders
protested the decision in letters to the OIA and to Secretary of the Interior
John Barton Payne. Charles E. Roblin, the tribe's allotting agent, told the
OIA that while "many speculators and prospectors" were trying to take
advantage of the Blackfeet, Lambert was the best candidate for helping
the Blackfeet exploit the "incipient oil boom" taking place in Montana.[101] Robert Hamilton explained to Payne that the destitution of the
Blackfeet reservation "can only be permanently relieved and amulior-
ated [sic] through the development of natural resources." He argued that
Indians could become independent of federal supervision only if they
were "encouraged to take the initiative," which the Blackfeet had done
by signing the Lambert lease. Normal department rules were not com-
patible with the wildcat territory of Montana, he insisted, telling Payne
that "unless we offer liberal concessions we cannot induce anybody to
come here and to develop the mineral resources upon this reservation."
Payne simply informed Hamilton that the department would consider a
lease from Lambert only if it did not exceed forty-eight hundred acres
and condescendingly told Hamilton that "it would be very unwise to
lease your entire tribal holdings" to one party or person under any circumstance.[102]

Support for the lease was not unanimous. Oscar Boy, a full-blood Carlisle School graduate, asked Payne to reject the lease. It was the government's responsibility to "keep the fires burning so that the wolves would
not devour us," he wrote. "Wolves" were prowling the reservation and
the Blackfeet needed the government's protection. Influential mixed-
bloods Levi Burd and Malcolm Clark also wrote to protest the lease,

largely because it would have denied them access to tribal oil lands.[103] The most prominent white to oppose the lease was Louis W. Hill, the president of the Great Northern Railroad. Hill acknowledged that oil development was "the last thing these Indians have left" and possibly the best means to alleviate the Blackfeet's "very destitute circumstances," but he complained to Payne that the "improvident terms" of the Lambert lease meant "the exclusion of all other operators and . . . the withholding of development for a long time."[104] Hill opined that the lease as written meant that Lambert could hold on to the land and pay only minimal penalties if he did not initiate drilling operations, a practice Hill apparently found distasteful. It is unlikely that Louis Hill, a resident of Minnesota, had the best interests of the Blackfeet in mind. His railroad company had reneged on a deal to offer free passage to Blackfeet in return for the tribe's granting a right-of-way, and it regularly failed to compensate Blackfeet for cattle killed by its locomotives. Hill, of course, also had his sights set on Blackfeet oil leasing, and he did not want to be one of those operators excluded from reservation development.

The BTBC realized that it would have to conduct oil leasing according to the dictates of the Interior Department, or its subordinate agency the OIA. Six weeks after Interior rejected the Lambert lease, the council voted unanimously to assign a forty-eight-hundred-acre oil lease to Louis Hill, but only after rejecting his first proposal; the council demanded and received a provision allowing it to cancel the lease if Hill did not commence drilling within a period of seven months from the date of approval.[105] The Interior Department approved the lease, but new Commissioner of Indian Affairs Charles Burke warned Frank Campbell, who had just assumed the Blackfeet superintendency, that the Interior Department still held final approval of any subsequent lease terms. The BTBC, in other words, would have to negotiate with Albert Fall, the new secretary of the interior, in setting the terms of its oil development. Interior had granted the tribal council that privilege to negotiate, Burke wrote, and he "hoped that the Indians will not abuse this privilege, because it is the earnest desire of the Office to cooperate with the Blackfeet Indians in leasing their lands."[106] The question of whether Albert Fall would be a friend or a foe of Indian leasing remained.

In April 1921 Hamilton sought Fall's sanction of the council's approval of four additional leases, explaining that if other leases were not signed along the lines of the Hill lease then "the wave of oil excitement in Montana may recede entirely and this reservation remain undeveloped as far as oil and gas are concerned." Hamilton told Fall that the council was concerned that businessmen like Hill would use their leases for "speculative purposes only," and he asserted the council's right to expand its oil leasing effort and to facilitate it on its terms to ensure that lessees would become developers rather than speculators.[107] Burke reminded the council through Hamilton that it must use department forms during the leasing process but gave it leeway to amend the lease with its own provisions provided that they "increase the obligation of the lessee." Burke justified the department's policy of discouraging large-scale exploration, telling the council that if oil and gas were discovered "you will not get the large cash bonuses which operators are willing to pay for leases in a proven field." This policy was not based on "mere theory," Burke wrote, but on the experience of the Osage Indians: "There a large portion of the income of these wealthy Indians is received from bonuses paid for leases on their lands."[108] On one memorable day in 1916, the Osage Nation earned $2.3 million in bonus money from the leasing of 108 tracts of land, many of them only 160 acres in size.[109]

Interior officials used the Osage experience as a model on which to base its Indian oil leasing policy, despite different geological and political factors on other reservations. Burke argued that "leases should not be made too rapidly in order that time may be given for development of the land already leased as higher bonuses will no doubt be paid for land leased in the future if the lands already leased are developed and prove productive."[110] On one hand, the OIA wanted the tribe and allottees to reap short-term benefits through bonuses, but on the other, it wanted to guarantee the long-term viability of the oil lands. The OIA's strict and contradictory policy dampened initial enthusiasm for oil exploration on the reservation and angered those Blackfeet eager to lease their new allotments and receive rental income. Campbell's passion and his training were in agriculture, not in natural resource development; he told Burke that there was "no one in this office that has had very much experience [in oil and gas development], and personally I have had none."[111] Campbell attempted to be solicitous of the tribe's needs in the matter of oil leasing, at least in the early stages of his tenure, but his hands were tied by the OIA, which failed to accommodate the varied needs of Blackfeet allottees and continued to limit the BTBC's authority to negotiate tribal leases.

The OIA rejected sixteen leases approved by the BTBC on behalf of Blackfeet allottees in late 1921 because the lessee in each case either could not post the requisite bond or offered an insufficient bonus.[112] Louise Dogears's letter to Burke captured the sentiments of many of the tribe's members frustrated by OIA policy. Mrs. Dogears, who described herself as a "full blood Indian, a widow, well advanced in years and without property or any means of support," told the commissioner: "I want this oil lease approved in order that I may have the rental used for my support under the supervision of the Agent. Under the terms of the leases, as I understand it, I would have received money sufficient to carry me through this long cold winter and possibly to prevent my death from hunger cold and insufficient housing and clothing. Does the Department intend to supply my needs in some other manner? . . . Why then should the Department refuse to approve this lease and thereby cause me to suffer from hunger, cold and lack of shelter?"[113] She attacked the OIA's optimism, its "impression that there was an oil field underlying" the reservation, complaining that the oil excitement was diminishing among oil operators "while it is evidently still running high at the Department." She asked Burke to meet her "almost criminally pressing" needs that winter.[114] Assistant Commissioner Meritt responded five weeks later by repeating Burke's argument that lease bonuses would be higher "*in the event*" [emphasis added] that oil was discovered. "The disapproval of the leases was therefore to the best interests of you and the other heirs," he explained.[115]

Another rejected lease affected eighty-three-year-old Mary Howard, who wanted to sell half her 12.5 percent royalty because, as Campbell explained to Burke, "she feels that she has not long to live and desires to sell a portion of this royalty in order to make her last days more comfortable."[116] Meritt told Campbell a month later that the OIA "does not approve of an Indian selling royalty or any interest therein" and thus would reject such a deal.[117] Meritt's explanation suggests that the OIA rejected the idea on grounds other than department policy, perhaps because such royalty sharing would necessitate unwanted changes in recordkeeping; either way, the OIA did not recognize Howard's right to sell what she owned. The OIA's policy amounted to a gamble that the Blackfeet would achieve a higher return on their oil assets—both tribal and individual—if the region could be determined to have oil rather than just the possibility of oil. Blackfeet like Louise Dogears, Mary Howard, and BTBC members were increasingly inclined to assign leases to those operators willing to make a minimal investment in reservation development in order to capitalize on the interest in Blackfeet lands. During the winter of 1921, the future for many Blackfeet had a short horizon.

Although the OIA's policy restricted the expansion of the Blackfeet's nascent oil industry, it also served to prevent the wholesale exploitation of the tribe's assets in some cases. The OIA rejected a lease offered to J. L. Sherburne, perhaps the wealthiest and most powerful white resident of Browning, because it contained neither bonus clause nor drilling terms and was not executed on the Interior Department's leasing form 5-371b; in addition, the land in question was scattered over six different townships, creating a problem of enforcement. The council approved the lease after initially rejecting it, suggesting improper lobbying on the part of Sherburne, a man known for insinuating himself into tribal affairs. A subsequent campaign in support of Sherburne's lease, conducted by aggressive mixed-blood oil boosters such as John Galbraith, failed to persuade the OIA to reverse its decision.[118] Preventing white operators like Sherburne from exploiting the oil excitement proved to be generally successful—with one major exception. In theory, the OIA was solicitous of the Blackfeet's concerns. In practice, it failed to protect tribal members. The OIA's test case was the Hill oil lease. Louis Hill, who had accused Lambert of speculating in Blackfeet lands, leased land for that very purpose. The lease he negotiated with the Blackfeet would frustrate them throughout the 1920s and engender lasting distrust of the Indian Office and the Department of the Interior.

Campbell's ignorance of oil matters and his focus on implementing the FYIP on other reservations resulted in a lack of coordination between the BTBC, the Blackfeet agency, and the OIA. Oil leasing in Montana was already a low priority for the OIA, in part because of reports issued by the United States Geological Survey (USGS) in 1912 and 1917 that had predicted there was only a slight chance of commercial oil production on the reservation.[119] BTBC members had concluded as early as 1923 that Campbell would not be a reliable aid to natural resource development and began to take matters into their hands by forming an oil committee to investigate the performance of its four lessees and to lobby for better enforcement of lease provisions. The Blackfeet involved in tribal oil matters perceived the problem to be, in part, the result of the Interior department's increasingly lax enforcement of these provisions. The "granting of extensions is to be deplored for the reason that the Department should earnestly cooperate with the Tribal Council in enforcing these various gentlemen to comply with the terms of their leases," oil committee members told Burke. Lessees were creating any excuse to justify their need for extensions, the committee charged, while the "true situation seems to indicate that these various lessees are trading among one another for advantages and tying up this vast acreage on the Reservation from future development."[120] The committee acted itself by notifying several lessees that it would cancel their leases if drilling did not commence. Meritt promised the committee that Campbell would investigate the leasing situation, but he warned that only the secretary of the interior had authority to cancel leases. The department finally acted on two leases in late 1923, canceling the John Galbraith lease and part of the Hill lease for noncompliance. The department thus took two years to cancel the Galbraith lease, and there is no evidence that the lessees paid demurrage charges as stipulated in the lease.

The committee became particularly impatient with Louis Hill and the Homestake Oil Company, Hill's development partner, charging that they had failed to drill within the prescribed period. In January 1923 Campbell reported to Burke that Homestake had abandoned its drilling site and made it "impossible to ascertain whether or not the required depth was reached" to avoid penalties. "The field," Campbell wrote, "has been given a black eye, so to speak, by these companies withdrawing from [it]."[121] The BTBC subsequently attempted to cancel the Hill lease, prompting a department hearing. Burke, Meritt, and representatives of the U.S. Bureau of Mines and USGS met with Homestake officials in April 1923 to determine whether the company had complied with a provision that its drill reach a geological stratum called the Kootenai formation, found at a depth of twenty-five hundred feet. No Blackfeet were invited to the meeting. Although government geologists contested Homestake's claim that it had reached the formation, Burke recommended that Secretary Fall cancel only half of the lease, leaving Hill 2,486 acres of prime land.[122]

Not content with a partial cancellation, the BTBC demanded that Campbell inform the OIA that it was unanimously opposed to Hill retaining "a foot of land" because he had "flagrantly violated the terms of his lease by suspending drilling operations."[123] Meritt responded to Campbell's protest by arguing that the OIA had no grounds for canceling the rest of the Hill lease because the well had reached the Kootenai formation, contradicting the conclusion reached by government experts, who, under normal circumstances, might be considered to have better knowledge of these scientific matters than bureaucrats Meritt and Burke. The department's decision meant, Burke stated, that Hill could "hold it" (the 2,486 acres) until March 12, 1931, without having to drill another well or pay penalties.[124] Burke gave a different answer in a 1926 report on Blackfeet oil leasing, writing that "some development work has been done on this lease [Hill's] but as far as the records show no well has been completed thereon."[125]

The abandonment of Hill's drilling operation and the government's refusal to secure lease compliance angered Blackfeet leaders and helped to dampen the enthusiasm of wildcatters in the region. The evidence indicates that Interior and OIA officials allowed Hill to breach his contract and retain control of a large area containing the promising Milk River Anticline, despite the protests of prominent Blackfeet and the opinions of government scientists. Three months after Burke and Meritt reviewed the Homestake drilling operation, the Senate Public Lands Committee began its investigation of Albert Fall's role in the leasing of the Teapot Dome naval oil reserve to private oil companies. The investigation resulted in Fall's imprisonment and the government's retention of the reserve. Given that Fall's office had authority over leasing on the Blackfeet Reservation, Burke's comment that tribal lands would be leased "under such rules and regulations and upon such terms and conditions as the Secretary of Interior may prescribe" takes on new meaning.

By 1926 the once-contagious oil excitement in Montana had virtually disappeared on the Blackfeet Reservation. The few tribal leases that were granted generated no royalty income for the tribe or employment for its members. No drilling had occurred on the reservation since the fall of 1925. The OIA again restricted Blackfeet leasing, hoping that a discovery of oil would trigger additional interest and generate more bonus money. The tribe received only $2,729.68 from oil leasing between 1921 and 1926, the product of five lease bonuses ranging from $500 to $719; oil leasing on restricted allotted lands netted $11,740.16 from forty-five leases, most of which the OIA eventually "disapproved."[126] The Blackfeet were naturally disappointed that no oil had been found, but they were also bitter that Campbell and the OIA had failed to represent their interests adequately.

Frustrated by the constraints and favoritism of the department's leasing system and the poor performance of tribal lessees, the BTBC looked for new ways to facilitate oil development on tribal land. In February 1927 the council considered a plan devised by oil booster John Galbraith, who proposed that the tribe mortgage its timber reserves to fund its own oil and gas corporation instead of relying upon a diminishing number of

white oil prospectors, a group that had up to that point shown little inclination to explore the reservation with any degree of seriousness. Galbraith's own lease had been voided in 1923, largely because his development partner failed to drill according to the terms of the lease. Galbraith
explained to the council that his personal experience with oil companies
and the Hill lease had taught him that "if we operate our own well here
we will know what is wrong with our money, and our well and why we
quit and what is wrong with our resources."[127] The council expressed interest in the idea of forming a tribal corporation. Full-blood councilman
George Starr told his colleagues, "The oil is here, it is all around us. . . .
You half breeds are just as smart as any white man and some are smarter
and we can do our own drilling, form a company and do our own work
and you can do it if you just get it into your neck that you can do it."[128] The
council voted to prohibit the use of tribal timber as collateral, but it
formed a new oil committee to explore other ways in which the council
might raise funds to expand the tribe's role in developing its resources,
with the hope that the tribe would eventually "own" the royalties.

Angered by the government's failure to promote Blackfeet resource
development, the tribe decided to try the oil business itself. But the
Blackfeet lacked capital, credit, and collateral; the FYIP and the financial
legacy of the government's irrigation projects had exhausted the tribe's
reimbursable funds. In August 1927 the new committee petitioned
Campbell to secure from Congress an appropriation of twelve thousand
dollars for inducing oil operators to drill on tribal land and invited
J. George Wright, superintendent of the Osage Nation, to tour its reservation and advise them on a sounder course of development.[129] Wright
was not optimistic about the viability of the council's plan to use public
money for oil exploration, and he reported to Campbell that the prevailing low price of oil in combination with the lack of infrastructure on the
reservation would make it difficult for the tribe to attract investors.[130]
The OIA ruled that it could not justify the use of public funds for Blackfeet oil development and refused to consider the oil committee's request.
Lacking proprietary, private, or public funds for the creation of a tribal
enterprise, the council was forced to rely on the standard leasing system.

The election of Herbert Hoover in late 1928 gave the tribe hope that
it might benefit from a different group of policy makers; Blackfeet leaders
had lost faith in Burke and the Interior Department primarily because of
the Hill lease controversy. Their hope was quickly dashed when the new
secretary of the interior issued Order No. 343, which applied Hoover's

oil conservation policy to Indian reservations as well as to public lands. The new policy, a reaction to depressed oil prices, disappointed Blackfeet who expected new lessees to strike oil, in part because oil continued to be pumped from fields next to the reservation. The policy meant not only that the Blackfeet's potential oil reserves would not be explored aggressively but that the Department of the Interior could cancel a series of recently signed leases. Hoover's policy greatly disturbed the council. Wolf Plume, a full-blood, lamented that "when Hoover took his seat we had a great deal of confidence in him that he would help us. . . . If he sits on that order, we will have nothing further to look forward to. He will take all the joy out of life."[131]

Council members feared that production in the Kevin-Sunburst field, which lay roughly eighteen miles east of the reservation's boundary, continued to drain their tribal reserves. The council sent a protest resolution to Hoover, telling him that "an emergency exists on this reservation both as to the needs of the Indians and the preservation of mineral rights and that the only relief immediately available is the development of the tribal oil lands." The council asked the president to exempt the Blackfeet from his conservation policy so that oil development could continue and thus ensure that "the Indians *now living* may participate in the enjoyment of the revenues to be derived from such development, and our people may be relieved from their present condition of poverty."[132] Interior summarily dismissed the council's request for dispensation, but it did approve a lease to the Browning-Fertig Oil Company after ruling that the tribe had signed the lease before Order No. 343 took effect.[133] The Browning-Fertig Oil Company, it should be noted, was managed by an acculturated Indian and three white businessmen, the kind of men the OIA supported.

The decade that began with the oil excitement of 1921, fanned by discoveries of oil on adjacent territory, ended with Hoover's oil conservation policy of 1929. The resolution that the business council telegraphed to the president in April 1929 captured a decade of Blackfeet hopes and frustration. They turned to Hoover and his new administration with the hope that he might help them achieve a greater state of self-sufficiency by facilitating the development of their natural resources. The council's act of emphasizing the words "now living" symbolized the deep frustration felt by all Blackfeet who had actively pursued resource development throughout the 1920s only to face favoritism from within the Department of the Interior and false prophets from within the business community. It was, perhaps, particularly frustrating for many of the tribe's elderly citizens, like Wolf Plume and Louise Dogears, who had survived the 1920s in part by adopting Campbell's agricultural program only to see the promise of oil dry up from a drought of political will.

Although the pro-Campbell faction assumed control of the business council in the 1927 election,[134] by late 1928 the majority of Blackfeet had lost confidence in Campbell and the OIA. Sen. Burton Wheeler addressed a large gathering in Browning in October 1928 to announce that a special subcommittee of the Senate Committee on Indian Affairs, of which he was a member, planned to hold hearings on Blackfeet affairs the following year. He told the crowd that Indians "were recently given the right of citizenship, but some 225,000 of them are still held in a virtual stage [sic] of bondage by the Indian bureau. Many cases have been called to my attention which reveal wholesale frauds and gross injustices in the handling of Indians' property." The committee intended to correct any abuses of the nation's "original Americans."[135] Acting Superintendent Forrest Stone wrote Burke the next day to warn him of the impending backlash against the OIA. He charged that Wheeler and Walter Liggett, the Senate investigator, had been coopted by Hamilton and his faction, and thus he did not expect a fair hearing. The mood on the reservation had swung against the OIA, Stone believed, and the result was that many of those Indians formally committed to the FYIP "had apparently changed their minds and were giving a great deal of credence to the theory that they were being very much abused by the government, and that the various investigators were going to correct many of these things and see that their alleged rights were protected." The attenuation of support for Campbell and the FYIP, Stone concluded, "has unquestionably weakened our administration and our influence with a great many of our Indian people."[136]

Campbell had told Burke in February 1924 that he would "appreciate the confidence that the Blackfeet Indians have in the Bureau, notwithstanding the fact that a great deal has been done here to discredit the Bureau among the Blackfeet people."[137] Intratribal political tension, Campbell's frequent absence from the reservation and concomitant neglect of oil and grazing resources, and the pending congressional investigation of Blackfeet affairs ate away at that confidence. It was no longer just the "Bolsheviks" of the Hamilton faction creating instability on the reservation but the inability of Campbell and his superiors to provide a comprehensive economic plan for the development of Blackfeet resources. Commissioner Burke would leave office in 1929 with the Meriam Report as his professional epitaph. Campbell, for all intents and purposes, had already left the reservation.

The primary debate among the Blackfeet in the 1910s centered on how best to use the reservation's physical resources: Should the tribe sell its surplus land to fund the expansion of a Blackfeet cattle industry? The rapid decline of that industry in the early 1920s, the general failure of government-sponsored agriculture, and the tribe's decade-long battle to spur oil production helped to precipitate in the late 1920s a new debate that centered on the federal government's supervision of Blackfeet political affairs and on its management of Blackfeet economic resources. For many mixed-bloods *and* an increasing number of full-bloods, the tribe had reached a point of diminishing returns from federal supervision. The basic problem on the Blackfeet Reservation was the degree to which the Blackfeet could rely upon the problematical notion of "tribe" to solve their problems if their home was divided into two politically and socially distinct communities. Had the reservation become a *place* populated by citizens and Indians, as James White Calf and Bird Rattler had argued at the dawn of the decade, a region defined by competing interest groups unable to bridge their cultural differences to address the political and economic problems that all Blackfeet faced as the decade closed? As those interest groups slowly began to coalesce in opposition to Campbell's one-dimensional agenda and absentee management, the Blackfeet's search for a modus vivendi to facilitate the proper use of their shared physical heritage continued.

2. "GIVE US A FAIR AND NEW DEAL"

1929–1934

> There is ample evidence that for a long period of years the head officials at the Blackfeet Reservation have been more interested in advancing the interests of a few whites and favored mixed bloods than they have been in conserving the property of the Indians. – Walter Liggett, Senate investigator, 1928

> Give us a fair and new deal as we know ourselves the old system is no success. – Rides at the Door, Blackfeet council member, 1933

The release of the Meriam Report in 1928 precipitated a series of reforms in the stewardship of the nation's American Indian citizens. Investigators found that the BIA was weakest in the area of economic development, which was "fundamental and in a sense underlies all progress." Most Indians earned less than one hundred dollars per year.[1] The report emphasized the need for the reform of Indian economies, recommending that "an experiment be tried . . . with the modern business device of the corporation. The corporation would own the property, keep it intact, and conserve and operate it as a great national asset." Government officials would serve as corporation managers until Indian leaders demonstrated their understanding of modern business methods.[2] The report recommended that tribes develop their natural resources in toto and use tribal funds as a "source of credit for enterprising members of the tribe." Investigators doubted whether a "well rounded program of economic advancement framed with due consideration of the natural resources of the reservation" had been attempted anywhere in Indian America. It certainly had not been tried on the Blackfeet Reservation. Only the Klamaths and the Osages could serve as role models. The Klamath Tribe had successfully developed its natural resources, and its people were now "anxious to get possession of their share of the tribal wealth so that they may use it as capital in individual enterprise." If "intelligent progressive Indians" like the Klamaths could develop tribal resources with the technical assistance of the Indian service, then other tribes might follow their example.[3]

The Meriam Report ultimately concluded that "thorough mature consideration should be given to the possibilities of using the corporate form of organization for tribal property that consists of great natural resources which cannot be economically administered or developed in small allotments."[4] The report thus laid out a "vision," previously lacking in federal policy, for the Bureau of Indian Affairs to foster the advancement of American Indians using both the assimilated and the tribal ideals of economic organization. This vision would later be embodied in the Indian Reorganization Act of 1934.

John Collier, the executive director of the American Indian Defense Association, urged Congress to follow the Meriam Report with an investigation of its own before instituting reforms in the management of Indian affairs.[5] S.R. 79, authorizing "a general survey of the conditions of Indians in the United States," passed on February 1, 1928. A subcommittee of the Senate Committee on Indian Affairs subsequently toured many of the largest reservations to get a firsthand look at the problems of Indian administration and the face of Indian poverty.

In June 1929, Sen. Lynn Frazier of North Dakota, the chairman of the Committee on Indian Affairs, informed Joe Brown, the chairman of the BTBC, that members of his committee wanted to hear "any claims, grievances, suggestions or recommendations" that the Blackfeet had to offer. Brown opened the July 16 BTBC meeting by reading Frazier's letter and telling those assembled that "if the Government has been mistreating the Indians in any way, this committee wants to know what that is." Brown listed several issues that he thought should be discussed—health, education, irrigation, and resource development—then opened the floor to suggestions. Robert Hamilton advocated the elimination of unnecessary and costly irrigation projects, which he believed diverted water to neighboring whites, and the creation of a million-dollar credit fund for individual investment. "Now is the time to send our views upon a fundamental and economic basis," he said, concluding that "if we get these big things through, we will make a long step towards a permanent relief towards self support, and you will not have to look to the Government for your needs."[6]

Oscar Boy told the gathering that the committee members were "big men, the last big men that are coming to visit you. Now we want to bring the good things that will bring home the bacon. . . . [I]f we should rake in what is coming to us for all the different kind of fees, we would not have to look for that million dollars, and the Indians will quit hollaing [sic]."[7] Oscar Boy referred to Campbell's inability or refusal to collect proper fees for water, timber, and oil leasing, and he believed that Hamilton's request for a government loan was thus unnecessary. "Bringing home the bacon" meant bringing home what was rightfully theirs. Hamilton's and Oscar Boy's speeches illustrate the different approaches to economic development among mixed-bloods and full-bloods and serve as another example of the competing assimilated and tribal ideals of economic organization. The OIA's bias against tribal investment had become painfully clear to Hamilton and other mixed-blood leaders during the 1920s. Hamilton's call for an imprest signaled his orientation toward individual investment. Oscar Boy wanted the tribe to facilitate investment for all Blackfeet using their community-owned assets.

Brown chaired a general meeting four days later, letting the mostly full-blood audience speak its mind. The speeches reflected three major themes: the need for the Blackfeet to put its grievances to the committee as one tribe, not as competing interest groups of mixed-blood and full-blood; the belief that the Campbell administration had not advanced Blackfeet interests; and the important role resource development could play in helping the tribe become self-supporting. Charles Reevis was the only speaker to assert the right of mixed-bloods to "represent their side," complaining that many could neither secure loans from independent banks nor receive the benefit of government loans to the tribe.[8] Most of the other speakers, though, called for witnesses to present the Blackfeet Tribe as a unified group. Peter Oscar was one of several full-bloods who admonished fellow Blackfeet to put aside differences at this critical juncture. "There is one nation on this reservation what you call Blackfeet, mixed bloods and full blooded Indians," he told them. "Help each other. . . . We must all work together if we are to accomplish something for our own benefit. The Government of the United States can't support you for all your lifetime."[9]

Oliver Sanderville, a seventy-year-old full-blood, offered the most pointed criticism of Campbell's administration. "We want a change," he demanded. "We are used too much like children—like a school teacher with a big stick saying I want you to say that. I want you to do that." The Blackfeet received no "protection from the office" while white lessees and trespassers enjoyed immunity from prosecution and penalty. Conditions on the reservation were going to get worse, he believed, "unless we get assistance from our Superintendents." He concluded his lengthy speech by saying, "Good law, American law and justice, liberty, that is my friend, and I got a good friend."[10] The Blackfeet's faith in Campbell's superintendency had eroded, but their hope that American justice would prevail remained strong.

The issue of resource development dominated the rest of the meeting. The committee hearing represented a real chance for the Blackfeet to discuss the development of the tribe's resources, as Campbell had failed to show any interest in doing so. Bullcalf argued, "We have oil possibilities here on the reservation, and we should look forward to getting developments on our oil resources, and this timber, and these canals, and things of that kind. If we could get these developments done, and [sic] then I am sure we would be self-supporting. Then we would have plenty of money to put in our pockets." Other speakers hoped that the government would "take the lid off" Blackfeet oil leasing and expand operations. Rides at the Door explained that he had seen an increase in drilling activity in neighboring territory and feared that "gradually those wells of Sunburst and Kevin will drain all the oil on this reservation" if the tribe did not develop it first.[11]

Prominent Blackfeet hoped that Congress would help cure the tribe's aphonic condition and support the tribe in its efforts to become a community of self-supporting citizens. Intratribal tensions remained, but the Blackfeet, on the whole, approached this one-day meeting with the committee with an unusual commitment to concentrate on the tribe's future as a cultural and political entity, however flawed it was. The appeal to unity reflected the tribe's frustration over ineffective oil leasing, its collective perception that it had a unique opportunity to secure some kind of justice for past BIA sins, and, for many full-bloods, the realization that Campbell's influence had waned to the point of no future return. The many poignant calls for unity on the basis of shared blood were extraordinary considering the animus generated by the recent factional conflicts, and they would be echoed throughout the 1930s as the Blackfeet debated, in the face of dramatic political and economic changes, the very nature of Indianness and, concomitantly, the notion of tribal obligation. The threat of the government's inevitable withdrawal of support, Peter Oscar inferred, necessitated a recognition of common interests based on economic need rather than differences based on blood and required a reconstituted tribal organization devoted to development of the tribe's shared physical heritage. A consensus emerged among both full-bloods and mixed-bloods that natural resource development would give the Blackfeet some measure of control over reservation conditions and that tribal resources should be developed by the tribe for the use of the tribe rather than allotted to individuals. The idea of self-support was a powerful one for many Blackfeet, especially for those who had known a degree of self-sufficiency, however tenuous, before the word "reservation" entered the Blackfeet lexicon. The tribe's natural resources, particularly the oil that was believed to be flowing beneath the reservation, had become for many Blackfeet the "new buffalo."

Senators Frazier, Burton Wheeler, and W. B. Pine of Oklahoma arrived in Browning on July 24 to hear the Blackfeet's grievances and suggestions. The Blackfeet who testified touched on such problems as persistent tuberculosis, fraudulent fee patent sales, and agency inaction on resource development. Blackfeet witnesses, with a few exceptions, denounced the FYIP, their opinions ranging from it being inappropriate for Blackfeet lands at best to corrupt in its intent at worst. But on the whole they looked to the future, not the past, emphasizing to the committee the need for a *real* industrial program. Several witnesses, including BTBC chairman Joe Brown, testified to the need for mechanical education to augment Campbell's reliance on agriculture, arguing that most Blackfeet simply could not survive as farmers in the harsh climate of northwestern Montana. Others testified to the problems associated with the tribe's development of its timber and oil resources. Robert Hamilton asked the committee for better protection and conservation of the tribe's timber, which he claimed was being stolen by whites near the Glacier National Park boundary. He also complained that Campbell and the OIA had failed to protect Blackfeet financial interests by approving the Louis Hill oil lease.[12] Other Blackfeet witnesses echoed Hamilton's contention that the government had failed to manage the tribe's natural resources in a responsible fashion.

The committee interrogated Frank Campbell at length about his controversial administration of Blackfeet affairs, detailing a litany of abuses of power, corruption, and neglect. The committee charged that Campbell, and Forrest Stone by extension, had fostered discrimination against Indians in favor of white labor and businesses, failed to adequately develop the tribe's natural resources, neglected to keep accurate records of land and business transactions, and done little to provide adequate health services. The subcommittee prepared for this interrogation by reading a report written by Walter W. Liggett, one of its field investigators. Liggett castigated Campbell and his predecessors, documenting improper fee patent sales and discriminatory leases of oil, timber, and grazing resources. He reserved most of his criticism for the agency's handling of the tribe's resources, emphasizing that the agents' inefficient accounting exhibited a lack of concern for the economic welfare of the tribe and an indication of outright fraud. He concluded that as a result of agency mismanagement the Blackfeet lands "do not bring in the revenue they should. . . . They are entitled to a bigger return and they could get it if the agency officials acted with the same zeal that they would display if employed by private interests. But, instead of attempting to get every possible penny for their Indian wards, in many cases they appear to be acting as though they represented the white lessees."[13] Liggett produced a well-balanced report, criticizing both bureau personnel and a clique of Blackfeet mixed-bloods while refuting charges of malfeasance made by disgruntled full-bloods.

Liggett discovered that between 1912 and 1929 more than two hundred thousand of the Blackfeet's most valuable acres had been sold after the Indian owners were given fee patents, charging that this land transfer was the result of a conspiracy devised by former superintendent Horace Wilson, the mixed-blood lease clerk Stuart Hazlett, and a "clique of covetous whites" who obtained the land at "absurdly low figures" by "more or less devious means."[14] The main beneficiary of this collusion was the Sherburne Mercantile Company, which acquired forty thousand acres of Indian land, partly through the manipulation of debts incurred by Indians at its general store. Many of the Indians who remised their land were, according to Liggett, "ignorant, absolutely illiterate, and wholly incompetent to conduct their own affairs," and thus most of the transactions were "conceived in fraud" and sanctioned by the Blackfeet's supposed guardians. These illiterate Indians, Liggett wrote, "were given patent in fees against their will and soon cajoled out of their property" that typically had "some particular quality which made it especially desirable."[15]

The allotment policy failed miserably on the Blackfeet Reservation, as it did elsewhere in the nation. But policies are designed and implemented by men and women. The BIA, to be more accurate, failed miserably to protect the interests of Blackfeet citizens. As Liggett put it, "There is ample evidence that for a long period of years the head officials at the Blackfeet Reservation have been more interested in advancing the interests of a few whites and favored mixed bloods than they have been in conserving the property of the Indians. Case after case can be cited where the officials of the Blackfeet Agency have failed to take steps to safeguard the rights of the Indians under their charge."[16] Besides successfully overseeing the dissipation of tribal land, the agency managed to spend most of the tribe's money. The Blackfeet had received $1.5 million from the sale of the Sweet Grass district in 1887 and another $1.5 million from the sale of the land from which Glacier National Park was created; the agency spent most of the funds on agency buildings and cars, a Catholic mission, and Indian irrigation projects. The agency exacerbated the problem by failing to give inquiring Blackfeet an accounting of these expenditures. Liggett received only a response from Forrest Stone that "there was no record of tribal receipts and expenses on the books of the Blackfeet Agency."[17]

Committee members repeated Liggett's charges of financial profligacy and impropriety over the course of the hearing. The fraudulent sale of fee patents occurred mostly during Horace Wilson's tenure, but, the committee charged, Campbell was superintendent for seven months during the period of active allotment, had done little to investigate the sales in order to make restitution, and had failed, along with his predecessors, to produce documentation relating to them. The committee repeatedly criticized Campbell and Stone for sloppy recordkeeping, a principal reason for the tribe's lack of confidence in government stewardship. Another reason was the instability of the agency staff; the tribe had had eight different superintendents between 1910 and 1929.[18]

Liggett and the committee focused on Campbell's mismanagement of the tribe's livestock herds and the FYIP. Liggett commended Campbell for his efforts to foster self-sufficiency among a mostly full-blood group through the FYIP, citing numerous examples of successful farmers who had nearly reached the point of being able to provide for their families without government assistance. Liggett was less than laudatory toward Campbell's leasing program, however, finding that much of the tribe's grazing land had been leased to large stock companies at below market rates and without competitive bids. Liggett found little direct evidence to support the theory that Campbell's FYIP program was designed to benefit white stockowners, but he did contend that Campbell had leased the Blackfeet's "exceptionally fine grazing grounds at an unfairly low figure." In addition, Liggett called the use of more than $1 million of Blackfeet tribal funds for irrigation purposes "an injustice." The theory that irrigation in Blackfeet country would solve Indian farming problems was "an errant fallacy," he wrote.[19] It was yet another program, and a very expensive one, devised by white bureaucrats to turn Indians into farmers on land that could not support them. Liggett concluded that "the Indians can hardly be blamed for questioning the business ability and integrity of their guardians."[20]

The committee questioned the agency's business ability and integrity as well, asking Campbell and Stone to explain why the majority of the leases granted stockowners were at 10 cents per acre (12.5 cents at renewal), 5 cents less per acre than on inferior grazing lands on other reservations and 20 to 26 cents per acre less than on private grazing reserves like those owned by the Northern Pacific Railroad. Campbell and Stone were unable to justify the leasing schedule. In addition, Campbell did not know how many cattle or sheep the lessees were grazing, giving the committee the sense that overgrazing of Indian land did not concern agency officials. Wheeler also questioned Campbell's personal use of the reservation for the grazing of his own sheep, which numbered, according to Campbell, between "1,500 and 8,000," an unusually broad range that reflected Campbell's habits of accounting in his personal and professional capacity of property manager.[21] State senator Frank McCabe, an ally of the Hamiltonians, argued that "an autocracy has developed here on the reservation. . . . The funds belonging to the Indians have been squandered and dissipated through incompetent administration of their affairs and the Indians get no justice and no consideration." McCabe testified that the Blackfeet agency lacked, more than anything, a modern approach to business organization: "They go into deals they don't know anything about, and when you try to get any data they don't seem to have any records like any other business or corporation would have. Any business organization of any kind would know whether or not their business was operating at a profit or a loss, and how the loss occurred or what was responsible for it, but the Indian Department has never been able to give any information to public officials or otherwise, which either goes to show [sic] or they don't care."[22] Wheeler then asked McCabe, "Which shows conclusively that there is either no management or poor management?" McCabe responded, "Yes, certainly." The committee tended to ask such leading questions, and it certainly was predisposed to find fault with agency administration, but it had been provided with enough examples of mismanagement and suspicious activities throughout the hearings to warrant the conclusion that impropriety and incompetence characterized Campbell's regime.

After spending the day reopening old wounds and uncovering new problems, the Senate investigating committee moved on to face another reservation's crisis of confidence and comfort, leaving in its wake a tribe angered by the government's neglect of its economic affairs and its natural resources. If the Meriam Report was to be used as a guide to bring Indian culture and economy into the twentieth century, then the place to begin, judging from the administration of the Blackfeet, was with the Bureau of Indian Affairs itself. If the OIA was to emphasize economic education, as the Meriam Report recommended, then it would need new teachers. Campbell and company were not likely to offer the kind of business education that would generate economic success for any people except white ranchers, traders, railroad tycoons, and oil developers. As Robert Hamilton had put it fifteen years earlier, "it looks as though the white man, in many instances, was the beneficiary of the reservation rather than the Indian."

Although the FYIP still had its supporters, by the end of 1929 its creator had left the reservation, leaving Forrest Stone, the acting superintendent of the late 1920s, in charge of the reservation; Campbell frequently had been absent from the reservation for more than eight months each year. Stone was thus responsible for some of the problems of the Campbell regime and yet was insulated from the blame. Campbell became, especially after the Senate hearing, the scapegoat for most Blackfeet who identified the failures of reservation management with his one-dimensional vision of agricultural prosperity. Stone had broad-based support among the main Blackfeet factions, however, and understood that the Senate committee hearing mandated better management of Blackfeet resources.

Stone had been with the Indian Service for thirteen years, ten of which were spent as supervisor of livestock and assistant superintendent of the Blackfeet Reservation. He focused his efforts on supplementing the subsistence agriculture of the FYIP with stock raising. Tribal members had petitioned Congress in November 1928 for a $1 million appropriation, stating that "it is the desire of the Blackfeet Indians to become self-supporting and not remain dependent" on the federal government.

Stone sanctioned the plan, which Congress ignored, telling Campbell that "there has been for many years a tendency on the part of a number of the Blackfeet people to want to get away from the Government and to disentangle their affairs from Government control," and he argued that a program financing sheep raising would facilitate that goal.[23] Stone also helped secure an increase in the tribe's grazing fees, but his cautious approach to reforming Indian-white economic relations undermined Blackfeet efforts to benefit from reservation resource development. Blackfeet leaders had protested for years the low rental rate of ten cents per acre. The tribal council passed a resolution supporting an increase of five cents per acre in February 1926, but the OIA refused to acknowledge it. The council again resolved in February 1929 to raise the rate. Stone decided to inform all lessees of Blackfeet grazing land of the rate increase and offer them a hearing to discuss the matter, telling the lessees, most of them large stock companies, that "the time has arrived when a higher lease rental should be obtained," while assuring them that a "friendly feeling" between the Blackfeet and the lessees remained.[24] Few companies protested the rate increase, and it became effective in March 1929. More Blackfeet protested the increase than did whites, as they believed the rate should have been raised to between twenty-five and fifty cents per acre.[25]

Stone thus failed to take an aggressive approach to a persistent inequity, either by applying the rate increase retroactively or by making it a unilateral decision by simply informing the lessees that their salad days were over. His diplomatic approach would have made sense if the Blackfeet grazing lands were of poor quality, but they were generally considered the best in the state. Field agent C. R. Trowbridge criticized Stone for his lax supervision and his opposition to secure competitive leasing through advertising or sealed bids, a process mandated by OIA regulations.[26] Trowbridge reported that Stone did not want to disturb the "agreeable relations" that he believed existed between the Blackfeet and lessees sympathetic to the Blackfeet's interests. For example, Trowbridge discovered that Frye and Company, which leased 84,200 acres at ten cents per acre, paid fifteen cents per acre for grazing on the Fort Peck Reservation while admitting that Blackfeet lands were superior. Stone justified his program by telling Trowbridge that he had "worked for many years to get a desirable class of lessees, men and companies who are in sympathy with our Indian work and the Indians' affairs," and did not want to risk losing this "class of lessees" by aggressively prosecuting lease

terms. Those lessees, Trowbridge responded, "are large livestock corporations and it is not believed they are swayed with sentiment."[27] Stone
thus began his official tenure as superintendent with little inclination to
alter a system that rewarded stock corporations for demonstrating "sympathy" for the Blackfeet's affairs while they abused their property. As a
result, Stone's management of Blackfeet grazing resources would come
under constant criticism throughout his superintendency, while the integrity of the leasing system became weakened from overgrazing, trespass, and inadequate compensation.[28]

Stone remained supportive of the FYIP. He reported to the Indian Office that the number of Blackfeet "rationers" had dropped from 1,620
during the winter of 1920–21 to 320 in 1928–29; 328 heads of families
were active in the program, though only 278 actually farmed. There was,
Stone intimated, an element of structural poverty on the reservation that
no program could address.[29] Stone advised that the FYIP remained the
best source of activity for many of the Blackfeet until employment could
be created and monies freed to provide sheep and cattle to the tribe to
supplement the program. Stone also recommended that the Montana
Extension Service help improve Blackfeet farming yields, explaining to
Commissioner Charles J. Rhoads that the Blackfeet would respond better to a state employee than a federal agent. "There is a growing tendency
on the part of our Indian people that they want to participate in the affairs
of the State, not only along educational lines but health lines and other
activities as well," Stone wrote.[30] Stone's comment served as an indictment of his own performance. The Blackfeet had become increasingly
dissatisfied with the federal Indian service; the Senate hearing and investigation had only reinforced their opinions.

Blackfeet full-bloods also remained supportive of the FYIP, though
they were skeptical of its ability to provide real economic progress. Full-
bloods and their chapter officers were physically alienated from the center of tribal economic activity in Browning and increasingly politically
alienated from the tribal council because of a growing population gap between full-bloods and mixed-bloods. By 1929, the number of mixed-
bloods had increased to 2,510 from 1,452 in 1914; full-bloods numbered
1,130 in 1929, down from 1,189 in 1914.[31] Although voting in council
elections did not fall precisely along blood lines, it did follow them
closely. Since the mid-1920s the FYIP chapters had served as a countervailing form of power to the BTBC. In many respects it had equal power,
given Campbell's loyalty to the program and his distrust of mixed-blood

leaders like Robert Hamilton. But without real constitutional powers each group could only press its respective agenda and, when possible, act together when the tribe's interests appeared clear.

At their annual conference in May 1931 chapter officers resolved to sustain the FYIP for another five-year term; the two-day conference included a dance and the dedication of the new Heart Butte community hall, where the meeting was held. Robert Hamilton and Joseph Brown of the "north side," the mixed-blood community of Browning, attended the meeting, as did Stone and Campbell, now supervisor of the OIA's new extension program. The speeches given during the meeting reflected both the cooperative spirit that prevailed for a time after the July 1929 congressional hearing and full-bloods' increasing dissatisfaction with federal supervision of tribal affairs. Mountain Chief, a Christian full-blood elder, opened the conference with a plea for unity: "Now, I am asking you full bloods—I want you to be friendly with the mixed bloods. . . . They are of the same blood as we are. . . . They are our tribe. . . . We all belong on the reservation and we should try to get along together as a tribe. Civilization has come over the Indians and we have reached the period where we have to do what the white man say, that is we have to accept civilization and the white man's way."[32]

Other speakers praised the FYIP and offered recommendations to the resolutions committee. The conference officers adopted without dissent the committee's twenty-seven resolutions, most of which related to the FYIP. But two of the resolutions, linked by recent events, stood out. They revealed the primary weakness of the FYIP: its inability to generate cash income for its participants. Resolution 1 requested that the government distribute any tribal money in the U.S. Treasury in per capita payments. Resolution 3 promoted the "development of oil and gas on the Blackfeet Indian reservation" and endorsed the tribal council's control of that development on both allotted and tribal land.[33] Neither resolution would have immediate impact. The tribe had very little money in the U.S. Treasury in 1931, and the OIA ruled that the tribal council could not manage oil leasing on allotted lands because the regulations governing such leasing differed from those governing tribal land. Here again, the OIA declined or more likely refused to consider adapting leasing programs to changing political and geophysical circumstances.

The Blackfeet remained bitter about the government's usurpation of tribal funds for irrigation and thus wanted more control over future expenditures. The passage of Resolutions 1 and 3 expressed the desire of chapter officers to minimize the federal government's future role in handling tribal finances and tribal economic growth. Full-bloods had become as frustrated as mixed-bloods by the centralized control of Blackfeet policy in Washington and sanctioned the council's expanded involvement in oil leasing. If oil development succeeded, as most Blackfeet believed it would, then the chapter officers and their constituents did not want revenue tied up in Washington or used for unwarranted and unwanted programs. In addition, the U.S. Court of Claims was due to render a decision in the suit filed by the Blackfeet and other Montana tribes to win compensation from the government for its failure to honor treaty obligations—what became known as the "Big Claim."[34] The Blackfeet thus were hoping for two windfalls and desperately wanted to ensure that they could control the distribution of any newfound wealth. The Blackfeet version of the depression had arrived early in the form of drought in the summer of 1929 and frigid temperatures in the winter of 1930, creating new distress and new demands for progress in the management of tribal resources.[35]

Oil leasing and the Big Claim also dominated BTBC meetings. In July 1932 the tribe's attorney visited the reservation to discuss a variety of legal issues. John G. Carter told the council that he believed a decision in the Big Claim would be reached within six months and result in a payment of more than $2 million to the tribe, provided that the government did not appeal to the Supreme Court. Council members expressed their appreciation to Carter for his firm's efforts but asked him to protect from government meddling whatever judgment the tribe received. Full-blood councilman James White Calf told Carter that in the event of a Blackfeet victory, "instead of putting it in banks or in Washington, I want to see this money given out to us in cash." Little Dog told Carter: "I hope you can get some money for us this coming winter, and that you can get this Big Claim through, for the sake of the old people, who have taken such an interest in it."[36] For many older Blackfeet, particularly full-bloods who lived during the nineteenth century, the Big Claim represented both monetary compensation and a form of belated justice for the traumatic period of reservation retrenchment; as a result, there was some resentment on their part that mixed-bloods would profit from such a long-running claim. Rides at the Door was equally concerned with the slow pace of tribal oil development. He asked the council, "Why is it that these wells on the outside of the reservation are developed and completed, and ours are not? Why is it that the Blackfeet reservation can't be developed?" Natural resource development, he told Carter, "will help set us on our feet." There was little that Carter could do to help the Blackfeet improve their leasing program, but he kindly offered that "after you strike oil here, you will have more legal business in Washington than you ever thought possible."[37] The council subsequently passed a motion to engage Carter's law firm to represent the tribe in any legal business that might arise from oil production, fee patent disputes, and other economic matters.

The Blackfeet's expression of interest in giving to the State of Montana the right to provide medical, educational, and agricultural services on the reservation and the council's engagement of a law firm to mediate land claims and allotment disputes symbolized the declining state of relations between the Blackfeet Tribe of Indians and the United States government. Full-bloods and mixed-bloods alike were tiring of the agency's and lessees' demonstrations of sympathy. They wanted demonstrations of economic progress instead.

Interest in Blackfeet oil lands had swelled just as Hoover's conservation policy took effect. A February 1929 geological survey indicated that the "Milk River structures . . . offer the best possibility of any known undeveloped structures in northwestern Montana," while concluding that previous drilling efforts were poorly executed and thus "the status remains as though none had been drilled."[38] Wildcatters like Louis "Tip" O'Neil, financed in part by Louis Hill, began producing oil near the reservation's eastern boundary in 1930, creating a new round of oil excitement on the reservation. The Texas Production Company, a subsidiary of Texaco, became active in the leasing of allotted oil lands in early 1930, signing five leases with allottees or their heirs for land near the Milk River Anticline, where Hill still clung to the only active tribal lease.

Forrest Stone submitted the new leases to the OIA for consideration but recommended against approval because company representatives refused to guarantee that drilling would begin within a reasonable period. Citing the Hill lease and calling it the most unsatisfactory lease in the tribe's history, Stone argued that the OIA had been "too free in the past in granting leases on our Indian lands without having any positive assurance that a test was going to be made." He recommended that the OIA approve a lease only if the company agreed to either drill within two years or risk forfeiting a fifty-thousand-dollar bond.[39] In a subsequent letter to Rhoads, Stone argued for disapproval because he believed that the department should discourage unscrupulous oil operators and encourage Blackfeet production. The Blackfeet, he explained to Rhoads, "are pretty much disgusted over the fact that they have never been able to get their oil fields properly tested to determine whether or not they have oil in commercial quantities. Their efforts over a period of years have been very intensive and determined but with the various companies they have entered into oil leases with, they have been repeatedly disappointed in the ultimate results." Oil companies had promised active development, but in every case failed to honor that promise. The Interior Department's approval of the five Texaco leases without sufficient bond to guarantee drilling would perpetuate the government's failure to protect Blackfeet interests and exacerbate the frustration of the BTBC and those Blackfeet who did not own an allotment in oil territory. Hoover's conservation policy created a divided oil policy on the reservation because it prevented the council from leasing tribal lands while allottees could sign any lease they wanted. Department policy thus unfairly penalized the tribe as an economic unit. Stone told Rhoads that he understood the logic of the conservation policy in a general way but also argued that the purpose of any oil leasing on Indian land "should be for the production of oil." He requested that the OIA "find it possible to support me."[40] Neither the OIA nor the Interior Department offered such support. Ignoring Stone's logical argument and passionate appeal for fairness, Interior officials approved the leases on July 2, in the process seemingly contradicting their own argument that the intent of the conservation policy was to discourage leasing. Hoover's policy, however, applied to public or tribal lands, not private land.[41]

Alarmed by new oil strikes by O'Neil and other wildcatters on the eastern boundary of the reservation, the BTBC undertook new efforts to generate production on Blackfeet lands in the summer of 1932. Levi Burd, a prominent Blackfeet businessman, lobbied heavily to increase Indian participation in the testing of tribal lands. Burd and Charles Buck petitioned the council in August 1932 to grant them the right to drill on forty-eight hundred acres of tribal land in the hopes that an oil strike would spur development elsewhere on the reservation. The proposal differed from standard procedure in that Burd and Buck would deposit $720 with the tribal council in lieu of a surety bond and retain the rights to the acreage for one year with the option of signing a standard lease after that period. Stone, eager to try anything to increase activity and improve the Blackfeet's leverage, supported Burd's idea, telling the council that it well

might "create a market for the allotted acreage. Other companies and individuals would come in." The council initially tabled Burd's proposition
after White Calf questioned Burd's motives but finally resolved to accept
it; Burd, White Calf argued, owned an allotment that was potentially
worth a great deal if oil was discovered, and he had invested in the Browning Development Company, a local oil company. Richard Sanderville
defended Burd's actions, offering that "Levi had done pretty hard work
for us; more than any of these mixed-bloods. Levi is benefiting the Tribe
while these others are not."[42] Stone wrote the OIA for approval, explaining that "only Mr. Burd and Mr. Buck stand to lose [money]." Interior officials agreed to waive the bond requirement and provide Burd
with a special exploratory lease.[43]

On the surface the decision served as a testament to Stone's persis-
tence as well as a high-level demonstration of sympathy to the council's
creative efforts to spur development. But it simply reflected the Interior
Department's continued bias against the Blackfeet's collective efforts to
develop tribally owned resources. This bias runs throughout the department's decisions in the 1920s and the 1930s. Only when acculturated
businessmen like Levi Burd and Charles Buck agreed to make an investment did officials consent to leasing alternatives. Department officials
routinely approved leases on allotted land despite entreaties from a veteran field agent that the Blackfeet oil leasing system required a uniform
strategy; Interior, in effect, served as a brokerage office for Blackfeet allottees at the expense of the tribe. The department refused to interfere
with the *individual's* right to make a contract, applying by fiat the logic of
market capitalism to the reservation political economy in yet another attempt to "break up the tribal mass."

As the BTBC tried to find new ways to circumvent government resistance and precipitate legitimate oil exploration, the Blackfeet ran into
opposition from a different antagonist: Montana's oil companies. Stone
attempted to auction the sale of six tracts of tribal oil lands aggregating
2,936.66 acres in early September 1932 but failed to generate any bids.[44]
Tip O'Neil, representing the Santa Rita Oil and Gas Company, offered
to sign a lease on the condition that the tribe waive the sliding scale of
royalty provision of the tribal lease; the sliding scale dictated that the
tribal royalty would rise from 12.5 percent to a maximum of 25 percent
once production quotas were met. Other prospective bidders also expressed dissatisfaction with the scale. The resistance and likely collusion
of local companies alarmed Stone and BTBC members, who convened on

October 3 to discuss the latest roadblock to development. The council resolved to survey all Montana oil companies to solicit their reasons for not
bidding. Nine of the twenty companies contacted responded, and all of
them indicated that the principal objection to the Blackfeet tribal lease
was the sliding royalty scale. The question of short-term versus long-
term benefits dominated the council's discussion of the survey results.
Levi Burd explained to council members the risks and expenses involved
in oil exploration and production and recommended that they offer Tip
O'Neil a lease without the sliding scale in order to determine the reservation's potential; if oil was found, the council could then reinstitute the
sliding scale. Several council members objected to the easy terms, believing that the potential for big oil strikes justified bigger royalty payments. White Calf and Rides at the Door, speaking for their full-blood
constituents, urged the council to waive the scale altogether. "We must
find something to get money for the people because of the condition that
will exist this winter," White Calf said. Rides at the Door's trip to the oil
fields on the reservation's boundary had given him hope. "I thought salvation had come to the tribe and they would live in plenty," he told his
colleagues. He too recommended that the council waive the scale but argued for its reinstatement once companies reached the production level
of five hundred barrels. The council unanimously adopted White Calf's
motion to waive the sliding scale and offered Tip O'Neil new lease terms
to induce him and his operation to cross the boundary line into Indian
territory.[45]

Stone, in yet another supplicatory letter to the OIA, explained that the
BTBC approved the O'Neil lease largely because it had to compete with
leases on allotted land that had no sliding scale; the council also continued to fear that its reserves were being drained by wells operating just
across the reservation border. Stone told Rhoads that if the OIA reviewed
the Blackfeet's history of oil and gas leasing, then it would "realize that
we have been confronted with some very serious obstacles and secured
some very discouraging results." The Blackfeet, Stone wrote, "have
never lost interest or hope in their oil prospects and have now come to the
conclusion that we must do something to stimulate the interest in the
tribal lands or otherwise any benefits that might be secured from the oil
and gas resources of the reservation will never be obtained during the
lifetime of our old people."[46] Stone had contended with the OIA's inflex-
ibility on oil leasing almost as long as the Blackfeet had, and his letter
spoke of the general frustration that prevailed on the reservation and of

his own frustration for being unable to facilitate oil production. This request is reasonable, he was saying, and perhaps the last chance for many of the tribe's older citizens to reap benefits from what was generally regarded as a potential source of income. Rhoads accepted the logic and the urgency of Stone's letter and secured permission from Interior to waive the sliding scale, giving the tribe a small victory after a decade-long struggle to secure assistance from its guardian in its search for "salvation."

By the end of 1932 the oil excitement was again at a high pitch. The decision to waive the sliding royalty scale and O'Neil's subsequent acceptance of the new lease terms gave many Blackfeet hope that oil would soon be gushing on reservation lands and royalties pumping into the tribal treasury; O'Neil was an experienced operator who had achieved much success in the neighboring Cut Bank fields. In late December, the *Cut Bank Pioneer Press* reported that "Stone sees prosperous days ahead for Blackfeet Indians through oil development." Stone did not think the Blackfeet would get as rich as the Osages, but he did say "the outlook at the present time appears exceptionally bright."[47] The newspaper reported in late February 1933 that tribal members "became richer" by nearly forty-eight thousand dollars from a per capita distribution of oil leasing bonuses. "This is the first of what is expected to be several 'melons' to be cut by the Blackfeet," the article exclaimed, predicting that by the end of 1933 "a steady stream of oil royalties will be flowing into the tribal treasury."[48] The Blackfeet finally saw oil flow on their reservation two months later, when O'Neil's well produced roughly seventy-five barrels of oil. On April 28, 1933, a group of Blackfeet, including several "[c]hiefs in full regalia" and the tribe's famous band, visited the tribe's first producing well to celebrate Mother Earth's new offering.[49] The first oil strike and the per capita distribution that resulted were not large by any means, but, after so many years of unfulfilled promises, they were tangible.

The John Collier era in Washington began the same week that the Blackfeet finally achieved a measure of success in oil production, two equally propitious events; Collier replaced Charles Rhoads on April 21, 1933, to begin the longest tenure of any commissioner of Indian affairs. The Blackfeet were familiar with Collier from previous visits and from his defense of Indian rights in the 1920s. The BTBC had resolved in March 1926 to thank Collier "for his valued assistance," offering its "undivided support in his good work and efforts, in disclosing to Congress the deceptive methods employed by said Bureau of Indian Affairs."[50] The council was waging war against Frank Campbell and his superiors in Washington at the time Collier, as executive director of the American Indian Defense Association, was battling the OIA and Congress over Pueblo land rights, Indian oil rights, and an Indian's right to due process.[51] Collier's persistent attacks on the allotment policy and the OIA's management of Indian resources had contributed to Secretary of the Interior Hubert Work's decision to conduct the investigation of Indian affairs that became the Meriam Report. Collier's subsequent testimony to the Senate subcommittee on Indian affairs in 1928 helped to convince Congress of the need for its own investigation. Collier had accompanied the subcommittee to Browning for its investigation of Campbell's administration in 1929. He sent Assistant Commissioner William Zimmerman Jr. on a similar journey to Blackfeet country in 1933.

The October 19, 1933, hearing differed in content and character from the one held four years earlier, in part because the well-traveled Senate committee was familiar with the problems facing the Blackfeet and because Stone's superintendency had not generated controversy as Campbell's had. Despite little progress in oil production and arguably no progress in grazing resource management, the tribe did not point to Stone as the principal source of failure but to the BIA, or, more generally, the federal government's guardianship of the Blackfeet Tribe.

When the subcommittee returned to the reservation, tribal leaders were united in their desire for organizational change. Both PFLA officers and BTBC members wanted expanded control of the tribe's financial and natural resources. Several weeks before the hearing began, Mountain Chief organized a meeting to discuss the committee's upcoming visit and the tribe's need for better representation in Washington. The eighty-five year-old full-blood leader told the gathering that the government was unresponsive to written communication and thus he believed that the tribe should demand better management of its natural resources. "We are tired of the leasing of our grazing lands and tired of outside sheep companies. We want to utilize our own resources and develop our oil lands," he said. Black Weasel added that the tribe had a right to know the status of its assets and its business and demanded that the government seek the tribe's consent before again "making disposition of our property." Rides at the Door, active in pursuing resource development for many years, called for a "'new deal' as we want to be treated the same as the white people. Give us a fair and new deal as we know ourselves the old system is no success."[52] The tribe's full-bloods, many of whom had supported the Campbell regime throughout most of the 1920s, had had enough of government supervision and became increasingly outspoken about the mismanagement of the tribe's appropriations and property, joining the chorus of mixed-bloods who had been pushing for more control of the tribal estate since the early 1920s. Those hardened views found expression in other tribal meetings and in the October 19 congressional subcommittee hearing.

The subcommittee first discussed the tribe's dormant irrigation projects, a particularly sore subject for most Blackfeet. The principal question facing the Indian Office and Congress was whether or not the tribe should abandon the projects that had been successful only in draining valuable funds from its treasury; if the Badger-Fisher and Two Medicine units were abandoned, then roughly eighty white families would be forced to move and Indian allotments in the district would be rendered worthless. While Collier's administration opposed the construction of new irrigation districts, it did not want to cancel unfinished projects that still might benefit Indians. Sen. Burton Wheeler believed it best to continue existing projects while waiving back charges for irrigated water. Wheeler ended one discussion of irrigation with an admonishment to the Blackfeet, telling them that in a few years the federal government was "going to release all of its guardianship over the Indian." Consequently, he said, "Indians have to know and they have to appreciate the fact that they will have to depend upon their own resources in the very near future. The sooner they go to work and realize this, get on a piece of land and become self-supporting, the better it is going to be for them."[53] Joe Brown, the sixty-year-old BTBC chairman, explained to Wheeler that the tribal council and the agency superintendent wanted to manage any newly organized irrigation districts: "We believe we can handle them more economically and to the better satisfaction of the Indian than the Reclamation Service."[54]

Brown, who enjoyed broad political support, urged the government to replace white workers with Indian workers when possible, another reflection of the desire of the Blackfeet to assume more responsibility for their affairs, the dominant theme of the hearing; of the seventy-three agency employees, only thirty-six were Blackfeet Indians. Brown also requested that Wheeler find funding to help the Blackfeet develop a tribal oil company and purchase another tribal herd. If the government would provide seed money for a tribal drilling operation, then "the Blackfeet themselves as a company [could] borrow money and drill these oil wells themselves and get 100 percent of the oil rather than get the 12 ½ percent that they get now." Wheeler discouraged Brown from pursuing such an idea, telling him that the oil industry was a "pretty hazardous occupation" and a financial risk. Wheeler continued to champion the allotment policy and a variation of Campbell's industrial program, but he also sanctioned greater Blackfeet control of reservation business affairs. "We ought to push as much responsibility onto them as we possibly can," he told Stone.[55]

While Wheeler opposed tribal control of oil development, he did support Brown's plan to expand the Blackfeet livestock industry, opining that "the only salvation for these Indians is for them to have their own farm and their own stock instead of leasing the land and depending upon the lease money that comes in." Brown had articulated the Blackfeet's desire for another opportunity to manage their own stock instead of leasing land to white stockowners. If whites could run their sheep from Washington state to Montana for summer grazing, paying taxes and grazing fees in the process, and then ship them to Chicago and still turn a profit, Brown asked, then "why can not we, the Indians who own the land and who do not pay these taxes nor do not have to pay for the grazing, make a success of the stock industry?"[56] Brown supported the efforts of the tribe to expand its oil and gas operations, but, like Wheeler, he strongly believed that tribal income should be produced from labor and not simply from leasing, particularly when the integrity of the tribe's oil and range leasing systems was difficult to maintain.

Stone also supported Brown's plan to rejuvenate the tribe's livestock industry, calling it "the ultimate solution" to Blackfeet problems. "We have an interest on the part of the Indians to handle his own affairs," he testified. "We have a commissioner who is in sympathy with the plan and I think we have a class of Indians who are able to carry it out." Stone testified that if the competent members of the tribe were given a chance to manage the livestock industry, tribal irrigation, and a proposed creamery plant, then within ten years the committee "would find the Blackfeet Indians very largely in control of their own industries." Stone ended the hearing by telling the committee that the time was right, at least on the Blackfeet Reservation, for a dramatic change in Indian affairs. "We cannot afford to lose the interest that they have right now to handle their own affairs," he said. "I never have seen a more genuine desire, and that is actuated not through any discontent that I can find, but through the confidence that they have in themselves in their ability to do it and I also have that confidence in them."[57] Stone would have found discontent if he had looked hard enough. But the Blackfeet, he knew, continued to look to a future they could influence rather than dwell in a past over which they had no control.

Tribal, congressional, and Indian Office leaders reached a consensus during the 1933 hearing that the Blackfeet Indians were able and willing to manage their business affairs. Senator Wheeler had remarked at the end of the hearing that "the Indians on this reservation are capable of taking care of themselves."[58] Walter Liggett, who investigated Blackfeet affairs for the 1929 senate hearing, had concluded four years earlier that "there has been a tragic failure to teach these Indians the true fundamentals of education. After many years in leading strings they are not equipped to cope with the conditions they are facing."[59] The truth lay somewhere between those opposing sentiments.

If the Meriam Report and the U.S. Congress recommended eventually "winding up the National administration of Indian life"—the "termination" of federal control of Indian political and economic affairs—then the Blackfeet Indians wanted it sooner rather than later, considering the state of affairs on their reservation. Given that the Blackfeet's physical and financial assets had declined so dramatically under white leadership, it is not difficult to imagine the bitterness and frustration they felt having to rely on incompetent, corrupt, or powerless white supervisors who consistently showed favoritism to their white neighbors. It is very possible that the Blackfeet could have done better than their white supervisors; their interest in improving tribal affairs was, to understate it, greater than that of their Indian agents.

Stone's superintendency was an improvement over Campbell's, but intruders, trespassers, and thieves continued to abuse Blackfeet resources. The Blackfeet's guardian offered neither legal protection against discriminatory leases nor restitution for the wrongs of allotment. Allotment had come and gone and taken with it a part of the Blackfeet's land base and a part of their economic future. The only vision for financial security, and thus cultural peace, lay in the development of tribal resources. What tribal leaders lacked, perhaps, were the structural tools of political economy, the political means to manage economic affairs that made sense given the specific climatological and cultural conditions of Blackfeet country, a way to balance the competing interest groups of full-bloods and mixed-bloods, farmers and ranchers, agriculturists and industrialists, pro-agency and anti-agency forces. This situation presented several questions for the Blackfeet. Who would organize and manage this vision? To what degree could the Blackfeet Tribal Business Council or other tribal organizations achieve some insulation from the vagaries and vices of agency administration while fostering independent control of political and economic decision-making, and in the process terminate federal supervision on their own terms?

The control of such decision-making lay for the moment in the hands of a distant administration and its local white managers. Cultural and political independence is born from the frustrations of living through such a neocolonial relationship. The word "termination" had not yet entered the lexicon of Indian-white relations, but its core meaning of Indian "self-support" had manifested itself in Blackfeet political speech. The idea of self-support dominated and animated discussions in public meetings, private conversations, and congressional hearings. The Blackfeet people may not have been ready to be self-supporting in 1933, but they were clearly ready to start trying. "[T]he old system is no success," Rides at the Door had said. The Blackfeet hoped that the political changes brewing far away in Washington would result in a "fair and new deal" for a tribe anxious about its future and eager to assume some control over it.

The Blackfeet Get a New Deal

The roots of John Collier's Indian New Deal lie in the administration of Charles Rhoads and J. Henry Scattergood, who, with the support of Secretary of the Interior Ray Lyman Wilbur, directed Herbert Hoover's Indian policy. Wilbur had worked with Indian reform groups since the 1910s and firmly believed in the assimilation of the Indian into white society; Indians, he said in 1924, "must as speedily as possible depend upon themselves if they are ever to amount to anything except dying remnants."[60] Rhoads accepted Hoover's call to serve as his Indian commissioner largely because Hoover agreed to support the central reforms outlined in the Meriam Report. Rhoads achieved considerable success in implementing some of the report's recommendations in the areas of health and education but less so in economic development and land reform. Indian health care became more accessible and geared to preventive treatment after the BIA hired more doctors and field nurses. Under the guidance of W. Carson Ryan Jr. the Indian Service enlarged its teaching staff and created a syncretic and flexible curriculum, which included the type of vocational training that Joe Brown had requested during the 1929 Senate subcommittee hearing. Ryan's approach embodied the cultural pluralism of John Collier that would find expression in the Indian New Deal. Just as Franklin Roosevelt extended some of Herbert Hoover's reforms, so too did Collier benefit from the reforms initiated by Rhoads and Scattergood.

Collier had been an early supporter of the Wilbur and Rhoads appointments, exclaiming in 1929 that "every condition favorable to a large reorganization of Indian affairs now exists."[61] Rhoads and Collier collaborated on a series of letters—sent to congressional committees shortly after Rhoads took office—that outlined the new administration's approach to Indian reform. Although Rhoads signed the letters, it is widely assumed that Collier wrote them. The second of the four letters outlined Collier's view on the "incorporation"—or reincorporation to be more precise—of Indian America. He suggested that the OIA give Indians "a collective responsibility for their tribal business and ultimately of terminating the present absolute responsibility of the Government for the management of [their] multitudinous properties."[62] Rhoads retracted his support for Collier's agenda when it became clear to him that it entailed reversing allotment and empowering tribal councils to manage tribal business without contributing to the tax base of local, state, and federal governments. Incorporation, for Rhoads, was another tool for the assimilation of the Indian into white America. For Collier, it was a tool for preserving the independence of Indian nations within the nation. Relations between Collier and Rhoads deteriorated during the remainder of Rhoads's tenure. Collier's criticism of Rhoads reflected both philosophical differences and Collier's strong will and sense of mission. Collier did not just see problems in the stewardship of the American Indian; he saw a viable culture in jeopardy. More precisely, he believed that preserving Indian culture would help regenerate white culture. Indian life, if properly reconstituted, could, he explained to Guggenheim Foundation members, serve to assuage the "troubled, frustrated but struggling Aryan individualized consciousness."[63]

It was this sense of mission and passion for reform that led newly appointed Secretary of the Interior Harold Ickes to select Collier as commissioner of Indian affairs in early 1933. Ickes defended his selection and Collier's philosophy by saying, "The whites can take care of themselves, but the Indians need some one to protect them from exploitation. I want a man who will respect their customs and have a sympathetic point of view with reference to their culture. I want the Indians to be helped to help themselves."[64] The Collier administration was thus poised to produce a New Deal for the Indian instead of the "false dawn" of Hoover's New Era. Collier acted quickly to push his agenda on an attentive Congress. Within six months the nation and its indigenous peoples saw a dramatic attempt to overhaul the ways and means governing Indian-white relations. In the reform-minded atmosphere of depression America, Collier and his dedicated staff assiduously promoted a vision of organizational change that would eventually be codified as the Indian Reorganization Act. The issue of tribal incorporation, delineated in the Meriam Report and in Collier's second letter to congressional Indian Affairs committees, became the cornerstone of his reform.

In early 1934, while Collier and his staff prepared a legislative agenda for Congress and an attendant public relations campaign to generate support for it, the Blackfeet considered the changes that were brewing in Washington. The 1933 Senate subcommittee hearing had created an expectation of BIA reform among interested Blackfeet, and they were eager to see what the new administration had to offer them. Their first exposure to the new regime was Collier's January 20 circular letter, which was sent to all tribes and their superintendents to introduce the philosophy of the Indian New Deal. Collier's twelve-page letter—simply entitled "Indian Self-Government"—first emphasized his hope that Indians would themselves contribute to the process of improving their affairs. The letter focused on the "evils of allotment" and the need for changes in land policy and local administration of resources to improve "the community life and political responsibility of the Indian," which had been "largely destroyed."[65] The establishment of Indian self-government and the concomitant expansion of economic opportunity were the twin goals of the program, he wrote. Tribes should be "organized and chartered as municipal corporations" and "entrusted with powers and responsibilities . . . exercised by a village or county government." Collier emphasized that his agenda centered on giving each tribe "the maximum measure of control over its economic life and, in particular, over expenditures of its own funds." Collier delineated the basic architecture and the checks and balances of an organized Indian community, providing a sketchy blueprint for the gradual termination of federal supervision. He recommended that state governments assume the responsibilities of education and health matters and that a reconstituted Indian community, if properly organized, ultimately should be given "complete supervision over its internal affairs."[66]

The First Blackfeet Debate

The BTBC convened on February 5 to discuss the letter and Collier's reorganization plan; nearly seven hundred Blackfeet attended the meeting, the largest gathering ever assembled for a discussion of political matters. Forrest Stone opened the meeting by summarizing Collier's letter and legislative agenda, which he called "an opportunity that will never be presented again." Stone reminded the Blackfeet that the tribe had lost 2.5 million acres of land in the last fifty years, arguing that Collier's policy would end the diminution of the tribal estate and give them "something to hand to your children." He raised the controversial issue of communal ownership, saying that the "matter of pooling your lands will equalize things, even though it does take a sacrifice on the part of some of you to do this."[67] Collier's proposal for Indians to remise their allotments to tribal ownership sparked a fierce debate. Few Blackfeet expressed a willingness to make the sacrifice. James Perrine, a supporter of Collier's self-government provisions, was skeptical about his land policy, declaring, "We are not Menonites [sic] yet." Despite this skepticism, Owen Heavybreast spoke for many of his fellow full-bloods when he criticized Perrine and other mixed-bloods who would benefit from the pooling of Blackfeet lands, saying that many of them had squandered a share of the reservation when they sold their allotments.[68] Hugh Jackson, a veteran of World War I, was the most outspoken, arguing that "it looks as if we want to be governed under a communistic form of government like in Russia. . . . I don't believe we should try any changes." The Blackfeet, Jackson said, "are living in the United States, and the system is that you have to own property by title. We are not in a foreign country, and we got to travel along with the people in the state of Montana. We got to live like the rest of them."[69] The constant shifts of Indian policy, despite its continued assimilationist thrust, had made some conservative Blackfeet suspicious of any structural changes in Indian administration.

Speakers did agree that the best economic policy remained the development of the tribe's oil resources. Despite some initial success the previous year, the reservation was not being developed in any fashion similar to neighboring Cut Bank; only three Blackfeet wells operated, compared with seventy in the Cut Bank fields, some of which, Perrine charged, continued to drain oil from Blackfeet reserves. Perrine raised again the prevailing argument that the tribe's future depended upon oil production. Collier's proposal failed to mention resource development, Perrine said, and he asked the council to convince the Interior Department that "this resource should be developed as quickly as possible so that the Indians here will receive the ultimate benefit. Then our reasons for assembling here to ask or beg the government for this and that would be eliminated, because we will then have our own subsistence."[70] Jackson and others supported Perrine's call for renewed attention to oil development, but some speakers raised objections to the idea of using proceeds from the anticipated Big Claim award to expand the oil industry. Charles Reevis told the council, "We have used other methods in the oil business and we have accomplished very little and now you want to take this $75,000 out of the big claim and put it in the oil business. We need that money for ourselves."[71] In addition to criticizing communal ownership and supporting oil leasing, the council expressed indifference on the issue of religious freedom, which Collier had promised in his plan; Christianity had been embraced, or at least had replaced for many the religious customs of the 1800s, and there seemed to be no interest in using the Collier bill to facilitate the rebirth of such customs.

There was great confusion about what Collier intended, on the Blackfeet Reservation and elsewhere in the country, particularly in regard to land consolidation. Reevis told Collier that his "letter and the policy advocated is not understood." The Blackfeet delegation selected to lobby Collier and the Congress, he wrote, opposed the policy and "will try to prevent the execution of its essential features on the Reservation."[72] Stone told Collier that despite "doing some pretty strenuous work" trying to explain Collier's intentions, "the feeling is running quite strongly against the plan." Stone did say that the plan had not been digested fully, and he hoped that "the voice of what might be termed 'the great silent masses'" would be heard once they discovered the plan's merits. Collier encouraged Stone to continue his discussion of the proposed legislation and to explain to the Blackfeet that "it is not the purpose of the bill to take land away from those who have it and give it to those who have not."[73] Blackfeet delegates made it clear that the bill as written appeared to allow a new Blackfeet community government to do just that. The kind of confusion and anger that Collier faced from tribes like the Blackfeet was a principal reason he initiated a series of Indian conferences the following month.

The Great Plains Congress

The debate on the Wheeler-Howard Bill—Collier's forty-eight-page plan was sponsored by Burton Wheeler and Edgar Howard of Nebraska, chairmen of the Senate and House Committees on Indian Affairs, respectively—began in the House on February 22, and in the Senate on February 27.[74] Collier announced during the first House hearing that he would be taking his reform program to the people it would affect by organizing a series of Indian congresses, the first time the OIA had given its charges an opportunity to consider important legislation before it was imprinted upon their reservations.

Eighteen members of the Blackfeet Nation joined tribal representatives of nearly sixty thousand Plains Indians in Rapid City SD on March 2, 1934, to hear Collier himself delineate the important facets of his vision of modern Indian administration; the four-day Great Plains Congress, or Rapid City Congress, was the first of nine conferences that Collier and his associates held throughout the country to address the concerns that had arisen in Indian America.[75] In his general remarks to start the conference, Collier emphasized the new attitude toward Indian affairs held by his administration and congressional committees. The OIA and Congress had the authority to pass unilaterally any legislation affecting Indians, he told the crowd, but they would not do so in 1934. "We intend to act in partnership with the Indians," Collier said, "and we are not going to act unless the Indians are willing to go with us." Collier and Secretary of the Interior Ickes had striven for the reform of Indian administration for many years, he said, and agreed that "it was the duty of the Indians themselves to determine what their own life shall be."[76] This pronouncement of faith elicited applause from those in attendance, who were as excited by Collier's words as by his presence in front of such a disparate collection of Indian leaders.

Collier attacked the "evils of allotment" before discussing the specifics of the Wheeler-Howard Indian Rights Bill. He attempted to clarify the issue of communal ownership, which had caused such a backlash among Indians concerned with losing title to land to the increasingly anachronistic idea of communal property; for many Indians, their allotment was all they had—both to live on and to produce rent from, as well as their only gift of inheritance. Despite Collier's impassioned exhortation for the end of checkerboarding and the need for land consolidation to make tribal estates economically productive, mandated property transfers of any kind for any reason did not appeal to the majority of the

Plains Indians in attendance. Collier received thunderous applause the following morning when he announced that the OIA leadership had decided to "recommend to the Committees of Congress that this transfer of title by the allottee to the community, this transfer shall be exclusively voluntary and that the compulsion feature shall be stricken out."[77] Collier faced opposition to mandatory transfers from both Indian groups and the congressional Indian Affairs committees and thus had little choice but to sacrifice that provision. Collier's decision, however, served as an example of his pledge to seek Indian input into the legislative process.

Collier's ideas about tribal reorganization got a better reception. The basis of the modern world, he said, was organization, which took form in corporations, associations, cooperatives, and municipal governments. Collier explained that "what is almost the heart of our plan" is the organization of the American Indian for "mutual benefit, for local self-government and for doing business in the modern, organized way." Reconstituted tribal organizations would still enjoy the "protective guardianship" of the federal government and the "privilege" of tax exemption, he promised, but they would also enjoy increased responsibility for the internal affairs of the tribe, access to the OIA's proposed credit system, and eligibility for the type of federal assistance contained in Franklin Roosevelt's New Deal legislation. No Indian group would be forced to organize, but if it did, Collier said to loud applause, it could "take over many of the things that are now being done by the Indian Bureau, and the money being spent on those things would be transferred to the organized body of Indians and they would spend the money and they would hire their own employees." Collier forcefully stressed the need for organization, telling his audience of Indian leaders and entrepreneurs that "in the United States, if you are going to do business and make money and protect yourself, you have got to do it in an organized way. Otherwise you are just out of luck. You don't make any money, you are not protected, and the other fellow eats you alive. You can't govern yourselves, you can't do business, you can't protect yourself, unless you organize." The American Indian, Collier told the crowd, was an example of Roosevelt's forgotten man, who had been carrying a "privileged class" and big business on his back. The Indian now had an opportunity to benefit from New Deal reforms designed to protect the common man.[78] Collier, sounding like a cross between Henry Luce and Dwight Macdonald, thus presented the philosophical heart of the plan: the need for Indian America to form countervailing or complementary organizations to those of white America. For Collier, the Indian New Deal was as much about class as it was about race.

After Collier reviewed his vision and the legislative version of it, tribal delegates were given a chance to ask questions of the panel and ten minutes with which to offer an "unofficial expression of opinion." Joe Brown opened this period on March 4 with a short speech, telling Collier and his associates that his delegation had tried to be a "good listener" so that its decision would be based on facts. "In the most part of this bill we are in favor of it, and I believe that if we can get together with some of the Bureau officials to work over the objectionable features that we have we are not far apart. Our Reservation is getting . . . so checkerboarded with white settlers that it looks like a man with the small pox," Brown said. He thanked the Collier delegation for its attendance and said to applause that he regretted "that our law permits a Commissioner to be appointed according to political affiliations" because "it is just too bad that we can't keep him there so that with his new program he can see it through and follow it up."[79]

The opinions expressed after Brown spoke were decidedly mixed. The Crow and the Northern Cheyenne delegations, for example, expressed their belief that their tribes could not operate successfully under the self-government provisions. Several delegations remained convinced that the bill would principally benefit landless mixed-bloods who would take advantage of full-blood assets through the vehicle of communal ownership; the factional fighting exhibited during the February 5 BTBC meeting was not uncommon in other Indian nations.[80] Others objected to the idea of community life itself, believing that the forces of assimilation were too strong to resist. Joe Irving, chairman of the Crow Creek delegation, argued that "the whole idea as to the self-government . . . is Socialism."[81]

Elderly delegates were given an opportunity to address Collier's delegation in their native tongue. Rides at the Door told the assembly that the Blackfeet Tribe needed the legislation to protect its resources from white predators. "My people now own a large area of oil land and we have now on our reservation three producing wells, and that is the reason I came here, and I want some law or protection whereby I can always hold that property intact so that no white man can take it away from me," he said to applause. Referring to the Collier delegation, he expressed hope that "with their protection and support, their guidance, we are not going to let any white man do like that to us."[82] The Blackfeet delegation was, perhaps, the most supportive and the most unified of those that attended the four-day conference; although they had not reached a final decision, Blackfeet delegates favored what they had heard. The delegation certainly gave Collier the biggest endorsement, both by offering a positive opinion of the bill during its allotted time and by adopting him into the tribe. During the last session, a Blackfeet delegate generated enthusiastic applause by announcing from the stage that the tribe planned to "adopt the commissioner" and make him a "leader in this community plan"; as a result the Blackfeet "expect him to do more for us," he explained. The Blackfeet gave Collier the name Spotted Eagle, the delegate said, because it "represents the Indian Reservations, the way they are checkerboarded. We hope that those spots will be rubbed off so that every Indian Reservation will be all in one spot."[83]

Collier ended the conference as he had started it, reminding delegates of the emphasis he placed on voluntary participation and the need for Indians to organize effectively to assert their rights in protecting their current assets and their future livelihood from the predations of white neighbors. He warned them not to listen to the local interests, who would call the bill communism. "Your interests," he said, "are, of necessity, in opposition to many local interests around you. You want to have the capital to put stock on your own lands and yourself enjoy the profits of the cattle business, and, of course, there are white cattle men and banks that don't want you to do it."[84] More important than the conference and the legislation, Collier told the delegates, was the idea that "Indians shall take the responsibility, here and now, of thinking out their own problems and arriving at their own conclusions, and determining their own future."[85] Self-determination through self-government was, Collier concluded, the means to the end of federal supervision as Indians knew it in 1934.

The Second Blackfeet Debate

The Blackfeet Tribal Business Council had tried to assume additional responsibility for the welfare of the tribe for two decades but had faced agency prejudice, favoritism, and in some cases informed opinion. Tribal, congressional, and BIA representatives had concluded in October 1933 that the Blackfeet were, in Sen. Burton Wheeler's words, "capable of taking care of themselves." The council now had an opportunity to act upon that judgment. Rides at the Door had said in 1933 that the Blackfeet wanted a "new deal" because "the old system is no success." The Blackfeet Tribe now had the option of choosing Collier's new system of political economy to reach its long-standing goal of self-support and self-governance. Collier's speeches at the Great Plains Congress appealed to the Blackfeet because they addressed several important issues besides the rather amorphous notion of self-government, delineating a new system of tribal economic organization that promised credit-starved tribal members access to a revolving loan fund. Collier's pronouncement that his legislation would enable an Indian nation to "take over many of the things that are now being done by the Indian Bureau," spend the money allocated for those activities, and "hire their own employees" mirrored the testimony of Blackfeet leaders during the October 1933 Senate hearing. But Blackfeet leaders had learned during the 1920s to read the fine print and, despite the promise held out by Collier's words and his actions, devoted considerable time to determining whether his plan would help the tribe achieve a self-supporting condition for its citizens.

The Blackfeet were more developed politically than most tribes. The BTBC had been in operation since 1915 and its constitution in place since 1922; the election process, however flawed, reminded the Blackfeet of their ability to foster change every two years. The type of centralized government that Collier proposed was not foreign to most Blackfeet, though it was not always acceptable to them. The internecine conflict between the business council and the FYIP leadership had died down, but the legacy of that conflict was a distrust of centralized control of tribal decision-making. Yet the experience that many FYIP leaders had with the opposite model, the disparate collection of chapter organizations, led many of them to oppose any alternative to centralized government.[86] The debate over which form of self-government the Blackfeet should adopt dominated the BTBC meeting of March 31 and three similar meetings held in the reservation's other voting districts.

Council chairman Joe Brown conceded at the outset of the March 31 meeting that many Blackfeet, particularly full-bloods, were "mixed up" about the Wheeler-Howard Bill, and thus he had invited Great Falls attorney Cleve Hall to help explain the council's proposed amendments. The principal question was whether the Blackfeet should sanction the charter of one central government or numerous self-governing communities. The question, as Hall put it to the council and more than one hundred Blackfeet in attendance, was "whether you would want a number of communities on the one reservation, bearing in mind that these communities take over the tribal funds and lands, or whether you would want one large community for the reservation."[87] The issue had been debated during the mid-1920s, as the north-side community, the mostly mixed-blood districts and the council they dominated, and the south-side community, which found political expression in the chapter organizations, struggled for political legitimacy. The Blackfeet now were faced with the need to define their community legally, to formalize the structure of governing within the physical boundaries of the reservation. Joe Brown predicted that confusion would reign if the tribe elected to charter more than one community government. "The whole bill means to gradually take over the range of government on your reservation," he told the crowd, and he recommended that the Blackfeet "control our government right here from this office." He asked those assembled to "imagine half a dozen governments existing on the Reservation, each one functioning under a president, secretary, its police powers, and its right to a certain portion of the tribal fund."[88] Hall agreed with Brown's assessment, adding that the expense of several governments would be prohibitive.

It would be quite natural to suppose that Chairman Brown and other mixed-blood council members would prefer the central government of the business council, but a consensus emerged that centralized decision-making was the only option to consider. Several influential full-bloods weighed in with support for one government. Bird Rattler, Many Hides, Weaselhead, and John Ground all testified to the need for one community government. Rides at the Door told the assemblage, "You all now realize the experience of that division of the reservation, known as chapter districts. You all know that you never got along good. There was nothing but continuous disagreement all the way through." The Blackfeet, Hugh Jackson added, "should call it one corporation—the Blackfeet Reservation."[89] Eighty-eight Blackfeet sanctioned the idea of one corporation, while twenty-four opposed it. There were a few holdover opponents who believed that "one community" meant the sacrifice of individual property and some who simply did not trust the mixed-blood leadership. Dick Kipp wanted a government like the one the Blackfeet had in the "old times," complaining that full-bloods were on the margins of tribal decision-making because they did not understand the English language. Kipp was the exception, however, as most full-bloods, particularly those who were currently or who had been active in the FYIP, voted to adopt one central government. John Oldchief answered Kipp by saying, "You

know I was president of a chapter. Today, I will throw that away. I am going to join this community self-government."[90]

Those Blackfeet active in the chapter organizations were both disillu-
sioned with the FYIP and probably wary of seceding from a government
influenced by the cohort of mixed-bloods involved in pursuing natural
resource development; the confusion that Joe Brown described at the
start of the meeting would have made it particularly difficult for full-
bloods to monitor the per capita distribution of funds from Court of
Claims awards and tribal oil production. While full-bloods held the idea
of tribal unity in high regard, they also understood that it was better to
work with the principals of any newly formed Blackfeet "corporation" as
members of that corporation than as leaders of competing communities
that lacked the requisite business skills for managing the kind of businesses that full-bloods needed to expand their economic horizons. Most
Blackfeet, then, vested their hopes in a reconstituted political community governed by one central government after thorough consideration
of the confusion a reservation of small competing communities would
create. No one, however, had an answer for James Fisher, who posed an
important question: "What would be the danger of getting a centralized
power?"[91]

The council also proposed eliminating the secretary of the interior as
a policing entity with the authority to effect changes in Blackfeet politics, fearing that a new Republican administration would expand its control of a reorganized tribal government. This amendment alarmed Superintendent Stone, who contributed his opinion after a long silence by
telling the council that "[i]n every community, every county or state,
there is some place a power over it [sic]. You could hardly leave that in the
hands of the community itself."[92] Stone argued that any government
needed checks and balances to guard against corrupt or simply incompetent administration. Hall answered that an autocratic interior secretary
was the worse option and that if the Blackfeet government did fail to
function, then it would "blow up" on its own. The amendment passed
over Stone's objections, an action that symbolized the Blackfeet's recognition of the need to control the operation of any new government and
thus to prevent the federal government from making wholesale changes
without the tribe's consent, the common denominator of the amendments; in several places the council simply replaced secretary of the interior with "three-fourths of the adult members of the tribe." Brown in
particular insisted that any future changes required "the consent of the

Indian." Brown also demanded that the tribe retain the right to determine the definition of Blackfeet, insisting that neither blood quotient nor residence status should affect the rights and privileges of anyone on the tribal rolls.[93] Blackfeet leaders agreed that the tribe needed statutory mechanisms to both terminate various Interior Department supervisory functions and protect the tribe's right to determine its social composition. The Blackfeet understood that not every administration would be as supportive of Indian sovereignty as Collier's.

At the end of a long day spent debating the tribe's future, the council endorsed the amendments presented and the Wheeler-Howard Bill that was then circulating in Congress. Brown and three other delegates were chosen to travel to Washington in late April to present the amendments to the House and Senate Committees on Indian Affairs in the hope that Congress would be as attentive as John Collier was to the wants and needs of the Blackfeet people.

The Blackfeet and the Senate Debate

Collier resumed his campaign for comprehensive Indian reform after touring Indian America, testifying before the Senate Committee on Indian Affairs on April 26. The controversial issue of mandatory land transfers and the scope of self-government were the principal points debated. Collier conceded to Senator Wheeler, the committee chairman, that the compulsory nature of Title III in the Wheeler-Howard Bill remained a barrier, citing the Blackfeet's protest as an example of the concern that had been persistently raised by many Indian leaders; the Blackfeet, Collier told Wheeler, wanted land recombination to be voluntary. Collier now had a very strong leaning toward making Title III a voluntary provision.[94] Wheeler had been an initial supporter of Collier's regime and a sponsor of his original bill, but by April he had lost faith in Collier's vision of a new Indian America and resolved to weaken it.[95] On several occasions, Wheeler asked Collier to clarify his intentions with regard to Montana's Indians. Collier's proposal to offer self-government to Montana Indians represented, Wheeler believed, "a step backward for them rather than a step forward." The Blackfeet and the Indians of the Fort Peck Reservation already exercised the form of government Collier was proposing and were "becoming more or less assimilated," he argued. If the government of the Blackfeet and other Montana tribes were to evolve toward the form of a "complete town government," he told Collier, then "it would bring about all kinds of conflicts between *your* [emphasis added] Indians and the white people and . . . it would set back the Indians."[96]

Joe Brown appeared before the committee two days later to address Wheeler's argument that the bill would set back the Indians. Brown testified that the tribe had studied the bill after the Great Plains Congress and would agree to accept it only if the voluntary nature of Title III was codified; the tribe would then "think it is a good bill," he said. Brown reviewed the tribe's experience with the FYIP, telling the committee that had government officials "done their part it would have been a success, but as it was, why, it was mostly a failure."[97] He expressed excitement about the proposed credit fund, which would provide Blackfeet with the money to buy enough stock and feed to help the chapter organizations expand; the Blackfeet, he said, "are aching to get a chance at that $10,000,000 that is in that bill." Wheeler expressed approval of Brown's enthusiasm for the FYIP and for advocating self-reliance to full-bloods. Sen. Lynn Frazier affectionately told him, "I believe you will make good too, Brown." Brown rejoined that "if we just had another chance we are going to make good. The older people have all received an experience and have learned something." Wheeler and Frazier, who had known Brown since the 1929 subcommittee hearing, seemed to have great confidence in his abilities. Responding to Brown's support for more Indian employment in the Bureau, Wheeler asked him, "You could take over the superintendency, more than likely?" Brown thought the job was too difficult for him and instead offered support for Forrest Stone, whom he thought was a "mighty good man."[98]

Wheeler quickly moved to his critique of the bill, telling Brown that he disagreed with Brown's assertion that the self-government provision of the bill would help the Blackfeet achieve economic and political progress. Wheeler argued that the Blackfeet already controlled most of Glacier County; Indians like Joe Brown were on the school board, were able to run for state senate as Joe Brown had done, and "practically run that community up there now." The Blackfeet were successfully assimilating into white society and its institutions, Wheeler told Brown, and if they were to create an Indian community "separate and distinct from the white community," then there would be "trouble between them."[99] When Sen. Elmer Thomas asked Brown if he intended to surrender involvement in the county government, Brown answered that the bill allowed the Blackfeet to participate in both the community and county government. He provoked laughter when he said that the Blackfeet would "take chances on what laws would be under the community government, because we would make them." Brown's response, however, was precisely what made Wheeler fearful of an indigenous form of Indian community government. If the Blackfeet Tribe passed its own laws, Wheeler countered, the result would be "a great deal of confusion and a great deal of bitterness and strife between two classes of people, which would be to the [tribe's] detriment." Brown offered to accept an amendment proscribing such a situation. Wheeler exclaimed, "We *will* [emphasis added] amend it." Frazier followed Wheeler's lead by telling Brown shortly before the session ended that "it seems to me that the best thing to do to handle a group like the Blackfeet is to assist them to take part in county government there, the regular county government, give them fair representation, and I believe they will get along all right." Brown responded that "the bill gives us that privilege. We do not have to go into this unless we want to."[100]

Joe Brown and the Blackfeet did not want to be handled by Congress. The pending legislation appealed to Brown and his people because it gave the tribe options for economic growth and the "privilege" to choose their own path based on their own reading of those options. Some Blackfeet may have been successful in Glacier County, but most remained the poor citizens of the county. The Blackfeet may have been dominating public life in Glacier County, as Wheeler claimed, but they were not dominating economic life. Without credit they never would. Without the right to negotiate with their white tenants they never would. Collier's plan gave the Blackfeet political power to negotiate with the state and the federal government, and it gave them access to credit, the essential elements of a political economy that the Blackfeet had been requesting for nearly twenty years.

Wheeler, for his part, ran the hearings using the Blackfeet Tribe as his model tribe. He was very familiar with conditions on the Blackfeet Reservation, having made official visits to Browning on at least three occasions during the previous five years; in addition, he vacationed in nearby Glacier National Park, where delegations of Blackfeet would often visit him and had once tried to invest in reservation oil leases in the early 1920s. His conception of Indian-white relations and *his* vision of organizational change were predicated, then, on these specific experiences with the Blackfeet Indians and, to a lesser extent, the other tribes of Montana. Although he clearly understood the varied nature of the country's Indian population, the sheer variety of the nations within the nation, Wheeler viewed the Blackfeet in many ways as a model for assimilation and acculturation. In his mind, as he told Collier and Brown on separate occasions, Indians were moving in the right direction within the institutional world of white America. Joe Brown's seemingly cavalier assertion of the Blackfeet's right to pass laws that superseded or contradicted county laws alarmed Wheeler, who in the end did not have that much confidence in Brown or his people to do the "right thing."

The Blackfeet and the House Debate

Brown told the House Committee on Indian Affairs several days later that the Blackfeet Tribe had been very opposed to Collier's plan during the delegation's February trip to Washington, principally because the tribe "had not had a chance to study it." But the tribe had spent considerable time since the Great Plains Congress discussing the bill in a series of meetings that had given all tribal members an opportunity to participate, with the result, Brown testified, that most Blackfeet now believed that the House of Representatives should pass the Wheeler-Howard Bill.[101] Brown told the House committee, as he had told the Senate committee, that "there are features in this bill that are very acceptable. They are extraordinary." He was particularly pleased with provisions advancing Indian education and Indian labor within the Indian Service, changes that he had been requesting for a decade. There were Blackfeet who could "fill every position on that reservation" except for chief clerk and superintendent, Brown said, and if the bill passed, then it would "not be long before we could develop men that would take those places." The committee allotted only fifteen minutes to each tribe, but Brown pressed his case for the legislation, telling the committee that the Blackfeet "do not know when we will get a chance of this kind, we do not know when we will ever get a man again in the chair of the Commissioner of Indian Affairs whose heart and sympathies are with the Indian."[102] Brown's endorsement of Collier provided an opening for Representatives Theodore Werner of South Dakota and Thomas O'Malley of Wisconsin, members of a contingent of pro-assimilation congressmen, who used it to continue their attacks on Collier and his conception of Indian self-government. Brown's request for more time turned into an interrogation.

Werner tried to chip away at Brown's support of Collier by asking him if he thought Collier had either created false hopes or blamed Congress for the Indians' problems during the Great Plains Congress. Brown answered that Collier had done neither. O'Malley implied that Brown and his people did not fully understand the legislation, despite attending the congress and holding several meetings on the bill. He asked Brown, "after what you say was a study of the bill and a discussion of it with members of your tribe, you are in favor of it?" Brown simply answered, "Yes, sir."[103] Werner also questioned Brown's cognitive abilities, asking him, "You say that you have given very careful study to this bill?" Brown simply answered, "Careful in my humble way. I am not a lawyer."[104] After facing Werner and O'Malley's lengthy contumely, Brown reemphasized the importance of the bill's protection of the Blackfeet's land base and its educational and financial provisions, in particular the revolving credit fund. This "wonderful system," Brown said, is "something that has been needed, because our credit system—we have none"; banks would not give Indians credit because the federal government held in trust the title to their land. Frustrated by the committee's lack of faith in his judgment and his people's ability to decide what was best for themselves, he finished his testimony by saying, "I think we could get together if we just all lower our sights a bit and cooperate. I believe we can put a bill through here that will satisfy the Indians."[105]

The Indian Reorganization Act

On June 5, 1934, Brown and BTBC secretary Leo Kennerly telegraphed to the Indian Office the council's unanimous approval of the pending Wheeler-Howard Indian Bill. Congress adopted the bill on June 16, and President Roosevelt signed it two days later.[106] While the final version of the bill—which became known as the Indian Reorganization Act (IRA)—contained enough important elements to satisfy the Blackfeet, Wheeler wielded his power in the Senate to ensure that Collier's vision of cultural pluralism and Indian self-determination devolved into Wheeler's defense of assimilation. After the formal hearings ended in early May, Collier negotiated a compromise with Howard and Wheeler, but by this time Collier had lost his leverage. It was Wheeler who dictated what the final bill would look like, going so far as to introduce a new bill, S. 3645, to replace the original, S. 2755. Wheeler told his Senate colleagues in June that the new bill contained no provision that "superimposes upon the Indians bureaucratic control from Washington. On the contrary, this bill proposes to give the Indians an opportunity to take over the control of their own resources and fit them as American citizens. . . . I, myself, think that this bill, as now presented, is the greatest step forward the Department has ever taken with reference to Indians."[107] Collier disagreed, calling the IRA a "very much modified, shortened, and amended version" of his original bill in his analysis of the act.[108]

Wheeler and his colleagues reduced Collier's forty-eight-page vision down to five pages and succeeded in deleting Collier's language of self-determination. The wholesale rejection of the Court of Indian Affairs represented the most conspicuous change. Although Collier and Indian leaders like Joe Brown had made it clear to legislators that Title IV was not the most important section of the bill, Collier nevertheless expressed disappointment at its exclusion; he argued that the rejection of the court "leaves law-enforcement on Indian reservations where it has always been—in confusion."[109] The IRA's provisions for education reform modified those of Collier's, emphasizing vocational training over higher education and providing for reimbursable loans rather than government grants. The complementary employment provision, however, promised greater access to jobs within the BIA than Collier's version; it authorized the secretary of the interior to create new criteria for the employment of Indians and provided that "[s]uch qualified Indians shall hereafter have the preference to appointment to vacancies in any such positions." The bill did, as Collier intended, legislate an end to the process of allotment, extend the trust period of existing allotments, and return reservation surplus lands to tribal control. The bill also permitted the creation of tribal political and economic organizations, allowing each tribe that adopted the IRA to develop a constitution and bylaws through which a central government could manage the domestic affairs of its members; such a government could employ a tribal attorney, manage tribal assets and land sales, and negotiate with federal, state, and county governments. In addition, each tribe could secure from the secretary of the interior a charter of incorporation to enhance the power of the tribal government to manage its economic assets. To assist in the creation of tribal enterprises, Congress allotted $10 million for a revolving credit fund, twice the amount Collier had requested.[110]

In sum, the IRA improved Collier's original bill in the area of economic development but weakened or eliminated important provisions for cultural development and self-government. The bill was imperfect, the result of a struggle between two competing visions of Indian Amer-

ica: one sought to protect Indians' right to construct their own version of
the American community, the other fought to sustain Indians' gradual
adoption of white mores and institutions, to "fit them as American citizens," as Wheeler put it. Congress wanted to assist America's Indian population in making progress, but it did not want to create nations within
the nation that held powers in conflict with the dominant society that it
wanted Indian citizens eventually to join. Joe Brown's assertion of his
tribe's right to pass laws symbolized for Wheeler, and other influential lawmakers, the danger inherent in Collier's vision of Indian self-
determination.

The Blackfeet Vote

Section 18 of the final bill embodied Collier's claim that he and his staff
would not "act unless the Indians are willing to go with us." The provision stipulated that the secretary of the interior must call for tribal referenda on the IRA within one year after the passage of the act. The IRA
would not affect any tribe whose majority of eligible voters rejected the
legislation, but once a tribe did so it could not claim any benefits provided under the law. Given that Congress had successfully weakened
Collier's reforms, the OIA leadership struggled to secure tribal votes on
the IRA before an even more hostile Congress took office the following
fall. Felix Cohen, the chairman of the OIA's Organization Committee,
told his colleagues in July 1934 that "it is important that a number of
tribes strategically located be actually organized before the next session
of Congress, since the failure to do this will subject the Indian Office to
considerable criticism."[111] The committee decided in September that
thirty-three tribes should vote on the IRA by October 27, 1934. The
Blackfeet Tribe, given its size and its relatively consistent support of the
bill's major provisions, became one of those tribes slated for an early vote.

The BTBC's June 5 approval of the Wheeler-Howard legislation would
have been rendered meaningless if a majority of the tribe's voting members did not support the IRA. The council organized a series of meetings
to inform Blackfeet citizens of the IRA's advantages and enlisted the aid of
Hall and McCabe, a local law firm, to analyze the bill to help the council
justify its vote for it. Cleve Hall simply recommended that the Blackfeet
vote for the IRA, adopt a constitution, and secure a charter of incorporation to gain access to the $10 million credit fund.[112] Forrest Stone sub-
mitted Hall's analysis to the OIA with the business council's request that
the OIA determine the report's veracity before the council distributed it

to Blackfeet voters. The Organization Committee called Hall's analysis "very creditable," though not as comprehensive as its own, and recommended that the council distribute it to its constituents for consideration.[113] The Indian Office tried to avoid coercing tribes or tribal leaders to adopt the IRA, choosing to support when possible the efforts of tribes like the Blackfeet to secure a second opinion of the act's merits.

The BTBC took the initiative for deciding the IRA's fate on the Blackfeet Reservation on September 11. Stone encouraged council members to support the act, telling them that the Wheeler-Howard Bill "is very important to the Blackfeet Indians. . . . We have discussed it from every angle. The time has come for you to decide whether you want it or not." Twelve of the thirteen council members decided that they wanted it and voted to petition the secretary of the interior to approve October 20 as the date of the tribe's referendum.[114] Stone told Collier two days later that "the Blackfeet are pretty well informed at present as to the provisions of this act. They have spent a good deal of time on it and have listened pretty carefully to the explanations that have been offered them by members of the council, employees, and leaders of the tribe aside from council members." Although the Blackfeet did not agree with all the IRA's provisions, Stone predicted that they were going to "accept it with the idea in mind that the good contained in the bill far exceeds the objectionable features."[115]

The Blackfeet proved Stone correct on October 27. Nearly 83 percent of participating voters supported the IRA; 823 Blackfeet voted for it, while 171 voted against it. A winter storm made it difficult for some Blackfeet to get to the polls, but 994 of 1,785 eligible voters turned out to cast their secret ballots; 114 of the 148 Blackfeet who mailed their ballots also voted for the act.[116] Collier wrote the Blackfeet one week later to make their decision official, telling them, "Secretary Ickes and I are highly gratified at the action taken[;] we wish to congratulate you upon the wisdom shown and the interest displayed by your people." Collier expressed confidence that the Blackfeet would begin working toward "the consummation of the program" that would give them the "opportunity for a life more secure and more free."[117]

A year after a Senate subcommittee judged the Blackfeet Indians to be capable of running their own affairs, the Blackfeet Tribe expressed agreement by overwhelmingly adopting the Indian Reorganization Act and thus grasped the tools of a modern political economy to realize its long-standing goal of self-support. The business council, under the steady and pragmatic leadership of Joe Brown, had created an environment in which debate and discussion could take place among the reservation's various factions and communities. The Blackfeet participated in an exercise of tribal democracy to "take the responsibility," as Collier told them they should, "of thinking out their own problems and arriving at their own conclusions, and determining their own future." The Blackfeet's widespread acceptance of the IRA was the result of an open and organized debate about the tribe's future and remembrance of a past largely influenced by the vagaries of OIA management. Blackfeet factions agreed during the IRA debate that in order to "decrease Federal overlordship," as Harold Ickes called the OIA's heavy-handed management of tribal affairs, the tribe had to assume greater economic and political control over the development of the reservation's natural and human resources by securing the tools of modern administration offered in the IRA. The IRA would give a reconstituted tribal council the authority to negotiate with other political bodies and conduct "business in the modern, organized way," as John Collier had said they must do to survive in twentieth-century America.

Recent historiography generally does not regard the IRA as a success or else it focuses on native communities that rejected it. It is important to remember the excitement the IRA engendered among the tribes that accepted it, as well as the spirited debate it created among those that did not. Many Indian leaders, like Joe Brown and Rides at the Door, considered the IRA to be the best legislative or political means to further their independence from federal supervision that had stifled economic progress and exacerbated tribal dissension. The OIA had failed for twenty years to provide the Blackfeet with a coordinated economic policy; it had debilitated the tribe's search for oil, neglected the tribe's grazing resources, and usurped tribal funds for costly irrigation projects in its zeal to turn the Blackfeet into farmers in one of the country's poorest agricultural regions. The Blackfeet, like their Flathead neighbors to the southwest, embraced the IRA because it gave them access to credit and the statutory power to stage elections to reduce or eliminate federal control of the tribe's financial and natural resources. Unlike their Crow neighbors to the southeast, Blackfeet of all degrees of blood had developed among themselves a confidence that they were capable of self-government. Adopting the IRA's machinery of political economy was a logical first step for tribal members committed to determining their own future.

It is important to note that the act received support from both mixed-bloods and full-bloods, though it is difficult to determine with any precision either the breakdown of voting by blood quantum or the reason nearly eight hundred eligible voters did not participate; the tribe's rate of voter participation fell just under the national average of 58 percent.[118] Some mixed-bloods objected that the IRA granted certain sovereign powers to the BTBC and thus expanded its role in the tribal economy; full-bloods, largely because of demographic circumstances, objected for the same reason. In most political communities, an unfortunately high number of voters elects not to participate in the democratic process because of cynicism, despair, or laziness. It was likely no different on the Blackfeet Reservation, particularly when one considers the history of Blackfeet-white relations of the preceding decades. This history, however, compelled more than one thousand Blackfeet to embrace the opportunity to alter the trajectory of those relations. For whatever reason a large number of voters did not have the same urgency. Snow-swept roads probably kept some people home. It is likely that both mixed-bloods and full-bloods, unfamiliar with or uninterested in the issues that day, simply chose to ignore the referendum. But they did not stay home because no one bothered to tell them of this opportunity. Leaders of both the BTBC and the PFLA represented their constituents' interests during key public debates and meetings. Tribal leaders and agency staff subsequently held a series of meetings in mixed-blood and full-blood communities, made themselves available to answer questions, and distributed appropriate information to inform the Blackfeet body politic of its voting options. The 1929 and 1933 Senate subcommittee hearings and the 1934 IRA debates on and off the reservation politicized Blackfeet citizens at a time when they as well as most Americans were looking for answers to a crisis of confidence and comfort. It was a good time to be political.

"[M]aking no decision at all becomes a decision," political theorist Benjamin Barber writes. "To be political is to *have* [emphasis in original] to choose—and, what is worse, to have to choose under the worst possible circumstances, when the grounds of choice are not given a priori or by fiat or by pure knowledge."[119] Hindsight should not preclude a broader understanding of the place where Blackfeet voters stood as they debated a historic opportunity to take a measure of control over their future. Regardless of what happened after October 1934 the Blackfeet made the right decision to adopt the IRA. In October 1934 the act made sense to a majority of Blackfeet voters. In spite of Burton Wheeler's claim that the

Blackfeet dominated life in Glacier County, there remained an infra-structure of white interests that had dug their heels into the soil of their lands. The Blackfeet needed to take the responsibility of managing and protecting tribal assets to ensure that "the wolves," as full-blood leader Oscar Boy called white ranchers and developers, did not devour any more of the tribe's natural resources and economic future.

PART 2

1934–1952

3. ON THE ROAD TO SELF-GOVERNMENT

The Incorporation of the Blackfeet Tribe of Indians,

1934–1935

There appears to be no doubt but that the tribe as a whole is very anxious to go ahead.... [A]t this time there appears to be a keen interest in the forming of the Corporation. – Warren O'Hara, superintendent, August 1935

I am confused about the Wheeler Howard Act. I do not know what it means. If you could tell me what we may expect from it, I would appreciate it. – No Coat to Harold Ickes, secretary of the interior, March 1937

Superintendent Forrest Stone was mostly absent from tribal deliberations on the Indian Reorganization Act, preferring, in the spirit of the act, to let the Blackfeet decide their own fate. He had told the Senate subcommittee in October 1933 that Congress should act quickly to reform federal supervision of the Blackfeet to take advantage of the "interest that they have right now to handle their own affairs." The Blackfeet had great confidence in themselves to do that, he told Congress, adding, "I also have that confidence in them."[1] In the spring of 1934, Stone examined the tribe's organizational makeup at the request of his Indian Office superiors. His report on Blackfeet FYIP chapters allowed him to elaborate on this expression of confidence. The report both endorsed the tribe's support of the Wheeler-Howard Bill, providing additional evidence of that support's depth and breadth, and served as a confession of a BIA employee who had faced for fifteen years the limitations of the "federal overlordship."

Stone argued that the FYIP had survived despite the "colossal handicap of government patronage that had warped" the Indian mind into servility. It existed as a "convenience of the government," he wrote, and as a result "government restrictions, regulations, and historical precedents as to procedure, always lay like a deadening hand on the spirit of the Indian belonging to and attempting to direct the efforts of his own people."[2] In a manner that became increasingly bitter in tone, Stone recounted the initial successes of the eighteen chapters and their subsequent decline into stasis. He described a mostly full-blood group of more than three hundred men and women who had been "united in a determined effort towards self-government with the hope in their breasts that as their abilities were demonstrated that more power and leadership would be given them by the Government, and that their progress would be aided at every step by the Indian Department. How hopeless it seems now when we look at thirteen years of effort on the part of these men and realize, as they realize, that it was only an idle dream and that regardless of the friends who were interested in them that the prevailing government 'system' could never at any time permit them to realize their cherished ambitions."[3]

After indicting the OIA for fraud, Stone proceeded to list the chapter's achievements, which included the rapid growth of grain production and livestock cultivation, construction of two flour mills, and dissemination of horticultural knowledge. In addition, the program facilitated the construction of community centers, the participation of women's auxiliaries, and improved social control that stemmed from a renewed respect for full-blood elders. The organizations had not only produced tangible growth in small-scale agriculture but had created a stronger sense of unity among a culturally depressed people who had been given an opportunity to lift themselves "out of the rut of misery and poverty" and pursue the goals of "good citizenship, self-support, and personal and community character development and enterprise." Some chapters did better than others, but all attempted to make progress. "The chapter has never failed insofar as the Indian is concerned," Stone asserted. "He has done his part and reached out for more control and for a freer hand in the management of his own affairs. The chapter has failed in the lack of cooperation given it by the government." Stone recounted his conversations with Blackfeet discouraged by the government's failure to correct flaws in the program, which would have helped them "go forward in a business-like way in the same fashion that a white person might progress." In addition to government inaction, the Blackfeet suffered from the lack of an "adequate financial system," a "great obstacle" to the modernization of their operation.[4] The IRA's promise of credit appealed to both full-blood and mixed-blood organizations.

Stone failed to mention his own role in the management of the program, discussing the government as though he had never worked for the Indian Service or been superintendent of the Blackfeet Reservation. But Stone had been a consistent and forceful advocate of the tribe's oil interests and, after Collier took office, a forceful advocate of Blackfeet self-government, testifying to that effect during the 1933 subcommittee hearing and in this report on the full-bloods' agricultural organizations. The Blackfeet had "a great desire to be self-governing," Stone concluded. What they lacked was a proper system. The Wheeler-Howard Bill represented such a system, Stone believed. He ended his attack on government policy and his defense of Blackfeet self-determination by writing, "There can be no mistake in community Indian government or controlled by the Indian leaders [*sic*]. To my mind, we cannot shift any part of our responsibility to a safer haven than the shoulders of these Indian leaders who will carry the load more creditably for the Indian people than the government has ever been able to carry it for them." It was time, Stone said, for the government to withdraw its "directing and controlling hand" and "put the responsibility squarely upon the Indian himself."[5]

Stone's second report about Blackfeet political organization, written in August 1934, lacked the bitterness that defined his report on the FYIP, perhaps because the Wheeler-Howard Bill had passed in June and was embraced by both BTBC and PFLA leaders. The BTBC represented the "entire Reservation," he wrote, though like the PFLA chapters it had "no authority" to manage tribal affairs; its functions included hearing complaints, issuing recommendations to the OIA, granting permission for the advertising of oil and gas lease sales, and approving grazing leases on tribal lands.[6] Stone reported that the BTBC generated "little complaint and little request for improvement or changes" from tribal members, though many of them had expressed a desire to see its authority expanded and "given more power" in tribal administration. Overall, Stone found that the tribe was content with the form of government and the election process. When prompted to describe the business council's weaknesses, Stone answered that he could not identify any. "It is difficult to imagine where an elective system can be improved upon. There is nothing that stands in the way of the Council exercising creative powers, when the Washington Office finds a way to give these powers to them."[7] Stone did note a growing sentiment among Blackfeet that women should be elected to future councils. Although several women were particularly active in the Blackfeet Indian Welfare Association, which endorsed council candidates and lobbied for financial support of Blackfeet education and employment, none of them had yet run for office.[8]

Stone also expressed concern about what he perceived to be a growing credibility gap between mixed-blood and full-blood leadership. Most Blackfeet granted little authority to the "hereditary chieftain," he wrote, and thus "as a matter of administration, it becomes increasingly difficult to try to administer the affairs of young, progressive, educated returned students, through the old full blood Indian who does not speak their language, who does not have their viewpoint." Although full-blood leaders were still accorded respect, Stone concluded that "as a social influence, or as a directing power, the day of the old hereditary chief is rapidly slipping away."[9] The IRA formalized the passing of an era, from a time when Blackfeet full-bloods dominated the sociocultural aspects of the Blackfeet Tribe of Indians to one in which a council of mixed-bloods dominated the political and economic management of the Blackfeet Corporation. The transition would be particularly hard on those Blackfeet who would come to believe that the "real" Blackfeet Tribe no longer existed. The challenge for all Blackfeet after 1934 would be to form a Blackfeet Nation that was responsive to the needs of both tribal and corporate members.

The Collier administration's central focus on organization, emphasized in OIA circular letters and at public meetings like the Great Plains Congress, resonated with the Blackfeet, who had successfully organized groups—such as the Blackfeet Tribal Business Council, the Piegan Farming and Livestock Association, and the Blackfeet Indian Welfare Association—that ultimately wielded little influence with federal agents. Organization came naturally to the Blackfeet then, but by October 1934, as Forrest Stone noted, the tribe wanted to empower its organizations to pursue specific economic goals rather than continue to act as pressure groups. The Blackfeet wanted additional political authority and power to manage tribal resources in place of a federal government that had failed to improve appreciably their economic lives. The IRA and its provisions for credit and tribal control of finances appealed to a cross section of Blackfeet, including chapter leaders and their full-blood constituents who, while maintaining a healthy skepticism of the business council and its centralized control of tribal affairs, desired a stronger tribal political presence on the reservation and in Washington. The Blackfeet

Nation took its first step toward the management and modernization of its reservation economy by adopting the IRA in October 1934. The business council, under the steady guidance of Joe Brown, would spend the following year trying to complete the political and economic reorganization of the Blackfeet Tribe as it evolved into the Blackfeet Corporation.

This process of incorporation suffered a serious blow in February 1935 when Forrest Stone announced his transfer to the Shoshone jurisdiction in Wyoming. Just two weeks before his transfer, he had been welcomed back to the reservation from Washington with a tribal dance and song and adopted into the tribe for his longtime service to the Blackfeet.[10] He had provided fair leadership to both full-bloods and mixed-bloods for most of those sixteen years of service and had helped the tribe generate the self-confidence that led to its adoption of the IRA. The Blackfeet were, perhaps, a victim of his successful stewardship. The delegation's performance during the Great Plains Congress and IRA hearings demonstrated a degree of progress in political development not shared by most tribes. The OIA sent Stone to Wyoming to produce similar results for a tribe that had failed to see the OIA's wisdom of adopting the IRA. The Blackfeet, while probably aware of this factor in Stone's transfer, protested the decision because the OIA made it without their consent. The unilateral decision in effect contradicted the essence of Collier's message of Indian participation in tribal management. While the IRA did not guarantee a tribe a deciding vote in the selection of its superintendent, Collier's message in various media had been that the OIA would consider the tribe's wishes, particularly in such an important area as agency personnel.[11] In addition, Stone was the logical person to help the tribe implement the IRA on the reservation.

Council members expressed their sadness and appreciation to Stone during their February 18 meeting. Rides at the Door, the tribe's most influential full-blood councilman, told him: "What I regret most is this: After you got us started on our feet, and then be moved away, that makes me feel sorry." Stone, Joe Brown said, "made us what we are today, as a Council." Brown listed Stone's various contributions to the improvement of the reservation infrastructure, which included home construction, roads, and a new telephone system. While he lauded Stone for his advocacy of Blackfeet welfare, Brown spoke angrily of Collier's betrayal. "As I look at this situation now, you that have attended the [Great Plains] Congress, and you that have had the opportunity to hear Mr. Collier talk down there, know that he said that it was to be his policy to let the Indians work in their own jobs, and select their own Superintendents. Now he has seen fit to make a change on our Reservation without even hinting to us that a change was to come about." Brown proposed that the council draft a resolution to Collier protesting Stone's transfer and stating that the tribe would hold Collier responsible for any failures of the post-Stone era. "If this new [superintendent] stops the progress of the Indian as he has been progressing," Brown said, "[Collier] should be held strictly accountable for it, because he has gone back on the statements that he made to us, and he hasn't given us an opportunity to have a voice in the selection or saying of who the new man might be." Losing Stone, he concluded, was "the greatest blow to this Reservation that we have ever had."[12] The council voted unanimously to adopt the resolution. Leo Kennerly, the council secretary, added that "removing Stone almost makes me want to turn 'radical,' as they call it, and join other Tribes in regard to the abolishing of the Indian Bureau at Washington."[13] Collier had antagonized his strongest supporters by removing from the reservation the man who had gone to the mat to secure greater Blackfeet relief and responsibility. Even if Franklin Roosevelt himself had replaced Stone, the council would not have forgiven Collier for breaking his promise to include them in the decision-making process. The BTBC thus deemed the government's early efforts at termination and the consequent empowerment of the tribe to be "unsatisfactory."

Collier's action created a sense of urgency among council members and other influential Blackfeet. James Fisher believed that Stone's departure would "draw the Council closer together" as it proceeded with the implementation of the IRA and Stone's parting suggestions.[14] The BTBC, and the Blackfeet people, lost a strong advocate in Forrest Stone, but the council had matured enough since 1929 to take a more aggressive stance in advancing the tribe's welfare. BTBC members had been working well together since Frank Campbell left the reservation in 1929 amid accusations from Senate investigators that he manipulated tribal elections. Freed of the bitter strife that Campbell's chapter leaders and Robert Hamilton's entrepreneurial faction engendered, the council had been able to concentrate on working to secure better grazing rates, expand oil leasing, and achieve greater responsibility for the tribe's economic affairs. A 1931 amendment to the original tribal constitution that extended the council members' term of office from one year to two also helped to stabilize the council's composition, improving cooperation between the representatives of the reservation's four districts.[15] Stone's departure did force the council closer together and thrust it into a more prominent role of representing tribal interests, the IRA's intent. The Blackfeet raised their expectations of the council as a result of the IRA adoption and Stone's departure. Although a new superintendent would continue to represent the Blackfeet's interests, the perception that the tribe had to contend for itself prevailed.

Joe Brown stepped into the void left by Stone's departure as the most influential man on the reservation. He was regarded highly by Collier and Stone, by members of Congress such as Sen. Burton Wheeler, and by his people, who continually elected him chairman of the business council. Despite the handicap of blindness in one eye and the lack of a solid education, Brown acquitted himself very well in front of congressional committees and tribal meetings. Educated only to the eighth grade during the 1880s, he overcame his feelings of inadequacy by hiring a tutor to help him with his diction and grammar. Brown was an active presence on the reservation, serving on the Board of Education while working for the government and running the council.[16] The council had such great confidence in Brown that it asked him in early April to serve as Stone's successor. Oscar Boy petitioned the council to nominate Brown, arguing that Brown was qualified to fill the position because he "understands the conditions of our people and is one of our own kind." Several council members supported Oscar Boy's petition and argued against accepting another superintendent from the outside. Despite the great respect the tribe accorded Stone, the IRA had influenced the Blackfeet to prefer indigenous leadership over that of the OIA, aided in large measure by Brown's considerable reputation and Collier's hypocritical actions. Brown did not support the idea, however, and declined to accept the nomination; he had told Senator Wheeler during the 1934 Senate debate that he did not think he was ready to assume the responsibility of the position.[17]

Brown *was* eager to lead the tribe as BTBC chairman. In March, he addressed Wright Hagerty's claim that the Montana State Relief Commission discriminated against the tribe, asserting the Blackfeet's right to receive the same amount of relief as white residents of Montana. Montana's governor responded to Brown's protest with an investigation, assuring Brown that the discrimination would end and allotting the tribe an additional five thousand dollars in relief funds.[18] Brown also led the fight to preserve the Blackfeet Strip, a six-mile-long stretch of Blackfeet land that bordered Glacier National Park. The National Park Service (NPS) had attempted for two decades to annex the land to expand the park's road system and hunting grounds, but since the strip contained the tribe's only timber reserve and numerous allotments the BTBC declined the invitation to sell the land. Brown had heard reports that the government planned to try again since Forrest Stone could no longer defend the Blackfeet. This rumor precipitated a series of meetings that again stirred feelings of vulnerability and betrayal among the Blackfeet.

The BTBC hosted a general meeting on May 2 to discuss the new threat to the territorial integrity of the reservation. Brown responded to criticism that he was not aggressively protecting the Nation's interests in an impassioned speech that left no doubt as to his leadership. Brown explained to the crowd that Collier had asked Acting Superintendent J. H. Brott if the NPS could annex the Blackfeet Strip. Brott in turn met with the park superintendent and with Brown, who registered a vehement protest. The three men concluded that Collier and the NPS should not take any action that would upset the tribe, as there was "considerable justification for the Indian viewpoint" against annexation.[19] The IRA required the government to secure Indian consent for any land sale, and thus the OIA and the NPS backed down after the Blackfeet protested their annexation plan. It was the process, however, that upset the Blackfeet, the idea that, as in the case of Stone's removal, Collier did not confer with tribal leaders before making a decision that affected the Blackfeet's fortunes and fate. The Blackfeet's specific criticism of government administration devolved into a general complaint about the "white man."

Brown considered the annexation plan another act of betrayal. "Why does the Government select the Blackfeet Indians to pick upon at this time? What have we done, what wrongs have we committed that they should turn around and treat us in this manner?" In a mocking tone, he criticized Collier for failing to consult Blackfeet leaders about the plan and for thus failing to recognize the Blackfeet Nation as a political entity. In addition, the government neither honored its treaties nor compensated the tribe when it broke those promises, and it never compensated the Blackfeet when it "killed old and indigent Indians and tore the babies from the breasts of mothers, heaped them up and burned them."[20] The government took Blackfeet lives and Blackfeet land and still was not satisfied. "They have us up here now," Brown continued, "on a little reservation, they allotted the lands to us and we have a little measly fifty thousand acres of tribal or timber land, and I say that underneath, the working of the white man is starting slowly to eat up that little reserve that you have—the little piece of revenue and property that you own as a tribe." Brown's normally solid support of Collier and the federal government vanished in this speech. The Blackfeet would no longer cooperate with the government on land sales. Brown concluded by saying to great applause, "I have come out in the open, I have laid my cards on the table and I am ready to defend my position. This might cost me my job, but I would rather be a respected citizen among my people than to be a dog in the Indian Service."[21]

Brown's oration served notice to his critics that he was willing to challenge anyone who threatened the Blackfeet's newly made promise of independent action and control of tribal decision-making. The speakers who followed Brown echoed his angry sentiments. Black Weasel captured much of this anger when he told those assembled that "the authorities in Washington, D.C. have got us Indians sold, that we are sceptical of all their dealings with us and to a very large extent we mistrust all that they propose, and eventually but slowly they are wising us Indians to the ways of the coniving [sic] white man."[22] Hugh Jackson, an army veteran, offered poignant criticism of the government's failure to honor its promises. The Blackfeet who had fought in World War I made a mistake, he said. Given recent events, "why would [Indians] be patriotic?" He had supported the IRA to "let the Indians run their own affairs" but now believed that the federal government would not let the tribe succeed. "You have been double crossed every damn time you start doing things. . . . The whole bunch of you are not competent, according to John Collier."[23] Such visceral criticism of the federal government had not been heard in Blackfeet public meetings since the late 1920s. Many of the tribe's political leaders had given up on Collier and what appeared to be his false vision of tribal empowerment.

Brown also announced during this two-day public meeting that the Court of Claims had rendered a favorable decision in the tribe's "Big Claim." Although Brown did not know the amount of the award, he indicated that the government would release the money if it decided not to appeal the decision. As the general mood of the meeting was one of mistrust of the government, the council and those attending the public meeting voted unanimously to adopt Brown's proposition that the tribe accept the judgment only if it resulted in a per capita payment. The tribe no longer trusted the government to use its money to good cause. As important, the tribe's right to use monies from such sources as Court of Claims judgments had been, as noted, a factor in its decision to adopt the IRA.

The Stone transfer, the annexation controversy, and the pending Court of Claims award hardened the tribe's position on government interference and weakened the tribe's resolve to continue along Collier's particular path toward self-support. The Blackfeet, who had vigorously defended Collier's program in Washington and at the Great Plains Congress, considered his actions a personal insult. The partnership between Indian and Indian Office that Collier had trumpeted at the Great Plains Congress seemed to be dissolving; the post-IRA honeymoon appeared to be over. Yet the events of April and May made the need for a Blackfeet constitution and charter even more pressing by reinforcing the notion that the Blackfeet needed expanded authority and power to both reduce government interference in tribal affairs and strengthen the tribe's ability to negotiate with the OIA for solutions to similar problems that would undoubtedly occur in the future.

The enthusiasm for reorganization simmered during the summer of 1935 as the BTBC concentrated on improving its leasing system and monitoring the annexation crisis. Warren O'Hara, who replaced Brott as superintendent in June, tried to rejuvenate the Blackfeet's initially keen desire for organizational change with the help of the Indian Organization staff responsible for helping tribes to codify IRA constitutions and charters. Once Blackfeet leaders became involved in the process of writing a constitution, they regained their confidence in the reorganization program; it reminded them of what was promising about the "new" OIA and the IRA.

The Indian Organization Unit—comprising Field Administrator in Charge Joe Jennings, Assistant Commissioner Fred Daiker, and Assistant Solicitor Felix Cohen, among others—toured the West that summer, meeting with leaders of the tribes that had embraced the IRA. Joe Brown and O'Hara first attended a conference in Billings on July 15, organized by Jennings to provide basic procedural information to those tribes marked for reorganization. The Indian Office hoped to simplify the implementation process by offering a sample constitution and charter to such tribes, though it understood that each tribe wanted to produce its own document.[24] Jennings and two associates accompanied Brown and O'Hara to Browning on July 16 to help the Blackfeet fashion their version of the BIA's model constitution. Inspired anew, in part by the enthusiasm and professionalism of the OIA staff, the BTBC worked with Jennings's team until 1:30 A.M. July 17 to produce a first draft of the Blackfeet constitution and selected a constitutional committee to make revisions the following day. Jennings became aware of the council's frustrations with the OIA, telling Collier in a letter of July 18 that councilman Little Blaze "caused a general laugh by saying that they had not heard from [O]rganization for so long that they thought the Wheeler-Howard Act had died out." Despite this frustration, he wrote, the Blackfeet demonstrated much interest and enthusiasm for the process and prospect of developing a viable constitution.[25]

Over the next two weeks O'Hara and the council distributed to the tribe copies of the council's first draft of the constitution and bylaws and held a series of public meetings to give the Blackfeet an opportunity to discuss it. O'Hara reviewed the proposed document with the help of the council members in whose districts the meetings were held, giving the process the imprimatur of local or community consent. "There appears to be no doubt but that the tribe as a whole is very anxious to go ahead," he told Collier in early August, noting the Blackfeet's splendid attendance at the meetings. O'Hara hoped for a quick ratification because he believed that "at this time there appears to be a keen interest in the forming of the Corporation."[26] Jennings, accompanied by Cohen and Daiker, returned to the reservation on August 12 to put the finishing touches on the first draft. The principal members of the Indian Organization Unit supervised the revision of the document to the satisfaction of the council, which voted unanimously to adopt the amended constitution and bylaws and to request that the secretary of the interior call for an election to decide their fate.[27] O'Hara later reported that "Mr. Jennings and Mr. Daiker most certainly won the hearts and the confidence of our Council and Mr. Cohen was very helpful in explaining the legal technicalities of the Act."[28] After an angry spring, Joe Brown and the council proved eager to continue on the road toward reorganization, their faith in the government renewed by the responsiveness and enthusiasm of Jennings, Daiker, and Cohen.

The council had to wait for more than two months before it could hold a tribal election to ratify the constitution. The OIA reviewed the Blackfeet constitution—as it did all constitutions before recommending that the Interior Department accept them for tribal referendum—but despite the assistance of Cohen and Daiker in drafting it, it was not until September 19 that the OIA made the formal request to Interior to accept the document and October 19 that the Blackfeet received formal notification of its approval. Most of the corrections to the Blackfeet version were minor, involving grammatical errors or poorly worded sections. Walter Woehlke, however, expressed concern to Daiker that the business council described in the constitution did not include a bonded treasurer. The document gave the council the "right to make expenditures of available tribal funds," but it did not outline the principal medium of distribution or ensure that the council would conduct the process in a proper fashion. Daiker asked Woehlke if he was "willing to pass," or accept the constitution as written, suggesting that the OIA might later try to require the council to offer financial assurances with a bond before the department agreed to "turn over any funds." Scribbling on Daiker's note, Woehlke answered, "Okay, let's take a chance on it although I'd like to know whether the treasurer's office was discussed by the framers of the document."[29]

Woehlke's concern was fitting, given that the IRA empowered the BTBC to control and distribute tribal funds. Woehlke did not believe that Joe Brown and the other framers adequately considered this issue; Daiker, who helped the Blackfeet write the constitution, apparently did not consider it either. The Blackfeet, for their part, left the question of expenditures an open matter. The constitution gave the council the right to "select subordinate boards, tribal officials and tribal employees, not otherwise provided for in this constitution . . . and to make expenditures from available tribal funds for public purposes," but it offered only that the expenditures would "be a matter of public record at all times."[30] The framers considered the question but did not assign fund distribution to the "white" office of treasurer.

After the OIA approved the document, the Solicitor's Office reviewed it before sending it to Ickes for final approval.[31] Frederick Bernays Wiener raised the sharpest criticism of the Blackfeet constitution, calling two of its provisions "extremely objectionable" and unlike any found in constitutions approved by the department to that point. Wiener, the acting solicitor, considered section 2 of Article V—the council's right to expel a member if nine or more members sanctioned it—a recipe for "unrestrained power, which may be used in undemocratic and tyrannical fashion." He argued that the provision did not delineate the possible offenses for expulsion, such as "gross misconduct or neglect of duty" (which themselves were vague), and thus the council had the "power to expel an unwelcome minority for no reason at all." Wiener likely viewed the minority in this case to be full-blood council members, who by demographic circumstances could find themselves expelled for having minority views; his concern was not unusual given the blood-based factional disturbances displayed on most reservations during the IRA debate. Wiener also criticized the Interior Department for failing to accord the process of writing constitutions the "serious and unhurried consideration that such a vital document deserves," complaining that the department's "whole desire seems to be to stampede the matter through on the ground that this has all been worked out with the Indians, and that a speedy notice of election is now the only desideratum."[32]

Given Wiener's general criticism of the constitution campaign, Solicitor Nathan Margold himself responded to his concerns. Although Margold recommended that Interior officials approve the Blackfeet constitution as written, he conceded that the council's power to expel members did not "give sufficient protection to minority viewpoints." He argued, however, that the council would not expel a member without a hearing and that most Indian constitutions already approved were no more specific about what constituted gross misconduct or neglect of duty; he also doubted that "the absence of these shadowy phrases will make any substantial difference in the practice of the Indian council." Margold admitted that he was "particularly reluctant to criticize a provision of minor importance in the Blackfeet Constitution" after speaking with John Collier, who had indicated, Margold wrote, that a "return of the constitution for minor amendments will probably encourage opposition to the whole organization program and invite a charge of bad faith." Margold did not, therefore, feel justified in overruling the Blackfeet framers or the OIA personnel who had assisted them.[33]

On the basis of Margold's recommendation, the Interior Department approved the constitution and ordered the tribe to hold an election within the following twenty-five days.[34] The review committees of the OIA and Solicitor's Office thus made no substantive changes to the Blackfeet constitution and bylaws. Collier apparently took heed of the Blackfeet's protests of his interference in tribal affairs and understood that any further encroachment on the tribe's fragile emotional constitution jeopardized Blackfeet reorganization.

O'Hara again took the constitution to the Blackfeet people, holding six meetings to explain every paragraph and every line in advance of the November 13 election; despite bad weather that included subzero temperatures and blizzards, the meetings were well attended. The tribe voted overwhelmingly to adopt the constitution by a vote of 884 to 157; 58 percent of the voting population turned out to express its opinion. The voting in the six districts was fairly consistent. The largest numbers of those who voted against it lived in the predominantly full-blood Heart Butte and Old Agency districts. But even in those districts the percentage voting for approval was no lower than 77 and 81, respectively.[35] The Blackfeet clearly favored a continuation of Collier's reorganization program despite as well as because of his diplomatic blunders.

The achievement secured by O'Hara and the BTBC did not come without a fight. The department's delay of approval gave their opponents a chance to lobby the tribe against the constitution. Both full-bloods and mixed-bloods absorbed the "poisonous false misrepresentations" offered by Levi Burd and his faction, O'Hara told Collier, forcing O'Hara to wage a campaign "as one would a real political battle." Burd's "lies and malicious attack" against Collier helped to persuade prominent Blackfeet to oppose the constitution and fight to repeal the IRA, O'Hara wrote.[36]

Burd was influenced in part by Joseph Bruner's anti-IRA propaganda and motivated by his own self-interest to oppose any structural reform of Blackfeet politics. Burd had campaigned for special dispensation for tribal oil leases in the 1920s and had been censured by the BTBC and Forrest Stone in 1934 for running sheep herds on allotments without the owners' consent.[37] He also served on the board of the Montana Stock Growers' Association, an organization that had opposed the IRA in 1934. O'Hara learned that Burd secured the support of Oscar Boy, the leader of a full-blood faction, and had offered to feed attendees of a meeting he staged in late October. O'Hara responded by hiring Oscar Boy as his interpreter, attending Burd's meeting to counter any objections Burd raised against the constitution and organizing a series of public meetings in all six reservation districts. O'Hara spent more than an hour at each meeting discussing the finer points of the constitution and answering the audience's questions. Joe Brown and the respective district's council members followed O'Hara to explain their support of the constitution. O'Hara and Brown "constantly hammered on misrepresentations," and by the end of each meeting, which culminated with dinner and a dance, they were able to "win the doubtful over." Burd's campaign likely confused some voters, but it also served to create a more robust educational campaign that could only have benefited the Blackfeet electorate as a whole. O'Hara's constitutional campaign probably would have failed

without Joe Brown's support. O'Hara told Collier that Brown in particular "cannot be given too much credit. He worked like a Trojan every hour
of the day and night during the campaign."[38] At O'Hara's urging, Collier
thanked Brown for his campaign work on the constitution and the forthcoming charter, the "foundation upon which to build a better civic and
economic structure for the Blackfeet Nation."[39] Collier's letter, in using
"Nation" rather than "Tribe," illustrated the OIA's growing recognition
of the Blackfeet's sovereign rights and served as a peace offering to someone whom Collier knew to be instrumental in the passage of the IRA and
the constitution. Collier still needed Brown's help to persuade the Blackfeet to adopt the charter of incorporation, the final structural element of
the reorganization program.

The argument against the constitution, and the IRA by extension, came
mainly from full-bloods, some of whom Levi Burd recruited for his campaign. Many of them simply resented mixed-bloods, particularly those
with less than one-half Indian blood, who stood to profit from economic
programs developed under the IRA. The constitution, dissenters argued
in a "petition of protest" sent to President Roosevelt and to their congressional representatives, would become an instrument for "landless
and part-blood Indians" to "determine matters which affect the rights
and privileges of the full blooded Indians." The petitioners were angry
that the landless and part-blood would share in tribal revenue and afraid
that a council operating under the new constitution would exploit their
minority status to gain access to their trust patents and the oil rights
owned by the allottees; the petitioners asked that "our rights and property may be protected and perpetuated to our heirs."[40] Assistant Commissioner William Zimmerman Jr. answered for Roosevelt, telling the
petitioners that they were misinformed. Every enrolled member of the
tribe regardless of blood quantum enjoyed the same benefits and rights,
he explained.[41] Zimmerman interpreted the law properly but failed to address the full-bloods' concerns. The protesters were resentful and fearful
of mixed-blood rule, not misinformed.

   Full-bloods suffered from a dramatic demographic disadvantage that
favored mixed-bloods by a four-to-one ratio and had become increasingly concerned about their minority status in the face of structural
changes that promised a further shift in the balance of power between
full-blood and mixed-blood communities. James White Calf, the son of
the venerated nineteenth-century chief White Calf, elaborated on the

full-bloods' concerns in a Washington meeting, telling BIA officials that his group feared that owners of trust patents would lose title to their allotments if Blackfeet tribal organizations or landless individuals defaulted on loans secured from the government's revolving credit fund. Their angst was a by-product of the IRA debate over community ownership, which full-bloods had vehemently opposed for that reason. BIA officials assured White Calf that no trust land could be taken as compensation for delinquent tribal or individual loans.[42] Despite the best efforts of Joe Brown and the BIA to assuage their fears, full-bloods imagined the worst-case scenario of a newly empowered tribal government jeopardizing the integrity of their isolated community. Somewhere between the self-interest of the mixed-blood Levi Burd and the desperation of an anxious full-blood faction lay the uncertainty and the promise of the new constitution.

It is important to note that the full-blood group that lodged the protest represented a minority of the reservation's full-blood population; White Calf's group lived in the Starr School community outside Browning, physically isolated from the full-blood communities in the Heart Butte and Old Agency districts. A majority of the reservation's voting full-bloods supported the constitution, as the returns from the November election showed. Yet the results of the January 1936 BTBC election, the first held under the new constitution, did not bode well for the balanced representation that had provided the tribe with a measure of political stability since 1929. The election, in which only one full-blood was chosen, validated and heightened the concerns expressed in the petition to Roosevelt. White Calf and Rides at the Door, the Blackfeet Nation's most prominent full-blood politicians, were not elected. White Calf, a two-term councilman, and Rides at the Door, a fixture on the council for the previous decade, lost in the Agency district (or Browning district) to mixed-blood candidates; Rides at the Door's defeat was particularly striking given his lengthy tenure and his consistent support for oil development. None of the three full-blood incumbents retained his seat, and full-blood candidates lost to mixed-blood opponents by wide margins in all four districts. In the predominantly full-blood Old Agency district, former full-blood councilman Mud Head received only twenty-nine votes, less than all the mixed-blood candidates. In the Heart Butte district, longtime councilman Richard Sanderville, a staunch ally of full-blood interests, lost by a two-to-one margin to newcomers James Choate and John Horn. Incumbents William Fitzpatrick, Wright Hagerty, and

Medore La Breche gained reelection in the Seville district, an almost exclusively mixed-blood district populated by farmers and ranchers; Hagerty was only one-sixteenth Blackfeet, while La Breche was only one-eighth. The only full-blood to gain a seat was Oscar Boy, whom the council had removed in April 1935 on the grounds of public drunkenness.[43]

At the same time, the election did not represent the subordination of a traditional "informal" political culture to an inchoate "formal" political culture.[44] Full-bloods typically placed three to five men on the thirteen-member business council before the 1936 election; since the late 1920s, PFLA chapter officers participated in both FYIP and BTBC administration, if elected to the council. The IRA and constitution debates had politicized the reservation; fifty-four candidates vied for the thirteen council seats, and roughly 85 percent of the tribe's voting population participated in the election.[45] Competition for council office rose in 1936 in part because the IRA granted the BTBC additional powers and in part because council members could earn per diem expenses and serve on tribal boards that distributed livestock and credit funds. The results could be seen either as an unhealthy slide toward the elimination of a full-blood political voice or as an expression of faith in the tribal idea. Some full-bloods likely voted for mixed-blood candidates because they viewed them as better able to advance the Nation's economic interests than full-blood candidates chiefly concerned with the maintenance of blood parity; contemporary observers of tribal politics routinely remarked on the absence of a full-blood voting bloc. Given the high turnout, it may have been that mixed-blood voters simply overwhelmed full-bloods on the basis of their demographic advantage.

Despite holding a minority position among the reservation's full-bloods, White Calf's faction had a legitimate complaint about the election process. The Starr School community lay within the Agency district, which mixed-blood voters and candidates dominated. Rides at the Door and White Calf received 146 and 138 votes, respectively, and placed seventh and eighth in this district, while none of the three successful candidates in the Seville district earned more than 100 votes. When White Calf lost his seat in 1934 and Rides at the Door failed to retain his in 1936, it must have appeared to full-bloods to be a disturbing trend, creating the kind of credibility gap Forrest Stone foresaw in his 1934 report on Blackfeet organizations. Reorganization failed to appeal to a close-knit community facing a decline in political power after nearly two decades of council representation.

The friction between White Calf's group and the rest of the reservation alarmed David Rodnick, a field worker with the OIA's Applied Anthropology Unit, who spent three months on the reservation in the spring of 1936. Rodnick warned the OIA that if it did not address the full-bloods' concerns, then "the Agency will soon have a negativistic and rebellious minority on its hands, uncooperative and suspicious of being discriminated against." He described the conflict as being between two groups that were "as different in culture as if they were distinct tribes." The Starr School full-bloods' principal complaint, Rodnick wrote, "consists in their not possessing any voice in their own affairs," suggesting that the tribe could eradicate conflict by "changing the council representation on the basis of actual communities existent on the reservation, rather than the present system of election districts" in which smaller communities like Starr School were at the mercy of larger mixed-blood communities like Browning. The full-blood would never achieve electoral parity because of simple demographics, he wrote, but in a fair system "some representation in proportion to his percentage on the rolls should be accorded him."[46]

The constitution granted the business council the "power to establish communities, and the basis of representation on the tribal council from such communities, subject to popular vote."[47] Rodnick's plan was thus legally possible, but naive. It is doubtful that a mixed-blood council would subscribe to any redistricting plan proposed by White Calf, whose protest amounted to an accusation that the council would act in bad faith even before it had a chance to prove itself. In October 1937, the council would narrowly defeat a proposition to make the district-based council election a general election, a plan that would have made it even more difficult for full-bloods to gain office.[48] In either scheme, full-bloods could no longer depend on the facility of a popular vote because of their declining numbers.

The Blackfeet constitution did not recognize full-blood and mixed-blood interests. Leaders like Joe Brown were not ready to declare the tribal name and idea dead, despite the wide gulf that yawned between the interests and cultures of the two groups. Most Blackfeet responded to the IRA largely because it put the Nation in a stronger position to compete with white businesses on and near the reservation. They reorganized the tribe not to divide full-bloods and mixed-bloods but to make the Blackfeet more independent of whites. Brown in particular opposed the government's attempt to legally define the Blackfeet Indian, refusing to accept the one-half blood quantum prescribed in the IRA. In January 1934, the BTBC had defeated a proposal initiated by Levi Burd to eliminate Blackfeet of less than one-half Indian blood from the tribal rolls, in part because council members thought his motivation was to reduce the number of Blackfeet eligible for Big Claim money. The respected elder Mountain Chief, wrapped in an American flag, answered Burd for many of his fellow full-bloods by saying, "I have many grandchildren amongst the mixed-bloods. I am not in favor of Levi Burd's ideas."[49] Brown, whose mother was a full-blood, informed the council two months later that "the mixed blood question" had been answered. "Throw it in a hole, cover it up, and not talk about it any more," he said. "I think just as much of [full-bloods], and I will work just as hard for them as I will for my own children."[50] The Blackfeet constitution made no distinction as a result.[51] Both full-bloods and mixed-bloods alike defended the notion of tribe by refusing to view the reservation in blood terms. By 1936, however, White Calf and his supporters no longer believed in that notion, only that a council dominated by mixed-bloods had ceased to represent their interests.

If the IRA was to transform a reservation comprising distinct Indian communities into a segregated municipality, then civic opposition to large-scale changes in local government administration was likely to develop, particularly from underrepresented interest groups that historically had managed to secure enough influence on tribal councils to keep their opinions heard in council deliberations. Rodnick believed that such civic opposition could be channeled properly if the friction between mixed-blood and full-blood could be ameliorated, writing that "much energy was wasted accentuating the mixed-blood full-blood problem" rather than improving the civic structure of the reservation. After spending a month among the Blackfeet, he reported a general lack of the community spirit that Collier had hoped the IRA would generate. Without the "feeling of something worth working for," he concluded, "this reservation is doomed, with a degenerated pauper feeling among many as a sequence." He encouraged agency personnel to inspire both cultural groups with a vision of "what the future can bring," first by publicly taking responsibility for past actions to clear an atmosphere permeated by anger against the BIA, and second by providing them with "whatever economic resources are available" to facilitate the creation of cooperative rather than individual enterprises. The IRA would fail on the Blackfeet Reservation, he was saying, unless the BIA remained a forceful advocate for change rather than simply serving in an advisory capacity to the tribe's new self-government. The full-bloods' resentment toward bureau personnel and mixed-bloods would not diminish unless "their economic situation is bettered." That resentment, he concluded, "is but an inner resentment of the full-blood toward his own inferior economic situation."[52]

The schism between full-bloods and mixed-bloods represented a serious problem for the tribe, but, as with the blood quantum of the "mixed-blood"—which included everything from one-sixteenth to fifteen-sixteenths—the issue was more complicated than a simple blood division. Mixed-bloods as a sociological group were a varied lot; many had full-blood friends, relatives, or ancestors, continued to honor full-bloods as valued members of the tribal community, or believed that it was important for all Indians to stand together against the predations of white business owners and the inaction of agency officials. And while White Calf's contingent of full-bloods would routinely protest the actions of the council and press for the repeal of the IRA in the coming years, many of the tribe's other full-bloods looked to the promises of the IRA rather than to the possibility of mixed-blood domination.

Conflicts between full-blood and mixed-blood factions took on a new dimension in the 1930s. As full-blood populations declined in relation to an expanding mixed-blood population, so too did their ability to secure equal participation in tribal politics to guarantee the fair distribution of government credit and revenues from natural resource development. The friction on the Blackfeet Reservation was not unusual, but it was highly visible partly because demographic shifts in the Great Plains were more dramatic than those in the Southwest, the "last stronghold of the full-blood."[53] The friction was also heightened by the aggressiveness of White Calf and members of his group, who wrote a series of letters to their congressional representatives requesting permission to send delegations to Washington or calling for investigations of mixed-blood councils in the hope of securing some influence apart from a BIA that had only encouraged them to participate in the tribe's nascent democracy.

Many BIA personnel treated full-blood Indians differently or viewed them in a more sympathetic light, largely because they viewed them as *real* Indians and as less capable than educated mixed-bloods of maneuvering within the organizational world of whites. But the realities of tribal demographics and policy-making meant that an enrolled tribal member of one-sixteenth blood who shared little enthusiasm for "Indian" culture or the notion of "tribe" had the same rights as a full-blood who had suffered the socioeconomic catastrophe of the reservation period and had an even greater chance to gain a seat on the BTBC. OIA officials such as John Collier and William Zimmerman responded to full-blood petitions and protests, and accompanying inquiries from Montana congressmen, by reassuring their writers that the Indian Office continued to look after the full-bloods' interests, while encouraging them to work within the new system. In response to an inquiry from Senator Wheeler about one such full-blood protest, Collier tersely answered, "The situation is this. The Indian Reorganization Act gives the Indians the right to organize and incorporate. Both of these have been done by the Blackfeet Indians. With a duly elected tribal business council operating under an approved constitution, naturally we should and do recognize this body as the official organization of the Blackfeet Indians." Despite being "deeply sympathetic toward the older Indian of the full blood type," Collier told Wheeler that the OIA did not feel it prudent to "extend privileges to any one group which may not be satisfied with the tribal set up."[54]

Collier's argument that full-bloods should work within the new system by electing their own representatives and exercising the rights and privileges granted by the new constitution was valid but not practical for groups like the White Calf faction, which had neither the council votes nor the signatures to initiate a tribal referendum to amend the constitution. And it had neither the council's support nor the financial resources to send a delegation to Washington to make the voices of its members heard. White Calf went to Washington without BTBC support.

Collier's response to factional disputes was informed by an ongoing discussion among members of the OIA's Organization Division on the issue of "blood rule" that culminated in the fall of 1938. The Cheyenne River Sioux full-bloods' protest of their IRA charter, which mirrored that of Blackfeet full-bloods, precipitated the extended debate. The Blackfeet Nation figured prominently in the discussion, reflecting the impact its leaders continued to have on the OIA's conception of reorganized tribal life.

Walter Woehlke's memo to Collier and Organization Division colleagues addressed the Sioux's fear that mixed-bloods would dominate new political and economic organizations and "dissipate the tribal assets

. . . by using it as security for IRA loans from which the full-bloods would derive little benefit." As a result of factional fighting, Woehlke reported, the Sioux's superintendent intended to adopt a "blood rule," proposing to conduct a "blood census" and administer "gratuity services" like relief, rations, and education loans according to a blood quantum system. Woehlke maintained that the OIA should seek statutory backing for a system in which Indians of one-half blood quantum or more would get most of the services.[55] Felix Cohen objected, arguing that superintendents faced a social problem rather than a biological problem. He contended that a group "referred to as 'full-blood' in reservation politics actually contains many mixed bloods. The lines of division are social and not simply biological." Cohen suggested that tribes address this social problem by buying out those Indians who wished to leave the reservation, which would "make the tribe a strictly voluntary group and . . . diminish the friction which always arises when individuals with a contempt for tribal ways are held within the tribe by legal or economic pressure." Cohen also believed it essential for the BIA to educate or, in many cases, reeducate full-bloods about the advantages of reorganization and thus find a middle ground for those Indians "too old or too old-fashioned" to avail themselves of the IRA's benefits. Cohen blamed social unrest partly on intransigent full-bloods who refused to adapt themselves to new forms of political organization or try to understand the "essentials of credit" that one needed to succeed in agriculture.[56] Like Collier, Cohen had limited sympathy for those Indians who did not make an effort to adapt to new reservation conditions.

Joe Jennings and Fred Daiker disagreed on the extent to which the BIA should intervene on behalf of full-blood groups that lacked, for whatever reason, access to the benefits of reorganization. Jennings supported Woehlke's position, arguing, as David Rodnick had, that if the BIA did not address the growing disparity of economic distribution and political representation, then it could expect "more and more dissension between the full-bloods and the mixed-bloods." The Extension, Health, and Education Divisions could not continue to supply gratis services to a growing Indian population because of static appropriations, he wrote, and warned that "unless a blood quantum is prescribed by Office policy or law" the full-blood population would receive fewer services and thus "become more and more aloof from the Indian Service and the organization movement." The Blackfeet Indian Council, he noted, had recently argued that the OIA could not legally deny an educational loan to a tribal member on the basis of his or her degree of Indian blood, portending a challenge from mixed-blood groups to any OIA program that attempted to distinguish between a worthy Indian and an unworthy one on the basis of blood quantum.[57] Daiker in turn countered that the OIA "should and must" recognize new tribal councils as the only legitimate political organization and warned that OIA interference in tribal disputes might destabilize duly elected political bodies and thus undermine the OIA's reorganization agenda; the Blackfeet's protest of the OIA's interference in the distribution of gratis services served as an example. Tacking closer to Cohen's position, Daiker asked his colleagues, "If [full-bloods] are not inclined to see their responsibility and duty, to bring about a better social and economic structure welded together in a program for the benefit of all, then how can we take this on ourselves?" There were many things "not subject to our control," he argued, expressing the collective frustration of a BIA faced with a choice between protecting a class of Indians resistant to change or a class of Indians that had faithfully adopted the most important elements of the government's prevailing Indian policy.[58]

The Indian Office found itself in a tough spot: it did not want to meddle in tribal affairs and yet felt inclined to assist minority full-bloods in making the transition to modern Indian life. The OIA continued to support the reorganized tribal governments in the face of both the BTBC's opposition to limitations on their control of tribal affairs and an increasingly aggressive campaign to repeal the IRA. Collier contested Sen. Burton Wheeler's claim that, in Collier's words, "the full blood ancient minded Blackfeet Indians, who are a minority of that tribe, have expressed discontent with the circumstance that the tribal government is too largely in the hands of the mixedblood majority." Collier maintained that Blackfeet full-bloods "grumble at the Act because it is making toward a more rapid assimilation or 'Americanization' of the tribe. Not because it is operating the other way, as Senator Wheeler seems to imply."[59] Collier seemed to have sacrificed the interests of Blackfeet full-bloods —and other full-blood groups by association—on the altar of the IRA, which, he asserted, offered great benefits to full-bloods and mixed-bloods alike. Although OIA leaders continued to consider full-blood complaints, as Collier did by meeting with Blackfeet leaders in the summer of 1938, Collier clarified the OIA's position in a letter to Sen. James Murray of Montana in which he stated that dissension between tribal groups "could be remedied to a very large extent if the [Blackfeet] full-bloods would actively participate in tribal matters by electing their own representatives on the Council and attending meetings and exercising other rights and privileges which are granted them under the constitution." As William Zimmerman had put it to Murray, "[i]t is a matter entirely within the hands of the Indians."[60] Representative democracy, as the IRA constituted it and as the OIA conceived it, became the invisible hand of postcolonial Indian administration.

The OIA and the Blackfeet Nation experienced a gestalt shift once the IRA became codified, reorganizing not only tribal political economies but their respective attitudes toward the question of what constituted a tribe of Indians. The tribal idea died hard for John Collier and his adherents. The forces of acculturation—frontier economic pressure, intermarriage, white education—made it difficult for some tribes, the Blackfeet in particular, to renew the community spirit or survival instinct that had held them together during the cultural and physical retrenchment of the nineteenth century. By 1934 the tribe as a cultural entity had become an anachronism on most Indian reservations of the Northern Plains. On the Blackfeet Reservation, the tribe as a political entity had just begun taking shape in the organizational form of the Blackfeet Corporation.

Indian Office policy, then, dictated that all Indians were to be treated equally as political entities, and thus it became incumbent upon each citizen of the Blackfeet Nation to secure an economic future through the instrument of tribal incorporation. Although many bureau officials were more solicitous of full-bloods than of "progressive" mixed-bloods, it became ultra vires to fashion a distinct economic policy for them. Ethnic considerations had ceased to be an issue in Indian Office policy. The adoption of a charter of incorporation would, on paper, grant all Blackfeet the right to borrow from a pool of government credit and give the tribe the power to expand its management of tribal economic projects, some of which could be directed at full-blood communities such as Starr School and Heart Butte.

As it did with tribal constitutions, the OIA offered a corporate charter to tribes organizing under the IRA, using the charter of the Flathead Indians as its model; the Flathead Tribe, the Blackfeet's southern neighbor, was one of the first groups to adopt a charter, doing so largely to gain access to the revolving loan fund, a dominant factor in the Blackfeet's decision to adopt the IRA. In December 1935, the OIA's organization committee debated the facility of the Flathead Charter and the problems facing the OIA's implementation of similar charters on a diverse set of reservations. The principal question revolved around the secretary of the interior's continued exercise of supervisory powers over Indians' financial and natural resources. Committee members informed Collier that the prevailing attitude on many reservations had become "one of increasing skepticism towards the promise of the administration that the Indians would be granted definite powers of independent action over tribal property and enterprises." OIA staff and field agents faced the "charge that Indian Organization is only another scheme of the Government to take control of the remaining resources of the Indian tribes into its own hands, and to perpetuate the control that it now has." Whites and Indians opposed to the IRA were spreading the specious charges, the committee stated, but it warned that if the charters did not embody the spirit of the reorganization movement—expressed at the Indian congresses and in numerous OIA circulars and statements—by codifying Indians' right to exercise independent action, then "the charter is an empty gesture and will be so regarded by the Indians."[61]

The debate amounted to asking whether the federal government was prepared to begin terminating its supervision of Indian resources. The organization committee, while arguing that Interior should retain some supervisory powers, advised Collier that the benefits of giving greater control to tribal leaders outweighed the risks of losing larger and more representative elements of "reorganized" tribes to the growing ranks trying to repeal the IRA. Members also argued that "the Indian who makes his own mistakes is likely to learn from those mistakes, and that the mistakes of the Indian Service personnel lead only to fruitless resentment and discord." This "process of education," assisted by technical advisers rather than bureaucrats, was the "only final solution to the economic problems of the Indian," the committee believed, echoing the findings of the Meriam Report.[62] The OIA, then, continued debating the principal ideas behind the IRA eighteen months after it passed Congress. At the heart of the act was the idea of self-determination, the notion that Indians should have the opportunity to make important decisions for themselves with minimal or no government interference.

The Blackfeet, judging from their public performances and private meetings during the IRA debate, were particularly keen on taking responsibility for the management of their natural resources and intent on reducing the discretionary power of the secretary of the interior to the level applicable to white citizens. The tribe's constitution granted the Blackfeet Tribal Business Council the authority to "manage all economic affairs and enterprises of the Blackfeet Reservation, including . . . the disposition of all oil royalties from tribal lands." This power, however, was contingent upon the tribe's adoption of a charter of incorporation. A delegation of Blackfeet led by Joe Brown spent nearly a month in Washington DC in late March and early April 1936 discussing the proposed charter and the pending distribution of the eighty-five dollars per capita payment from the Court of Claims decision; the delegation's lobbying effort, Brown said, helped to "jar [the eighty-five dollars] loose" from the General Accounting Office. The tribe welcomed the delegation home on April 20 with a victory party. Delegates spoke of their struggles in Washington trying to get the Big Claim money and other funds for tribal development. Warren O'Hara added some humorous anecdotes before announcing that he was resigning to join the new Social Security Administration in Washington. O'Hara had proven himself a worthy successor to Forrest Stone, but like Stone he left soon after steering the tribe though a difficult period of decision-making. Both departures interrupted progress in tribal deliberations while reinforcing the notion that the tribe needed to depend on itself for leadership and direction.

The charter devised by O'Hara and the Blackfeet delegation received intense scrutiny from the organization committee, which convened in William Zimmerman's office on April 1 to offer "criticisms" of the document. The language of the Blackfeet charter followed closely that of the model Flathead charter, and its provisions were generally agreed upon by department representatives of the Solicitor's Office and the Land and Extension Divisions. Allan Harper and Fred Daiker raised minor objections to elements of section 5, which delineated the "corporate powers" of the tribe, and section 8, which established criteria for the distribution of per capita payments.[63] Supervisor of Indian Credit H. M. Critchfield suggested that the committee modify provisions of section 5 outlining the process of securing loans and the subsequent distribution of loan monies to ensure access to government funds from agencies other than the Interior Department.[64] The organization committee agreed to restructure section 5 to encourage the Blackfeet to secure funds for economic development from as many sources as possible, heeding Critchfield's warning that the Revolving Credit Fund was underfunded and politically vulnerable.

Robert Marshall, chief of the Forestry Division, offered the most strenuous criticism of the charter, raising the question of termination of federal control of Indian resources. Marshall's "major tremendously serious objection," as he put it, centered on section 6, which established a schedule for the "termination of any supervisory power reserved to the Secretary of the Interior." He argued that this section "makes possible and almost inevitable that at the end of 10 years the Secretary will lose his control over the conservation of the natural resources of this reservation." Marshall expressed concern that Indian councils would subordinate their tribe's welfare by selling timber reserves for profit, writing that "it is the working out of the obvious economic principle that people do not voluntarily give up *present personal private profit for future general public welfare*." Marshall's objection reflected the wearied opinion of a man both frustrated by the abuse and misuse of private and public natural resources and uncertain of the integrity of the Indian councils that were poised to assume control of valuable assets. Marshall unfairly equated Indian stewardship of natural resources with white mismanagement of public and private land, neglecting to take into account both the general cultural history of Indian land management and the Blackfeet Nation's specific policy against mortgaging or selling its timber reserves for investment purposes. His criticism was not unreasonable, however, given the changing composition of Indian councils and the enormous stakes involved in their stewardship of natural resources.[65]

The organization committee subsequently grafted onto section 5 a provision that mandated a tribal referendum on any sale of tribal assets valued at more than ten thousand dollars, giving Blackfeet citizens some protection against BTBC profiteering. The committee focused on Marshall's more serious concern about the premature termination of federal control of resources and funds, the most contentious issue of the debate proceedings. The committee decided to ignore Marshall's warning about the danger of terminating the department's control of tribal assets as outlined in section 5(b) because the Blackfeet delegation "insisted that this provision be terminable." Marshall also waived his objection to terminating federal control of "corporate dividends," or per capita payments. Marshall and Daiker did succeed in preserving the secretary's right to control the amount of corporate lending, capping tribal indebtedness in section 5(d) at one hundred thousand dollars to protect the financial integrity of the Blackfeet Corporation.[66]

The most significant change in the charter's final version, then, was the authority granted the BTBC to request the termination of the Interior Department's supervision of natural resource development, contracts, loans, fund deposits, and per capita distribution.[67] The original version had provided that the council could not make such a request until the end of a ten-year period. The final draft reflected the Blackfeet's demand that the secretary of the interior approve at any time after charter ratification a tribal referendum on termination, which required for its passage a majority vote at an election in which at least 30 percent of Blackfeet adults participated.[68] If the secretary rejected a termination request after the ten-year period the tribe could overturn his or her veto through apopular referendum of resident adult Blackfeet, which would pass if two-thirds of the voters supported the measure. A revised section 6 represented the principal difference between the Blackfeet and Flathead charters. Joe Jennings considered it a worthy improvement to the Flathead charter, explaining to Zimmerman that the spirited debate on Blackfeet termination criteria had produced a "more flexible" provision that "should permit more easy adjustment of the relation between the Department and the tribe as changing circumstances develop the capacities and abilities of the tribe."[69] The BTBC thus received a statutory guarantee that the tribe had the right to exercise the "power of independent action" in the administration of certain tribal affairs and had secured the right to terminate the government's supervisory control over other functions if it could convince the Blackfeet people of its necessity. Although the BTBC did not intend to exercise this right in 1936, it understood the importance of having the option codified in its charter. Securing the authority to exercise such options was what motivated Brown and other Blackfeet leaders throughout the reorganization process.

The BTBC approved the new version of the charter on June 4 by a vote of ten to two.[70] Ickes notified C. L. Graves and the BTBC on July 18 that the department had formally approved the Blackfeet's charter and called for an August 15 election. Graves and his staff distributed copies of the charter to interested Blackfeet and with the BTBC's help lobbied them to adopt it. Supporters encountered expected resistance from Starr School full-bloods who had made their position clear throughout the previous year, but they also found that white traders actively distributed propaganda warning that those Indians voting for the charter would lose their allotments and their share of the Big Claim.[71] The Blackfeet Nation adopted the charter on August 15 by a vote of 737 to 301. The Seville, Little Badger, and Babb irrigation districts, populated mostly by mixed-bloods, offered nearly unanimous support for it, while only 25 percent of the voters in the Starr School precinct supported it. In the predominantly full-blood Old Agency district 64 percent of the voters supported the charter, the smallest level of acceptance in the four major precincts.[72] The tribe's support of reorganization had clearly declined since June 1934. While the number of voters participating in the various IRA referenda stayed relatively constant, only 737 Blackfeet voted for the charter in contrast to the 884 that supported the constitution in October 1935 and the 823 that voted to adopt the IRA in October 1934.[73]

This declining support stemmed from the results of the 1936 council election and from the economic conditions that prevailed on the reservation while the tribe waited for the benefits of reorganization to materialize; some Blackfeet voted against the charter because of a delay in the distribution of Big Claim monies. No Coat's letter to Secretary Ickes, whom he had once met in Glacier National Park, captured the frustration of many elderly Blackfeet. "I am confused about the Wheeler Howard Act," he wrote. "I do not know what it means. If you could tell me what we may expect from it, I would appreciate it."[74] Acting Secretary of the Interior Charles West answered No Coat by informing him that under the IRA the Blackfeet "have an opportunity to help plan and work out those things which should be done on the reservation for the interest of all concerned. Heretofore those matters were handled by the government for you." The IRA, he wrote, also enabled Blackfeet to secure loans to purchase livestock, improve homes, and generally to "provide for themselves." West preached patience, telling No Coat that because the IRA was just beginning "the full benefits are not apparent, but as time goes on and your people and our employees work together we have every right to look forward to progress and advancement by the Indians of the Blackfeet Reservation."[75] The charter vote completed the reorganization of the Blackfeet Nation. As the declining support for the charter suggested, the Blackfeet were getting increasingly impatient for signs of "progress and advancement."

4. FEEDING THE "SECOND BUFFALO" AND THEMSELVES: The Contours of the Blackfeet Economy, 1934–1940

> The Blackfeet are always industrious and hardworking people but they have nothing to do today. If you give us cattle then we will always have something to do and the White Father won't have to do anything more for us. . . . The buffalo are gone forever and can never come back, but my people can still be happy if you give them a chance to raise this second buffalo. – Mountain Chief to Robert Marshall, forestry chief, 1935

> We were flooded with applications for loans from families who were thoroughly disgusted and discouraged with the uncertainty of living conditions. These people were, and still are, anxious to get away from these emergency relief programs and establish themselves on their land where they hope, with the aid of loans, to be able to feed and clothe their families as it should be done. – John Krall, Blackfeet extension agent, 1937

Difficult living conditions prevailed on the reservation for most Blackfeet during the Great Depression, especially for those in communities outside Browning. As the Blackfeet people debated the charter during the summer of 1936, Extension Division workers surveyed the outlying communities of the reservation, visiting about half of its 820 families. They found homes in great need of repair and lacking basic necessities like furniture and household staples, noting that many of them "are nothing more than shacks which are not fit for summer shelter, let alone a protection against winter storms. A good tent would be a palace compared to some of these places." Workers also reported that "in most cases the food was as scarce as the furniture."[1] In early 1936, 63 percent of the reservation's population received government rations or some form of relief, though half of those recipients were "mentally and physically disabled," and 10 percent of those on relief performed labor to earn their rations.[2]

In response to American Indians' continuing economic depression, the federal government tried to provide tribes with a coordinated program of labor, rehabilitation, and relief to boost reservation income and employment. The Indian New Deal—which mirrored the national New Deal—came to the Blackfeet people in late 1933 in the form of Public Works Administration (PWA) and Civilian Conservation Corps (CCC), or Emergency Conservation Works (ECW) projects, which attempted to improve the reservation's infrastructure through the building of bridges, roads, and water mains, and to rehabilitate their forests and grasslands as well as those of neighboring Glacier National Park. By 1935, ECW crews had organized three major camps and numerous "community camps," which housed temporary workers and their families. The ECW's forestry and conservation projects emphasized fire control measures and improvement of grazing ranges. Blackfeet men also worked on CCC and ECW projects clearing roads and trails of burned and fallen timber, which was allocated to the Blackfeet for home building.[3] The OIA encouraged Indians across the country to supervise the various operations, citing the Blackfeet as a good example of those Indians who "demonstrate their fitness for promotion." The OIA also reported that Blackfeet women were "so quick to grasp the opportunity to work" that ECW personnel designed rotating shifts of thirty-hour weeks to accommodate them; more than seventy Blackfeet women sewed old buffalo coats, made clothing for schoolchildren and crib mattresses for infants, and canned berries and other foodstuffs for the winter months.[4] The Blackfeet were grateful for the opportunity to work and to generate cash income, however small the amount.

The actual distribution of the Big Claim money in late 1936 also boosted Blackfeet incomes. Congress passed Senate Joint Resolution 243 on June 20, 1936, authorizing a per capita payment of $85 to each of the 3,950 enrolled tribal members; the federal government first deducted $4,032,155.61 for its investment in property, food, and buildings, essentially making the Blackfeet pay for the services and goods the government had provided since 1855.[5] Without Congress's approval the money would have gone directly to the tribe's U.S. Treasury account without passing through the reservation, where, one could argue, the Blackfeet needed it. The Blackfeet finally received their long-awaited checks in November 1936. The "entire State [Montana] speculated as to how this money was going to be spent," the tribe's extension agent reported, adding that "[h]undreds of second hand cars were brought in to be in readiness for the first pay day."[6] Reports of Indians buying these cars and other extravagances circulated in newspaper accounts of the big payday. The *Glacier County Chief* addressed these reports in its November 20 issue, noting that "contrary to the general belief that the Blackfeet Indians who are receiving the Big Claim money are spending it foolishly, comes the report from the business houses in Browning . . . that the Indians are buying clothing for their children, food for their families, and improving their homes and furnishing their rooms with modern and necessary furniture and equipment."[7] Extension workers also reported that Blackfeet spent wisely, buying mostly livestock, clothing, and furniture. They helped one group of 113 families buy, among other things, 27 milk cows, 174 horses, 3 wagons, lumber for home repair, blacksmith tools, and livestock feed. In addition, extension workers found that many younger Blackfeet invested their money in education, paying for enrollment at the various Indian schools.[8]

The Blackfeet's participation and performance in the various New Deal projects illustrated their desire to work and learn new skills. Their judicious use of Big Claim money indicated that they were more inclined to invest in livestock and necessities than to waste it on luxury items like automobiles. The Indian New Deal projects and the Big Claim distribution represented, however, a short-term solution to the long-term problems of unemployment and underdevelopment of reservation resources. Veteran BIA employee Oscar Lipps called the Blackfeet Reservation a "hard country in which to live and to make a living." Because of a difficult climate and an expanding population, the Blackfeet situation, according to Lipps, "presents one of the most difficult economic problems to be found anywhere in the Indian Service." He was not optimistic that the government could do anything but "subsidize this reservation and maintain it as an almshouse—a paupers nursery." Agency, tribal, and BIA personnel agreed, he wrote, that the solution to the Blackfeet situation was a comprehensive economic program emphasizing livestock cultivation, irrigation development, and population control.[9] Such a bleak assessment of the Blackfeet's economic future heralded a painful first stage of self-government. Tribal leaders would spend the rest of the decade trying to fashion a workable economic program while balancing the needs of an evolving and growing body of politicized citizens who had developed great expectations for progress after two years of discussions, debates, and decisions about the IRA and its institutional mechanisms for change.

Despite the promises of oil development in the early 1930s, by 1936 the tribe's leasing program had generated only an annual $10 royalty for each Blackfeet, a negligible amount and a small percentage of the average $162 per capita annual income.[10] Interest in the reservation's potential remained high, especially after Tip O'Neil's successful strike in April 1933, but the tribe had to compete with white-owned oil lands in the Cut Bank field—an area of exploration and development that included the eastern part of the Blackfeet Reservation. In 1934 the BTBC had removed the requisite $25,000 bond because it "marred development," calling for "better inducements for operators to come in and lease our oil lands."[11] The council liberalized its leasing policy in August 1936 in the hope of convincing existing oil operators to continue their drilling projects. The BTBC had won some concessions from the OIA and the Interior Department to make tribal oil leases after the tribe adopted an IRA constitution and charter, but it still needed OIA authority to advertise for bids and faced Interior's right to veto those leases. Acting Solicitor Frederic Kirgis cautioned officials to use the veto "primarily as an education device to check up on mistakes, honest or dishonest, that may be made by the tribal officials in the exercise of their new duties." The OIA and Interior must earn the tribe's respect, he wrote, or face a vote on termination of their powers after ten years had elapsed.[12]

Felix Cohen had advised Kirgis that the department could not appear heavy-handed in its use of the veto; BTBC leaders had made it clear to Cohen that the "question of tribal management of oil resources has always been uppermost in their minds." Reorganization had promised Blackfeet Nation officials the prospect of managing important aspects of tribal leasing programs, Cohen told Kirgis, and thus excessive regulation would "be used with telling effect by opponents of administration policies who have told the Indians of the Blackfeet Reservation that the Department will never carry out the promises embodied in constitutions and by-laws."[13] Written during the height of IRA opposition, Cohen's words were not taken lightly.

The BTBC made those words ring true the following month. Frustrated by the OIA's delays in securing bids and approving leases during the short drilling season, several council members sanctioned a showdown with the OIA. Medore La Breche told his colleagues, "Here is our chance to find out whether or not we are really self-governing and how much power we have."[14] Although the council passed a resolution supportive of the IRA in April, it contended that the OIA discriminated against the Blackfeet by not acknowledging its request for faster development. Council members debated whether to advertise on their own a large group of oil tracts. Joe Brown convinced the council that any action taken without department approval would scare off potential bidders unwilling to get in the middle of a political conflict, but the council's hardened attitude ultimately led to productive changes in its ability to control both production and revenue. The BTBC finally received authority to advertise the sale of oil leases in September 1937, though it was too late in the year for most developers to begin drilling.

Cohen's memo to Kirgis precipitated a general review of the department's "proper interpretation of constitutional and charter provisions." Cohen in particular emphasized to Organization Division staff the need to help tribes develop both sources of revenue and the mechanics of managing such revenues for tribal benefit.[15] A Blackfeet delegation had raised this issue during a visit to Washington in February 1937 by asking the OIA to modify its standard oil lease to permit revenue to go directly to the tribal treasury rather than to the agency superintendent. The Organization Division staff, divided on the issue, debated the facility of this change both for the Blackfeet and for other incorporated tribes. The decision to grant the Blackfeet the right to manage their own funds would set a precedent that would thus become one of "broad policy." Some officials felt that revenue was best managed by superintendents, fearing "malfeasance or misfeasance" on the part of tribal officials. Assistant Commissioner John Herrick maintained that the OIA was "honor bound to give the Blackfeet the privilege of handling money" because it had adopted the IRA, an instrument designed to give control of such functions to tribal leaders.[16]

Cohen supported Herrick's position but argued against using the new Blackfeet lease as a model. The Blackfeet, with Cohen's help, had devised the new lease and thus understood its provisions and the logic behind them. If the OIA simply mailed this form to other tribes, he wrote, they would have no understanding of the organic process that created it and thus would not understand the process of leasing itself. Cohen recommended sending the Blackfeet lease to oil-producing tribes, telling them that "they have as much right as the Blackfeet" to devise their own lease while suggesting that the Blackfeet lease was "worth some study."[17] Cohen had helped the Blackfeet devise their constitution and charter, and he seemed to appreciate the Blackfeet's willingness to study the documents and forms of self-government and adapt them to their own physical and political climate. This internal debate amounted to yet another OIA referendum on the IRA—to decide whether or not the OIA should trust tribal governments with tribal revenue. For Herrick and Cohen, the OIA had no choice if the reorganization program was to survive.

After several rounds of negotiation the BTBC received permission from Interior officials to use the new lease. The OIA proved to be very accommodating by providing "what the Blackfeet Tribal Council desires," adopting Cohen's and Herrick's approach of giving leaders an opportunity to learn by doing.[18] The council also got stricter drilling terms codified in the lease, which addressed its frustration with oil speculators who simply waited for the soft market to rebound. The council had been trying for fifteen years to compel delinquent lessees to honor their drilling terms. The OIA proved to be willing, for the first time, to prosecute such lessees.[19] The OIA and its big brother the Interior Department finally became advocates of Blackfeet interests, in large part because the IRA had given the Blackfeet Nation a legal foundation on which its diplomatic requests for change could rest. Reduced market demand and the attendant low prices diminished production incentives during the mid-1930s, however, affecting the tribe's leverage in lease negotiations. Although the Cut Bank fields remained more active than other Montana fields, the loss of Canadian markets created a basic problem of supply and demand; in 1937, roughly 50 percent of the oil produced in Montana was unsold.[20] And though the council continued to pursue oil leasing, the expectations of a bonanza on the scale of what Osage Indians achieved had virtually disappeared among the Blackfeet who had shared in the oil excitement of the previous decade.

The leasing of allotments and tribal land to stock companies also provided some income in 1936, but here too such income—roughly thirty-two dollars per person in 1936—was hardly enough to provide anything but subsistence. Although it appears that Forrest Stone did an adequate job of securing payments from grazing lessees, he failed to reform Blackfeet grazing regulations or pursue with any zeal the prosecution of trespassers. Council members repeatedly complained about overgrazing and trespassing to Stone and his successors. Some prominent Blackfeet stockowners like Levi Burd contributed to the problem by trespassing on Indian allotments or, in Burd's case, subleasing to white stockowners.[21] The checkerboard nature of the Blackfeet Reservation made it especially difficult to enforce lease provisions. Extension staff concluded in 1935 that "effective practicable grazing management was impossible, and lessees were left largely to their own devices."[22] Overgrazing by white stockowners and the ravages of the northwestern Montana climate degraded portions of the tribe's best grazing land. Despite these administrative and environmental problems, Montana and Washington stockowners continued to lease Blackfeet lands, especially after the dust bowl began to invade other ranges in the Northern Plains.

The principal problem with the tribe's grazing program was that few Blackfeet used the reservation's fine grazing lands. Between June 1935 and June 1936 tribal members leased only 122,075 of the 923,364 acres available to Indian and white stockowners, or about 13 percent of the tribal range, and they leased only 11 percent of the 38,666 acres of tribal land available for grazing. Blackfeet allottees used an additional 194,156 acres. In sum, the Blackfeet utilized only 28 percent of the 1,117,520 acres of reservation rangeland.[23] Those Blackfeet who did lease tribal or allotted land varied greatly between a few large lessees and many small lessees. Only twelve of the fifty-six Blackfeet leasing reservation land between June 1935 and June 1936 had more than one lease. Only six had more than two. The largest Indian lessee on the reservation was Wright Hagerty, the one-sixteenth Blackfeet councilman from the Seville district, who had ten leases totaling 22,141.46 acres, representing 18 percent of all Indian leases and 18 percent of the total acreage leased by Blackfeet during this period.[24] The numbers suggest that the Blackfeet could elevate their economic standing by adopting the land use patterns of white stockowners and successful Indian lessees, but only if they got capital, training, and adequate supplies of winter feed.

During the 1930s, the BTBC tried to ensure that the tribe's natural resources were managed properly and fairly. Chairman Joe Brown believed, however, that the Blackfeet needed to earn income through labor rather than simply to wait for the per capita distribution of oil and grazing revenues. To rely upon the latter would mean that the Blackfeet had merely traded the federal government's form of relief for the business council's. Brown understood that a stable economic foundation could come only from a long-term "program of work." Senator Wheeler and Forrest Stone had sanctioned Brown's philosophy of work and economic agenda during the October 1933 Senate subcommittee hearing. Brown had tes-tified to the Blackfeet's desire for another opportunity to manage their own stock, arguing that if white stockowners from Washington state could turn a profit after paying taxes and grazing fees to the tribe, then "why cannot we, the Indians who own the land . . . make a success of the stock industry?" Stone called Joe Brown's goal of creating a livestock in-dustry "the ultimate solution" to the Blackfeet's problems; Wheeler said it was the tribe's "only salvation."[25]

Brown also found backing from Assistant Secretary of the Interior Oscar Chapman, who believed that the Blackfeet had "what it takes to make an ideal setup for the stock business, except the capital." White men, he told Wheeler in June 1934, leased the best land and reached the economy of scale necessary to mount a profitable operation largely be-cause they had access to capital. Chapman championed the Wheeler-Howard Bill—then pending in Congress—and its $10 million revolving credit fund as the Blackfeet's best hope to become self-supporting. With-out cattle or credit, he concluded, the Blackfeet "cannot hope to be suc-cessful."[26]

Reservation surveys conducted later that year indicated that full-bloods and mixed-bloods alike were eager to become stockowners. Al-though many full-bloods continued their agricultural pursuits under the aegis of the Piegan Farming and Livestock Association, most continued to believe that the Five Year Industrial Program would provide only a subsistence living. Some of the FYIP adherents had already started small flocks of sheep or cattle and sought to expand their size to create a cash in-come. Mountain Chief, the tribe's oldest hereditary chief, told forestry chief Robert Marshall in April 1935, "The Blackfeet are always industri-ous and hardworking people but they have nothing to do today. If you give us cattle then we will always have something to do and the White Father won't have to do anything more for us. . . . The buffalo are gone forever and can never come back, but my people can still be happy if you give them a chance to raise this second buffalo."[27] Full-blood councilman Little Blaze gave political expression to Mountain Chief's views when he voiced opposition to the National Park Service's proposal to stock the Blackfeet Reservation with buffalo, as the Crow Indians had done on their reservation. Little Blaze told his colleagues during the BTBC's April 1935 debate on the buffalo question, "From the census rolls you will no-tice that there are more mixed bloods than full bloods. In the days when the full blood got the most benefit from the reservation was in the days when the buffalo were here, but they are gone now, and so are most of the full bloods. What we will get the most benefit from now is the cow."[28] After initially accepting the proposal in January 1934, the council rejected it in favor of expanding cattle and sheep ranching, largely because of the fencing costs and the need to preserve tribal land for the cattle herds that had grown considerably since January 1934.[29]

Blackfeet stock numbering in the tens of thousands nearly all died in the harsh winter and dry summer of 1919–20. In January 1934, the Blackfeet owned only 2,500 head on a reservation that extension personnel estimated could carry more than 40,000.[30] Most enterprising Blackfeet thus seized the opportunity to renew their livestock operations with cattle provided by the government in late 1934. Besides giving the Blackfeet a number of slaughter cattle to supplement food relief, the federal government sent the tribe a large number of drought relief cattle purchased from drought-stricken areas in southern Montana and Wyoming. The Extension Division had lobbied the government for months to provide funds with which division supervisors could purchase and distribute cattle through local administrators. Although the dust bowl extended to the southern part of Montana, the Blackfeet's rangeland remained productive and their feed supplies remained high, thus meeting Extension's main criteria. The Nation expected a sizable herd but got considerably fewer than the 20,000 head requested by agency staff. The Nation's allotment, which included 4,419 head of grade cattle, 828 head of purebred beef cows, and 276 head of purebred Hereford bulls, was distributed to 550 different Blackfeet. The terms of the Cattle Repayment Program (CRP) gave the Indian allottee title to the animals after three years, provided that the new owner reimbursed the BIA one calf for each head of cattle given, which in turn would help other needy Indians with "foundation stock."[31] Much of the herd was thin and very weak when it arrived, the tribe's extension agent reported, and the subsequent loss during one of the worst winters in many years was very heavy. By July 1935 more than 1,000 of the grade beef cattle had died, as had 38 Hereford bulls and 109 purebred cows. Blizzards in late March and early April also killed many of the calves produced by a belated breeding program.[32]

In February 1935, when it had become clear that the losses would be higher than expected, the BTBC attempted to retain the calves that were due as repayment and secure more of the relief cattle. The OIA determined that the tribe had benefited from the cattle program more than "perhaps any other reservation" and refused to grant the tribe dispensation or additional cattle because "less fortunate Indians" needed them. Collier reminded the Blackfeet that the OIA had given them "an opportunity to enter the cattle business on a scale which should make them self-sustaining." The council tried again, this time submitting photographs of the heavy snowfall and reports of subzero temperatures.[33] Although the losses mounted and the OIA ignored the council's requests, the Blackfeet had received the essential ingredient of a new cattle business. Stock raising became the tribe's principal economic focus during the Indian New Deal.

The agency distributed the cattle to those Blackfeet "best equipped to handle them," an inherently inequitable plan.[34] Distribution clearly favored residents of the predominantly mixed-blood Browning district; they received 64 percent of the bulls, 66 percent of the purebred Angus and Hereford cows, and 60 percent of the grade cows. Browning stockowners also suffered fewer losses during the harsh winter; by July 1935 they had lost 11 percent of their bulls, 9 percent of their purebred cows, and 20 percent of their grade cows, in contrast to stockowners in the predominantly full-blood Heart Butte and Old Agency districts, who lost on average 19 percent of their bulls, 21 percent of their purebred cows, and 29 percent of their grade cows.[35] The difference in both the distribution and survival rates reflects several factors, perhaps the most salient of which was the inexperience of Heart Butte and Old Agency residents. Many of them had relied more on dry farming and sheep raising than on cattle grazing and thus had less experience, fewer facilities, and insufficient hay supplies. Although the better survival rates in the Browning district probably reflect this experience, it is also possible that Browning stockowners received the healthier segment of the relief herd; Melvin Strang, superintendent of livestock, centered his activities in the Browning district, as did Joe Brown, the government stockman.

Despite the seemingly sound nature of the distribution policy, it discriminated against those Blackfeet living in communities other than Browning who had little background in stock raising but great enthusiasm for it. David Rodnick, the anthropologist who studied the tribe in the spring of 1936, argued in his final report that such discriminatory practices made good sense given the cultural differences between full-bloods and mixed-bloods. The Blackfeet's "economic rehabilitation," he wrote, "is closely tied up with adoption of white monetary attitudes. From that point of view, the mixed-blood represents far less a risk than the full-blood." Any investment in stock programs, he insisted, "must be proportionate to the amount of training given."[36] Yet Rodnick also warned that any comprehensive program should be both well funded and equitable or it would produce "jealousies among those left out" and aggravate the existing conflict between mixed-bloods and those full-bloods who perceived them to be the beneficiaries of administration largess. The "culturally handicapped" full-blood, he maintained, "should receive better care and attention than he has received so far." Rodnick offered a bleak assessment of the tribe's future: "The complexities of the economic and cultural situation are such as to make it seem improbable that any panacea will be found within the next few years that will end once and for all the intense poverty of the reservation and the great lack of incentives such as are found among American Whites. These problems can be solved over a period of time, if ample loans and a considerate personnel are forthcoming." He noted that although most Blackfeet were eager to work, their good "work attitudes" would not help them with stock raising unless they got training from "efficient corps of farmers and extension agents."[37]

John Krall, the tribe's extension agent, shared Rodnick's belief in proper training and education but not his pessimism about the Blackfeet's chances for prosperity. Although the tribe owned the physical necessities for stock raising, Krall found after assuming his position as agent in June 1936 that most Blackfeet stockowners had not yet learned the "real underlying fundamental principles" of successful livestock cultivation. Like other government officials, Krall appeared to be impatient with older full-bloods and intent on reforming the attitude of a new generation of Indians, both full-blood and mixed-blood. His first step was to instill in "the minds of the small children a sense of individual responsibility," which, he claimed, most Blackfeet lacked. Krall blamed both Indians and the government, which had "made them a dependent people by nursing them when they cry, with the Politician working in the back ground and figuring out the balanced ration to keep up the milk flow."[38] Krall's plan for weaning the Blackfeet from the government's teat began with the 4-H program, which he emphasized more than any other economic program. He organized a program of instruction to educate young Blackfeet in "Farm mechanics, Animal diseases, Breeds and Breeding, Livestock Management," and crop production that was "adapted to this climate."[39] Krall both ended the FYIP as Frank Campbell had envisioned it and remodeled it for a new generation of Blackfeet whom he believed needed to combine livestock production with subsistence agriculture to prosper. Krall also tried to change the Blackfeet's attitude toward government relief, indicating that certain families would no longer get free seeds or other government aid if they did not heed extension workers' instructions. Krall delineated three groups that required close supervision: the "shiftless," the "next most shiftless," and the "semi-failures," which represented about 30 percent of the reservation's rural population. Krall concluded that less than half of the Blackfeet farm families had made an earnest effort to succeed in dry or irrigated farming and thus decided that the government should distribute free seeds only to "a few widows and to fullbloods who really try to grow gardens."[40] He reported that his staff's advice was also "resented and branded as coming from a swivel chair artist who knew nothing about stock raising." Such people were told to follow instructions or risk losing their cattle to "those who would cooperate."[41] If the Blackfeet continued to lack confidence in the extension program, he argued, then future progress would be stunted. Krall attempted to fight through the Blackfeet's cultural resistance to farming and white advisers with a program of tough love, coercing when necessary and encouraging when possible.

Despite the extension staff's difficulties establishing sustainable farm and stock-raising programs, some of which stemmed from such coercive administration, its successes helped to reduce the number of families completely dependent on government relief from 762 in 1934 to 120 in 1937.[42] In many ways, the tribe's extension agent had become as important to the tribe as the superintendent. Krall cooperated with other BIA divisions and New Deal agencies to help the Blackfeet secure loans, relief supplies, and surplus equipment for their abandoned irrigation projects. Krall's tenure as the state director of rehabilitation and resettlement in Montana helped him to facilitate the distribution of federal loans on the reservation and to secure the Blackfeet's fair share of federal relief; he used his knowledge of lending regulations to expedite rehabilitation loans from the Resettlement Administration and his familiarity with programs like the Distribution of Surplus Commodities to get as many relief supplies as possible. Like other well-meaning federal programs, Krall's failed to realize all of its goals. The cornerstone 4-H program showed "practically no activity" because of staff shortages, Krall wrote in his 1937 annual report, hardly an auspicious start to engendering a reorientation of agricultural and social values. His enthusiasm for the 4-H program waned, apparently, when he realized how difficult it was to produce functional gardens in Blackfeet country.

Krall's enthusiasm for the livestock industry remained high, however, and he tried to work within prevailing cultural domains by encouraging full-bloods to raise sheep rather than cattle. He discovered that full-bloods, as well as some mixed-bloods, responded better to the quicker returns in sheep raising; the biannual payments reduced the incentive or the need for these ranchers to sell all or part of their foundation herd. Resettlement Administration loans and a good market for lambs and wool in 1936 helped to induce several cattle owners to turn to sheep. Blackfeet sheep herds swelled to nearly 10,000 head in 1937, sparking the creation of a Lamb and Wool Producers Association that helped sheep owners to use leases and workers' time more efficiently. As a result, sheep owners earned $11,220 for the 51,000 pounds of wool produced, an increase of nearly 400 percent from the year before, and roughly $10,000 from the sale of 2,000 sheep, an increase of 250 percent from the previous year.[43] White sheep owners grazed more than 130,000 head on Blackfeet lands, evidence that Indian owners could succeed if they organized along similar lines.

Krall reported that the reorganization of the tribe's livestock program was the highlight of extension activities in 1937.[44] This reorganization was due largely to the actions of the Blackfeet Tribal Business Council. Alarmed by the large number of cattle sales, the BTBC established two ordinances in October to protect foundation herds. The first ordinance required white cattle traders to secure a permit before buying Blackfeet cattle, and those Blackfeet wishing to sell ID (Interior Department issued) cattle had to obtain a permit before selling them. The second ordinance required Blackfeet who butchered cattle to retain evidence of ownership in an effort to reduce cattle rustling.[45] The BTBC passed these ordinances on the recommendation of the newly created Livestock Board, which had discovered during its survey of the reservation's livestock that too many stockowners had jeopardized their foundation herds by selling cattle indiscriminately. The board sought to promote the industry and ensure that those Blackfeet fortunate enough to get government cattle kept their herds healthy and their repayments on schedule. It had the authority to repossess ID cattle from those Blackfeet who operated in "poor faith" or sold their cattle without permission from the board and the agency office, and to give the confiscated stock to those Blackfeet "making an honest effort to develop an economic herd."[46] The actions of the Livestock Board and the BTBC helped to preserve foundation herds, regulate livestock commerce, and enhance efforts to reduce trespassing and cattle rustling. They also helped to persuade OIA officials to delay the tribe's repayment of ID cattle until the fall of 1942 in order to give Blackfeet stockowners a better chance to create "economic herds" and thus ensure the growth of what virtually every government and tribal official believed was the best means of creating a "self-sustaining economy."[47]

The BTBC remained supportive of Collier's agenda, reacting harshly to congressional efforts to repeal the IRA. The council expressed surprise and disappointment upon hearing about the repeal campaign, asserting that "it would be disasterous [*sic*] for us if the Reorganization Act were to be repealed at this time."[48] After voting ten to two in April 1937 to protest repeal, the council informed Collier, Senator Wheeler, and Senator James Murray that the tribe was making progress under the IRA and wanted an opportunity to "give it a fair trial."[49]

The BTBC had become, Superintendent Graves reported, "the real voice of the people and is very much interested in helping to solve the problems of the Reservation. This is a sincere desire on their part to be of value to their people."[50] Besides championing the livestock industry and natural resource development, the BTBC had striven since the passage of the Nation's corporate charter to organize tribal affairs along the lines of modern municipal management. The council reorganized its fiscal affairs by designing a budget for the expenses of the corporation and electing a treasurer, which the corporate charter required; it also exercised its constitutional rights to establish a Blackfeet Indian court and jury to adjudicate tribal matters and levy fines, issue ordinances governing hunting and fishing within the reservation's boundaries, and promote the creation and sale of tribal arts and crafts.[51] The council also added a deputy game warden and range rider to the tribal government and gave fish and game commissions to thirteen salaried employees, reflecting the council's eagerness to enforce the physical boundaries of its new sovereignty.[52]

In addition, the council redefined itself by forming various committees to contend with its new responsibilities. The council had become increasingly committed to establishing itself as a political body with the influence and responsibility equal to that of the agency superintendent. The council established a grievance committee in early 1937 to provide a forum for Blackfeet with complaints about employment discrimination, leasing irregularities, and government negligence; after investigating a complaint the committee either adjudicated it or referred the person to the superintendent or the Indian court. The council formed other committees to explore the feasibility of economic programs. One such committee, formed in late 1937, eventually secured the OIA's approval to use ten thousand dollars in tribal funds to start a sawmill operation, which provided lumber at cost for home building and other construction projects.

The most important new committee was the Recommendation Committee on Loans (later designated the credit committee), which decided which Blackfeet applicants got what part of the tribe's allotment of the Revolving Credit Fund (RCF).[53] Joe Brown produced the tribe's first loan application in September 1936 with the help of credit agent H. D. McCullough and field agent Donald Hagerty. The Blackfeet Corporation requested a loan of two hundred thousand dollars to fund the tribe's economic rehabilitation. The BTBC submitted financial statements, résumés of tribal leaders, plans for managing credit disbursement and collection, and details of an "economic development program" to justify the loan. The economic program, the first articulation of a Blackfeet political economy, consisted mainly of expanding the tribe's livestock industry by providing loans to individuals at 3 percent interest, but it also emphasized improving reservation ranges, helping tribal members to "finance sound business or commercial enterprises," and assisting cooperative associations and tribal enterprises. In addition, the tribe asked for nearly seventy thousand dollars to aid the resettlement of twenty families to eastern irrigation districts and proposed the eventual use of two hundred thousand dollars to resettle an additional eighty families. The program would succeed, the authors wrote, when the tribe's rangeland was "entirely used by Indian stock," agricultural lands were "utilized by Indian farmers," and independently financed business enterprises were created by Indians for Indians.[54] The agenda was ambitious, but it was instinct with the Blackfeet's increasing confidence in their ability to fashion economic development using tribal resources and labor in combination with an infusion of government credit.

McCullough's accompanying letter to the OIA reflected this confidence, indicating that "the aims and objectives of the Economic Development Program appear sound, the security all that the Charter authorizes, and the material resources awaiting development and use by the Indians ample." The BTBC, he wrote, seemed to understand its responsibility and appeared eager to be "helpful and conservative" in managing its credit program; the council had sanctioned the use of progressive loans, which provided annual installments to a borrower if he or she demonstrated satisfactory progress, and had encouraged the use of extension and credit division staff to ensure fiscal and agricultural success. But McCullough recommended that the OIA provide only one hundred thousand dollars, largely because he did not believe that the administrative apparatus was sufficiently mature to distribute two hundred thousand dollars in a timely and efficient manner.[55] Despite the council's promise that the corporation would use all diligence in instituting efficient lending practices, the ultimate success of the program, he wrote, was "dependent to a considerable extent upon the initiative, resourcefulness and managerial capacity of the borrowers."[56] The loan committee would therefore distribute money to those applicants who demonstrated "white monetary attitudes," as David Rodnick had put it, a criterion that would restrict lending. McCullough also did not support the council's plan to populate the proposed Two Medicine Irrigation Project, arguing that structural rehabilitation should precede "colonization." The OIA naturally adopted McCullough's recommendation and approved a loan of one hundred thousand dollars on December 8, 1936. The Nation accepted the amount on February 18, 1937, and began the distribution process the following April.[57]

The five-person credit committee, elected in April 1937, had an enormous responsibility. The tribe's enthusiasm for reorganization had come largely from its desire for economic independence. Most Blackfeet lacked the credit to either expand or begin a small livestock or farming operation. The committee therefore received a great number of applications for RCF loans—most of which were for livestock purchases—and thus it had to be judicious and fair in its decision to approve or reject Blackfeet dreams of advancement; extension agents had final authority to submit loans to the Interior Department for approval, but they generally accepted the committee's recommendations. McCullough's review of the credit committee's performance found that it accepted the first loans with "little consideration for the soundness of the plans or the ability of the applicants to repay," though it was now "considering each loan application carefully and doing quite efficient work." He noted that the Blackfeet Nation was the only tribe in his jurisdiction to use a paid tribal officer—treasurer Asa Armstrong—to keep credit records, which were "particularly well kept."[58] Actually, the council's early decisions on loan applications do not appear to be as frivolous as McCullough indicated.

The committee accepted only five of the first ten applications, three of which were for the purchase of farm seed. The committee rejected one application because the "property [collateral] listed is not on Reservation and security is not sufficient" and approved another contingent upon a satisfactory inspection of the property.[59] The committee, like many white municipal organizations and private lending operations across the country, would make mistakes; the unpredictable weather patterns of northwestern Montana almost guaranteed an unstable credit program. It could hardly do worse than many Montana county governments, which in 1933 were $2 million in debt.[60]

The RCF program had a great impact on the tribe in several ways. Krall noted that when RCF funds became available, "the agency was flooded with applications for loans from families who were thoroughly disgusted and discouraged with the uncertainty of living conditions. These people were, and still are, anxious to get away from these emergency relief programs and establish themselves on their land where they hope, with the aid of loans, to be able to feed and clothe their families as it should be done."[61] He concluded that the RCF had given Blackfeet farmers and ranchers a new lease on life and "may be the deciding factor in putting these people on a self-supporting basis."[62] The RCF program also made the IRA seem more real to the Blackfeet. It had been two and a half years since the tribe had adopted the IRA, and between that time and April 1937, when the BTBC first considered applications, the Blackfeet had seen little material benefit. The IRA did not hasten the expansion of oil development. It did not improve the Blackfeet's grazing system. The federal government provided the relief cattle. And though the IRA empowered the tribe to receive the Big Claim fund in per capita form, it did not generate the award. The benefits of the IRA had been, therefore, chiefly political or, more accurately, psychological: the constitution and charter provided the tribe with a better sense of self, that of a nation with new powers of sovereignty, of a nation of laws. But it was the opportunity to borrow money at low interest rates (typically 3 percent) for a five-year period that turned the IRA into something compelling and tangible. The RCF program thus helped to preserve the tribe's commitment to its reorganization program at a time when it was most vulnerable.

By most accounts—including those of Graves, McCullough, and Krall—the BTBC had done a respectable job of building a foundation from which a modern Blackfeet Nation could develop some degree of economic self-sufficiency. The official OIA committee investigating the progress of reorganization on Northern Plains reservations—led by field representative C. E. Faris, a former livestock supervisor, and H. Scudder Mekeel, the head of the OIA's Applied Anthropology Unit—concluded that "everything was going along as well as could be expected at Blackfeet, with reservation resources so limited." Faris and Mekeel also described a reservation still suffering from hunger and discontent, reporting the "constant and growing problem of keeping the Indians fed and alive" and the consequent congregation of Blackfeet in and around Browning, where rations were easier to get. Some full-bloods still felt "out of the picture in the reorganization program," despite agency and council efforts to include them.[63] Supplemental farm loans averaging about one thousand dollars had been granted to several dozen Blackfeet in late October; many of them, including the largest loan, went to full-bloods.[64] In November, the council used RCF and tribal monies to assist the expansion of the tribe's arts and crafts cooperative, an organization of mostly full-blood women.[65] And in early December, in order to address White Calf's persistent complaint that it neglected full-bloods, the council unanimously approved his petition to give Starr School residents preference in non-WPA employment. There is no evidence that the council or the OIA systematically isolated full-bloods from the benefits of the reorganization program. Full-bloods Joe Ironpipe and Richard Sanderville served on the credit committee and worked to ensure that BIA credit agents visited each reservation community to discuss the Blackfeet's various borrowing options. The first step for both full-bloods and mixed-bloods was to determine what options existed in the lending program and then take the necessary measures to become eligible to exercise them.

Although most white observers of tribal reorganization agreed in late 1937 that "the tribe would not care to operate without the [IRA]," as Krall put it, it had become clear that a growing number of Blackfeet did not agree with the BTBC's political management of the IRA's resources and had become impatient with the pace and the nature of economic reform; they saw the council's emphasis on livestock production and irrigation as discriminatory and called on the BTBC to distribute oil revenues and treasury monies in the form of per capita payments. In addition, the new livestock regulations probably angered some Blackfeet who may have seen the BTBC's nascent supervision of reservation affairs simply as a substitution of the OIA's.

The dominant issue causing friction among Blackfeet in late 1937 was the council's decision to use tribal funds to expand the "rehabilitation" of the tribe's irrigation program rather than distribute the money in a per capita payout. Graves, Krall, and other BIA officials, including John Collier, encouraged and supported the council's decision.[66] The issue was, as usual, one of long-term economic planning versus short-term individual needs, a dilemma that affected many Indian tribes facing persistent poverty. Tribal leaders like Joe Brown and OIA officials like John Krall had become increasingly concerned that as the livestock industry expanded, the tribe needed to use its existing irrigation projects to guarantee the production of sufficient quantities of winter feed for those cattle. The proposed rehabilitation program was designed to provide farming opportunities in the neglected irrigation districts while preserving the Nation's water rights. Despite the Department of the Interior's ruling that the tribe had a prior right to 284,300 acre-feet of water and the Bureau of Reclamation's opinion that the Blackfeet needed all those acre-feet to achieve any measurable agricultural production, white ranchers and farmers operating south of the reservation had been clamoring for Blackfeet water for decades, arguing that the tribe did not need the water that flowed through the reservation because the irrigation projects were dormant.[67] Without winter feed, the Blackfeet would never establish a viable livestock industry. Without water rights, the tribe would never grow that winter feed.

On November 5, the BTBC debated allocating RCF and tribal funds to rehabilitate one of four neglected irrigation projects. Several senior OIA officials attended the meeting after touring the Two Medicine Irrigation Project (TMIP) and reservation communities. Assistant Commissioner John Herrick offered the OIA's view, telling the council members, "You men have it in your hands to make or break the Blackfeet Tribe. The choice of the people is before you today as to whether or not the whole Tribe is going to have a chance to rehabilitate itself and work back to some sort of decent standard of living, cleaning up these slums that we see around here, or whether you are going to have to give up entirely and establish a warehouse and pass out rations." He presented rather stark options: either the Blackfeet pursued the expansion of the livestock industry or they would become perpetual wards of the emerging federal welfare state. "The question," Herrick said, "comes down to winter feed."[68]

Tribal leaders like Joe Brown and Richard Sanderville had lived through the first period of irrigation construction, a time when the government had little compunction about draining valuable tribal funds in its futile and misguided effort to make yeoman farmers out of "idle" Indians. In the 1910s the OIA rammed irrigation down the Blackfeet's throats at no risk to the government. In the late 1930s the reorganized Indian Office sought a partnership with the Blackfeet by offering to contribute federal funds from its Land Acquisition Program to buy white-owned plots, Civilian Conservation Corps–Indian Division (CCC-ID) funds to restore the structural integrity of decayed canals and ditches, and Indian Relocation and Rehabilitation money to improve the homes on the proposed project, as well as to offer the services of farm managers to help transform the region into the Blackfeet's breadbasket. The council in turn had to pledge its support by using thirty thousand dollars in RCF funds and roughly twenty-seven thousand dollars in matching tribal monies, seventy-five hundred dollars of which would be earmarked for the arts and crafts cooperative. In return, the tribe would get a chance to maintain its water rights, reclaim Blackfeet lands from white ownership at federal expense, create the foundation for agricultural production of winter feed for the only real tribal industry, and relocate dozens of families from the crowded, slum conditions of Browning to the promise of a new beginning farther east. It was an attractive option and an important decision for the tribe. Blackfeet leaders, though embittered by the government's past reclamation efforts, understood that irrigation was a fact of life in the American West and that the livestock industry needed a reliable supply of hay to survive Blackfeet winters. They also had families willing to move to the irrigation districts and families willing to improve their existing allotments if given farm loans. Joe Brown noted to the OIA contingent that "people come in all the time to find out more about [the Rehabilitation Program]. I meet people down town every day who ask me about it and who seem very much interested in it."[69]

The BTBC voted unanimously to both accept the government's offer of financial assistance and to use tribal funds to rehabilitate the TMIP, choosing it over three other dormant projects largely because of its proximity to railway transportation. Richard Sanderville, the elder statesman representing the Heart Butte community, had earlier proposed the repair of the Birch Creek project for use by full-bloods. Although disappointed with the council's choice, he graciously acknowledged that "the important thing is to save our water rights." John Herrick answered him by saying, "Not only to save the water, but to save the tribe." The council voted, on Graves's recommendation, to reserve 284,300 acre-feet of water for use by the Blackfeet Nation to protect its water rights.[70]

The OIA approved the council's recommendations in late December and added another $25,000 to the pot, raising the government's stake to roughly $120,000. It also offered to codify the council's request to reserve the 284,300 acre-feet of water and to defend the Nation's claim in court if necessary. The Department of the Interior issued a press release on December 27 to announce the accord. Calling the Blackfeet Nation "one of the most important in the Great Plains area," the announcement applauded both the Blackfeet's initiative in devising the program and the role of IRA money in funding it, presenting the tribe as an example of the IRA's success; the OIA and its main policy needed all the good press it could get in 1937. The object of the Blackfeet program, the release stated, was to rid Browning of its slum: "As in the case of urban slums, Indian reservations have their shacktowns, and the Browning shacktown is typical in that it is inhabited by Indians who have been driven into destitution by years of drought and depression."[71] The relocation of families to Two Medicine would serve both as urban renewal of the Nation's capital and economic rehabilitation of its hinterland.

The BTBC made the right decision in November 1937, taking advantage of the government's offer to *give* money outright and lend RCF monies at 1 percent interest to provide the tribe with a platform for economic development. It also understood the importance of protecting from thirsty white communities the Nation's water supply, a natural resource arguably more valuable than oil. The council thus started the Blackfeet on the road from reorganization to rehabilitation in a reasonably efficient and judicious manner. The decision to invest in the rehabilitation program, however, had a significant impact at the polls the following January. Although many Blackfeet wanted to participate in the program, there were many more who thought it either discriminated against their communities or diverted per capita income from them during the brutal winter months. The council's focus on irrigation and livestock angered Blackfeet who either did not want to relocate to a distant corner of the reservation and raise hay or had neither the inclination nor the resources to raise livestock. The BTBC's December 27 resolution asking the Indian Office to approve a per capita distribution was too little, too late.

On January 11, 1938, ten of the thirteen BTBC incumbents lost their seats, most of them by large margins; voting participation was very high despite icy travel conditions. The *Glacier County Chief* described the election by opining, "In analyzing the returns, it is plain to be seen that the people were wanting and did demand new blood in the council. There was evident at all times, a strong undercurrent of unrest and dissatisfaction with present conditions, brought on by wide spread destitution, lack of work, etc. The people wanted a change. This feeling of unrest and discontent expressed itself at the polls in striking terms."[72]

The change in representation in the Browning district was most striking. All four of the Browning council members lost the election. Joe Brown, the respected council chairman, lost by nearly a three-to-one margin to newcomer Stuart Hazlett, as did longtime council secretary Leo Kennerly. Mixed-blood business leaders Hazlett, Levi Burd, John Wren, and Mae Aubrey Coburn, the first Blackfeet woman elected to the council, took their places. Although the tribe elected two full-bloods and Richard Sanderville, creating a slightly better balance between mixed-bloods and full-bloods, the new council also contained five mixed-bloods of one-quarter blood or less. It would be unrealistic to expect any political body to reverse a community's economic fortunes in less than two years, but despite doing a reasonably good job under difficult circumstances the council was rudely disbanded by voters who had failed to see the benefits of reorganization. The Blackfeet did not reject the IRA so much as the people they believed had failed to implement it properly. Joe Brown and the council had aggressively asserted the Nation's sovereignty by passing regulations governing the use of natural resources and establishing its own law-and-order machinery. Although the credit committee had given RCF loans to several council members, it apparently did not practice an egregious form of political favoritism, denying on one occasion a large loan of tribal funds to businessman John Galbraith.[73] In July 1937 it had approved a resolution presented by the Blackfeet Indian Welfare Association (BIWA), which asked the federal government to release Blackfeet treasury funds in per capita payments.[74] The council had made similar requests in the past, but such payments required an act of Congress, which generally frowned on them. The returns suggest, therefore, some other factor at work.

It could be argued that that factor was the return of the one-eighth native, Stuart Hazlett, who brought with him modern political strategy. Born off the reservation in Choteau, Montana, Hazlett had been fired as agency lease clerk by the Indian Service in 1919, accused of selling Blackfeet fee patents to local whites at low prices under dubious circumstances. Since his termination, he had lived in Great Falls, Montana, and in Seattle. He wrote the OIA periodically to inquire about reservation opportunities, as he did in 1925 by asking about oil leasing. In June 1937, at the age of fifty-six, he moved back to the reservation to participate in the tribe's reorganization program.[75] Less than one year later Hazlett ran for a council seat and garnered the highest number of votes in Blackfeet political history; with his 528 votes in the Browning district, he received nearly 200 more than Mae Coburn and 330 more than Joe Brown, who had been council chairman since 1927. It was a stunning victory for someone who had demonstrated little regard for his fellow Blackfeet for most of his adult life. A business council led by Joe Brown was no longer "the real voice of the people," as Superintendent Graves had claimed in November. Hazlett assumed that role after waging an aggressive campaign to gain political power.

Hazlett first appeared on the political stage in July 1937 when he presented to the council the BIWA's aforementioned resolution, which insisted that the government distribute tribal oil revenues and the balance of the Big Claim award that Congress had allotted for development purposes.[76] The BIWA, created as a community alternative to the BTBC in late 1932, pressed for Indian employment on WPA and CCC projects, solicited relief supplies, and asserted the tribe's right to monies held in the U.S. Treasury, all worthwhile and popular activities. BIWA founders included mixed-blood businessmen John and William Billedeaux, and Mae Coburn, who was elected to the BTBC along with Hazlett in the Browning district, where most of the BIWA's members lived. The BTBC sanctioned its existence in January 1933 despite concerns that the 175-member group intended to "overpower" the council.[77] The organization, though recognized by agency personnel and the BTBC, had no authority to represent the tribe's economic and political interests. Hazlett and Coburn parlayed their BIWA activities into election to the BTBC, the only political force managing the new Blackfeet economy.

Although most of the candidates continued a trend among Blackfeet politicians by attending or sponsoring holiday parties, Hazlett was the most aggressive and creative of the candidates. He actively sought the full-blood vote by accompanying a full-blood delegation to Senator Wheeler's vacation home in September to protest labor discrimination and by offering financial support for the Starr School Christmas party in December.[78] Well before December, when most candidates began to lobby voters, Hazlett had initiated a quiet campaign to impugn the reputation of the BTBC and associate it with government inaction and incompetence, using the *Glacier County Chief* as the medium for his message. Each month between August 1937 and January 1938 Hazlett contributed several "articles" or "comments" that addressed labor discrimination, irrigation, and the general state of Blackfeet affairs. The *Chief* had never printed guest editorials before Hazlett's began to appear in August 1937 and rarely printed anything with a byline, but it saw fit to endorse Hazlett and his views by prominently displaying his opinions.

After first attacking John Collier and his "cohorts and courtesans" for discriminating against elderly Indians, Hazlett took aim at the agency staff for its administration of tribal resources. The Blackfeet, he wrote, had reached "such a low estate that as mendicants and beggars they so belittle themselves as to docilely accept any or all things handed them by a system that is the very fountain head of hypocracy [*sic*], deceit and evasiveness. The putridness, the rottenness of this system, the czaristic or autocratic attitude of some of our officials combined with the evasiveness must and shall be done away with for all times. . . . As to the System, I want to say in closing, that this is not the last you shall see or hear of all this—there is plenty more of it coming and in doses you shall not like."[79] Hazlett's critical tone is certainly ironic given his dismissal for selling the fee patents of noncompetent Blackfeet nearly twenty years earlier. Although Hazlett's subsequent pieces were less vitriolic, he continued to attack the OIA, the Blackfeet agency, and the BTBC, which had failed to protect the tribe from "heartless and mercenary interests." Hazlett's first articles focused on the "absolutely destitute condition" of Blackfeet fullbloods; his tour of full-blood communities made him the unofficial leader of what he called the tribal "underdog." It was to this destitute constituency that he directed his attacks on the council's plan to rehabilitate the TMIP, which became his cause célèbre. Although he called the TMIP "a laudable purpose and under ordinary circumstances well worthy of commendation," Hazlett argued that it was folly to divert money from Blackfeet citizens during the winter and improper to use tribal monies to benefit "a selected few." The public, he maintained, favored the distribution of oil money and the balance of the Big Claim award.[80] Hazlett's subsequent articles on the water question took a different tack, however. He condemned the OIA for letting the irrigation projects deteriorate and claimed that the reconstruction of the Blackfeet's irrigation capacity would not only protect the Blackfeet's water rights from white aggrandizement but would be a "benefit . . . bestowed upon the entire community—more hay; more grass; more crops and possibly more workless Indians having jobs or homes."[81] Hazlett tried to appeal both to poor full-bloods and mixed-bloods and to those Blackfeet interested in long-term economic development. He could champion the popular per capita payments while endorsing the rehabilitation of the Blackfeet's irrigation system, criticizing both the BTBC and John Collier in the process.[82]

In December, Hazlett's rhetoric became heated again. He attacked the business council, which consisted of "yes-men" who were "slowly awakening from their Rip Van Winklean sleep." Castigating the council members' lack of "ability, character, resourcefulness and tact," Hazlett told voters "to say who shall represent you, a collection of reactionaries as we now have or . . . a new body consisting of aggressive, clear-thinking individuals whose sole aim shall be the protection of tribal rights."[83] His final calumny—entitled "New Blood Wanted"—took on an even more critical tone: "It goes without saying that the present council has not during its existence originated a single idea looking to improving conditions on the reservation! A close check of their record will show clearly that every act or deed on their part has been at the instigation of others— foreign or alien thought has been governing their every action. . . . Your conscience will tell you that new blood, new thoughts, new ideas are needed or else we are doomed to another spell of official dictation and passive indifference."[84] It is presumed that Hazlett's rhetoric found its way into his campaign rallies, which may have been even less restrained than it was in print. Hazlett shrewdly avoided making ad hominem attacks; by attacking the council as a whole he avoided angering voters who still felt some loyalty to their council representative. But never before had another Blackfeet attacked in public the Nation's elected officials. It is a testament to the novelty of Hazlett's campaign that neither Joe Brown nor any other council member chose to respond to Hazlett's spurious and captious attacks.

Like many politicians, Hazlett found it easier to attack incumbents than to delineate a viable new program; he offered not one new thought or new idea during his war of words against the OIA and the BTBC. Some of Hazlett's causes were just, and his arguments for them persuasive, but he never described how he would improve reservation conditions other than to assume office, deliver per capita payments, and support the irrigation projects that the Brown regime had earnestly developed for two years. Rather, he exploited the tension that existed between supporters of rehabilitation and relief. Joe Brown in particular stressed the importance of pursuing long-term solutions rather than simply providing short-term relief payments. Where Brown failed in his administration of the Blackfeet economy, and where Hazlett succeeded in his political campaign, was in striking a balance between the two options. In a letter to the public published by the *Glacier County Chief* shortly after the election, Hazlett asked tribal factions to set aside personal differences and opinions and concentrate on improving living standards. He told Superintendent Graves and the OIA, "we want to work in harmony with you. Forget for the time being the picture that has been painted by *us* [emphasis added] and give us an opportunity to demonstrate our worth." And from the tribe as a whole, Hazlett asked for patience: "It is entirely out of the question to expect us to make changes over night. Certain programs are in the process of formulation, programs that will prove of benefit to each and every resident of the reservation but time is required to put these plans thru. . . . I, for one, refuse to be rushed."[85] After brazenly sowing the seeds of political acrimony, Hazlett's propitiation secured the cooperation he needed to further his agenda, and he buffered himself against criticism by acknowledging the difficult problems his council faced.

The new business council, like its predecessor, proceeded to steer the tribe toward the eastern part of the reservation where the TMIP lay waiting for repairs and Blackfeet settlers. After assuming additional power by securing the chairmanship on February 3, Hazlett led a delegation of three mixed-blood and two full-blood council members to Washington in early March to secure funds for the new regime's economic program. The centerpiece of that program was the TMIP. With funds for physical rehabilitation in place, the delegates focused on getting money to fund the emigration of Blackfeet to TMIP lands. One of Hazlett's priorities was the emancipation of the tribe's treasury funds, which in March 1938 amounted to $159,465.86.[86] The agency's use of Blackfeet money for white-oriented programs had not only gravely reduced tribal funds but also fueled the tribe's desire for greater control of its finances. The IRA had appealed to Blackfeet largely because it gave them better access to government credit and, theoretically, better access to their own money. The delegation proposed using $125,000 of those treasury funds for a program of "industrial assistance" that involved adding $50,000 of tribal funds and $50,000 of government funds to the tribe's existing revolving credit account, forming a land management enterprise to improve TMIP farm units and creating a "supplemental credit enterprise" (known as the Production Credit Association) to provide loans beyond the purview of the Department of the Interior. In addition, the council proposed allotting $25,000 for a fund that would "provide improvements for selected clients." The delegation's plan involved, therefore, the withdrawal of nearly all funds from the Nation's treasury account.[87]

Hazlett thus continued his predecessors' main project but championed the expansion of tribal investment and credit sources to facilitate its development. Hazlett, in contrast to his campaign attacks, praised OIA staff members in an effusive letter of thanks to Assistant Commissioner William Zimmerman. The Blackfeet's experiment in self-government could succeed only with the OIA's help, he wrote, and with it the Blackfeet would "make history among Indians." He asked only that the OIA "give us a chance to prove our worth."[88] OIA officials generally supported the delegation's rather broad economic program. R. S. Bristol, acting director of extension and industry, called the delegation's plan "constructive." John Collier thought that the delegation worked diligently to devise a workable plan to help Blackfeet families become permanently self-supporting, and in early April he approved the inclusion of the $125,000 request in the Department of the Interior appropriation bill. In June, Congress granted the tribe the funds in reimbursable form. The tribe could thus borrow its own money, but it could not *have* it.[89]

While the tribe waited for the money it needed to improve its economic future, the BTBC continued its reorganization of political affairs. OIA officials had informed Hazlett that if he acted on his promise to "clean house," then he would be allowed to do so only by firing tribal and not BIA employees.[90] In the "spirit of cleaning up," the council reorganized the credit committee and livestock board by discharging Brown-council appointees serving five-year terms, formed a labor board, hired councilman Sam Bird to monitor tribal credit operations, and chartered the Blackfeet Corporate Building Enterprise to provide construction loans for TMIP "clients."[91] The council also formed a new oil and gas committee—comprising Hazlett, Levi Burd, and Wright Hagerty—to monitor leasing and production as well as a committee to manage the tribal sawmill. Hagerty, who had served on the previous council, recommended that "the entire Tribal set-up be dispensed with," but no one else supported this radical idea.[92]

The death of the tribal judge of the Blackfeet Indian court in June sparked another debate about the tribal "set-up." The salaries of the treasurer, game warden, tribal court judge, stenographer, and two deputy game wardens represented 67 percent of the 1938 tribal budget. Council member Brian Connolly (one-quarter Blackfeet) recommended, as Hagerty had, that the council "save . . . tribal funds by discontinuing, not only the position of Tribal Judge, but also all other positions paid for from tribal funds." The council, however, voted by six to four to retain the judgeship and, by default, the other tribal positions. Connolly's motion may have reflected a growing suspicion on the part of some council members that Hazlett's leadership did not bode well for tribal finances. Shortly after the council elected Levi Burd to the judgeship at an annual salary of eighteen hundred dollars, Connolly motioned that "all bills and obligations incurred by the tribal corporation be presented to the Council for approval before being paid."[93] Hagerty and Connolly, both wealthy stockowners of low Blackfeet blood quantum, were either intent on securing guarantees that council members and tribal employees be held accountable for their actions or interested in proscribing the tribe's regulation of the reservation economy from which they profited handsomely in order to establish their brand of laissez-faire agricultural capitalism. Although the council resisted calls to dismantle the tribal set-up amid debate on the Blackfeet Corporation's organizational structure, the council's reforms ran contrary to Hazlett's call for intratribal harmony and represented a portent of political turnover and instability.

Hazlett's new economic program earned him the OIA's commendation, but his aggressive pursuit of tribal monies to fund that program did not endear him to OIA officials monitoring Blackfeet reorganization. In an April 1938 letter to Superintendent Graves, John Herrick recommended that the BTBC use a recent allotment of oil revenues to expand its credit operations or fund tribal enterprises and "avoid in every way possible needless expenditure of Tribal moneys in unproductive ways [and] keep their administration costs in line with their legitimate needs."[94] Hazlett responded by claiming that Herrick lacked confidence in the council. Herrick, in turn, tried to mollify him by writing, "Naturally we have a friendly anxiety to see that things go well. The Blackfeet Council . . . is starting out on a new path, and this Office would be lax in the performance of its duties if it did not proffer counsel and advice. You will agree with me, I think, that Indian tribes have not always used their tribal assets to the best advantage in the past, and the letter was merely meant to convey—not a question as to the right of the Council to use the money as its judgment dictated—but merely a suggestion as to what a wise use would be."[95]

Herrick's friendly anxiety cut both ways. On one hand, it reinforced an old notion that the BIA did not think Indians could handle their own affairs, particularly in the area of fiscal management. For the Blackfeet, who had seen the BIA itself fail to use "their tribal assets to the best advantage in the past," Herrick's argument was hypocritical and thus absurd. On the other hand, Herrick's statements reinforced the idea of a Blackfeet and BIA partnership. Hazlett's vicious electioneering against the OIA in late 1937 probably offended BIA employees who had strenuously tried to improve the tribe's legal and economic condition. Hazlett's aggressive stance once in office likely did not enhance his reputation with key policy makers, who had come to respect the quiet insistence of Joe Brown's diplomacy; Herrick would not have written a similar letter if Brown had remained in office. And given Hazlett's rapid rise to power, OIA officials were generally wary of his motives.

The sparring between Herrick and Hazlett grew out of a dispute over the council's request to supplement its 1938 budget. Herrick had complained that the BTBC's budget relied upon "capital assets"—Class A monies held in the U.S. Treasury—rather than anticipated revenue. Hazlett replied by arguing that Blackfeet self-government was in an "experimental" stage. Although he admitted that "[m]istakes and errors of judgment have unintentionally been made," Hazlett blamed the budget shortfall and consequent supplemental request on the previous council's unfamiliarity with financial administration and justified the unforeseen expense of holding special meetings of the BTBC and its credit committee on the need to organize the TMIP in a timely fashion. Hazlett had a legitimate argument that tribal officials were learning how to budget expenses and estimate revenues from unpredictable sources like fishing and hunting permits, oil production, and court fees.[96] Both Graves and Acting Commissioner E. J. Armstrong supported Hazlett's defense; Armstrong approved the revised budget because Blackfeet self-government was indeed new and revenue projections devised by Joe Brown's council had fallen short through no fault of the new council.[97] The OIA's problem with the council's finances was part procedural and part prophylactic. The tribe's charter stipulated that the use of its Class A funds required the approval of the secretary of the interior. The budget adopted in 1937 had been based entirely on anticipated revenue and not on the use of capital assets like treasury funds. The OIA also did not want the tribe to use its Class A funds to pay tribal salaries and per diem expenses, as Hazlett intended.

The issue of "special council meetings," the only item on which the council overspent, also troubled department investigators and Blackfeet groups opposed to the tribal bureaucracy. Blackfeet full-bloods led by James White Calf had become alarmed by the council's expenditures and had organized a petition drive to persuade the secretary of the interior to approve a referendum amending the Blackfeet constitution and charter to limit the expenditure of tribal funds, prevent the appointment of unnecessary tribal employees, and improve full-blood council representation. A separate petition asked for a per capita payment. The department's failure to foster these changes, the petition warned, would "cause the general breakdown" of the IRA on the Blackfeet Reservation.[98]

Hazlett and other council members from the Browning district had won the support of Starr School voters in the January 1938 election by promising to produce per capita distributions and reform the electoral system to facilitate full-blood representation. By early May, that constituency had turned against the council. Hazlett defended himself by telling Herrick that the complaints came from "disgruntled politicians and pool room habitués," a group of "smart" mixed-bloods and young full-bloods "too lazy to earn an honest dollar," who tried to persuade the "poor old full blood Indian" to adopt their view of the council. Hazlett asked that the OIA consider the source of the complaints and give council members and him, in particular, a chance to succeed. Herrick agreed, politely responding that the OIA planned to address the complaints and "satisfactorily dispose of the things which have been troubling you."[99]

OIA officials gave Hazlett that chance until it discovered in November 1938 that the council had sufficient money to maintain operations and thus did not need a supplemental appropriation from its Class A account; the audit also revealed excessive per diem payments and an overpayment to tribal judge Levi Burd.[100] This news prompted Herrick to write an admonitory letter to Hazlett, which set off a new round of diplomatic anxiety. Herrick described himself as an adviser and affirmed his belief that the council must succeed or fail according to its exercise of responsibilities delineated by the tribe's corporate charter, but he informed Hazlett that reports of financial irregularities had disturbed the OIA. Citing the council's lack of wisdom in its distribution of finances and patronage, Herrick told Hazlett that "these things should be corrected" by practicing fidelity to the provisions of the charter and limiting council salaries, including the chairman's.[101]

Hazlett responded by criticizing the OIA's forced appropriation of tribal and individual monies to pay for the services of the U.S. Geological Survey (USGS) and the Blackfeet hospital. On September 8, 1938, the

BTBC adopted a resolution from its oil committee criticizing the OIA's attempt to collect 10 percent of mining revenues earned by IRA tribes to defray the cost of USGS supervisory activities, costs that the BIA usually absorbed.[102] The OIA's letter had indicated that reimbursement required the consent of tribal councils. The BTBC, exercising a right established in the Blackfeet constitution, did not grant that consent.[103] The council's resolution stated that the fee was "excessive and far out of proportion to the amount of services rendered," arguing that the tribe's oil fields "have been brought into production without the aid and assistance of the Geological Survey. Some go so far as to say that they were brought in despite the objections of the U.S.G.S."[104] Despite Hazlett's signature lack of self-restraint, he made a good argument that the OIA's policy amounted to taxation without consultation or regulation. William Zimmerman reminded Hazlett that Congress mandated the reimbursement policy, warning him that if the tribe did not comply, then the OIA would no longer authorize USGS operations on the Blackfeet Reservation. He asked Hazlett to consider the implications.[105]

The issue of Blackfeet consent became a topic of discussion within the OIA ranks. During the September 8, 1938, meeting that produced the protest of the USGS tax, the BTBC also adopted a resolution protesting Circular Letter 38468, which had notified tribes that Congress's 1939 Appropriations Act required them to pay for hospitalization. Joe Jennings, alert to hiccups in the reorganization program, told Collier that protests like the Blackfeet's would become the norm if the OIA did not revise its system of distributing information about policy changes, whether they were initiated by the OIA or mandated by Congress. "Too frequently policy changes in Indian administration have been made without the Indians being informed of the desirability of such changes," Jennings wrote. "Would it not be better," he asked Collier, "to give the councils the opportunity to express their viewpoint before we have the *fait accompli*?"[106] Fred Daiker agreed, arguing that the process of delivering such sensitive information should be "one of careful explanation and education," written with Indians in mind rather than BIA personnel, and distributed to a variety of Indian organizations and in group meetings where the policy changes could be discussed. But Daiker also believed that the Blackfeet complaint derived mainly from the fact that the tribe objected to the idea of being charged at all, and he recommended that the OIA justify the policy change by explaining its role in the process.[107]

The OIA had initiated the policy change, however, not Congress. Collier informed the House Appropriations subcommittee that the BIA intended to charge modest fees for hospitalization and "real-estate administration," because the "well-to-do Indian ought to help pay for his own services." Collier maintained that the policy would not deny an Indian access to health care but would "bring in some compensating revenue."[108] Since there were many in Congress who would have liked to repeal the IRA and could not, it appears that they decided instead to alter the federal relationship with Indians by charging them for services whenever possible. In the face of sustained opposition to the reorganization program, Collier conceded such changes. The process of implementing the new system of charging Indians for improvements to their communities' health, economic, and welfare programs may have been accompanied by more "careful explanation and education" than in the past, but the resistance to paying for those improvements remained. To Indians, who were mobilized to reverse bad economic conditions largely attributable to OIA mismanagement and politicized by the reorganization program's emphasis on intergovernmental negotiations and the sovereignty it created, these mandated costs seemed anachronistic, impolitic, and untenable. In the minds of Blackfeet leaders like Stuart Hazlett, the new policy was a unilateral termination of federal services.

Diplomatic relations between the OIA and the BTBC worsened in the fall of 1939. Although the council's intransigence aggravated the conflict, Blackfeet consent and OIA education turned out to be very protean and short-lived propositions.[109] In response to the council's refusal to accept its decisions without question, the OIA publicized the results of a September audit of the Blackfeet Corporation's books, an audit initiated in part because of sustained full-blood protests.[110] The audit and the OIA's distribution of its findings precipitated spirited debate among tribal members on the eve of council elections, focusing attention on the activities of the Hazlett council and the BIA's role in Blackfeet politics. Collier clearly intended to influence the tribe's perception of the business council's integrity and thus the January 1940 election. He told field agent Charles Heacock after the election that the OIA had been using "diplomatic means to try to make the members of the Council see the error of their ways. Mr. Hazlett, for example, had frequently been exhorted by [OIA] staff to turn over a new leaf to handle tribal funds with due and proper care. [The] audit showed that our preachments had not been heeded and a sharp reprimand seemed entirely in order." That reprimand took the form of a public letter to the BTBC. Collier admitted to Heacock that "it was realized that this letter was sure to create a stir" among the Blackfeet.[111]

Collier's October 31 letter summarized the results of special agent Marvin Clark's September audit, which discovered fiscal irregularities involving "rubber checks," missing funds, and personal loans to council members and their relatives amounting to $5,510.95, of which only $330.12 had been repaid. Some of the loans were small. Edward Bigbeaver and William Buffalohide each received $40. And some were large. Mae Coburn's husband got $1,000. Quarter-blood councilman John Wren and his white wife borrowed $1,624.45 to pay off a mortgage. Collier also condemned the council's salaries, which had consumed $10,020 of the tribe's budget; the council chairman's $1,800 salary was a new feature of the tribal budget thanks to Hazlett. Collier was particularly distressed that Hazlett had instructed the tribal treasurer to disburse funds without the council's approval, which violated the terms of the charter and jeopardized Hazlett's bond. Collier told the council members that the audit disturbed him very much. He blamed those "actively responsible" but also admonished those council members who had become "passively acquiescent or took the attitude of 'washing their hands' of the matter." Collier decided not to initiate drastic legal action against the council after hearing from Superintendent Graves that the council was addressing the problems delineated in the audit. A portion of the funds had been reimbursed, but more important, the council's passage of several resolutions that reformed the corporation's fiscal practices indicated to Collier that council members wanted to "straighten matters out and to act properly in the future"; one resolution sanctioned the transfer of tribal funds to an agency account, giving the superintendent improved "scrutiny and control," while another prohibited loans to tribal members from the tribal treasury. Collier held Hazlett responsible for any missing funds and warned his colleagues that he would seek justice if financial improprieties continued.[112]

Collier had instructed Superintendent Graves to give the October 31 letter a wide distribution to ensure that large numbers of Blackfeet became aware of their council's actions. The *Glacier County Chief* published both Collier's letter and Hazlett's scathing reply in its November 17, 1939, issue. Hazlett's letter to Collier mixed apology, righteous indignation, and political grandstanding. Acknowledging the council's failure to maintain proper books, Hazlett blamed the previous council. Although the council had approved the personal loans in good faith, he promised Collier that he had expedited their repayment. But Hazlett refused to abide by Collier's "outrageous and unholy proposition" that he make up any financial shortfall, arguing that such an action would amount to confessing that he stole money. Collier's intent was to "meddle in Blackfeet politics" and create a "rubber stamp council," Hazlett charged, complaining to Collier that the "Indian office through you is making a herculean effort to control Blackfeet votes at the coming election. Apparently Bolshevik Russia has nothing on the Indian department and then you talk of the Reorganization act and selfgovernment—there is no such animal." Hazlett was indeed correct that Collier attempted to influence Blackfeet political affairs; Collier admitted it after the election. Hazlett exaggerated the tribe's opposition to the IRA, however, by claiming that "if given an opportunity the Blackfeet as well as many other thousands of Indians would throw the act in the garbage can tomorrow morning. . . . 90 per cent of the Blackfeet are and always have been opposed to the act."[113]

Hazlett shifted blame for the council's mismanagement and favoritism onto a piece of legislation supported by a majority of Blackfeet voters. He continued to reinvent Blackfeet political history and himself in a subsequent letter to the *Chief.* After acknowledging that his previous letter contained "a few inaccuracies" and was not based on "official figures [and] documents," he argued that the IRA was "imposed upon the Blackfeet against their will" through high-pressure salesmanship. Hazlett, in a desperate attempt to salvage his damaged reputation, presented himself as the defender of Blackfeet sovereignty, citing several instances dating back to the 1910s in which he alone defended the Blackfeet against Collier, Congress, and other Washington "henchmen."[114]

The OIA had decided that Hazlett and his colleagues were not the type of Indian leaders it wanted managing the reorganization program on the Blackfeet Reservation, a decision that ran counter to the spirit of the IRA. Although the council's actions were arrogant and corrupt, adjectives that could easily describe the OIA's previous administration of Indian affairs, the OIA failed to embrace Joe Jennings's argument that "Indians should be encouraged to make their own decisions even if their progress is painfully slow and most disappointing at times."[115] At the same time, the OIA rightly focused attention on the council's important fiduciary and moral obligation of properly managing valuable tribal funds and preserving the tribe's privilege of getting federal credit monies. Though meddlesome, Collier's sharp reprimand to the council served to arm Blackfeet voters with relevant information to help them make their choice in the January election. Few Blackfeet protested Collier's actions.

More important, the OIA was not alone in pressing the issue of financial mismanagement. The White Calf faction had asked Collier as early as the spring of 1938 to investigate Hazlett's council for financial improprieties. As Hazlett and Collier traded accusations in late 1939, other Blackfeet leaders began voicing their opinions. Councilman Brian Connolly distanced himself from Hazlett and his supporters and condemned the actions of some of his colleagues in letters printed in the *Glacier County Chief*. James Brown, a mixed-blood entrepreneur, bemoaned the mudslinging and asked candidates to tell him how they intended to deal with the reservation's problems rather than simply "tearing the other fellow down."[116] Hugh Jackson, the tribe's gadfly hovering over the stink of political corruption, reminded Blackfeet voters that they alone could affect the outcome of the pending council election. In a series of letters to the *Chief*, Jackson admonished voters to consider the council's misuse of tribal funds, criticizing "mercenary" and "nepotist" council members and their "fat payroll." He asked his fellow Blackfeet, "When your councilman whizzes past you in a new shining gas buggy, don't it sort of seem to you that some of your money missed your pants pocket or stocking?" The best way to preserve the tribe's financial integrity and their rightful share of tribal revenues, he told voters, was to "sing another song when January rolls around. We cannot afford to store the grapes of wrath indefinitely." Jackson was no friend of either Collier or the IRA, which he called communistic, and his principal or at least subsidiary motive was to facilitate the per capita distribution of oil revenues. But his mocking criticism of the political aristocracy made it difficult for Hazlett and others to present themselves as virtuous Blackfeet politicians victimized by Collier and his "henchmen."[117]

Collier's letter served, as he intended, as a catalyst in the destabilization of the Hazlett council. Field agent Charles Heacock reported that Collier's letter both sparked reforms in the BTBC's procedures as a result of tribal complaints and served as a convenient target for council members, who tried to deflect the letter's criticisms by claiming that Collier's interference abrogated the principles of the IRA. Although some full-bloods remained hostile to the IRA, Heacock found no evidence of any "organic trouble" with the act. Tribal leaders remained in sympathy with it; their critical letters, while suggesting otherwise, were written "primarily to attract voters." He noted that Hazlett's attempt to blame government interference and his Blackfeet political opponents had mostly failed. Hazlett's articles in the *Chief* were received with a "great deal of amusement on the part of many, and needless to say, with a 'grain of salt' by all." Heacock and other BIA staff decided to keep a low profile, however, to "avoid any risk of implicating the administration in the election."[118]

Hazlett's credibility with the OIA had diminished. As Heacock soon discovered, it had also diminished with the Blackfeet themselves, whose support for Hazlett and other council members crumbled in the face of mismanagement, broken promises, and a specious defense. White Calf had argued as early as March 1939 that the "Indians' confidence [in the BTBC] has been thoroughly shattered by wild meaningless promises." One full-blood elder captured the faction's sentiments by saying, "you promised us everything as sweet as sugar. . . . I do not like anything you have done. You have made liars of yourselves and fools of us."[119]

Collier and his colleagues were not disappointed when Hazlett failed to retain his council seat on January 16, 1940. Hazlett received only 112 votes, 416 fewer than he received in 1938. Joe Brown regained his seat by winning 477 votes, more than any other candidate. Levi Burd barely survived, winning the final seat in the Browning district by only 9 votes over BIWA founder William Billedeaux.[120] The two full-blood incumbents—Bigbeaver and Buffalohide—lost their seats largely because they failed to produce per capita payments as promised. Only five of the thirteen incumbents retained their seats, though John Wren, Mae (nee Coburn) Williamson, and Sam Bird did not run, perhaps because they realized they stood little chance of reelection. Mixed-bloods Connolly and Hagerty survived the political shift despite their wealth, in large measure because they were better insulated from political change in the Seville district and because they had publicly objected to the growth of the Blackfeet bureaucracy.

The political system worked on January 19. Although the corruption practiced by Hazlett and other council members was relatively minor compared with historical acts of mixed-blood exploitation, the favoritism and fiscal infidelity created a genuine fiducial crisis. Hazlett and others who failed to keep campaign promises and manage tribal finances responsibly were not reelected. Collier told Heacock that Hazlett's ouster from and Brown's return to the council indicated that Blackfeet affairs were "headed toward a condition of somewhat greater stability." Collier, like Heacock, was "not at all pessimistic about the fate of organization among the Blackfeet."[121] But the election, and Hugh Jackson in particular, raised the tribe's consciousness of class differences. Jackson attacked council "aristocrats" and "elites"; Hazlett and his highfalutin language, John Wren and his white wife, and Mae Coburn Williamson and her oil-rich husband were all perceived to be ill suited to represent the interests of the Blackfeet Nation of Indians. The rich got richer during the Hazlett years. Jackson's descriptions of women and children wearing ragged clothes while council members enjoyed their beer and drove their cars obviously struck a chord with tribal members struggling to achieve a decent standard of living.

It remained to be seen whether the economic system would work. Full-bloods had fewer options for growth, perhaps because of their social organization and lack of collateral for loans, but the council's agenda of reinvesting tribal revenues into the rehabilitation program also affected mixed-bloods like Jackson, who wanted per capita distributions to further individual investments or to simply make old age more comfortable. The project, according to both council and agency staff, was designed "essentially for the resettlement of younger couples." Older mixed-bloods like Hugh Jackson were not physically able to participate in the program. James White Calf and many of his followers were neither physically suited nor culturally inclined to leave an established full-blood community. Many Blackfeet, both full-bloods and mixed-bloods, did not have sufficient collateral or political pull to secure a loan. The discriminatory nature of the rehabilitation program, therefore, ran along lines of age, class, and ethnicity.

There were thus two economies evolving on the Blackfeet Reservation: an artificial economy that depended upon welfare from tribal and federal sources in a system that offered little promise of structural change, and an organic economy that rested on the hope of a "rehabilitated" reservation suited to self-sustaining agriculture and able to withstand the rigors of northwestern Montana winters.[122] Each economy contained elements of the other: the artificial economy depended in part on the benefits of tribal oil production, while the organic economy depended in part on the "corporate" welfare of government credit and investment. The artificial economy remained a tribal economy, embracing the tribe as both developer of natural resources and provider of welfare payments; the organic economy evolved as an assimilationist economy, asserting the need for individual investment and adoption of "white monetary attitudes."

Indian Organization staff had discussed the issues of welfare and rehabilitation in late 1937 while the tribe debated its commitment to irrigation projects. H. Scudder Mekeel had recommended that the OIA replace Superintendent Graves with a "welfare man" who could address the needs of Blackfeet unwilling or incapable of participating in the rigorous work of irrigation farming or livestock cultivation.[123] John Herrick disagreed: "On the contrary, [the superintendent] should be the best extension and industry man we can find, and the Office should support him actively, particularly in bringing about the rehabilitation and development of the irrigated lands which are the key to the Tribe's economic welfare." Herrick believed that the tribe's resources—grazing range, arts and crafts, and oil—would consistently provide the Blackfeet with an income, "provided they are properly developed." Acting Commissioner E. J. Armstrong wrote in the margin of Herrick's memo, "I agree. The welfare end of the problem should be purely incidental to economic rehabilitation end."[124] The choice, as Herrick had put it to Blackfeet leaders in November 1937, was whether the tribe would try to rehabilitate itself or "give up entirely and establish a warehouse and pass out rations." OIA leaders recognized that certain Blackfeet groups and individuals would derive direct benefits if the tribe adopted the rehabilitation program but maintained that "in indirect benefits . . . the money [for rehabilitation] will work a greater good to the whole Tribe."[125] As the decade closed, the OIA remained optimistic about the "fate of organization" on the Blackfeet Reservation. An unfortunate element of structural poverty existed among the Blackfeet, officials argued, which could be ameliorated through relief but not eliminated. The OIA's and BTBC's philosophy of trickle-down agricultural economics prevailed.

Rex Kildow, John Krall's successor, wrote in his January 1939 extension report that "while the seperating [sic] of relief from extension has not been definitely accomplished we feel that rapid strides have been made during the year toward that end."[126] Kildow believed that his overworked staff—comprising a livestock supervisor, farm agent, stockman, and two Blackfeet farm aides—needed to concentrate on meeting its twin goals of expanding the tribe's livestock industry and furthering the resettlement of young families to irrigation districts. His small staff was charged with helping 826 Blackfeet families derive benefit from three main economic programs—the Revolving Credit Fund, the Rehabilitation Program, and the Cattle Repayment Program. Kildow estimated that "33% of the [826] families are in a position to be rehabilitated, the other 67% are aged people, and other families for whom the Rehabilitation Program could not be successfully carried out for various reasons." Of the families "worth" rehabilitating, about 100 were operating successfully with RCF funds and another 50 or so had developed an economic herd through the CRP. The remaining 125 families still needed extension's help to achieve a similar level of self-support.[127]

Kildow's delineation of "worthiness" both supported and contradicted Herrick's and Armstrong's commitment to the Rehabilitation Program. On one hand, he fostered the expansion of the tribe's inchoate middle class by segregating a minority of Blackfeet families deemed capable of becoming productive and devoting an incommensurate amount of resources to them. On the other, he admitted that a majority of the Blackfeet people had no economic future and that he could do nothing about it. This assessment, coming from the federal agent principally responsible for overseeing the tribe's economic development, did not bode well for political unity.

The decision to invest in the future rather than ameliorate the present carried a cost, as council members discovered in the 1938 and 1940 council elections; Hazlett had confidently told OIA officials in early 1938 that "[w]e are looking to the future, let the present look out for itself," an attitude that contributed to his dismissal.[128] The lesson of both elections was that the pursuit of the economic greater good was not enough to ensure a measure of political stability. Hazlett and his colleagues had failed both to honor campaign promises and to address the growing class-based disparity that became an unintended, though foreseeable, consequence of the distribution of RCF money, CRP cattle, and tribal investment in the Rehabilitation Program. The first period of self-government had created an agonistic tension between a political majority and an economic minority. The exigent task of new councils was to create a political economy that balanced rehabilitation and relief and thus to address the needs of those who had begun new lives in eastern Blackfeet country and those literally left behind by the centrifugal forces of change.

Although the market for crude oil remained soft until 1940, when demand for gasoline from Canadian and American armed forces stimulated greater drilling activity, the Blackfeet treasury enjoyed increasing returns from rentals and bonuses. The tribe earned about $100,000 per year in the late 1930s, representing both economic and political progress. By 1943, sixty-four tribal leases were producing roughly $300,000 for the Blackfeet treasury; fifty-four allottees earned another $150,000.[129] The BTBC thus became responsible for managing an evolving political economy increasingly based upon community-owned oil revenues. The growth of tribal revenue set off a new debate about income distribution more fractious than that over the Rehabilitation Program. The BTBC found itself faced with new pressures to produce a long-term investment program while satisfying the short-term needs of an increasingly out-spoken minority. During the 1940 council election campaign, Hugh Jackson publicly raised the call for per capita distribution of oil monies. Prominent Blackfeet full-bloods issued similar calls in the ensuing years, declaring that oil revenues belonged to the Blackfeet people, and in par-ticular to full-bloods. The promise of oil was the unifying force on the Blackfeet Reservation in the 1920s and 1930s. The profit from oil would be the most divisive issue in the 1940s and 1950s. The success of the oil industry both served as a reminder that some Blackfeet benefited more than others and exacerbated the class distinctions and social inequality that emerged in such visceral fashion during the 1940 election.

5. "RECONCILING THE OLD MEN TO THE NEW WAY": Income Distribution in an Infant Democracy, 1940–1945

> Most of the older generation full bloods are not familiar with the ways of tribal government under constitution, bylaws, and charters, either by custom or through ability to read English. We are smaller in numbers and hence are out-voted. . . . This way of tribal government is not of their making. The way of bringing justice through tribal government as constituted is therefore closed. Other means must be found if the appeal must be carried to Congress itself. – Full-blood petition of protest to Congress, 1942

> [The IRA] gave us powers that we had never had before. It gave us the chance to use our funds; it gave us the chance to get credit and we have under it all of those things and they have helped us, and we fear that if the act were thrown out and we had to go back to the old system that we could not get the advantages that we have now. – Joe Brown to congressional subcommittee, 1944

Michael Walzer writes that citizens of democratic communities need a "shared understanding of what sovereignty is and what it is for."[1] The problems that surfaced during Stuart Hazlett's brief BTBC regime initiated a period of political introspection that induced changes in the relationship between the BTBC and the people it was designed to serve and protect. The newly elected business council gathered on February 1, 1940, to hold a frank discussion about the growth pains of the tribe's infant democracy and its need for improved management of financial assets and communication with its citizens. The meeting emphasized the evolving relationship between the people and the council this political body had elected. Participants attempted to define more precisely just what Blackfeet sovereignty and Blackfeet democracy meant.

Veteran field agent Charles Heacock offered support for Blackfeet sovereignty, relating to the council and an audience of mostly full-bloods the BIA's reluctance to criticize council actions to avoid "meddling in tribal affairs." But since the council had asked for advice about avoiding serious mistakes in tribal administration, Heacock promised to "sometimes say things that might hurt"; BIA agents had to walk a fine line between providing advice and engendering ill-feeling by appearing coercive. In response to Heacock's principal recommendation to establish a budget based on accurate information and to address the need for public disclosure of the tribe's finances in the wake of audits pointing to BTBC graft, the new council voted to examine the affairs of the Blackfeet Corporation and adopted a resolution that read in part, "[O]wing to the dissatisfaction and dissension of [tribal members] and the failure of preceding councils to inform the people of the financial status of the corporation, such as . . . expense of the tribal council and committees, and numerous other expenditures that have been unknown to the members of the tribe . . . and to prevent present and future irregularities, and to clarify the atmosphere of dissension . . . be it resolved that all present tribal employees, and committees be indefinitely suspended."[2]

The resolution to investigate tribal affairs and provide "the people" with information about the corporation's operations reflected the severity of the political dissension that had erupted during the council election. Such conflict had been mostly absent since Frank Campbell's "meddling in tribal affairs" exacerbated tribal factionalism in the mid-1920s, a period that ended with public calls for tribal unity. The February 1 meeting produced similar calls. Many of the tribe's full-blood elders addressed the council to plead for its understanding of their status and their need for assistance. These full-bloods, many of whom had served on the BTBC during the 1920s and early 1930s, had formed the ceremonial committee to represent their concerns to a predominantly mixed-blood council when it became clear that Hazlett had broken his promise to include them in political deliberations and to issue per capita payments. Respect and equitable revenue distribution were the objects of their desire.

Full-bloods objected to the IRA largely because it created a government that cost money to operate—money that could go directly to tribal members—and because they had little say in the operation of that government. Full-bloods felt neglected, Wades in the Water told council members. "It is the full-blood and 'Indian Blood' that put you on the Council," he said, adding, "My advice to you is to consider this carefully and give the full-blood a little more power." He admonished the council to view the tribe as a family and full-bloods as valued relatives. Wallace Night Gun explained that full-bloods strenuously objected to the council's closed-door sessions. "In the future do not shut us long-haired Indians out and shut our braids in the door," he said. "Open the doors so that we will know what the council is doing."[3]

Dissidents also asked the council to open the books. Black Weasel complained that "all of our Tribal money and oil money goes toward that Wheeler-Howard Bill" while elderly Blackfeet went hungry. White Calf, the most vocal critic of the tribal government, asked the new council to manage the tribe's money more carefully and to "ask the people what they want to do with this money. It is the people who have hired you to do the work for them." Full-bloods, and by extension other tribal members facing similar economic conditions, continued to hope for an oil bonanza. The seventy-four- year-old White Calf said that the Blackfeet "are called the oiled Indians of today and right now every one in this room should be sitting with a lot of money in his pockets. . . . We are standing on riches."[4] As the 1938 election demonstrated, many tribal members wanted the council to distribute oil revenues to the people rather than invest them in rehabilitation programs that benefited a small segment of Blackfeet society. And as the 1940 election made clear, the perception existed that the council misappropriated these revenues by spending that money on exorbitant salaries and rehabilitation loans for "white people"—Blackfeet with little Indian blood. For many Blackfeet, both mixed-bloods and full-bloods, oil, not cattle, was their "second buffalo." Despite their complaints, the elders expressed faith that the democratic system would work and that council members would honor the idea of tribe, or "family," by distributing any income that the council could derive from the land. Heacock defended the IRA, telling ceremonial committee and BTBC members that "most of the trouble lies in the people not knowing how to use the instruments of self-government to make their wants known." The Blackfeet had the power to change or amend the constitution. The "first lesson" a democratic people learns is "the use of the referenda [sic]," Heacock said. The IRA constitution, he added, was an "organ through which the voice of the people can be heard."[5]

The "open" council meeting of February 1 produced a renewed sense of hope in the democracy of the Blackfeet Nation and a new look at the operation of the Blackfeet Corporation. The budget-investigation committee recommended reducing the council's per diem expenses and the salaries of tribal employees, consolidating the stock board and the credit committee, and the apprenticeship of an Indian "girl" to the tribal credit clerk so that she could eventually assume the position. The council adopted these recommendations, with one exception; it voted against consolidating the livestock and credit committees, instead reorganizing the credit committee by appointing to it a member from each district. The council also resolved to prohibit its members from holding paid tribal positions while in office, addressing the complaints that council members had "double-dipped" in the tribal treasury.[6] Heacock told John Herrick that the February 5 BTBC meeting was "one of the finest meetings of its kind I have ever had the pleasure to attend. . . . One can only marvel how rapidly a total situation considered by many to have been hopeless, can change for the best." The new council seemed determined to "turn over a new leaf" and effect meaningful reforms, partly on the strength of a renewed "Indian public opinion" that had emerged from the "intense political activity" of the January 1940 election. Heacock believed that this "marked change for better government offers reassurance in democratic institutions for Indian people."[7]

John Collier focused on Indian democracies in his 1941 annual report, writing that one of the OIA's goals during wartime was "the continued but sharpened emphasis upon training Indians in practical democracy through increased participation in self-government." Previous Indian policy had succeeded in "destroying [the] local democracy of the Indians," he argued. The IRA now provided the democratic tools for the "rebuilding of [Indian] social organization," which would serve as an example to countries fighting fascism abroad.[8] The Blackfeet Nation's success in reconstituting its political community along constitutional lines required the effective participation of all factions to ensure that they maintained what Carole Pateman called "feelings of political efficacy."[9] Heacock's defense of the IRA and its instruments for change would not be lost on full-bloods and mixed-bloods alike as the debate on the distribution of oil revenues evolved over the course of the following decade.

Heacock, the Blackfeet's democratic "trainer," was encouraged by the measures the BTBC took to assist the minority faction after the February 1 meeting. The council took an active stance on including full-bloods in its deliberations and giving aid to their communities. During a March 6 BTBC meeting, held to select a delegation for a pending trip to Washington, the council allowed members of the ceremonial committee to contribute to the delegation's agenda. The speakers reemphasized the full-bloods' desire for direct distribution of oil revenue rather than loans and expressed opposition to any rehabilitation program that might jeopardize the integrity of the oil fields. Supported by a large crowd of full-bloods, the speakers also demanded full-blood representation on the delegation. The council agreed to this request and offered to pay their expenses. Theodore Last Star and White Calf were selected in a separate vote of full-bloods.[10]

It is important to note again that Blackfeet full-bloods did not constitute an active and homogeneous voting bloc. Only twenty-two bothered to participate in the vote to elect the delegates. Dissidents typically had once served on the council and had lost their seats largely because of changing demographic circumstances, and those protesting council activities tended to be the same persons from the same community. Nine of the thirteen full-blood delegates to council meetings came from White Calf's Starr School community, and even Starr School full-bloods disagreed over policy.[11] Thus the political opposition was not organized reservation-wide but was based partly on proximity to established mixed-blood communities. Earl Old Person, who grew up in the Starr School community, noted that while Starr School and Heart Butte full-bloods "knew each other," they did not necessarily organize political campaigns or protests together.[12] Each community had its own political ecology and patterns of economic organization. The Heart Butte and Old Agency communities were more independent of mixed-blood communities, a legacy of the Five Year Industrial Program. Heart Butte residents could typically elect a full-blood through whom they could channel grievances and requests and thus feel involved in the political process.

The White Calf delegation raised its concerns during the March 20 conference with OIA officials in Washington. BIA agent George Fox's postconference memorandum indicates that officials explained in detail several important issues to the full-blood delegates. For some full-bloods, this meeting was the first time someone had bothered to address the confusing issues posed by reorganization. For example, on the matter of the council's management of hunting and fishing rights, full-bloods believed that such control abridged their treaty rights. OIA officials explained that tribal regulations served to protect Blackfeet sovereignty by prohibiting trespassing by whites and other Indians. White Calf and Last Star seemed to be satisfied with the explanation. Confusion of this kind pointed to a general lack of communication between factions and, on White Calf's part, an inherent inability to trust any action of a mixed-blood dominated council. The group discussed less successfully the more intractable problems of minority representation and the full-bloods' attendant opposition to the IRA. Mixed-blood delegates complained that mixed-blood candidates prevailed in some predominantly full-blood voting districts, suggesting that full-blood candidates did not campaign aggressively or that their agenda was less appealing than that of mixed-bloods. In response to the familiar charge that the IRA discriminated against full-blood communities, OIA officials suggested to White Calf and Last Star that their opposition resulted from "a lack of understanding of the IRA." The discrimination, "if it exists," Fox wrote, stemmed from the administration of RCF monies rather than the architecture of the act itself. Indian Office officials could do little but encourage the BTBC to be more aware of the full-bloods' complaint of discrimination in the administration of the RCF program and in the expenditure of other tribal monies and for both tribal groups to continue to discuss the IRA and its provisions for constitutional change.[13]

While in Washington, Burd, White Calf, and William Spanish testified during a congressional hearing on a bill recommending assistance for needy Indians. They faced a generally accommodating House Committee on Indian Affairs. Rep. John C. Schafer of Wisconsin asked Burd if the record on Indian Affairs "more than parallels the atrocities and so-called concentration camps abroad?" The historical record, Schafer said, was that "the white man took the Indians['] land, debauched their women, killed many of them, and herded the survivors in concentration camps which we now call Indian Reservations." Burd simply responded by saying, "if there are any people that are neglected, it is the Indians."[14]

The Blackfeet's testimony never reached the visceral level of the committee members'. Schafer's description of Indian reservations as concentration camps may have offended Burd and White Calf; it painted the Blackfeet as powerless victims. Burd and White Calf wanted to focus on the year 1940 and the tribe's future rather than relive the past. When Rep. James O'Connor of Montana asked Burd what *he* thought the government should do to relieve distress and help the tribe become self-supporting, Burd emphasized the need to establish balance between relief and rehabilitation measures in the Blackfeet's dual economy: "The first thing, I think the Government should supply enough credit so that we could carry on our program that we are working on under the Reorganization Act. In the next place, I think a bill of this kind . . . would solve the problem up to a point where in 4 or 5 years time the younger generation and the younger Indians, who are using this credit, could take care of their own fathers and mothers and grandfathers." Burd reinforced the tribe's commitment to the reorganization program, and to the Revolving Credit Fund in particular, but he argued that in the meantime the "older Indians and the middle-class Indians" needed aid. Most of the older Blackfeet lived in single-room shacks. Most had little to eat.[15]

Burd did not place blame on either the BIA or Congress but rather argued that the government's rations were insufficient. Burd and Spanish contended that the new federal welfare system had failed to protect elderly Blackfeet. Many of the older Blackfeet could not pass the government's medical test to become eligible for CCC projects and were "just out of luck." The tribe's relief problem was exacerbated by the Montana state government's refusal to accept responsibility for the welfare of the state's Indian residents. State and local officials appeared to believe that it was the duty of the federal government to take care of Indians, and thus the Blackfeet did not receive the kind of state-supported auxiliary relief that meant the difference between starvation and relative comfort. Despite the problems of federal relief distribution, both Burd and Spanish agreed that the BIA should retain control of Indian welfare because it understood the "set-up" and the tribe's needs. Rep. John Murdock asked Spanish, "You hear a good deal about submitting the Indians and all relief work for that matter to the State. That would be an unfortunate thing, would it not?" Spanish answered that he would prefer not to "depend on Montana," as Murdock had put it. Both Spanish and Burd thus argued against terminating federal control of welfare under the terms of the Johnson-O'Malley Act, sharply contrasting the message of the two delegations of California Indians that followed the Blackfeet.[16] Blackfeet leaders, at least for the moment, remained optimistic about the "fate of organization" on their reservation and about the BIA's ability to help take care of the tribe.

Burd testified during the hearing that the older Indians and the middle-class Indians needed assistance. "Older Indians" typically referred only to full-bloods. It is unclear what he meant by "middle class." Perhaps, given the nature of the hearings, he was referring to mixed-bloods who also struggled to achieve a decent standard of living. Given his wealth, Burd may have classified as middle class all mixed-bloods and full-bloods who had some income production. The sixty-two-year-old businessman was an interesting choice to shepherd the tribe to greener pastures. He had championed oil development and succeeded in stock raising during the 1920s and 1930s, though he earned in the process the enmity of agency superintendents who charged him with grazing trespass, subcontracting, and organizing opposition to the IRA. Although he coopted full-blood leaders to an extent greater than other mixed-blood leaders, he was, as a half-blood, perhaps more genuinely interested in helping their communities and in preserving tribal harmony, two related activities. He had survived the purge of the Hazlett council, despite benefiting as a salaried judge and getting a five-thousand-dollar RCF loan, in part because he kept a low profile and in part because he appealed to diverse constituencies. But he was also one of the Blackfeet Nation's wealthiest citizens. He and Wright Hagerty, the one-sixteenth blood councilman, each enjoyed a net worth of more than one hundred thousand dollars. In 1942, Hagerty and his wife Grace had a combined net worth approaching five hundred thousand dollars, earning their money in sheep ranching and oil and grazing leases. One need not calculate these sums in 1990s dollars to know that by any standards—rural or urban, Montana or New York—they were wealthy. The presence of these men on the council reinforced the notions of class differences not only between full-bloods and mixed-bloods but among mixed-bloods as well. And they reinforced the notion that the council itself was an instrument for this wealth and would continue to prove so.

Hugh Jackson's editorials of the 1940 election campaign revealed an emerging class consciousness that related to the reorganization of the tribal political economy and to attendant changes in the notion of tribal obligation. For full-blood groups like White Calf's, the BIA remained their chrysalis. The challenge for elites like Burd and Joe Brown was to reorganize the reservation political economy to the point at which the Blackfeet Nation could emerge fully from this cocoon and become the true guardian of "the people." The success of this transformation required the attenuation of an incipient class stratification that threatened to undermine the Blackfeet's evolving democratic community.

Since 1936, the BTBC, and its development partner the BIA, had clearly focused on creating long-term programs of work to establish a real middle class, a group of Blackfeet who could depend upon their own labors and investments rather than on government relief. Extension agent Rex Kildow reported in early 1940 that the Cattle Repayment Program (CRP) initiated in late 1934 appeared to have furnished many enterprising Blackfeet with sustainable economic herds. Livestock sales conducted through Blackfeet cooperatives in 1938 and 1939 raised profits between 10 and 40 percent higher than individual sales. In addition, the Blackfeet sheep industry exceeded all expectations. Lamb sales rose by nearly 60 percent between 1938 and 1939.[17]

Despite such progress, a centralization of economic power was occurring on the reservation. The average income derived from livestock sales did not present a "true picture of the situation," Kildow wrote in 1940, noting a disparity between small and large operators that belied the idea of widespread economic advancement and the notion that economic success fell strictly along ethnic lines.[18] Although more Blackfeet managed cattle herds larger than twenty head than in previous years, fewer Blackfeet actually participated in the revolving livestock program. Between late 1934 and late 1939, the number of Blackfeet contract holders fell from 556 to 280. Shifts in ownership occurred over the five-year period, but consolidation of livestock wealth occurred most rapidly in 1939: between January 1939 and January 1940 the number of small contract holders (those with fewer than twenty head) dropped from 196 to 121; Blackfeet owning more than twenty head rose from 69 to 122. Some did very well; those families owning more than a hundred head rose from 2 to 6. There were several reasons for this consolidation, which Kildow called "necessary." The drought conditions that had ravaged lands south of the reservation for most of the 1930s finally visited the Blackfeet in 1936, making it difficult for some stockowners to maintain their herds; others simply sold the original allotment of cattle for reasons of survival or quick profit. The BTBC and the livestock board enforced the principles of the CRP by shifting some of the heifers from less productive contract holders to those more "interested" and "capable." Certain Blackfeet, as Kildow pointed out, simply were "not cattle men." Full-bloods in particular preferred to raise sheep; in contrast to cattle raisers, sheep owners received two incomes a year—from lambs and then from wool. Here too the more successful and aggressive sheep owners such as Wright Hagerty expanded their operations while small operators "dropped out or were liquidated."[19] Similar economic consolidation occurred on other reservations. Collier noted in his 1941 report that "as in white society, so among the Indians, there is a tendency for a concentration of wealth. On many of the reservations, 10 percent of the Indians own from 75 to 85 percent of all the livestock, and control this same proportion of the range resources."[20]

Burd tried to balance the demand for the release of oil income and the need for continued tribal investment in irrigation and livestock projects. He suggested in a letter to Collier that the tribe buy cattle with oil revenues and distribute them to heads of families rather than release the money directly; it was, he wrote, "not always best to pay some Indians all their money at one time."[21] The OIA refused to consider Burd's plan, arguing illogically that a distribution of cattle bought from oil income served merely as a substitute for a per capita distribution of cash. It asked the council instead to invest tribal revenue in "income-producing activities" that would "provide a much larger return for the members of the tribe as a whole."[22] As in the 1920s, when the Indian Office refused to expand oil leasing on the grounds that higher bonuses *might* eventually result from planned and prudent development, the OIA failed to adapt to changing reservation conditions. The council was stuck in the middle of a divided tribe, facing political pressure to satisfy struggling constituents needing income and enterprising constituents needing capital while trying to invest tribal funds wisely without much guidance from the OIA about how to advance income-producing activities.

The council itself was divided. Several council members had nearly come to blows in April 1940 over a disagreement on expenditures. A minority faction within the council led by Brian Connolly campaigned to remove Burd as council chairman and engineer the transfer of Superintendent Graves. Connolly charged that "tribal moneys [*sic*] are being used, and many say squandered, for a favorite handful of 'insiders and Court favorites' at the expense of over 4,000 members of the tribe." He warned the OIA that his group would "continue to stir and agitate" until it took action.[23] Burd resigned the chairmanship in February 1941 amid charges that he had improperly benefited from livestock sales to tribal members. An OIA investigation determined that Connolly's charges were unfounded and discovered that Connolly himself had profited from livestock sales while in office. Further, no council ordinances prohibited such sales; Burd protested that his council duties should not prevent him from making a living. Most council members ran businesses of one kind or another. Some were more successful than others, which created the effect of invidious distinction. Connolly, judging from various reports, was a contentious man and, judging from the records of various BTBC meetings, not predisposed to offer practical solutions to difficult problems; the OIA eventually sued *him* for grazing stock on allottees' land without permission.[24] In protecting his own political agenda and economic position, Connolly attacked both "internal elites" such as Burd and "external critics" such as BIA officials.

The OIA also rebutted Connolly's charges that Superintendent Graves and Extension Service staff discriminated against various applicants for RCF loans. According to Acting Commissioner Allan Harper, several applicants had been denied loans by previous credit committees and had thus "brought considerable pressure to bear upon their councilmen. Probably this influenced some of them to charge the Superintendent with showing partiality."[25] But the Extension Service, isolated from reservation politics in Washington DC, had little cause to discriminate on any grounds other than the practical ability of a borrower to achieve a modicum of success with the loan. Discrimination, using another definition, means being judicious. The conflict between the BTBC credit committee and extension workers, therefore, transcended parochial concerns. Tribal credit committees could recommend loan applicants but did not have final authority; the system was designed to prevent the kind of discrimination Connolly claimed the BIA staff practiced. Councilman George Pambrun complained that extension workers neglected to provide ongoing service to loan clients and had given some loans to Blackfeet with little experience in stock raising without inspecting the clients' assets and capabilities. "The records of the Extension Service looks [*sic*] darn good in Washington, D.C. but they look pretty darn sad on the reservation," he asserted. Extension's control of the loan process made the credit committee obsolete, Pambrun argued. "What use is there for a Credit Committee?" he asked. He believed that the BTBC could run the RCF program better than the Extension Service because the council was "better acquainted" with loan clients and the climate they faced. The Extension Service staff's recommendations and the BTBC's lack of control created considerable dissension between the two groups. Pambrun, in the kind of terminationist language that would mark his career as a BTBC representative, urged his colleagues to "get together and strive to eliminate the Extension department."[26]

Pambrun's comments reflected both legitimate concerns about the RCF and rehabilitation programs and his own bias against white administrators. Many of the original settlers of the Two Medicine and Badger-Fisher irrigation projects had little experience with stock raising and had struggled accordingly, but the BTBC had selected them in part because they were willing to relocate and literally break new ground. The BTBC's struggle with the Extension Service—certainly the most visible and dominant of any BIA group on the reservation—over control of loan distribution became, much as oil leasing had, the source of considerable dissension between a council intent on taking charge of tribal affairs and an OIA skeptical of the Blackfeet's capacity for self-management, despite its claims to the contrary. There was, therefore, an evolving disjunction between the idea of self-government and the practice of it, a disjunction that would grow as the debate on the Nation's right to terminate federal control became prominent.

In his 1942 reservation survey, BIA agent George Fox argued that since the Nation's adoption of the IRA the BTBC had been "struggling with many new problems which have become its responsibility, problems that vexed the Indian Service for years, and since the Service itself has not found a solution to them it is hardly to be expected that they would be solved in a few years by the council." Council members showed a "real desire to promote tribal welfare," in both its forms; BTBC graft, Fox believed, was "the exception rather than the rule." Despite the Blackfeet's limited experience with the "art of self-government," Fox wrote, "the general picture of council operation over the years does not compare too unfavorably with the pictures of other units of local government[,] and, in fact, with the record of the Indian Service itself in the matter of administration of tribal affairs." County governments in Montana, Tennessee, and elsewhere were deeply in debt, he noted. He thus concluded that it would be unfair to "criticize too harshly an inexperienced people who are struggling not only with routine matters of effecting satisfactory procedures in tribal government but who are also struggling with the fundamental economic problem of promoting human welfare through the utilization of tribal resources." Fox remained optimistic about Blackfeet reorganization. He believed the council needed to facilitate tribal and private development of natural resources through cooperative ventures with both federal and tribal officials. The lack of cooperation between Blackfeet and BIA personnel alarmed Fox, who attributed dissension largely to the imprint of the BIA's past failures on "Indian memory and Indian consciousness."[27]

Fox did see signs that the council was prepared to consider long-term programs of work, noting to a colleague that council members probably wanted to "get the [oil] income committed in order to take the heat off themselves that is being applied by their constituents."[28] Council members received constant pressure from these constituents—many of whom came from extended families—who wanted either tribal loans for hay, school uniforms, and other necessities, or per capita payments. Many of the loans were for good causes, but their proliferation created budget problems and the perception of favoritism. The council could not avoid releasing per capita payments, given the demand for them; councilman Leo Kennerly made the argument in late 1941 for the timely release of oil money to help "the poorer class of people."[29] By doing so, however, the council risked setting expectations of annual distributions. The BTBC issued small payments each year until 1945 while focusing on supporting the rehabilitation program with funds for land and livestock purchases as well as home and irrigation construction. The distribution of community assets in democratic states, Michael Walzer writes, "is what social conflict is all about."[30] The Blackfeet political community not only had failed to solve the problem but had become politically paralyzed by it.

Economists typically recommend the allocation of financial resources for long-term development programs rather than cash distributions. What is important in this analysis is how the Blackfeet themselves viewed the issue of income distribution, especially since oil production connoted, for full-bloods in particular, an offering from Mother Earth. Many Blackfeet, mixed- and full-bloods alike, did not believe they would benefit from the BTBC's trickle-down cattle economics, which they considered discriminatory because, as noted earlier, the rehabilitation program favored young mixed-blood families. Older tribal members of high blood quantum saw these families, by virtue of their age, limited Blackfeet blood quantum, and financial wherewithal to start new operations or expand existing ones, as the least worthy of receiving the proceeds of the tribal estate. Tribal members also could not depend upon successful Blackfeet individuals to serve as catalysts for diffused economic growth. Mixed-bloods like Wright Hagerty and Levi Burd made money by exercising their "preference rights" to secure favorable lease terms, thus benefiting from tribal programs, but they did little to stimulate development by reinvesting the money in community development or job programs; Burd stayed active politically, while Hagerty remained on the periphery of tribal activities, in part because of his wealth. In addition, successful stockowners paid no tax to the tribe, and due to the BTBC's negligence, some borrowers of tribal funds never repaid their original loans.

The conflict that raged between the respective supporters of the rehabilitation program and per capita distributions, or "sustained economic enterprises" and "subsistence economic orientations," thus had class, cultural, ethnic, and generational dimensions. It is therefore easy to understand the criticism leveled against the BTBC's economic agenda. Historians of Indians' political economies have noted the effect of an unstable political environment on the viability of long-term economic development.[31] But both factors feed off each other. Interior Department officials later recommended to BTBC leaders that the council separate its political and economic functions. How this separation would have succeeded in minimizing dissension is hard to determine; all decisions affecting the distribution of limited tribal income would have been political decisions. An economic development board composed of Blackfeet stockowners and business leaders, or an "independent" business manager as Interior suggested, may have been separate from the BTBC, but such a board or manager also would have been separate from the voters. And per capita payments, while not a source of stimulation to an economy lacking consumer goods production, nevertheless provided the means for individual investment. A family of five (the average family size on the Blackfeet Reservation) could use its combined payment for the purchase of livestock, farm seed, or other useful purposes; for example, some Blackfeet invested their 1936 Big Claim distribution in education.

As noted in part 1, the BIA refused to facilitate the expansion of Blackfeet *tribal* organizations, sponsoring instead the activities of wealthier Blackfeet who presumably had the business experience to create economic opportunity. The IRA empowered the Blackfeet's duly elected government to pursue tribal projects—land and livestock purchases, credit lending, and the arts and crafts cooperative, among others— which it did, with varying degrees of success, under the guidance of men and women with some knowledge of livestock and business operations. The BTBC's funding of collectives and individual stockowners represented a middle ground between the wholesale distribution of tribal assets and individual economic sovereignty. Given the human and natural ecology of the Blackfeet Reservation, that ground proved to be unstable. The BTBC's challenge was to create a stable political economic environment that could balance the needs of the two factions and stimulate growth in their respective economies.

The BTBC had begun to assume a greater role in the distribution of welfare monies in 1940, in part because oil revenues made it possible and in part because many Blackfeet were leery of becoming dependent on county or state welfare services. The BIA hired a social worker in 1940 to help the tribe administer its relief load. Kate Smith reported that the BTBC's tribal welfare committee had given her "splendid cooperation" in formulating a tribal relief program during her first two years. The Nation's assumption of welfare services had created "a very wholesome attitude" among Blackfeet normally tied to the "old idea that they were entitled to help because they were wards of the government." Smith devised, at Charles Heacock's urging, a tribal public welfare program that categorized Blackfeet families on the basis of income, employability, and eligibility for federal programs such as Aid for Dependent Children (ADC), Old Age Assistance, and Aid for the Needy Blind; state welfare tied eligibility to rental income levels, and thus some Blackfeet preferred to avoid dealing with county agents.[32]

The advent of World War II and the generation of significant oil revenues shifted even further the responsibility for welfare and relief work from the federal government to the tribal government. In 1942, Congress reduced its appropriation of federal relief money for Indians by 20 percent, forcing the OIA to find alternative funding sources and to ask the Blackfeet, and other tribal corporations with revenue streams, to assume the burden of taking care of its citizens. Fred Daiker, the OIA's director of welfare, informed Superintendent Freal McBride that the council needed to assume responsibility by "assisting its own people" and by allocating tribal funds for "the old and indigent, unemployable, and emergency cases." The Blackfeet's action would "enable this Office to provide more adequately for those Indians where no tribal funds are available. . . . We hope that the tribe will accept this responsibility. Not that it helps this Office, but because it helps and provides for its own people."[33] The Blackfeet were doing better than most, he wrote, indicating that the Blackfeet owed it to their fellow Indians. It thus became de facto policy for the OIA to shift the relief burden onto tribes able and willing to support it. The Blackfeet were willing to do it and increasingly able to do so as oil revenues rose. Nevertheless, the added burden created tension between tribal leaders who wanted to use the tribe's Class A (U.S. Treasury) funds for relief purposes and OIA officials who tried to persuade them to protect the tribe's capital by using its Class B (tribal treasury) funds. The amount requested and allotted from Class A funds varied depending upon reservation conditions. In 1943 the tribe received $250 in Class A funds, using $12,029.16 of Class B funds to cover the relief load; in 1944 the tribe did not request any Class A funds.[34] But when the BTBC asked for $12,000 from its Class A account in 1945 the OIA balked. During the war years it became increasingly difficult for some tribes to access their Class A accounts because the government needed the cash reserves to wage war; in 1944 Congress limited to $100,000 the expenditure of *all* Indian Class A money. The OIA elected not to release any of the tribe's Class A funds in 1945 partly because of Congress's cap. If the Blackfeet got $12,000, Daiker told McBride, then "other tribes who are not so fortunate as the Blackfeet with such [a] large income . . . are entirely dependent on the $100,000 item." The OIA, Daiker admitted, also was not in sympathy with the idea of using Class A funds for relief purposes.[35] Such a position was arbitrary, as William Zimmerman put it, but it prevailed because of the OIA's resistance and Congress's restrictions. The OIA thus forced the Blackfeet Nation to assume a greater financial burden while restricting its means to shoulder it.

Daiker also questioned McBride on the kinds of relief listed in the tribe's budget, particularly the appropriation of $10,000 for an emergency sickness fund and $10,000 for burial expenses. McBride explained that the Nation had voted by referendum to create a sick fund and a funeral fund from which all Blackfeet would receive $150 for burial expenses regardless of their economic station. Like per capita distributions, this form of welfare discriminated against poorer Blackfeet simply because those who could afford funerals were eligible whether they needed the money or not. But the vote served as a symbol of the Blackfeet's attempt to preserve certain aspects of the tribal ideal, a way to take care of their own. McBride explained that the BTBC supplemented ADC and other federal programs for those Blackfeet needing glasses, dental work, and special surgery, and the BTBC allocated money to pay for "free milk given out at playgrounds."[36]

The BTBC, acceding to public opinion in cases like burial expenses, took an activist role as welfare provider, trying to fill the deficits created from gaps in the safety nets of state and federal programs. The BTBC and the OIA danced their respective jigs each budget season. Although the council agreed to cap Class A relief expenditures at four thousand dollars per year, the OIA continued to question allotments for the funeral and sick funds, presumably questioning whether the council would spend the money for those purposes. But despite continuing friction over access to Class A funds, diplomatic relations between the BTBC and the OIA were not suffused with the bitterness of the Hazlett years. Council secretary

George Pambrun answered an OIA inquiry about the funeral and sick funds in a methodical and courteous manner, explaining again that the tribe had voted by referendum to create the funds. "We shall be glad to explain further if you wish to have us do so," he closed.[37] Council members had accepted their public responsibility to disburse tribal monies fairly and efficiently. Once charged with providing tribal welfare, however, they would brook no meddling from the OIA in how they did it.

The Blackfeet, like most Americans, mobilized during the war years to both contribute to the nation's cause and take advantage of the opportunities it presented them. More than 250 Blackfeet men and women served in the military in 1943, including most of Charles Reevis's and Joe Brown's children. In early 1942, the Blackfeet superintendent held meetings in the various reservation communities to discuss ways in which tribal members could contribute to the war effort. Twelve community victory committees subsequently formed to spur production of agricultural products for the war machine.[38] Blackfeet also contributed more directly to the war effort. More than 300 Blackfeet, mixed-bloods mostly, migrated to defense jobs in California, Oregon, and Washington, while another 300 or so Blackfeet, most of them full-bloods or near full-bloods, earned income in Washington state's fields of hops and berries, thus helping to feed the nation and its armed forces.[39] The BTBC facilitated this off-reservation employment, providing grants for persons seeking defense work and allotting three thousand dollars in tribal funds to help Blackfeet workers obtain training for defense jobs.[40] Representatives of Boeing and West Coast shipyards recruited in northwestern Montana, advertising for trained mechanics in the *Browning Chief* (originally the *Glacier County Chief*).[41]

CCC-ID representatives helped place Blackfeet in vocational schools to learn mechanical trades, carpentry, and plumbing, and they worked with the state employment office to ensure that Montana received its quota of defense jobs. The tribal council's national defense board provided loans to help Blackfeet attend these schools; Joe Brown made a special effort to ensure that Heart Butte and Old Agency full-bloods had an opportunity to get job training if they qualified. Once employed, Blackfeet could apply for defense or emergency loans of roughly $50 from the council's revolving national defense employment fund to pay for transportation or living expenses; borrowers in turn agreed to tithe 10 percent of their earnings and any money due them from leases or per capita distributions.[42] Brown, a member of the local Selective Service board, traveled to

Seattle in late 1941 to check on the living conditions of Blackfeet laborers and was authorized to extend additional loans to those in need. The council lent tribal money for other defense-related matters. James White Calf, for instance, got $150 to help bring his son home from Europe. In addition, the BTBC donated tribal money to the local Red Cross chapter and to the Browning War Mothers Club, which sent care packages to soldiers, purchased $10,000 in War Bonds, and allocated monies for the planting of victory gardens.[43] In short, the Blackfeet people and the BTBC made every effort to help oil various parts of the nation's war machine.

Despite the migration of able-bodied defense workers and service personnel, income levels rose on the reservation during the war years. Between 1942 and 1944, total individual income rose from just over $950,000 to nearly $1.4 million. Much of the increase was in unearned income—per capita payments, royalties, and lease rentals—though wage income also rose from about $650,000 to $740,000.[44] Family income rose, demonstrating that a middle class was slowly forming: the number of families with more than $1,000 in annual income increased from 400 in 1942 to 550 in 1944; families earning less than $500 decreased from 150 to 35 during the same period. The average income for each of the roughly 800 resident Blackfeet families amounted in 1943 to $1,232.[45]

It is difficult to compare such figures with those for white rural families. Agency personnel compared the 1943 figure with the $965 median net income earned by the nation's farm families between 1935 and 1936, noting that the Blackfeet income in 1943 was "35% above that median."[46] Although the comparison is untenable given the effect of war production on agricultural incomes, the figures indicate that the RCF and CRP clearly had produced general progress in the Blackfeet economy, yielding solid dividends both for individuals and for four livestock cooperatives. Between 1937 and 1945 the Blackfeet Nation used $883,658 in RCF monies. In comparison, Sioux Indians of the Pine Ridge and Rosebud Reservations borrowed just $350,930 during the same period. The Blackfeet figure is significant in that half of the $883,658 was in addition to the federal government's original loan. The fund, therefore, was indeed revolving. In January 1944, the Blackfeet RCF had a surplus for the first time. Loan repayment improved dramatically as well. Of the 576 RCF loan agreements signed since 1937, 403 had been paid in full by 1945, an excellent number considering that 138 new loans had been made in 1945; the rate of repayment of the "troublesome" Special Loans to Aged Indians increased as well.[47] The program's success stemmed from increased demand for agricultural products and the improvement of loan administration, made more manageable in part because wartime employment and military service reduced case loads.[48]

The RCF loans ranged from the $45 given to Rides at the Door to the $8,934 allotted to mixed-blood Eva Hannon. Most of the larger loans went to mixed-blood "clients" of the TMIP, but full-bloods received a proportionate share. Roughly one-third of the loans went to full-blood clients, while mixed-bloods of one-half blood or more received another third.[49] Nearly one hundred families owned flocks of about three hundred head by the end of 1943 because of the RCF. A full-blood partnership grazing sheep borrowed $2,000, pooling its money with other full-bloods who had received loans to form a sheep herd numbering about eighteen hundred head. Twelve full-blood borrowers were able to repay the principal and the interest on schedule, earning slightly higher prices for their wool than those selling individually. This full-blood cooperative combined efforts with other sheep owners, those who had secured loans through other federal programs, to sell a large amount of stock. All the full-blood sheep owners were "pleased with their credit relationship with the tribe," according to credit agent H. D. McCullough. Twelve families, mostly Blackfeet of full- or three-quarters blood, settled on the Badger-Fisher irrigation project. All of them were "greatly pleased at having the opportunity to participate in such a program," according to the extension agent.[50] Some small operators had quit, however, because they lacked "sufficient interest to face the hardships" and strenuous labor of running sheep under the "severe climatic conditions common to the area."[51]

The availability of defense jobs and the heavy demand for agricultural products also were determinant factors in the reduction of welfare rolls and expenditures during the war years. Net relief expenditures in 1943 were down 95 percent from 1940; the number of Blackfeet receiving rations declined from 905 to 174 between 1940 and 1942, and those receiving surplus commodities dropped from 3,300 to 1,851 during the same period. Seventy-five elderly Blackfeet received Old Age Assistance funds; another 173 received ADC monies.[52] These payments were not large, but in combination with per capita payments, supplementary tribal assistance, and, for many families, lease income from grazing permits, the Blackfeet as a nation and as individuals had made important strides toward achieving the goal of self-support, aided in many ways by an activist business council. After the important January 1940 council meeting,

1. Canvas teepees and wagons along lower St. Mary's Lake, ca. 1911. Courtesy of William Farr.

2. Blackfeet Agency, Montana, Willow Creek, 1911. Courtesy of William Farr.

3. First Graduates of the Five Year Industrial Program, Heart Butte, 1921. Courtesy of William Farr.

4. White Grass Chapter, Piegan Farming and Livestock Association, ca. 1924. Courtesy of William Farr.

5. Superintendent Fred C. Campbell and Heart Butte Farmers, 1920s. Campbell is standing, fourth from left. Courtesy of William Farr.

6. Dedication of oil well, ca. 1928. Courtesy of William Farr.

7. Logging crews, 1930s. Courtesy of William Farr.

8. Digging water lines, Blackfeet Agency, 1934. Courtesy of William Farr.

9. Blackfeet full-bloods at Carroll College, 1941. From left: unidentified, Adam Whiteman, Theodore Last Star (?), Rides at the Door, unidentified, Chief Bull (Richard Sanderville), Leo Brown (Joseph Brown's son), Wades in Water, Julia Wades in Water, Fish Wolf Robe. Courtesy of the author (thanks to Lorraine Brown Owens).

10. Full-blood elders in front of Mint Pool Hall, Browning, ca. 1940s. From left: Mike Bad Old Man, Eddie Double Runner, John Mountain Chief, Good Gun, Arrow Top Knot, Rides at the Door, Lazy Boy, Black Weasel, Green Grass Bull, and James White Calf. Courtesy of William Farr.

11. Three generations of Blackfeet women. Courtesy of William Farr.

12. Singers at Sun Dance Encampment, 1943/44. Courtesy of William Farr.

tribal leaders began providing welfare to those who could not for whatever reason prosper through livestock production. This support was in the form of direct aid and discretionary loans to both full-bloods and mixed-bloods who lacked requisite collateral for RCF loans. Council members adopted Joe Brown's motion to distribute ten thousand dollars in new rehabilitation grants to assist "old Indians" who wanted loans for horse teams, wagons, and other items (what became known as the Special Loans to Aged Indians) and voted to allocate to full-blood communities most of the relief funds provided by the federal government. The council also paid for dozens of full-bloods to get rheumatism treatment at the Flathead hot springs and attempted to give full-bloods a more visible political presence, agreeing to permit two elected representatives of their ceremonial committee to attend meetings as nonvoting members.

Although relief monies expended during the war years dropped considerably, they went disproportionately to full-bloods; though representing only 18.3 percent of the tribe's population in 1943, 72 percent of the 112 families receiving direct relief were full-blood, and another 14 percent were of three-quarters blood.[53] Factional problems thus remained despite increases in tribal welfare, employment, and family income. A vocal and insistent minority group continued to protest the council's administration of the IRA, charging discrimination against full-bloods and mismanagement of tribal finances.

John C. Ewers surveyed the tribe's cultural makeup for the agency's 1943 analysis of reservation conditions. Ewers had come to the reservation in 1941, after studying with Clark Wissler at Yale and working briefly with the NPS, to curate the new Museum of the Plains Indian, which was built partly with tribal funds. By 1943 he had become quite familiar with Blackfeet full-bloods, many of whom served as "informants" for his ethnohistorical studies. Ewers argued that the economic status of the full-blood group—in which he included "the great majority of those of a high degree of Indian Blood"—could be addressed only if the "difficult problems for social syncretism" were honestly assessed. Chief among them was the continued practice of certain customs, which created various "impediments to self-support": the interference of full-blood summer dances with agricultural production, the practice of the "give-away" to those less fortunate as a way to enhance social prestige, and the "less-ambitious" family choosing to rely upon the more ambitious for support rather than learning to "stand solidly upon its own foot [sic]." Ewers celebrated the survival of these beliefs and customs, writing that in the face of colonizing influences these full-bloods had "outlived the hostile officials." But the result of this sustained cultural resistance, Ewers believed, was that "in the march of the Blackfeet towards self-support, the full-bloods generally bring up the rear." Ewers considered full-bloods as "a minority group highly conscious of its existence as such—the poorest group economically, the least able to make success of farming, the least qualified for employment for wages, the least able to take advantage of educational opportunities, the least able to understand the intricacies of tribal business, the poorest fed, the poorest housed, with the most limited use of English." He did caution against taking such "generalities too far," arguing that the full-blood group contained many elderly Blackfeet "beyond the age of economic rehabilitation." Younger full-bloods had demonstrated an interest in taking advantage of New Deal reforms and the ability to succeed in livestock production. In contrast to full-bloods, many Blackfeet with less than one-half blood "have long since arrived," Ewers wrote. Just under 45 percent of the tribe's population had less than one-half blood, and as a rule this class displayed "little knowledge or interest" in traditional Blackfeet practices, was better prepared to earn a living, better able to understand formal economic and political institutions, and thus more capable than full-bloods of dominating economic and political life.[54]

Ewers believed that any progress in Blackfeet social unity depended upon the "sympathetic assistance of the more acculturated Indians on the Reservation and of the Indian Office." Despite the BTBC's improved solicitude of full-blood concerns, the issues of oil revenue distribution and political representation stubbornly remained a cause of intratribal tension. Hugh Jackson wrote John Collier in late 1941 to protest the BTBC's expenditure of tribal oil money on council members' salaries and expense accounts. One of Jackson's full-blood friends told him, he wrote Collier, that "they, the *real* [emphasis added] Indians are ignored and penalized under the present set up, insofar as it pertains to having anything to say about their tribal money. . . . Your honor my pure blood friends positively want their oil money paid to them in cash." Jackson indicated that if tribal revenues were "paid out to the rightful owners annually" then discord would disappear. He also warned that if the Blackfeet failed to get the proceeds from "*their* [emphasis added] oil lands" then there would be another "shake-up" in the coming election.[55] The protest against the council's use of tribal funds was both economic and cultural in origin. Full-bloods and mixed-bloods like Jackson objected to mixed-bloods and mixed-blood council members profiting from "their" lands, in part because full-bloods more than any other group had retained their individual allotments and an attendant belief in the sacredness of land. Blackfeet who had sold their allotments had, in effect, given up their rights to earn any income from the land or the oil that lay beneath it.

Assistant Commissioner William Zimmerman responded to Jackson by telling him that the Blackfeet "should be cognizant of their rights under the constitution and of their responsibility in the matter of exercising their influence to see that good government is obtained." He reminded Jackson that his own warning about a possible political shake-up was the answer to his complaint, advising him to exercise his right to vote and effect changes in the constitution.[56] Zimmerman gave a similar response to other letters of protest and petitions. He told John Yellow Kidney in December 1942 that full-blood protests against political discrimination were not warranted; most council members were mixed-bloods because the tribe was "composed largely of mixed-bloods." Zimmerman added that, since the election of three full-blood council members in January 1942, "the proportion of full-blood councilmen is greater than that element of the total population bears to the tribal membership. In other words, the full-bloods already have slightly more than their share of representatives on the council, from a strictly numerical standpoint." Zimmerman also defended the council's "substantial" efforts to provide the Blackfeet with assistance, arguing that it had done its best given the limited resources with which it had to work. Zimmerman patiently and promptly answered letters from full-bloods, explaining the new reality of Blackfeet political life, but neither he nor any other OIA official could reassure these writers that they received fair treatment. Yellow Kidney had argued that "the full-bloods own the reservation." Zimmerman could only explain that under the terms of the IRA "all members of the tribe have [or] own an interest in the reservation."[57] Yellow Kidney's arguments were, perhaps, more untenable or anachronistic than other full-bloods' protests, but the sentiments were the same. Full-bloods, either of an ethnic or a social grouping, considered themselves, as Jackson had argued, the "real Indians" and the "rightful owners" of the reservation and its oil.

There were thoughtful arguments made about the full-bloods' views on post-IRA reservation life. One such statement appeared in a petition that accompanied Yellow Kidney's letter asking for redress. Petitioners argued that under federal supervision full-bloods had received a "fair share of tribal income." Much of the tribe's income now went to cover the BTBC's growing expenses and projects that benefited "the strong and English speaking Indians," several of whom were "merely politicians who often favor relatives and friends." In addition, petitioners claimed that most of the per capita payments went to "Indians who do not need the money." The primary beneficiaries of tribal money were, the petition stated, "mixed blood Indians whose sole need could be fulfilled by the revolving credit loans. A small part of the total income goes to those in desperate need in the form of relief. Most of these are among the full-bloods." The petitioners asked the OIA to reduce council expenses and direct the savings to "the poor, old, and helpless Indians," arguing that it was impossible for full-bloods to effect change themselves as the OIA continually admonished them to do, because "[m]ost of the older generation full bloods are not familiar with the ways of tribal government under constitution, bylaws, and charters, either by custom or through ability to read English. We are smaller in numbers and hence are out-voted. . . . This way of tribal government is not of their making. The way of bringing about justice through tribal government as constituted is therefore closed. Other means must be found if the appeal must be carried to Congress itself." The author closed by writing that "the older and childlike full blood Indian has often less to fear from his conqueror than from some of their own people who have acquired [a] mixture of other blood—the white man's cunning."[58] The petition indicated that there was no chance of reconciliation between older full-bloods and mixed-bloods, regardless of the mixed-bloods' actions; there was no engagement, no dialogue, no hope. If one considers the relations between the full-blood contingent and the mixed-blood council to have been a continual diplomatic negotiation, then a stalemate had occurred.

Actually, 1942 was a good year for full-blood representation. As Zimmerman had pointed out, three of the five full-blood candidates were elected to the business council, all of them coming from the Heart Butte district. In addition, thirteen prominent leaders organized an honorary council to attend BTBC meetings, replacing the ceremonial committee. Zimmerman urged the council to educate the Nation's citizenry and give full-bloods an opportunity to be heard to reduce social conflict: "The effectuation of real self-government is a slow, tedious process and one that requires almost infinite patience and education. Complaints like those raised by Mr. Yellow Kidney are not to be unexpected. . . . It is not so important that a protest arises but the real test of the council is how fairly and constructively it can deal with such complaints to the end that uninformed or misinformed members of the tribe gain an understanding of what representative self-government really is."[59] The BTBC responded by incorporating full-bloods' political views in its deliberations, agreeing to consider full-bloods' written requests and inquiries about council policies and offering to release the minutes of its meetings to preclude any argument about a mixed-blood conspiracy. Judging from the minutes of BTBC meetings, council members did provide full-bloods with opportunities to discuss funding for delegations to Washington, per capita payments, and land claims, and they agreed to their requests for council funding of traditional full-blood celebrations like the annual Fourth of July encampment, emergency loans for fuel or clothing, and beef rations. Joe Brown and other BTBC leaders had taken to heart the OIA's admonition to foster factional peace, and, more important, they acted in accord with their own desire for tribal unity; the council, under Brown's guidance, was trying to develop a modus vivendi and to reduce social tension. For mixed-bloods like Brown, whose mother was a full-blood, helping the elderly "long-hairs" was not seen as a burden but as an honorable obligation, as loyalty to the very idea of social obligation to all tribal members.

Unconvinced, however, the full-blood faction took a different tack in 1943 by calling for agency control over council rule. Faction leaders met with Sen. Burton Wheeler at his vacation home in the summer of 1943 and discussed their fear of being "turned loose" from government supervision; the ceremonial committee had begun discussing this prospect as early as May 1940.[60] Wheeler, in the process of introducing another bill to repeal the Wheeler-Howard Act, encouraged the full-bloods to present their views to Congress and the BIA whenever possible. Charles Reevis subsequently wrote Collier to request funding for a full-blood delegation to present its side of the issues in Washington: "As you know there is a movement on foot to take the Indians who desire to handle their own affairs, and I know that there are many Blackfeet who desire to remain under the protection of the United States. Many of the Indians who say now that they wish all their property turned over to them will sing a different song in a few years when their property is gone. We want to keep ours as it is . . . in trust."[61] Reevis included a petition, signed by 328 Blackfeet, that asked for the Interior Department's *expansion* of control and supervision of tribal affairs and a greater distribution of oil royalties in per capita form. Zimmerman answered for Collier by calmly refuting Reevis's arguments. Addressing Reevis's complaint of council favoritism in the distribution of loans, Zimmerman reported that full-bloods got 128 of the 378 RCF loans. Another 125 of the 378 went to Blackfeet with between one-half and a full degree of blood. The rest of the loans went to Blackfeet with less than one-half Indian blood, though these recipients received a greater percentage of the actual RCF dollars. Zimmerman concluded by offering to assist Reevis's group in preparing amendments to the Blackfeet constitution that would limit the council's expenditures and by encouraging him to participate in the tribal elections scheduled for January 1944.[62]

Zimmerman's letter is a model of patience, information, and respect for the minority viewpoint, but his advice pertained to working within a system that most full-bloods had ceased to recognize as legitimate. "The mixed-bloods are taking everything away from us," one full-blood told John Ewers. Although full-bloods lagged behind the mixed-bloods economically, the informant's statement to Ewers related as much to political as economic aggrandizement; full-bloods objected to what they considered an improper representation on the council.[63] A 1945 petition signed by both full-bloods and "half-bloods" argued that

> down through the centuries the Chiefs and the elders had authority and commanded the respect of the other members. . . . Gradually, the authority of the Chiefs and the rights and privileges of the elders of the Tribe have been almost swept away; and since the adoption . . . of the [IRA], the unity of the Tribe has almost disappeared, and has tended to break up the Tribe entirely and thus scatter abroad [its] members . . . many of whom, because of their lack of education and because of their desire to retain many of their ancient customs, become easy victims of designing men; and, as a result, the welfare of the real Indians, who constitute the real Tribe, is in a bad situation.[64]

The full-bloods' protests were not invalid, but their argument of racial or ethnic discrimination rested on shaky ground. Full-bloods clearly remained the poorest citizens, however, and were thus the most sensitive to class differences. But, as this petition indicates, they had come to recognize that they were on common ground with "half-bloods" as well. In this context, there was a diminishing disjunction between class and ethnic differences. In his analysis of Blackfeet cultural conditions, Ewers argued that between the full-bloods and the "near-whites" existed a large group of Blackfeet "nearly half-white and half-Indian. Some of them tend toward the full-blood characteristics, some toward those of the near-whites."[65] He described the fluid nature of social and political alignment based on economic progress, the shifting ground of Blackfeet class relations. Between these two poles of racial and cultural imbalance lay this large group of Blackfeet—the silent Blackfeet majority, as it were—compellingly drawn to the goal of economic security rather than to an amorphous blood or tribal loyalty that had failed to provide commensurate political advantage, a protean demos that increasingly responded to issues of class rather than race or ethnicity. The exploding population of mixed-bloods sharpened the full-bloods' sense of cultural self. The incipient class consciousness affected full-bloods and mixed-bloods alike and reinforced a politics of difference that was based on economic rather than cultural considerations.

The protests and petitions of the minority group likely contributed to the decision of the Special Investigating Committee of the House Committee on Indian Affairs to visit the reservation during its summer 1944 tour of Indian America, part of Congress's renewed effort to answer the "Indian question." The tour also was designed to drum up justification for Senator Wheeler's IRA repeal bill and to generate support for terminationist legislation initiated by Republican critics of John Collier and his BIA. The BIA came under fire in 1943 from both houses of Congress, in part because it was weakened by appropriations cuts due to the war and because the ideological nature of the war stimulated a new round of assimilationist activity among Indian Affairs committee members. Senate Partial Report 310 followed Rep. Karl Mundt's introduction of House Resolution 166 calling for an "investigation of Indian conditions," both serving as attacks on Collier and as programmatic blueprints for dismantling the BIA. Although Sen. Elmer Thomas submitted the Senate report, Wheeler contributed to its writing, one of several actions he took to deconstruct the Indian New Deal bureaucracy.[66] Mundt, Wheeler, and Rep. James O'Connor of Montana spent August 4 in Browning hearing both council members and their detractors debate the relative merits of the IRA. The act's most ardent congressional foes thus confronted its most assiduous Indian defenders. The hearing, then, provides a good look at the contours of an emerging shift in Indian-white relations.

O'Connor, the committee chairman, explained at the outset that his committee's goal was to "try to rehabilitate the Indians so they may be assimilated into the American way of life and not be in the reservation like a concentration camp; for, after all, a reservation is only a step or two from a concentration camp."[67] Such visceral imagery appealed both to critics of the IRA and to critics of the BIA. With one exception, full-bloods criticized the IRA and the BTBC's distribution of tribal revenue. Some witnesses simply testified that the IRA should be "abolished" and "erased." Reevis exposed the weakness of his faction's position when he testified that after ten years "my people do not understand [the IRA]. . . . Each year we just cannot understand it. I want to get rid of the [IRA]." He labeled the IRA "a nuisance."[68]

Wheeler encouraged these critics, as did O'Connor, who noted that "real Indians, fullblood Indians" should have the right to send delegations to Washington. Wheeler and Joe Brown sparred over the IRA's merits, as they had ten years earlier during the 1934 hearings. Brown reminded Wheeler that the tribe had adopted the IRA because "it gave us powers that we had never had before. It gave us the chance to use our funds; it gave us the chance to get credit and we have under it all of those things and they have helped us, and we fear that if the act were thrown out and we had to go back to the old system that we could not get the advantages that we have now." Brown also defended the council's record as a loan agency and its members' right to secure loans themselves, provided that they met the requisite criteria. Most council members were ranchers and farmers; they derived little income from political service. William Buffalohide and Joe Ironpipe supported Brown's testimony, countering that of Reevis and White Calf. Ironpipe, the BTBC vice chairman, vigorously defended the council's distribution of RCF monies, arguing that it was the Extension Division that had final approval on all loans. "We are trying to be fair with the Blackfeet Tribe, in fact more than fair," he said, listing for the committee the kinds of services given to full-bloods: loans, relief, beef rations, and financial support of cultural events.[69]

Mundt alone seemed interested in examining the actual details of the IRA's operation and the reason for full-bloods' discontent. For instance, he asked Middle Rider why he disliked the IRA. Middle Rider told him that he had had two horses before it passed and that now he had none.[70] Mundt also seemed more aware of the need to find a middle ground between "competent" and "incompetent" Indians, maintaining that "the problem before us is how to apply an Indian program which will do justice to both groups." Though an ardent assimilationist, Mundt showed a greater respect toward Blackfeet sovereignty than did Wheeler and O'Connor. Mundt urged the BTBC to help Congress "take care of the Indian problem" by transferring as many "competent" Indians as possible "from the tribal status onto the white man's status." And he asked it to determine when the tribe could "administer and finance its own affairs without any help whatsoever from the Indian Office, provided we can work out a system to give you the authority. We want this reorganization to come from you."[71] Mundt, in effect, argued that the IRA did not go far enough in expanding self-government, and he encouraged another reorganization of tribal affairs to ensure that the Nation could get the proper authority to manage the Blackfeet Reservation like any other rural community government.

Leaders of both tribal factions did agree that the Blackfeet should assume various BIA functions. The prevailing attitude among the Blackfeet, according to Brown, was that the BIA should be "cut to the bone." Leo Kennerly wanted "an organization of our own, run by our own people without any strings attached from the Washington office." Kennerly led a pro-termination faction, which "recommended the complete abolishment of the Indian Bureau as the business conducted through that channel can be conducted by our local tribal council." Kennerly indicated that the tribe would soon exercise its right to request the termination of certain supervisory functions of the Interior Department, a provision with which Wheeler was unfamiliar.[72] Tribal leaders considered the Extension and Forestry Divisions particularly expendable. Brown elicited applause when he testified that "capable and competent" Blackfeet could perform the functions of those divisions and do them "more economically." This argument played better with committee members than did his defense of the IRA. O'Connor and Wheeler had become alarmed by the increase of BIA personnel on Indian reservations; O'Connor noted that he saw a "regular city here of official residences."[73]

Wheeler and O'Connor refused, however, to acknowledge the tribe's support for the IRA. O'Connor told the crowd that he and Wheeler "do not think it has been working satisfactorily . . . [so] I want you to feel that we are with you in that respect." He disingenuously claimed that "the opinion here, apparently almost unanimously, is that you are opposed to the continuation of this act." Councilman Richard Grant, annoyed by such grandstanding, asked O'Connor an interesting question: "Mr. Chairman, have you anything in mind that you are going to present that will be better than the Wheeler-Howard Act?" O'Connor answered, "I do not believe that anybody has thought through on the matter and has figured out something to take its place."[74] Mundt offered only that the tribe could hold periodic referenda on whether to continue the act or, as Wheeler put it, "get out from under it." Brown and his colleagues generally supported the idea of putting any issue to a vote, whether it was a referendum on reservation liquor sales or an amendment to abolish the IRA. "That is democracy," Brown told Wheeler. Neither dissenting members of Congress like Wheeler nor disgruntled Blackfeet like Reevis discussed or delineated alternatives to the IRA. It is ironic, of course, that the very people Wheeler and O'Connor defended were the people least likely to assimilate into the American mainstream. While defending "real" Indians who would never become "white" culturally or economically, terminationist congressional representatives remained hostile to leaders such as Joe Brown, who shared their intellectual inclination for assimilation and the concomitant termination of federal supervision and had a genuine solicitude for full-bloods and their needs.

If the Blackfeet had not adopted the IRA in 1934, then the tribe likely would not have experienced growth in agriculture and ranching, nor would it have succeeded to the extent it did in oil leasing. Certainly the tribe's government, the BTBC, would have had less money to distribute to its constituents in the form of gratis services, such as rations, relief grants, and supplemental funds for housing and health, and much less to distribute in the form of per capita payments because of Congress's opposition to such payments. For at least a decade the BTBC and groups like the BIWA had been petitioning the OIA and Congress to release its Class A funds, usually with little success. If the tribe had not adopted the IRA, then either Congress or the OIA would have controlled the distribution of oil revenues. Thus full-bloods would have had an even harder time prying money from the tribal accounts, even if one considers that an increased number of Blackfeet would have joined the protests. The political effects of not having an IRA would have been an increasing centralization of mixed-blood power, producing a cycle of BIA intervention and mixed-blood resistance. The federal government would have become, therefore, a stronger and increasingly coercive presence in the reservation political economy. Some tribes, the Arapahos in particular, succeeded without the IRA. The Blackfeet, as tribal and OIA leaders continued to argue, and as economic data suggests, did better by being "under it."

The Blackfeet Nation's constitution and its right to call referenda remained the best instruments, as OIA personnel had argued since 1935, for changing patterns of tribal income distribution, political representation, and economic investment. Accordingly, in March 1945 the BTBC organized a constitutional convention to consider amendments to the Nation's governing political framework and to prepare for changes in Indian-white relations. After the August 1944 subcommittee hearing George Pambrun and Leo Kennerly had met with OIA officials in Chicago to discuss the ways and means of improving self-government on the reservation. From the hearing and the meeting with OIA officials, BTBC leaders like Kennerly, Brown, and Pambrun had become keenly aware that Congress was eclipsing Collier and the BIA in political influence, and they reasoned that the Blackfeet Nation needed to prepare for changes in federal supervision on its own terms—a reflection of the BTBC's pragmatic approach to intergovernmental relations. Brown and other council members had read House Report 2091, the product of the House subcommittee's 1944 tour, which had outlined an agenda for voluntary termination of federal supervision and trust protection. The balanced report acknowledged both the benefits of the IRA and the need for a measured approach to the integration of "competent" Indians into the American mainstream. Although terminationist in spirit, it reflected Mundt's belief in noncoercive assimilation and thus the important recognition that one could not legislate changes in Indian affairs as if Indians were a homogeneous socioeconomic entity.[75]

On April 23, 1945, Joe Brown welcomed BTBC members and twenty-five delegates from the reservation's various communities to open what would become a nine-day meeting; the gathering represented a good cross section of Blackfeet leaders, including nine influential full-bloods, and Mary Salois and Mae Williamson, the Nation's most influential women. Brown told the delegates that the Blackfeet should be ready to offer their own recommendations for another round of reorganization when "Congress change[d] policies." Kennerly added, "We have been held back by the Indian Office on the things that we would like to do and it is not our constitution that stops us." Although the Blackfeet were better prepared than most tribes to make progress in self-governance, Kennerly said, the council wanted to "put more teeth" in the tribal constitution to do it.[76] Full-blood delegates were encouraged to take their copy of the constitution out of the trunk and to get acquainted with it before beginning discussions about changing it. For BTBC leaders, the convention represented a chance to discuss in public and in detail the constitution's benefits and thus defend the IRA and the council, both of which had come under heavy criticism since 1942. The convention became a referendum on the IRA and an opportunity to strengthen its instruments to face the changes many leaders felt would begin drifting west from congressional corridors in the coming years. The Blackfeet people, they believed, needed to prepare for these changes as they would prepare for annual snowstorms or else face the consequences of getting buried politically.

In his review of House Report 2091, Brown explained to the gathering that while Congress wanted to reduce the BIA's operations, subcommittee members had discovered during its grand tour that "Indians are not ready to be turned loose" and that Congress thus had not "discharged its obligation to the Indians." Despite this assessment, Brown asked tribal members to take pride in their accomplishments; the Blackfeet had made greater progress and were "smarter" than most Indians, he said. He asked the assembly to consider how they had progressed since the turn of the century. When Congress complained about Indians' poor education and health, it did not refer to the Blackfeet Nation. The Blackfeet had progressed on their own by seeking higher education, and as a result, tribal members were attending college, teaching school, and filling positions in the county government. Blackfeet politicians had succeeded in securing federal funds for a reservation hospital during the 1930s and were now taking care of their people with a sick fund created by a democratic vote. The Nation's leaders were always planning ahead, Brown believed, largely by taking responsibility for tribal affairs using the IRA constitution as a guide. The IRA constitution "protected" the Nation's citizens from "the white man's intrusions," Brown stated, and he urged the gathering to make use of the convention to strengthen this legal foundation and ensure continued progress on Blackfeet terms. Addressing the full-blood delegates, Brown affirmed that council members were "just as red-blooded and their feeling for you people is paramount, and they are doing everything that is humanly possible to help you."[77]

Brown had been a powerful force for the sustained integration of the tribe on racial and cultural terms, consistently extolling the value of blood unity and respect for elders; he had worked with FYIP leaders during the 1920s and retained considerable influence with full-bloods, in some ways resembling a hereditary chief. Theodore Last Star responded to Brown's statement by saying that full-bloods were relieved to hear that Congress did not plan to "turn us loose in the very near future" and asked all delegates to get together and devise a workable reservation economy. Mixed-blood Francis Guardipee expressed sadness that blood brothers had failed to grasp the meaning of the word "cooperate." He said it was time for leaders to operate on the "cancer" threatening tribal unity and "prove to the outside that the Blackfeet Indian is capable of looking after his own business."[78] The prevailing sentiment was that the Blackfeet Nation had to move toward self-termination—or self-determination, to use its vernacular cousin—on its own terms. If it did not, Congress would dictate the terms and control the process.

Members of both factions spoke urgently about providing returning veterans and younger Blackfeet with a viable program of work and establishing a diversified economic agenda in the event the tribe's oil supplies dried up like a dust bowl grazing range. Brown invited Theodore Haas, the BIA's chief counsel, to discuss the status of the tribe's funds and the council's power to distribute them. Haas used the phrase "benefit the tribe as a whole" several times during his talk, emphasizing the need for coordinated development that would ensure a steady revenue stream not contingent upon sustained oil flow. OIA officials were concerned that if the tribe's oil revenues decreased or were "spent entirely on per capita payments, it is possible the future Blackfeet generation may be in a critical condition." Per capita payments jeopardized a tribe's capital wealth, Haas argued, likening them to selling one's cow rather than its offspring. He sanctioned instead investment vehicles like war bonds, land purchases, and livestock enterprises. "You know much more about your reservation than I do," he concluded, "but I know that some of your leaders could plan the proper use of these Tribal funds in a better way than just distributing them and not investing them." Other IRA tribes had succeeded in generating tribal wealth "through a wise use of their tribal income. I know that you can do the same," Haas said.[79]

Brown was especially grateful for Haas's "independent presentation" of financial options. He told the delegates that Haas "explained to you . . . the sentiments that have been in my head for many years . . . but I was prevented from expressing those views because if I did, you would be on my neck, particularly so with this per capita payment that we have been making here every year." Brown had felt such enormous pressure from the people to turn the Big Claim into per capita payments in 1936 that he in turn pressured Congress to make the eighty-five-dollar payment. "Today that money is all gone," he said. Brown acknowledged that the pressure for per capita payments would continue, but he cautioned delegates that "it is just as Mr. Haas told you, that unless you put your money into something to bring your money back, you are sure to fail, as soon as your oil wells dwindle down and that is sure to come. Your income will be exhausted."[80] Brown defended the BTBC's programs, which matched his personal vision of sanitary homes, improved health, and expanded stock operations, by outlining the council's funding of home construction, medical treatment, and repayment cattle.

By explaining to the full-blood faction and other interested Blackfeet where their money had been going, Brown succeeded to a great extent in presenting a view of the council as well-meaning in its control of the reservation economy. He admitted, however, that a certain segment of the tribe did not wish to support stockowners and wanted the cash instead. Brown thus failed to satisfy those Blackfeet who could not secure loans because of insufficient collateral or those who had little inclination to begin a stock enterprise, as well as those of the perennially disgruntled minority who continued to believe, as Reevis put it, "that the Superintendent's office is a good place to deposit our money. The Blackfeet Tribal office cost too much on overhead expenses."[81] Reevis's attacks led to an extended discussion of the IRA and a nonbinding vote on its future. Twenty-eight of the thirty-four delegates present voted to retain the IRA. A surprising number of full bloods stood in support of it. Six full-bloods stood to reject it, though two of them praised the act's ability to help younger Indians; Juniper Old Person captured the ambivalence of older full-bloods when he said that "my children got a start under the Wheeler-Howard Act and I feel proud of them and they will feed me."[82] Both the vote and the subsequent testimony of full-bloods indicated that the meeting succeeded in educating several Blackfeet "uninformed or misinformed" about the IRA's value. Many of the delegates told Joe Brown afterward that they learned for the first time what the council did with tribal funds. As a result, Mae Williamson recommended that the council hold similar meetings once a year to air grievances and keep the Blackfeet citizenry informed about the council's activities.

Although mixed-blood council members dominated the important resolutions committee, in the spirit of tribal unity they sanctioned the right of the older Indians to determine the tribe's membership requirement, an important role for full-bloods complaining of mixed-blood influence and their own loss of status in tribal decision-making. Kennerly told full-bloods to codify a blood quantum dividing line, which would allow them to decide who could be a "member of the Blackfeet Tribe." The membership committee recommended that Blackfeet with one-sixteenth degree of blood or greater should retain eligibility for per capita payments and other benefits; in addition, enrolled members had to maintain residence or a regular presence on the reservation to receive those benefits. The vote of the delegates was nearly unanimous—thirty-four to two. Several committee members were loath to exclude anyone with any Blackfeet blood, and delegates tacitly agreed that exceptions could be made to the new rule if circumstances warranted them. This elasticity reflected the heightened ambivalence of full-blood delegates forced to circumscribe the very notion of Indianness despite the deleterious effects of heirship problems and their avowed resistance to the influence of "white" Indians on tribal affairs.[83]

The membership committee also recommended to the general convention that the tribe continue to elect thirteen representatives to the council rather than reduce the number to five or nine.[84] The motion to retain thirteen members carried unanimously. The attendant motion to elect these thirteen by popular vote passed by twenty-seven to nine, though to amend the constitution the tribe would have to hold a referendum later that year. Leo Kennerly sanctioned the popular vote, arguing that Blackfeet soldiers were fighting and dying in Europe to preserve democracies in which "the majority shall rule."[85] There was, as could be expected, some dissatisfaction with this measure. Peter Grant Blackface, for example, claimed that the popular vote would allow greater manipulation of candidates in predominantly full-blood districts. The nine votes against the measure may well have come from full-bloods who understood quite clearly that in their traditional political system and in their extant demographic situation the word "majority" had no meaning. For all this, though, the convention yielded a civil meeting of informal and formal political cultures and provided full-bloods a chance to help define "the real Indians, who constitute the real Tribe."

The delegates also voted to create a scholarship fund of five thousand dollars to help Blackfeet attend college. In addition, they elected to assert the tribe's right to run the extension program, to allocate three hundred thousand dollars to expand the tribal livestock and oil industry, and to sanction the "issuance of certificates of competency to qualified members of the tribe desiring to renounce membership."[86] The last measure is of singular importance. An undercurrent of terminationist thinking surfaced during the meeting, both in the resolutions adopted and in the speeches emphasizing the Blackfeet's right to manage their own affairs. An interesting social disjunction thus found political expression during the convention: full-bloods decided which Blackfeet could retain tribal membership, while a nonbinding resolution offered successful Blackfeet an opportunity to resign that membership. Although it became easier for some full-bloods to accept the IRA and the Blackfeet government it produced, responding favorably to self-terminationist arguments was another matter. Some full-bloods feared that an expansion of self-government initiated by members eager to divide the tribal estate would both reduce their sustained access to tribal revenue and create political conditions in which their release from government supervision would become codified against their will.

Full-bloods expressed these sharpened fears in several postconvention meetings with BIA officials. Despite the BTBC's dissemination of information and what appeared to be improved interfaction relations, members of the Reevis group went to Chicago to seek succor from the Indian Office. In May, Reevis, John Yellow Kidney, and three other delegates met with new commissioner William A. Brophy, field representative D'Arcy McNickle, Felix Cohen, and Walter Woehlke to present what they called "their list of complaints against self-government." The faction continued to protest the BTBC's ethnic composition, complaining that the IRA had forced the tribe's transition from a political system led by "hereditary leaders" to one led by young mixed-blood council members. "Full-bloods were not accustomed to selection of representatives by popular election" or "familiar with the white man's methods of democratic politics," delegates claimed, and thus after the tribe adopted the IRA the older "uneducated full-bloods . . . suddenly lost [their] leadership and influence and became a minority."[87]

It is important to note that the delegates ignored the thirty-year history of the BTBC—on which leading full-bloods like White Calf and Rides at the Door had once served—and the extant makeup of the council to which they were opposed; the 1944 council contained three full-bloods and three members with a blood quantum higher than one-half, as well as four half-bloods. The problem for the Reevis faction was that the full-blood council members supported the IRA and opposed their agenda; they were also younger and better educated than Reevis and Yellow Kidney, sixty-eight and seventy-five years old, respectively. The Reevis faction contained, with the exception of Reevis himself, mostly older first-generation uneducated full-bloods. OIA officials tried to defend the IRA and its flexibility, encouraging the group to exercise its right to form a subsidiary organization, such as a "full blood welfare organization," and try to secure funds with which it might administer programs on a local basis. Brophy told Joe Brown after the May meeting that though OIA officials did their best to mediate the dispute and help with "reconciling the old men to the new way," it remained the BTBC's "grave duty" to reduce social conflict by responding to the concerns of its critics. "In effect," Brophy wrote, "the council is on trial before its own people."[88] Brophy visited the reservation that July to continue discussions and sanctioned Felix Cohen's proposal to foster a separate full-blood organization chartered to assist older Indians. Reevis failed to act on Cohen's idea or offer any substantive proposals of his own except one that would distribute to tribal members 85 percent of all gross revenue. The protests continued.

The OIA responded by sending D'Arcy McNickle to the reservation in early November to mediate the ongoing civil conflict. McNickle, a Flathead Indian and one of the founders of the new National Congress of American Indians (NCAI), spent four days meeting with the minority group and the council it opposed. The IRA was not "magical," McNickle explained, but it did grant Indians the right to manage their own property and finances and to foster independent decision-making. The Blackfeet's constitution was "a living thing" and could be changed, just as the U.S. Constitution had been amended. McNickle emphasized the need for all Blackfeet to "think for themselves" and not "wait for the government to do things for them."[89] Several of the speakers referred to McNickle as a white man or as the "little boy"; McNickle's Indian heritage appeared to have little effect on most full-bloods. And most of them had little interest in the feature of independent decision-making that McNickle championed. White Calf spoke for many when he said that he wanted to be protected by the BIA. This isolationist wing had no interest in becoming a "full-pledged" citizen. "I am going to stay an Indian," Chewing Blackbones said. The fear of termination dominated full-blood testimony, as did the council's misuse of tribal funds. "The money problem is the only thing that causes trouble among the Blackfeet," Three Calves told McNickle. Three Calves asked the gathering, "Why is it I wear such poor clothes when I come from an oil community[?] Everyone should have an equal share in the oil money. I am almost starving, and the poor mixed-bloods are in the same position." Other witnesses exhibited a similar class consciousness. Chewing Blackbones said he remained poor while wealthy Blackfeet drove "a shiny car."[90] McNickle pointed out that Reevis's proposal to transfer oil revenues to the agency superintendent for distribution could backfire if a new Congress decided to use the money to pay for the local administration of Blackfeet affairs: "All you people seem to harbor the opinion that it would be nice if the Government were handling your money. But it *would not* be what you think, I can assure you." The Blackfeet could become "beggars" if Congress began "spending it for you," McNickle added.[91] George Pambrun had told full-bloods a day earlier, "You folks have to learn to look ahead and not just think of today."[92]

For many of the older full-bloods like Three Calves and Chewing Blackbones, several years was a long time to wait for an investment to produce dividends. For more than two decades these elderly Blackfeet had waited for the oil excitement to turn into a cash bonanza. Now that the money was flowing, they did not want to wait and did not think they should have to wait. Many could not wait. Full-bloods remained divided on the issue of the IRA and the council, however. Several speakers, perhaps swayed by the constitutional convention, offered that they wanted to "hang with the council" and admonished dissenters to examine the tribal books if they suspected corruption. Wades in the Water, the former chief of police and a longtime political activist, asked his fellow full-bloods why no one blamed the BIA. "Stop criticism of the Council," he said, urging them to recognize its accomplishments.[93] The constant criticism angered Joe Brown. "You [full-bloods] do not give us credit for any help whatever," he said. As in April, Brown passionately defended the IRA and the BTBC's expenditures on tribal health, education, and economic programs, offering that "any member of the Indian race is privileged to examine any business handled through the Tribal Council."[94] Brown had heeded the OIA's call to respect minority viewpoints and address full-bloods' complaints. He got little respect in return. For a man who devoted much of his adult life to tribal politics and economic development, and who acknowledged during the meeting that he had little time left to give the tribe, the criticism was particularly painful.

Joe Brown's "exceedingly able presentation" should have "satisfied any listener as to the earnestness with which the council has gone about its business," McNickle informed Zimmerman after the meeting. As for Reevis, the council's principal antagonist, McNickle told Zimmerman that he had "smoked him out of the position he had been taking and he was looking for a new base from which to operate."[95] McNickle also thanked Brown directly for doing "everything humanly possible" to facilitate a productive discussion of tribal affairs. McNickle urged Brown to continue his efforts to foster confidence in the council among those

Blackfeet in outlying districts and to foster educational programs. Like Brown, McNickle placed great emphasis on training young people to assume important positions on the reservation. Lastly, he recommended that Brown keep Reevis and other disgruntled Blackfeet involved in the political process. He noted the "time, effort and money you have already expended in behalf of achieving harmony in the Tribe." Keeping the minority group involved, he wrote, would be a "cheap investment" in a more stable future.[96]

Blackfeet full-bloods received a fair hearing in Washington and in several public meetings devoted mainly to addressing their dissatisfaction with tribal affairs; they enjoyed both the vigilance of the OIA and the solicitude of the BTBC. By the end of 1945, the council leadership and the OIA had convinced some members of the minority group that the IRA worked and that the BTBC had at least tried to make it work for their benefit. The council helped fund their annual encampment, paid for special medical treatment on many occasions, and included political groups in most council meetings. Not once during the subcommittee hearing, the constitutional convention, or the public meetings did a full-blood complain of religious or cultural persecution. Blackfeet full-bloods fared better than their counterparts did on reservations like the Rosebud, where full-bloods faced a mixed-blood council hostile to traditional customs.[97] Records indicate that full-bloods did not face discrimination from council loan boards, though some applicants were handicapped by a lack of collateral. Full-bloods received more RCF loans than did Blackfeet with between one-half and full blood and those with less than one-half blood, though their actual dollar total was much less than the other groups'. The statistics of lending on the Blackfeet Reservation point to a relatively equitable distribution of RCF monies, especially if the full-bloods' demographic disadvantage and general lack of requisite collateral are taken into account; council favoritism, to a certain extent, affected the shape of the lending program, but it did not impair it or prevent widespread participation.[98]

Both Brown and McNickle used the word "disgruntled" to describe the full-blood faction, which would remain critical of the council, "egged on in part by Charles Reevis," as McNickle put it. Given the dispute over his blood quantum, his unrealistic proposals for full-blood control of the BTBC, and his ill-advised transfer of funds to agency control, Reevis seemed to offer little to his group or to his tribe. He had at one point threatened to "segregate" full-bloods from mixed-bloods, a proposal that would have further isolated full-bloods from reservation affairs. At the same time, Reevis and full-blood leaders succeeded in waging a remarkable campaign to keep the "poor Indian"—both mixed-blood and full-blood—involved in and the object of Blackfeet politics. It was, in a sense, a campaign for civil rights in the context of tribal affairs. Most important, the minority group had legitimate complaints about the BTBC. Under pressure from his colleagues, George Pambrun was forced to repay a delinquent loan secured from tribal funds. A shadowy character named C. R. Teter, under contract to the council to sell oil contracts and ensure white oil operators' fidelity to lease terms, created grave questions about the council's management of tribal oil assets. A related problem involved the granting of "preference rights" to oil tracts to certain tribal members—notably Levi Burd and Wright Hagerty, the wealthiest Blackfeet—rather than seeking the highest return from competitive bidding. In 1944, Kennerly, Brown, and Pambrun had warned the OIA that oil operators were attempting to bribe council members and influence council elections, charges that Superintendent McBride considered more a reflection of the Blackfeet's sensitivity to oil profits than an actual incidence of corruption.[99] These problems affected not just full-bloods but all tribal members who depended on oil revenues—whether for per capita distributions or for tribal loans—in part because the problematic situation reflected a tendency of some council members to ignore BIA proscriptions or exploit weaknesses in the Blackfeet constitution and charter. Most Blackfeet, then, faced a termination or at least a suspension of federal control outside the IRA's parameters and beyond the purview of the Interior Department's political authority to regulate economic affairs.

As the BTBC continued to respond to external forces pushing the idea of termination, these protests became louder. The BTBC's assumption of BIA functions, however gradual, meant more expenses for the tribe and thus less money for per capita distribution. It also meant less federal guardianship and thus less vigilance against mixed-blood domination or exploitation of the economy. The idea of self-support no longer appealed to all Blackfeet. Many full-bloods had previously embraced the promise of a self-supporting condition created largely by the money produced from tribal oil fields. Self-support for aging full-bloods, and mixed-bloods to an increasing extent, had become impossible, either on their own or through family networks; resources were stretched too thin by the practice of the give-away. Full-bloods in particular decided that they stood a better chance of surviving with the government of the white man than with a self-governing tribal council composed of mixed-bloods and even unsympathetic full-bloods. A big gulf loomed, therefore, between those choosing guardianship and those pursuing "full-pledged" citizenship. The tribal ideal, the loyalty to the notion of tribal obligation, remained important for many Blackfeet leaders struggling under pressure from the OIA and their own sense of social responsibility to preserve racial harmony and mitigate class conflict to create the stable future of which D'Arcy McNickle spoke, even as they individually pursued the assimilated ideal. The tribal ideal was increasingly less valid for those who considered themselves "the real Indians, who constitute the real Tribe." The full-bloods' fear of being "turned loose" and their diminishing political power were obviously related issues. McNickle's visit represented the literal and symbolic arrival of a new breed of Indian—well educated, progressive, impatient for Indian control of reservation functions, and interested in enlarging the scope of Indian politics to a national context. Several full-bloods spoke against pan-Indian organizations like the NCAI (which held its second convention on the Blackfeet Reservation just two weeks before the McNickle meeting), in part because they feared that tribes with "very small property" would seek help from the Blackfeet and reduce the tribe's assets. Given demographic and political trends, full-bloods' efforts to mitigate their minority status faced serious obstacles. Faced with a sympathetic but mostly inert Indian Office and a sometimes recalcitrant BTBC, the minority group had nowhere to go except the voting booth. Despite making the empty threat to "segregate," full-bloods politicized by recent public meetings chose to stay and fight using the tools of the IRA, the fountainhead of their discontent.

In late 1945, the Blackfeet Nation voted on two important measures, one economic, one political. Mixed-blood entrepreneur John Galbraith had for two decades championed the idea that the Blackfeet should invest in their own oil operation and claim 100 percent of the profits rather than the 12.5 or 17.5 percent typically earned. In January 1944, largely on the strength of his promise to increase per capita payments significantly, Galbraith gained a council seat, through which he began lobbying anew for a tribal oil venture. In November, the council dispatched him and Leo Kennerly to Washington to secure a Reconstruction Finance Corporation (RFC) loan for tribal drilling. Such an investment was extremely risky given the costs associated with oil exploration and the uneven history of drilling on tribal land. As a result, RFC officials declined to provide a loan simply on the basis of oil prospects, but they did agree in principle to granting a loan using a portion of existing oil revenues as collateral. Section 5(g) of the Nation's corporate charter prohibited the use of such revenue as collateral for loans, however, and thus the BTBC decided by unanimous vote to put the charter amendment to a referendum. After first rejecting Galbraith's proposal, council members resolved that they should not "make a final decision without enabling the members of the Tribe to express their views in a referendum." Despite reservations about Galbraith as a businessman and the project itself, Interior approved a referendum on a modified proposal to borrow two hundred thousand dollars using 10 percent of tribal oil income as collateral.[100] On October 3, 1945, Blackfeet voters soundly rejected the measure by a vote of 543 to 55.[101]

The margin of defeat indicated that Blackfeet voters had their own concerns about Galbraith, his proposals, and the council's ability to manage a difficult operation in competition with white experts. Voters, at least those willing to go to the polls, sent the message that oil development was best left to white businessmen. The council's granting of preference rights to wealthy Blackfeet probably convinced many voters that an Indian-run operation would suffer from favoritism and from corruption, given the allegations that white oil operators meddled in council elections. In a larger sense the vote also served as a rejection of the idea of self-termination. Voters decided, in effect, to retain government supervision of their oil resources. It is telling that the proposal generated such little support. Mixed-blood voters outnumbered full-bloods by a large margin, and thus the decision had less to do with blood-based factionalism than with class issues. Voters concerned about losing tribal loans or per capita payments elected not to take a risk. On November 30, Blackfeet voters defeated by a vote of 532 to 244 a similar referendum that proposed the sale of the Nation's "participating royalty interest" in drilling contracts for a lump sum. The BTBC, in a sense, tried an end run around the previous vote; the council could have used the proceeds from the sale to invest in a tribal oil industry.[102] A clear majority of the Blackfeet electorate again expressed its disapproval of the council's economic agenda.

The political referendum held on November 30 fared better. Arguments for amending the constitution to permit the election of council members by popular vote rather than by district residents had been made since 1937. A 1938 referendum passed by a wide margin, but the Interior Department disallowed it because officials did not approve the election, as the Blackfeet constitution required. It is questionable whether the popular vote would increase full-blood representation, as supporters like John Galbraith claimed. It seemed to follow that full-bloods concentrated in the Old Agency and Heart Butte districts would protect their local political position rather than take their chances reservation-wide.[103] It did make sense, however, to Starr School full-bloods like James White Calf, who had been overwhelmed by mixed-blood voters in the Browning district in which Starr School rested. But by 1945 a consensus had emerged among both full-blood and mixed-blood political leaders that the Nation should adopt the popular vote amendment. Some proponents argued that it would reduce full-blood discrimination; others asserted that every Blackfeet had the right to vote on each candidate because the financial stakes of council management were so high. A referendum amending Article III, section 2 of the Blackfeet constitution, approved by the secretary of the interior this time, passed by a vote of 515 to 305 on November 30. The measure needed only the secretary's approval to make the Blackfeet one of just four Indian nations to amend their IRA constitution.[104] Oscar Chapman, assistant secretary of the interior, failed to see the wisdom of the change, however, believing that the amendment would further reduce minority representation. He asked Superintendent McBride to assemble full-bloods and poll their views on the proposed change before he would approve it.[105] A large number of full-bloods gathered on January 11, 1946, to debate the merits of the change. Eighteen of the most influential leaders of the "minority group" stood to support the amendment; only Charles Reevis had reservations. McBride searched for any of the 305 Blackfeet who had voted against the measure, finding only 2 among the 135 assembled. Satisfied that Blackfeet full-bloods supported the constitutional amendment, Chapman approved it on January 18.[106]

In the January 22, 1946, council election, the first conducted under the new system, just three of the thirteen incumbents were reelected. Joe Brown survived, though he garnered the fewest number of votes of the thirteen elected; Brian Connolly and Charles Higgins of the isolated Seville district also retained their seats.[107] Not one of the three Heart Butte council members won reelection. And not one true full-blood won a seat, though the three new council members from Heart Butte were of eleven-sixteenths, thirteen-sixteenths, and three-quarters blood quantum, respectively. Charles Reevis, though half-blood, was the most vocal leader of the "full-blood" group elected to the council. Full-blood incumbents

William Buffalohide and Joe Ironpipe received little help from Starr School and Heart Butte voters, who supported as many mixed-bloods as full-bloods; Starr School voters gave full-blood activist Theodore Last Star only six votes, while Heart Butte voters gave him just twenty.[108]

Although biological full-bloods, Buffalohide and Ironpipe no longer enjoyed the support of the minority faction because they defended the IRA and because their success as ranchers set them apart from less successful full-bloods. According to John Ewers, "there were endless dual differences that are submerged in any effort to classify tribal members as full bloods or mixed." Citing Ironpipe to illustrate the difficulty of determining factions based on blood quantum, he wrote that one "cannot generalize about the Blackfeet."[109] Given the minority group's inconsistent voting behavior and its heterogeneous composition (its constituents' range of blood quantum), the result of the first popular vote supports the argument that full-bloods, both social and biological, failed to vote as a blood bloc and voted instead based on economic considerations. The rout of the incumbents probably had more to do with the ousted council's December 1945 decision to forgo per capita payments in favor of livestock purchases than with the formation of a new voting alignment. Voters were angry that they did not receive the Christmas bonus they had come to expect. Blood considerations had not become meaningless, but the socioeconomic gap between full-blood and mixed-blood had narrowed further, making such ethnic or racial considerations less prominent and thus less useful for explaining political activity. The voters' rejection of two referenda on tribal oil development in late 1945 represented the growing divide between Blackfeet economic factions, and the election of Charles Reevis in January 1946 reflected the creation of a new tribal entity: the socioeconomic full-blood.

During the 1940s, the influx of oil revenue and the attendant social conflict over the distribution of it sharpened the debate over how fair the Blackfeet democracy really was, especially to "persistent minorities" like full-bloods; it raises the question posed by political scientist Peter Jones as to "whether persistent minorities should regard their position as unfair or merely unfortunate."[110] And what was Blackfeet democracy? A typological examination might find it demonstrating attributes of several different kinds of democratic systems posited by political theorists. For the purposes of this analysis it is best to consider two basic democratic models, which David Held defines as "direct or participatory democracy (a system of decision-making about public affairs in which citizens are directly involved) and liberal or representative democracy (a system of rule embracing elected 'officers' who undertake to 'represent' the interests and/or views of citizens within the framework of 'the rule of law')."[111]

Since colonialism had destroyed Indians' "local democracy," John Collier emphasized in 1941 that with the IRA, Indians could create "practical democracy through increased participation in self-government."[112] Collier likely meant that Indian political leaders would increasingly participate in managing tribal resources and performing governmental functions, though, given his embrace of traditional or "local democracy," he also hoped that such self-government would include a high degree of citizen participation in any decision-making process. But he had assiduously defended the IRA by claiming that Indians had the right to change the composition of tribal councils and constitutions through regular elections and referenda, saying little about rebuilding a framework for what theorists like Held, Carole Pateman, and Benjamin Barber call "participatory democracy." In practice, especially on reservations like the Blackfeet, Collier counted on "representative democracy" to provide social peace and distributive justice.

How the Blackfeet themselves viewed their democratic process and its rules for decision-making is fundamentally important. Political leaders of all factions had come to an understanding in 1934 that the IRA provided the best possible political system for the Blackfeet Nation. This consensus was in part engendered by full-blood leaders of the Piegan Farming and Livestock Association, who agreed that the tribe's representative democracy, strengthened with the sovereign powers offered in the IRA, presented a good alternative to the PFLA's flawed system of participatory democracy. In the 1940s, democracy for Blackfeet leaders like Joe Brown and Leo Kennerly meant the right to vote for candidates and on referenda; they supported, above all, a system in which "the majority shall rule."[113] In contrast, full-bloods asserted the right to assume council representation based upon their historical role as tribal leaders. Reevis's proposition to assign six full-bloods to the BTBC each election period angered mixed-blood leaders who defended the integrity of representative democracy. Francis Guardipee attacked Reevis's idea, telling him, "If it ever happens that the mixed-bloods get mad, we can out vote you anytime we want to, and don't forget that. As it is now, we do everything we can to help you."[114] Mixed-bloods like Guardipee and Joe Brown became impatient with full-blood leaders like Reevis (especially Reevis himself, since he was a half-blood claiming to be a full-blood) who refused to acknowledge the council's efforts to address the minority group's concerns. That Reevis proposed his electoral scheme during the consociational constitutional convention particularly disturbed mixed-blood leaders, who had set up the convention in part to allow full-bloods to participate in tribal decision-making. Mixed-blood leaders who valued full-bloods both as political equals and as cultural figures understood that to deny their voice in the democratic process would be to deny their "claim for status" and thus lower their self-esteem.[115]

The constitutional convention was intended to bridge real and perceived gaps between the Blackfeet's informal and formal cultures, to provide a forum for what Benjamin Barber calls "ongoing participation in talk" and "public thinking," the literal and figurative lingua franca of participatory democracy; this "talking" environment was especially important to full-bloods, who preferred face-to-face discursive discussions rather than parliamentary debates and dictates.[116] The convention's "educative function" was thus to reinforce in all participants the idea that the connected notions of Blackfeet tribal membership and democratic citizenship could create the common ground of Blackfeet citizenship through which common goals and goods could be produced.[117]

The irony of the full-bloods' situation was that they ended up on the winning side of virtually every important election in the 1940s. Full-bloods supported the referenda to establish the sick fund and the funeral fund and helped to reject the council's two proposals to invest tribal money in proprietary oil production. And on two important occasions the minority group was given an opportunity to influence fundamental dimensions of self-governance: during the constitutional convention the council granted full-blood leaders the power to define tribal membership, and in a separate meeting ordered by Oscar Chapman, full-bloods were effectively given the opportunity to veto the constitutional amendment establishing a popular vote. In neither case did they elect to deviate from the majority position. In addition, only six of the fifteen full-blood delegates to the convention voted to reject the IRA during a nonbinding vote. Full-bloods thus participated to an extent greater than their "minority group" status indicates. They remained a demographic minority in the context of representative democracy, failing to secure, at least in every council election, proportional representation. However, in the more important realm of participatory democracy, which the series of referenda could stand to represent, they emerged as members of the clear majority.

Superintendent McBride was pleased with the Blackfeet's political activity of late 1945, telling Commissioner Brophy that "it is evident from recent elections that the Blackfeet Indians are doing some thinking on items presented to them for decision."[118] Blackfeet had voted against investing their money in a tribal oil operation, elected not to sell the tribe's share of oil contracts, and decided to alter their electoral scheme to allow every voter a chance to determine the BTBC's composition. Charles Heacock was less sanguine about the prospects of Blackfeet democracy. Although no longer officially associated with the tribe or the BIA's field staff, he protested the popular vote amendment after it passed in November. Heacock had been a vigorous defender of the IRA when he first began counseling the tribe on matters of self-government. The IRA constitution was, he had said in February 1940, an "organ through which the voice of the people can be heard." Through the "use of the referenda," he told council members and their detractors, the tribe could exercise its democratic rights to amend the constitution.[119] But in December 1945 he called the popular vote amendment "an invitation for increased manipulation by designing elements" that would further reduce minority representation on the council. The IRA, he now argued, "placed a legal tool in the hands of the ruling clique, mainly mixed bloods. . . . In the hands of at least seven of thirteen councilmen lies constitutional authority for the sole direction of [tribal] wealth."[120] Yet Heacock's 1940 call for Blackfeet to exercise their democratic rights through referenda had encouraged full-bloods and mixed-bloods alike to go to the polls and vote to circumscribe the council's economic agenda. Full-bloods were given a chance to make their voices heard in late 1944 and early 1945. They gambled, perhaps out of desperation, that the new voting scheme would enable them to increase their presence on the council and thus restore a measure of credibility and authority to their status-deprived leaders. They exercised their democratic rights as best they could given their large demographic disadvantage, as did a significant number of mixed-blood voters equally unhappy with the council's economic program. For many Blackfeet of all degrees of blood, then, the per capita payments derived from oil production were essential psychological and financial gifts from Mother Earth. When they did not receive a payment in December 1945, they returned to the polls the following month to make the voice of the people heard.

Heacock was right about the council's ability to control the distribution of the tribe's revenue. He had lost his faith that the Blackfeet people could make their political system function to prevent the council from making improper distributions and investments. Creating a sustainable democracy, then, was the challenge that the Blackfeet Nation faced as it tried to remain intact as a political and cultural community under growing internal and external pressures. Each source of pressure threatened to alter once again Indians' relationship with the federal government and thus redefine the meaning of Blackfeet citizenship.

6. "WE HAVE A WAY TO MAKE CITIZENS OF THEM": The Politics of Blackfeet Self-Termination, 1945–1952

> So we feel that if you will just let us take care of ourselves and not put too many stumbling blocks in our road, then we are going to come out all right. – Joe Brown to House Subcommittee on Indian Affairs, 1947

> We feel as if we were convicts trying to find protection and our only view is to go back to the United States Government for that protection where the Tribe would be benefited by the Interior Department's rules and regulations. We have no grudge against any of our Tribal members, half breeds, three quarters or one sixteenth, but it looks to me as though they want to get out from under the Inte rior blanket and emancipate themselves so they can get away from the Blackfeet Tribe. – Louis Plenty Treaty to Harry S. Truman, 1952

Judging from most historiographical accounts, the Indian New Deal ended with John Collier's resignation in January 1945.[1] When Collier left office, American Indians lost a champion of their right to associate for cultural, economic, and political advancement. They also lost an advocate in Congress, someone with the requisite conviction to pursue and protect adequate funding to match this vision of socioeconomic renewal. Congress, by 1944, had become less willing to provide this funding or to support his vision; as World War II evolved into the Cold War, assimilation became more of a policy than a philosophy, and tribal rights became subordinated to national interests. Collier himself had become more accepting of congressional propositions for terminating federal supervision of Indian affairs during his final years in office, in part because he believed that the Indian New Deal had provided American Indians with a political and economic platform from which they might prosper independent of federal support and rely like any other American community on the rewoven social contract of the Roosevelt New Deal. Politically then, in the face of mounting congressional opposition to the BIA and increasing calls for reform from Indians themselves, the momentum of the Indian New Deal came to an end, even as its economic, institutional, and programmatic legacy continued. After Collier resigned, a cohort of assimilationist congressional leaders from the West introduced a spate of bills calling for the reduction or withdrawal of federal services on individual reservations and cuts in the BIA bureaucracy, mirroring the call for reform issued by an emerging Indian elite intent on realizing the goal of true tribal sovereignty.[2]

Increasing pressure from both external political forces and influential Blackfeet citizens forced the Blackfeet people to address the issues of termination. By the end of 1945 three main Blackfeet political groups had formed in regard to federal administration: extreme terminationists, led by Brian Connolly and Leo Kennerly, who espoused a rapid withdrawal of all things BIA; moderate terminationists like Joe Brown and George Pambrun, who championed a reasoned and gradual transfer of federal responsibilities to tribal, county, and state organizations; and segregationists like James White Calf and Charles Reevis, who refused to consider any alternative to federal wardship, largely because they did not trust the council to manage the tribe's political economy in a fair manner. This tripartite factionalism created a crisis of authority on the reservation as each group sought to convince OIA and Interior officials that their group represented the true interests of the real Blackfeet Indians. Ultimately, the tribe had to rely on the institutional machinery of the IRA, which remained, however flawed, the best mechanism for the reform of Blackfeet political and economic administration.

Joe Brown continued to represent the council's terminationist agenda, in part because Kennerly failed to secure reelection in January 1946. Brown was less emotional about the BIA presence than either Kennerly or Connolly, both of whom resented the very idea of the BIA. Brown simply maintained that the Blackfeet could do the BIA's work and should have the right to do it. He articulated his moderate philosophy to the House Subcommittee on Indian Affairs during its April 1947 hearings on the "emancipation bills" proposed by Rep. Francis Case of South Dakota and Rep. Wesley D'Ewart of Montana. The advertised intent of the bills was to free Indians—in particular Indian war veterans—from property restrictions by providing them with a "certificate of emancipation" and a patent in fee to their land, which they could then sell or mortgage to raise capital. The thrust of the legislation was to revive the competency commissions inaugurated by Cato Sells, who was commissioner of Indian Affairs in the 1910s. The emancipation of trust land, not the Indian, was the goal of most congressional reformers.[3]

Yet the lifting of property restrictions was not solely the domain of white congressional males. The Blackfeet and other Indians, particularly veterans, were hampered by their inability to secure mortgages or other forms of credit because the government held their land in trust. Many veterans returned to reservations that faced a declining pool of government credit or to those that lacked adequate tribal revenue to allow for proprietary loans. The BTBC extended credit to veterans through its various lending programs and granted them "preference rights" in its distribution of tribal cattle, but it had limited funds for distribution. Given that the Blackfeet enjoyed greater financial resources than most other Indian nations, it is not surprising that increasingly acculturated veterans would find restrictive and hopeless an environment that failed to provide opportunity commensurate with expectations created during wartime. But allowing for fee patenting, and thus exposing owners to real estate taxes, was not a cure for economic ills if development programs did not follow. And given the tragic history of previous trust emancipation campaigns, it was not unusual for critics to label such bills coercive and regressive. William Zimmerman testified that he was "troubled by the probable loss of Indian land which might result from the wholesale removal of restrictions." Emancipation bills were, he argued, unnecessary, and they jeopardized the progress made by constitutionally empowered governments.[4]

Brown expressed general agreement with the principles of the Case bills, but, like Zimmerman, he contended that the IRA had given the Blackfeet the tools they needed to move within the white world and sufficient protection for those who were not ready to do so. Brown especially objected to a provision that would permit tribal land to be sold if two-thirds of the Blackfeet electorate voted to sell it. The Blackfeet, he said, were surrounded by railroad, oil, and even government interests intent on taking pieces of the reservation, and he feared that their wealth could influence such a vote. The BTBC would preserve the Nation's land base at all costs and, through its Land Purchase Enterprise program, even enlarge the tribal estate. His Indian community did not need the "civil rights" proposed by Case but rather the authority to exercise existing rights codified in the IRA. "The powers are there," he said, "but when we go to carry them out we are interfered with [by the BIA]." The Extension Division, which controlled credit operations, created most of the conflict on the reservation; the lending process took too long and went through too many stages, Brown complained. The Blackfeet could handle the responsibility of managing the "economic development of our reservation," he contended, in part because Blackfeet education had produced capable high school and college graduates who were now filling positions in the county government and court system. "So we feel that if you will just let us take care of ourselves and not put too many stumbling blocks in our road, then we are going to come out all right."[5]

Brown argued that those reservations ready "to be turned entirely loose" should embrace the bill. The Blackfeet, however, simply would not profit from it. This argument reflects in part Brown's belief in the retention of tribal organization, the idea that one need not own land outright to meet the criterion of citizenship. He supported the individual's right to sell land while opposing a blanket policy that mandated it, fearing another round of governmental coercion. Under the Case bill, he told the committee, "you are emancipated whether you like it or not"; under the IRA, he claimed, "we have a way to make citizens of them." Although the Case bill did not legislate blanket emancipation, Brown, a veteran of previous termination campaigns, understood that the underlying principles of the legislation made it likely that the Indian's privilege would devolve to a government policy; the government's "forced" fee patenting of the Sells era, Brown testified, made the Blackfeet wary of any emancipation program.[6] Brown, the leading intellectual voice of his generation, would push for reductions of government control during the remaining years of his distinguished career and continue to argue that Indians should make their own way at their own pace; termination should be an organic process rather than the mandate of politicians insulated from the vagaries and vices of neocolonial administration. The sale of land was ultimately a personal issue, Brown believed, and one that the tribal government could not control and that the federal government should not dictate. For Brown, the matter of emancipation was best left to Indians themselves.

The Blackfeet prided themselves on being alert to the prevailing political winds and tacking close to them in an attempt to harness and adapt them to their particular political environment. Tribal members had embraced the idea of self-support, or self-termination, for more than two decades, out of confidence in themselves and out of fear that the federal government would make the decision unilaterally. A dominant question for the Blackfeet Nation emerged after 1945: Was the Nation as a whole ready to accept reduced government supervision of its affairs and thus assume political and economic responsibility for its citizens, or was termination important only for elites like Brown, Kennerly, and Connolly, as the ultimate manifestation of their battle for sovereign rights and their agenda of gradual assimilation? Given the Nation's constellation of interests that fell along class, ethnic, and generational lines, finding an answer to this question would prove to be difficult.

During the war years the BTBC had worked effectively with BIA officials to create workable budgets and to allocate oil money for long-term development projects that promised to expand cattle and sheep ranching, the only enterprises considered appropriate to the physical environment of Blackfeet country. The council had "set its own house in order" with the help of Charles Heacock, who spent months working with council members to convince them of the need for proper accounting and budgeting. Heacock warned his superiors that the BTBC "would be naturally suspicious of what they might consider any attempts to usurp their rights with respect to programming their tribal income."[7] Council members were willing to consider suggestions to improve their administration of financial resources, but they reserved the right to decide how to use them in the Blackfeet context. The relationship between the BIA and the BTBC thus continued to be cooperative but also ambivalent. The BTBC's attitude changed after the war. Emboldened and politicized by the series of meetings held in 1944 and 1945 to review the tribe's reorganization program, council members took the next step in that program. The council announced its intentions in a December 7, 1945, resolution that called for the elimination of the "many duplications" that existed between the BIA and the BTBC, which had created "problems of jurisdiction," inefficient leasing practices, and unnecessary costs. The council wanted to handle oil and range leasing "exclusively, subject only to the approval and consent of the Secretary of the Interior" because the BIA had failed to take proper care of the Blackfeet's business.[8]

In a letter to Sen. James Murray, Commissioner William Brophy called the resolution "one of the most interesting documents to come from any tribe as a direct result of the Indian Reorganization Act." The

BTBC was the first tribal organization to raise specifically the question of duplication of service. Maintaining that it was the BIA's intent to "build up the authority and responsibility of tribal councils," Brophy argued that the BTBC had "made progress in developing as a legislative body within the scope of its tribal constitution" and had "shown initiative in developing plans for the use of its tribal resources." But he cautioned that the council had made some errors of judgment and that "some members have not been above gaining profit at the expense of the tribe. There is the further difficulty that a large minority of the tribe, a minority made up of full-blood members, regularly protest the activities of the Council and express a desire to have all tribal and individual affairs handled by the Indian Service." In a draft, Brophy told Murray that he disagreed with the council's contention that "the tribal machinery has developed to such a point that the Indian Service is no longer needed on the Reservation. . . . The time may come at Blackfeet sooner than at most reservations when the Indian Service can safely withdraw. But that time has not yet arrived."[9]

William Zimmerman also thought that the Blackfeet were not ready for termination. During his infamous testimony to the Senate Committee on Post Office and Civil Service in February 1947, he placed the Blackfeet Tribe in his second category of termination readiness; the Blackfeet and eighteen other tribes needed between two and ten years to join the Klamaths, the Menominees, and eight other Indian groups he considered capable of surviving without federal services. Zimmerman proposed three termination programs to fit Indian America's diverse population (the so-called Zimmerman Plan): individual termination for those Indians who no longer wanted to be a federally recognized Indian, tribal incorporation for those tribes that had not adopted IRA charters, and the transfer of federal services to state jurisdiction or tribal control.[10]

Blackfeet leaders focused mainly on exercising the third option after the war. The BTBC's principal intent was to reduce BIA influence on the reservation and federal control of oil and range leasing. The BTBC had made a serious effort to accommodate the needs of the minority faction during the war, but, in line with OIA recommendations and its own belief in the need for long-term program goals, the council extended the CRP and the RCF, the Blackfeet New Deal's principal economic programs. The BTBC became increasingly aggressive in its management of tribal livestock programs in 1945, choosing to ignore several nonbinding referenda that demonstrated the tribe's general opposition to tribal investment in livestock, in part because binding referenda had circumscribed the council's role in oil development. The cattle population on the reservation jumped from 12,649 head in 1944 to 17,158 head in 1945, largely because the council decided in December 1945 to forgo a per capita distribution and spend more than $110,000 on bulls and heifers for distribution to those Blackfeet with adequate hay supplies. In March 1945 the council had created the Blackfeet Repayment Cattle Enterprise (BRCE), a variant of the government's CRP, with a new shipment of 2,344 head procured from the government for distribution to 226 Blackfeet families and 51 4-H clubs; the BRCE assumed responsibility for repaying the government on an annual basis.[11] As a result, the number of families owning cattle rose from 278 to 316, roughly one-third of Blackfeet resident families. The number of families active in sheep ranching dropped from 68 to 34; the sheep population declined dramatically from a high of 40,580 head in 1943 to 16,196 in early 1947, largely because a number of inexperienced operators lost money. The number of families reporting agricultural income remained steady between 38 and 40 percent. But the number of families earning more than $1,500 rose steadily after the war, from 158 in 1945 to 181 in 1948. The middle class—those Blackfeet families earning between $500 and $1,500—fluctuated between 29 and 34 percent of all agricultural families during the same period.[12] In 1950, the extension staff would estimate that 145 Blackfeet families receiving RCF loans were self-supporting. Another 280 families had become "partially" self-supporting because of participation in the RCF program.[13]

It is difficult to determine with precision the degree to which the RCF loans in particular created self-supporting conditions because enterprising Blackfeet had also borrowed from the tribe, the Production Credit Association, and, for those with fee patents or sufficient collateral, from private banks; and the word "partial" is as inexact as the label "mixed-blood." Despite such qualifications, since the inception of the RCF program in 1937, 603 Blackfeet individuals had borrowed money at affordable rates, repaid the money to a high degree, and prospered to a greater extent than possible without such access to credit, the lifeblood of any business organization or individual enterprise. Nearly half of the dollars lent to Blackfeet went for livestock, feed, and farm machinery.[14]

After the war, Blackfeet political leaders became increasingly confident of the tribe's abilities to manage its economic affairs. Despite progress aided in part by the Extension Division's efforts, Blackfeet leaders resented the presence of its workers. As the 1944 House subcommittee hearing demonstrated, most Blackfeet wanted to reduce the BIA's presence on the reservation and to replace white workers with Indians. Blackfeet terminationists had singled out the extension service for reduction largely because it controlled credit (for better and for worse) and was the most visible presence on the reservation. Extension workers became commonplace in white farm communities during the New Deal and beyond, representing both an intrusion of government into farmers' lives and the extension of support to traditionally insular communities increasingly faced with economic pressures created by an evolving and politically unstable global marketplace. On the Blackfeet Reservation, among a people searching for increased political and economic control, the Extension Division served as a mobile reminder that the Blackfeet Indians needed whites to tell them how to farm, how to manage money, and how to raise livestock.

The BTBC's campaign to terminate federal supervision of reservation management had several other root causes. The OIA's refusal to acknowledge the council's requests for input in the selection of the agency superintendent certainly affected its terminationist mindset. The issue had surfaced as early as the mid-1920s, but it became more divisive once the tribe adopted IRA machinery and assumed the mantle of governmental responsibility. When the BTBC nominated Joe Brown for the superintendency in 1942, it asserted that other tribes, notably the Crows, had contributed to the decision to appoint their superintendents and warned of "considerable friction" if the Blackfeet council was not granted the privilege to do so.[15] Instead, the OIA promoted Freal McBride, superintendent of Blackfeet schools, a concession of sorts and a good choice, as it turned out; McBride generally worked on the sidelines of Blackfeet political affairs, serving in an advisory role during the expansion of the wartime reservation economy. The BTBC again raised the issue after McBride died in an automobile accident.

The OIA's appointment of Warren O'Hara to replace McBride seemed, on the surface, another safe choice. As superintendent in the mid-1930s, O'Hara had helped the Nation craft its IRA charter and constitution, from all accounts providing an environment conducive to debate and discussion. He did earn the enmity of reactionary mixed-bloods who feared that the BTBC would expand its control of the reservation economy. In August 1948, the council, led by Brian Connolly, one of those reactionary mixed-bloods, resolved that it "strongly suspected [O'Hara] of maladministration of office." The council wanted the position "declared vacant and filled by a qualified person, *mutually* agreed upon" by the Blackfeet Nation and the Interior Department. Interior officials denied the council's request. They had already cleared O'Hara of impropriety after Connolly accused him of intimidating candidates in the January 20, 1948, council election and favoring the interests of oil operators over those of the Blackfeet. Connolly had been a divisive influence on the council since 1938, championing unproductive causes, attacking bureau personnel and programs, and defending himself against charges of trespassing and fraudulently obtaining tribal livestock.[16] Connolly opposed the BIA presence on the reservation, but, unlike Brown, he did not have a vision of bicultural tribal unity. A wealthy rancher from the rural Seville district who described himself as "far better off than many of my Indian brothers," Connolly was less interested in forming a responsive democratic government than in expanding the council's control of the reservation economy by neutralizing BIA and Interior "technologies of power and surveillance."[17] Joe Brown the democrat no longer defined the personality of the council; Brian Connolly the libertarian did.

The BTBC's campaign against O'Hara and the BIA in general reflected not just the personal battles of Brian Connolly but an emerging conflict between a new group of council members (of which Connolly was the most vocal) with ideas of self-government and veteran BIA officials like O'Hara who resisted the implementation of those ideas. The contours of Blackfeet factionalism had changed during O'Hara's interregnum; the divide was now based largely on the role of Blackfeet government rather than on bureau government and on the distribution of economic assets rather than on the economic agenda itself. The incorporation of the Blackfeet Nation that O'Hara had fostered in 1935 and 1936 had altered Blackfeet conceptions of tribal responsibility. O'Hara himself did not oppose the idea of self-termination, but he did not trust Connolly or his laissez faire approach to reservation management. In contrast to McBride and his advisory role, O'Hara played the role of advocate, pushing for tribal self-government in a series of clashes with the BTBC that aggravated an already tenuous relationship between the two political bodies and led to Connolly's charges and O'Hara's eventual resignation because of exhaustion and frustration.

This clash of philosophies began with the first postwar council, elected in January 1946. Peter Vielle, a fifty-year-old half-blood, issued a public statement to tribal members in a March 1946 piece published by the *Browning Chief*, in which he wrote that he wanted to "instill into your minds at this time this fact. You all know that the Blackfeet Business Corporation is a business enterprise and should be treated as such, and not as a relief organization or medical or dental society. . . . You are wards of the United States government. They should shoulder your relief, medical and dental care. Remember this: You're not wards of the Blackfeet Tribal Business Council. You are a participating corporative member and you are entitled to any dividends that I hope some day we will be able to pay you."[18] Vielle stressed that the original purpose of the Blackfeet corporation was to distribute tribal monies to those willing to invest in enterprises that would enable them to become self-supporting. The new council intended to reduce tribal indebtedness to preserve its lending authority and sustain this mission. It did not consider itself responsible for running a welfare state. The council subsequently voted to dismantle the tribe's welfare and law and order programs. Connolly in particular insisted that the tribe spend oil income only on per capita payments and administrative expenses; he had always pushed for limited tribal government, arguing in 1938 that the council should eliminate "all . . . positions paid for from tribal funds." The council's fiscal philosophy of 1946 both exposed the Blackfeet Nation's evolving class structure and mirrored the country's growing conservatism and the concomitant attenuation of Collier's Indian New Deal by Republicans eager to deconstruct the nascent welfare state. The council's actions represented a dramatic shift in attitude toward tribal organization from that of its predecessor, which during the constitutional convention had seemed to value the minority group's input in political decision-making. The first thing members of a political community owe each other, Michael Walzer writes, "is the communal provisions of security and welfare."[19] Vielle's comments heralded an emerging struggle between corporate and political conceptions of the tribal community and their attendant notions of social obligation.

The attempt by mixed-blood political elites to downsize the Nation's commitment to "ward Indians" dismayed OIA officials, who continued to claim, as William Zimmerman did in response to Vielle's declarations, that "with an income such as is available at Blackfeet [Reservation] it is the moral, as well as the legal, responsibility of the tribe to provide for its own people and to supply funds for the needy."[20] The Indian Office again argued that it had neither the funds nor the inclination to subsidize the Blackfeet or other Indian nations with revenue streams. The council protested that the OIA's decision amounted to discrimination against the

Nation simply because it had financial resources. Thus neither side was willing to accept responsibility for the welfare of ward Indians. The issue of regularized welfare payments divided the council, but its members did not elect to restore funding for them. Superintendent O'Hara assumed the responsibility of sustaining the welfare and judicial programs, engendering hostility from council members for ignoring their decision and thus supplanting their authority and aggravating the Blackfeet populace by raising fines to fund the tribe's reorganized law and order setup.[21]

The council elected in January 1948 softened its attitude toward relief payments, securing a contract with Glacier and Pondera Counties to administer a welfare program under the aegis of federal supervision; these county welfare agencies began distributing tribal and federal funds to ward and nonward Indians in September 1949.[22] The council's agreement to provide a fixed amount of tribal funds under the terms of the contract solidified its financial commitment to Blackfeet welfare, but it also underlined both its disinterest in managing the program and dealing with individual cases and its terminationist belief that the OIA could better serve Blackfeet interests by transferring responsibilities from the federal level to the state and county levels.

The fight over relief reinforced the council's position on the government's "power of control" and its conception of the tribe as a corporation; it continued to oppose the use of tribal funds for relief in favor of expenditures for per capita payments and corporate operations. Vielle acknowledged to Commissioner Brophy that "the Council is responsible for their people," but he asked for available army surplus materials, commodities, and other gratis rations rather than accept responsibility for the tribal welfare program; the council was committed to serving the tribe by replicating various functions of the superintendency but not to devoting an inordinate amount of its Class B funds for direct relief. Council members distinguished between emergency relief and institutionalized welfare, arguing that the federal government should provide the latter. Blackfeet leaders resented the relief the federal government gave to Europeans, calling for a domestic version of the Marshall Plan in Indian America. While acknowledging the need for such relief, Vielle asked Brophy, "how about our own people[?] I believe relief should begin at home."[23]

Council members rightly charged that the federal government prevented the tribe from using its own monies for economic development while the government invested billions abroad; in a cruel twist, the government essentially used Blackfeet money held in the U.S. Treasury to finance the Marshall Plan because Congress's $75,000 cap on all Indian withdrawals from the Treasury amounted to appropriation by fiat. In an April 1949 letter requesting funds to aid a comprehensive rehabilitation program, council members told Zimmerman that "the Blackfeet Nation is poorer than any nation of Europe aided by the Marshall Plan, poorer than any of the nations that our boys helped to free from dictatorship. Yet, we ask no charity. We ask only a chance to build our own future to free ourselves from economic subordination . . . and the right to expend our own funds."[24] For patriotic Blackfeet fresh from the killing fields of Europe or grieving the loss of those who died there, the "economic subordination" practiced by the government amounted to a form of racial discrimination. Blackfeet politicians had always resented how difficult it was to extract money from its Class A accounts. The issue became especially heated after the war and greatly contributed to the council's terminationist mindset.

The council also resented government interference in its release of Class B funds for per capita distributions, which it used to supplement relief. Council members, exhibiting a corporate view of income distribution, believed it improper to distribute oil revenues directly to certain classes of Blackfeet. In keeping with its newly articulated corporate mentality, the council issued per capita payments in November 1946 and in April 1947 rather than continue to fund a social worker and a tribal welfare program. It therefore treated each tribal member as a shareholder who would get the same dividend from any revenue generated from tribal enterprises. The April distribution produced resistance from O'Hara, who classified the distribution as a per capita payment rather than as a relief payment; the tribal charter prohibited the BTBC from spending more than 50 percent of its annual budget on per capita distributions. By calling the April payment a relief payment the council would not have to credit it against the budget.[25] Paul Fickinger, BIA area director, argued that the "usual thinking of the tribe is that everyone needs relief, which of course is wholly [sic] fallacious," and he complained that the relief was "distributed discriminately."[26] It *was* "usual thinking," as per capita and funeral funds were not distributed on a means basis. This approach may have made sense at one point in the tribe's history, but such was not the case in the 1940s because the wealthiest Blackfeet got the same amount as the poorest. The actual distribution also caused logistical and accounting problems, particularly during the winter months when the poor needed relief the most. But the idea of a *tribal* distribution remained a very appealing one to most Blackfeet, as did the Nation's right to determine the rules of dividing its income among its citizens.

The fight over welfare, law and order, reservation employment, and control of tribal monies crystallized the terminationist thinking of men like Brian Connolly, Joe Brown, and George Pambrun, mixed-blood political elites with varying degrees of commitment to the notion of tribe and its cultural value. The BTBC's terminationist mindset found expression in congressional hearings and in a series of council resolutions asking for the termination of the government's authority to regulate tribal economic affairs. The question facing the Blackfeet Nation as the internal debate on termination began dominating its political affairs was whether self-support in the form of enhanced sovereignty was simply a tool for what Charles Heacock called the "ruling clique" or the vehicle through which all Blackfeet citizens could enjoy an added measure of comfort and economic opportunity. "Self-determination," Stephanie Lawson writes, "can indeed be a democratic concept, but it is not necessarily so. On the contrary, it can function as a useful banner under which all kinds of unpleasant ideologies and patently anti-democratic activities can be justified."[27]

As with the Menominee and Klamath reservations, there existed on the Blackfeet Reservation a growing disjunction between middle-class mixed-bloods and poor Blackfeet of both full-blood and mixed-blood. Blackfeet were either "Indian-oriented" or "White-oriented," to use Malcolm McFee's sensible though somewhat restrictive dichotomy.[28] Termination divided these two groups more than any other issue, partly for cultural reasons and partly for economic reasons. George Spindler and Louise Spindler wrote of the "self-conscious attempt" of the predominantly Catholic mixed-blood "elite-acculturated" Menominees to minimize their Indian heritage. Termination was for most Menominee elites a way to divide tribal wealth and dissociate themselves from "native-oriented" Menominees to complete the process of assimilation, a legalistic purge of Indianness.[29] Klamath elites also pushed hard for termination. Wade Crawford, whom John Collier appointed superintendent in 1933, had long advocated termination, in part as a way to divide the tribe's natural resources on a pro rata basis.[30] Federal officials looked favorably on Klamath and Menominee termination because of the tribes' timber resources and the avid support of aggressive tribal elites, many of whom mirrored the white middle-class values of BIA bureaucrats and members of Congress. The Blackfeet Nation differed from the Klamaths and the Menominees in two principal ways: it lacked their liquid natural resource wealth and, unlike those tribes, had incorporated under the provisions of the IRA. The BTBC, lacking control of extensive resources, would thus face less pressure from federal officials for termination and, lacking the option of a pro rata distribution, less demand from tribal members for termination. But the BTBC did have the option of exercising the right to secure limited or graduated termination of federal supervision using the IRA charter. Regardless of the federal government's interest in termination, Blackfeet politicians and voters could thus depend upon the democratic system created by the IRA to help determine the Nation's postcolonial future.

The BTBC formally committed the tribe to a scheduled termination of the Interior secretary's supervisory powers and the expansion of the council's powers of self-government on December 8, 1947, with its promulgation of Resolution No. 20. The resolution, adopted by a vote of nine to zero, read in part: "The Blackfeet Tribal Business Council now feels that after twelve years of operation under the supervisory powers of the Secretary of the Interior . . . the members of the Blackfeet Tribe can successfully conduct their affairs without such supervision by the Secretary of the Interior . . . and they now feel that they are ready to take this step towards such self-government."[31] Specifically, the council requested the termination of the secretary's supervision of tribal business affairs contained in sections 5(b) no. 2, 5(f), 5(g), 5(h), and section 8 of the tribe's charter. Section 5(b) no. 2 required the tribe to get the secretary's approval on leases, permits, and contracts relating to tribal land; section 5(f) prohibited the tribe from making business contracts in excess of ten thousand dollars without the secretary's approval; section 5(g) gave the secretary control of lending operations; section 5(h) allowed the secretary to set the terms for the deposit of tribal funds; and section 8 stipulated that the tribe needed the secretary's approval to make individual per capita payments of more than one hundred dollars or distributions that totaled more than "one-half of the accrued surplus."[32]

The secretary thus had the authority to regulate most areas of tribal economic activity; the tribe did have the discretion to make oil leases for periods of more than ten years, but the secretary still controlled the overall terms of oil development. The OIA officials who designed the charter in 1936 did so with the intent of circumscribing the BTBC's financial activities in order to protect the credit worthiness of the Blackfeet Corporation. The council members who approved the document did so without knowing that within ten years the charter's dollar limits would cease to relate to tribal revenue. And the council increasingly wanted the discretion to invest tribal revenue in tribal enterprises or distribute it in per capita payments. Whether the council needed new terms of operation had mattered little because the original limits remained in place. The council now had the right to eliminate those limits. If the secretary approved the election, then the resolution would be ratified by a majority vote provided that "at least [30 percent] of the adult members of the Tribe" participated. If the secretary declined to approve the election or failed to respond to the election request within ninety days, then the council could override the secretary's veto and hold a popular referendum. In this scenario, however, the Nation would adopt the termination order only if approved by two-thirds of the eligible voters.[33] Adoption of the referendum required the approval of the Blackfeet people either way, but the Interior Department had the powerful option of placing a heavier burden on the referendum's supporters by vetoing the election. The department-sanctioned election would require roughly 250 votes in favor of termination; without the department's support, adoption would require nearly 1,050. BTBC members had fought hard in 1936 to gain the right to call an election to terminate the secretary's supervisory powers. They would have to fight hard in 1948 to secure the secretary's support or to find a way to persuade two-thirds of the Blackfeet electorate not only to participate in the election but also to support their goal of expanded self-government.

The council's termination agenda both gratified and alarmed OIA officials, particularly William Zimmerman, who had followed the shifting contours of Blackfeet factionalism since the mid-1930s. On one hand, the resolution symbolized the progress created as a result of OIA programs and guidance; it validated the Indian New Deal and the IRA. On the other hand, it highlighted the disjunction between two evolving sociopolitical tribal groups: elites on the council and the growing middle class, which had benefited from both OIA and BTBC economic programs, and the less successful "minority group," which included both full-bloods and mixed-bloods unable for whatever reason to take advantage of Indian New Deal reforms. Zimmerman initiated an investigation of the BTBC's record in advance of the secretary's decision. Recent audits of the tribe's finances had shaken his confidence in the council. The audits—conducted by the Great Falls firm of Douglas Wilson, Ferris, and Company—criticized the council's management of oil leasing and revealed "unbusinesslike practices and possibly some dishonesty on the part of individual members of the council." As a result, Zimmerman told a BIA colleague, "We have not been satisfied with the manner in which the Blackfeet Tribal Council has conducted the affairs of the Tribe."[34] Zimmerman was chiefly concerned with the removal of Interior's control of section 5(b) no. 2, which related to oil and range leasing. He did not object to a withdrawal of the supervision outlined in sections 5(f), 5(g), and 5(h), which related to the "disposition of the income." Zimmerman understood that once the Nation generated income, the OIA had the recourse of the audit to track its distribution, a way to follow the money and identify corrupt or incompetent fiscal management. But if the Nation, or the BTBC to be more precise, managed oil and gas development, it would become difficult, outside of using legal measures, to identify such unbusinesslike practices.

O'Hara did not support Resolution No. 20, arguing that if the Nation's self-government was not sufficiently mature to sustain its welfare and judicial programs, then it was not ready to enlarge the scope of its management of financial and natural resources. The BTBC passed the resolution, he told Interior officials, "at the instigation of a minority group who consistently attack anything the [federal] Government attempts to do"; a separate council faction opposed the resolution but wanted the Blackfeet people to decide its fate. Most Blackfeet, O'Hara opined, opposed self-termination. He predicted that a succeeding council would likely rescind the resolution and thus preclude the need for an approved referendum.[35] O'Hara soured on Blackfeet democracy during his second tour of duty, telling Zimmerman that the BTBC had created chaos by violating provisions of the charter and constitution, practicing unsafe lending that benefited council members or their relatives, damaging the integrity of the tribe's RCF program, and misappropriating funds. "I am convinced," he wrote, "that these people cannot operate under the Wheeler-Howard Act, simply because they will not comply with the terms of [it] and there seems to be nothing which can be done to block them."[36] The council elected in January 1948 did rescind the resolution by a vote of ten to one; only Connolly remained in support of the measure. New chairman Henry Magee opposed Resolution No. 20, as did most of his colleagues, who agreed that the tribe was not ready for the termination of federal supervision. Magee feared that "unscrupulous individuals" would control the council if the amendments passed. Connolly, according to Magee, sponsored the resolution because he opposed any form of government supervision of Indians.[37] As a result, the OIA quietly backed away from a full review of the council's management of tribal resources, perhaps the new council's intent. But the OIA's preliminary investigation revealed that the BTBC had failed to respond to suggestions made by the Nation's own auditors from Wilson Ferris. Lacking legal authority to compel the BTBC to improve its fiscal management of the Blackfeet Corporation, Zimmerman sanctioned the use of "moral suasion" to do so, expressing confidence that "the tribe, once it's conscious of the situation, will insist on a greater degree of responsibility in its elected officials."[38]

By August 1949, however, the Magee council had come to adopt Connolly's aversion to government supervision, reversing itself by declaring its intent to hold the referendum election; a majority of council members now claimed that the secretary of the interior had prevented the Blackfeet people from deciding for themselves the merits of Resolution No. 20. The council voted nine to four to issue Resolution No. 18, which requested an election along the same lines as Resolution No. 20; in addition, the council resolved to reduce the number of council members from thirteen to five. Connolly's aggressive pursuit of termination likely influenced the reversal, but the decision stemmed largely from the Magee council's own battles with federal officials over their decision to restrict the tribe's access to its Class A funds and to government RCF monies. As the BTBC's fiscal performance worsened, the BIA had tightened its control of funds, prompting Magee and other council members to embrace the termination of that control. Paul Fickinger, now BIA regional director, supported the reduction of council size but not the reduction of federal power. He cited the Wilson Ferris audit and an anticipated follow-up audit requested by the council, which promised to expose additional financial irregularities. Treasurer Iliff McKay had resigned in September 1949 after a Wilson Ferris accountant found a sixty-five-hundred-dollar shortfall.[39] Fickinger charged that council management had been "growing steadily worse in recent years." Besides granting unsecured and unregulated loans to themselves or to other influential Blackfeet, what Fickinger called "misuse or theft of tribal funds," council members repeatedly violated provisions of the Nation's corporate charter. Fickinger used the word "subterfuge" on several occasions in his analysis of BTBC activities. Most council members were capable of fostering sound business practices, Fickinger believed, but they lacked "integrity and will-ingness . . . to work wholeheartedly in the interest of the tribe, rather than taking advantage of the opportunity for personal gain." And unless the electorate changed the constitution to permit the recall of council members, the Blackfeet faced the "dissipation of their assets."[40]

The Interior Department failed to respond to the BTBC's resolution within ninety days, effectively vetoing the council's request for an election. Although it chose a moderate position by not publicly vetoing the measure, the department's inaction nonetheless served as a form of electoral manipulation. By ignoring the BTBC's request the department called into question both the council's integrity and the Nation's sovereignty. The BTBC promptly issued a new resolution setting March 7, 1950, as the date for the referendum election.

The Blackfeet Nation's termination election would be the first conducted by any Indian group for any reason, and it thus became critical for the BIA and the Interior Department, despite their opposition to it, to help stage a fair election. Secretary of the Interior Oscar Chapman told chairman Magee that in spite of his disapproval the tribe could proceed with the election provided that it adopted a series of procedures to ensure that the election would hold up under intense scrutiny. Chapman emphasized that voter participation would be restricted to permanent residents of the reservation, and he insisted that the council educate Blackfeet voters on each of the amendments.[41] Chapman attempted to appease the council, telling Magee that while the Interior Department applauded the council's goal of self-termination, it could not endorse it until the council demonstrated its commitment to sound fiscal management. The termination amendments, he argued, "may well jeopardize the interests of the tribal members." Chapman's letter underwent several revisions; the first draft's harsh language and sharp rebuke criticizing the council's behavior were deleted in favor of more assuasive language.[42] Chapman did not want to antagonize a tribe trying to reduce its dependence on the government, the de jure goal of federal Indian administration. But he also did not want to encourage a council seemingly unable to foster self-reliance without jeopardizing the Blackfeet people. Chapman recommended that the council separate its political and economic responsibilities and reform its operation by hiring an independent business manager. Chapman told Magee that "since the Business Council is primarily a political body its task of business management is more than usually difficult." As managed, the Blackfeet political economy was at odds with itself. The BTBC had formed as a pressure group to secure investment and facilitate development of the tribe's resources. Empowered by the IRA to further tribal control of the reservation economy, by 1950 the BTBC had not satisfied its white advisers that it could handle additional responsibilities; it had failed to administer RCF monies properly, adequately support tribal welfare and judicial programs, and establish the requisite confidence of the Blackfeet electorate.

The BTBC postponed the referenda the day after its March 2 meeting revealed the depth of the electorate's disapproval and the council's own deep divide over the matter; council members nearly rescinded the original resolution calling for the election, falling short of the requisite number of votes to satisfy parliamentary rules. Connolly continued his aggressive campaign to push the termination amendments and to discredit all forms of government support, calling BIA area counsel A. B. Melzner—invited by BTBC chairman Henry Magee to advise the council on proper election procedures—a government "stooge." Magee defended Melzner's presence to the applause of other council members and a large crowd of Blackfeet; Connolly appeared to have few supporters outside his district. Both mixed-blood and full-blood speakers stood to criticize the council and its violation of the constitution; the amendments would simply have codified actions the council had undertaken extralegally. The principal difference expressed in the various speeches was that full-bloods wanted to abolish the council and the IRA constitution, while mixed-bloods wanted to reform them. Mixed-bloods, both citizens and council members, proposed new eligibility requirements for office, including an education criterion, strict residency rules, and "good moral character." In their minds, the council and the IRA were not imperfect in the same way as the leaders who employed the IRA's provisions to the detriment of the Blackfeet citizenry.[43]

The division within the council, the stridency of Blackfeet citizens' opposition, and the scrutiny from BIA and Interior officials compelled the council to postpone the election until June 20. Chastened, it decided to hold separate referenda for each act of termination, giving voters the option to preserve certain of the secretary's supervisory powers. The council subsequently distributed to tribal members voter handouts detailing the various amendments and the council's justification for them. The introduction to the list of amendments stated that the referendum required the participation of all voters because "it is, perhaps, the most important question to be voted upon" since the elections on the IRA constitution and charter. The supervisory powers of the secretary of the interior were designed, the introduction read, to

> act as a check on the actions of the council in order to prevent wasteful spending to some extent and hasty action or action taken by the council which would not be, in the opinion of the Secretary of the Interior, for the best interests of the majority of the members of the tribe. These powers reserved to the Secretary of the Interior were intended to act as a guide for the council during their formative years of tribal government or until such time as the members of the Tribe gained sufficient business knowledge to manage their affairs in a business like manner. Whether this point has been reached and these powers are of no use to the council other than to create additional administrative detail, or "red tape," is up to each of you to decide.[44]

Each amendment was clearly written and provided examples of the effect of the specific act of termination. The language emphasized the red tape the council faced in its attempts to handle contracts, loans, and bank deposits. The explanation for referendum no. 5, for instance, stated that amendment no. 5 would allow council members to "pay out any amount of money in a year without approval of the Secretary of the Interior, or any other government agency as long as they had the funds to do so."[45] Like many stock prospectuses, this description contained a "forward looking statement." At the same time, the council clearly demonstrated its intent to run a fair election by distributing what Melzner called "clear, simple[,] understandable" instructions and by providing Blackfeet voters with an important option of choosing partial termination rather than a wholesale rejection of the secretary's supervisory powers.[46]

On June 20, voters defeated the council's proposals to terminate those powers. Four of the five amendments were rejected by at least 65 percent of those voting. A bare majority of voters actually supported the fifth— an amendment to section 8—but for adoption it required a two-thirds majority. A separate *nonbinding* referendum supporting regular distribution of per capita payments in excess of approved budgets passed by the widest margin and was the only measure to draw sufficient voting support to meet the constitutional terms for adoption. The variance in voting totals for the measures, which ranged from 787 for one of the termination measures to 1,193 for the nonbinding referendum, suggests that lingering questions about termination prevented some voters from making clear-cut decisions. The section 8 amendment to terminate Interior's right to limit per capita distributions attracted the largest vote of the binding termination measures and the only majority vote—476 for and 450 against. But 267 additional voters who participated in the comparable nonbinding referendum failed to commit to this termination of section 8, suggesting that there was great ambivalence about the issue.[47] In the BTBC election held the same day, the Blackfeet elected for the first time an entirely new council. Voters restored George Pambrun and Joe Brown to office and, also for the first time, elected two women, a result that the *Cut Bank Pioneer Press* called "a tribute to the good sense of the voters."[48] More Blackfeet ran for office than in any other election; eighty candidates ran in 1950 compared with only twenty-nine in 1942. Political interest and activity remained high; voter confidence in the council remained low.

It is not surprising that council leaders wanted to terminate various powers of the federal government, given its refusal to grant the BTBC expanded control of the Nation's operations. And it is not surprising that a majority of Blackfeet citizens did not sanction that expansion of council power, given the council's poor track record managing and investing the Nation's money. Superintendent Kildow told Fickinger that the defeat of the amendments "clearly indicates that [Blackfeet voters] are not satisfied with the present form of self-government to the extent that they are willing to entrust the Tribal Council with the supervisory powers now held by the Secretary of the Interior."[49]

Why did the Nation reject a measure of independence from the BIA? Had the "minority group" become the majority group? Kildow sensed among voters "very little desire for the termination of the supervisory powers." Unlike the popular vote amendment of 1945, there was little support from below for the termination amendments. Full-bloods had complained about the council since the late 1930s, charging favoritism, corruption, and discrimination. The BTBC meeting of March 2 demonstrated that the animus against council leadership had broadened. Class politics, couched in cultural terms of full-bloods and mixed-bloods, underlay protests and public meetings. During one such public meeting, council leader Leo Kennerly objected to the notion that "rich members are being shown partiality," while acknowledging the Nation's poverty; he admitted that "[80 percent] of the people here and not the full-bloods alone, can be classed as very poor."[50] Full-blood elders, therefore, had simply assumed the mantle of leadership of a burgeoning class-based opposition that transcended the "minority group," an appellation based solely on demographics.

Politically active Blackfeet were particularly disturbed by the council's 1948 investment of one hundred thousand dollars of tribal money in a cooperative store, devised in a manner to avoid having to get secretarial approval of the contracts. The council's action violated section f of the charter's corporate powers provision limiting the council's authority to make contracts to ten thousand dollars.[51] In a widely unpopular decision, especially among full-bloods, the council gave to John Loewen, a white man earning thirty-six hundred dollars per year at a competing Browning grocery store, a very generous contract to manage the new store. The contract's provisions included a six-thousand-dollar annual salary, three weeks' vacation, and a potential profit-sharing bonus of two thousand dollars. The contract also provided that the council would base Loewen's bonus on gross sales, giving him incentive to maximize his profit against that of the Nation.[52] Superintendent O'Hara noted that "a great many Blackfeet Indians are against this venture" and opined that "the Tribe not only stands to lose a large sum of money on the original plan but further still, if the venture is a losing one, there is nothing to prohibit the Council's appropriating more money from time to time to keep the thing alive." He called the council's plan "a very dangerous venture" with little chance of success given the council's lack of marketing experience and the competition from white merchants.[53]

Protesters might have overlooked the contract's deficiencies had the store earned a profit for the Blackfeet. Once operational, however, the store ran at a deficit. According to Wilson Ferris auditor Howard Gaare, "[i]t was impossible to run the business, because people did not pay for the goods. The [Blackfeet] customers thought they owned the store."[54] And as O'Hara had predicted, succeeding councils threw good money after bad. By September 1949 the store venture owed the Nation $92,597.66, largely because of high salaries and what auditors called customer "favoritism," or subjective pricing.[55] Although the council stopped the heavy bleeding, the store continued to run in the red and thus generated among interested parties less than sanguine views about its future. The store controversy appeared to have made a difference in the 1950 council election. In response, the new council issued its own report attributing the loss to "excessive salaries," theft, nonpayment, and extended credit, but it elected not to initiate any reforms other than to establish routine audits and expressed optimism that the store could eventually turn a profit.[56]

The BTBC's repeated failure to implement suggestions from BIA field personnel to strengthen the fidelity of the tribe's administrative operation also angered a cross section of Blackfeet citizens. The problem stemmed in part from the council's resistance to accepting advice from extension workers charged with supervising most aspects of the tribe's credit program. The BIA attempted to defuse this tension by giving the council more leeway in its lending program in July 1948, granting to the Magee council the authority to administer RCF loans under two thousand dollars without the approval of BIA personnel. The authority was revoked soon after the council provided 211 "hay loans" in one day, many of them to people who owned no livestock.[57] The council's action undermined the integrity of the Nation's entire RCF program, turning it into one of the worst in the plains states; it damaged the council's ability to secure new funds and engendered a new round of hostility with the Extension Division that ultimately precipitated the Magee council's decision to call for the termination election. The BTBC's persistent criticism of the division's control of the RCF program seemed inappropriate given its own undisciplined performance providing "hay loans," many of which were never repaid. The Magee council also distributed "tribal emergency loans" of between five and twenty-five dollars, most of which went to full-bloods.[58] The loans served either as a supplementary per capita payment or as an advance against an anticipated one. Despite good intentions, such distributions were not regularized and thus open to abuse. During the unusually harsh winter of 1950, the council distributed a portion of its tribal funds in the form of a per capita advance.[59] Blackfeet from outlying communities traveled to the Nation's welfare office during a blizzard only to discover that the funds were insufficient to give everyone a loan. According to Gaare, some Indians collected two checks. Others returned home empty-handed.[60]

The council also ignored most of the suggestions given by Wilson Ferris auditors. The company's accountants faced two principal problems, according to Gaare, who audited the Blackfeet Nation's books between 1946 and 1955. Auditors had to "start from scratch in setting up records" when they assumed the task in 1946. Once a new council took office, however, it would elect a new treasurer and reorganize the recordkeeping system, and most of the treasurers had little experience in accounting procedures. Gaare and his colleagues tried to standardize procedures to reduce the effects of this turnover, but they faced resistance from the new chairman and new treasurer. The second problem stemmed from BTBC leaders' resistance to adopting standard fiscal practices.

Council members were intent on establishing their own system, despite the handicap of implementing accounting methods without adequate training or guidance. Gaare noted the Blackfeet's tendency to reject white advice, explaining that council leaders "wanted to do it by themselves, [and] wanted to run it themselves."[61] The problems of the Magee council, then, were endemic to Blackfeet politics. Newly elected council members agreed with many of the criticisms leveled by BIA officials and Blackfeet voters during the termination and council election campaigns of 1950, and they contributed their own criticisms. But the Magee council was certainly not the first to be charged with incompetence and impropriety. The Wilson Ferris audits tracked the BTBC's financial misdeeds back to 1942, though questionable dealings had begun during the Hazlett years, when wealthy council members of low blood quantum helped themselves to financial favors. Some of the council members elected in 1950, particularly new chairman George Pambrun, had themselves been charged with impropriety during previous terms; both Pambrun and Joe Brown had been negligent in repaying loans secured from tribal credit funds.

The constant turnover on the council, the members' lack of financial education, and their resistance to white advisers and "white" administration contributed to the BTBC's poor performance. Howard Gaare also attributed the council's problems to the constant pressure council members faced from relatives, friends, and constituents to release funds in per capita payments or loans, most of which were never repaid. For example, Gaare confronted treasurer Iliff McKay after he discovered the sixty-five-hundred-dollar shortfall. McKay replied that he was indeed "guilty," explaining to Gaare that he "took the money and gave it to people who asked for it." In Gaare's mind these distributions were not corrupt but an Indian form of resource distribution, a modern form of the traditional give-away that characterized Blackfeet social relations.[62] Other contemporary observers of Blackfeet politics such as Felix Cohen, John Ewers, and William Fenton all argued that what appeared to white officials to be corruption was actually a syncretic form of cultural tradition. Fenton, who investigated Blackfeet factionalism in August 1950, described a "pay-off problem" that was "related to the problem of gift-giving" and the maintenance of status. Echoing Gaare's comment, Fenton said that council members got "pressure from relatives to give them benefits." Government officials considered the council's distribution of assets a "Tammany bribery scheme," but Fenton argued that such was not the case.[63] Felix Cohen, the Blackfeet Nation's attorney, described to new council members the "resentment which white officials have so often expressed against the generosity that Blackfeet Indians and their tribal leaders have always shown towards those of their own people who are in need or distress. We have a hard job ahead of us, in trying to combine Blackfeet generosity and white man's business practices." Cohen persuaded the council to make public the auditor's reports of council finances, an action that was "a necessary part of progress." And he asked BIA officials for patience, arguing that the tribe needed time to find the proper balance between the Indian's culture of generosity, practiced in the give-away of tribal loans and per capita payments, and the "white monetary attitudes" and accounting practices that demanded a more objective approach to resource distribution.[64]

Yet in the context of constitutional democracy, the provisions of which governed the entire Nation rather than certain bands or social groups, BTBC fiscal behavior was corrupt and BIA officials rightly expected some reform of its practices to mitigate social and political tensions and help break a long-running cycle of dissension. Cohen effectively claimed what Stephanie Lawson calls "errors in cross-cultural understanding," a common defense against external criticism.[65] But the problem and the practice of council give-aways was endemic and not isolated to one or two professional politicians. BIA staff thus struggled with the problem of how to facilitate the reform of Blackfeet politics, how to balance its mission to foster Indian self-support without sacrificing the interests of the "minority group" or infringing upon tribal sovereignty. The personnel, the mission, and the methods of the BIA changed in the late 1940s, all of which coalesced during the Blackfeet's termination election and dramatically altered the trajectory of Indian-white relations.

As the termination election drew closer, so too did the BIA's scrutiny of the BTBC's performance. Fickinger, a magnet for Blackfeet complaints about the council's actions, pressed his superiors to clarify both the government's responsibility toward disgruntled tribal members and his options for policing or prosecuting council members guilty of breaking rules or laws. Fickinger's query signaled a shift from the Zimmerman regime, which had drawn the line at the application of moral suasion to council members suspected of mismanagement or misappropriation. For Zimmerman, the last vestige of Collier's New Deal team, the tribe had to learn from its mistakes and use the democratic tools contained in its constitution to correct them. Although he found the council's actions disturbing, he preferred to leave reform in Indian hands.

Fickinger and Superintendent Rex Kildow met with Zimmerman, D'Arcy McNickle, and other BIA officials in late April 1950 to review the Blackfeet election and discuss its implication for Indian-white relations in the coming decade. The BIA contingent examined the BTBC's contracts and banking procedures but focused on its attempts to circumvent controls on per capita distributions, a source of contention between the two governments since oil revenues had reached a level where distributions were possible. The Blackfeet charter limited per capita distributions without secretarial approval to those amounting to less than one-half of the tribe's accrued surplus funds.[66] As indicated earlier, BIA officials routinely accused the council of juggling revenue figures by adding Class A monies to its balances to justify a higher distribution amount. Council members tried to avoid getting secretarial approval largely because they knew they would not receive it and because they had lost interest in cutting through red tape for approval for per capita distributions demanded by their constituents. This was one charter violation most Blackfeet chose to overlook.

McNickle summarized the meeting in a letter to Dillon Myer, the new commissioner of Indian Affairs, by reporting that the "record is discouraging at many points and unless corrective actions are taken at once the assets of the Blackfeet Tribe may be seriously depleted." McNickle suggested that the government might need to "seek an injunction or mandamus in the Federal Court" and pursue subsequent violators with contempt proceedings. To do so, McNickle cautioned, the government would need convincing evidence of criminal or civil violations.[67] Myer instructed Fickinger to continue his investigation of charter violations and to revive constitutional amendments sought by a full-blood delegation in late 1949 that had never reached the election stage. He thus answered Fickinger's query about the government's role in Blackfeet affairs by directing him to investigate the tribe's political leaders for misdeeds and possible prosecution and to strengthen the council's political opposition.[68]

Fickinger responded by sending to council members a series of letters that criticized the tribe's BRCE, RCF, and tribal loan programs; the letters subsequently found their way to the Blackfeet electorate less than two weeks before the June 20, 1950, elections. Fickinger listed the various charter violations outlined during the April BIA meeting and demanded immediate reform. His paternalistic and threatening tone concerning a *tribal* enterprise not initiated by the BIA, and the distribution of letters—which contained damaging phrases like "poor judgment," "by subterfuge," "financial loss to the tribe," and "direct violation"—to potential voters on the eve of the tribe's most important election since the IRA years symbolized the arrival of a new BIA and a new era of intergovernmental relations.[69] The partnership between the BTBC and the BIA that New Dealers like Zimmerman had fostered devolved to a form of increasingly hostile diplomacy between council leaders and men like Fickinger. Notable was Fickinger's use of "U.S.A." in describing the federal government's contributions of credit and cattle; it suggested that Blackfeet were not true, patriotic Americans. Fickinger's letters served as a frontal assault on the BTBC's integrity. He wrote in one letter, "Frankly, I have been extremely disappointed at the manner in which Blackfeet Tribal Business Councils have administered the affairs of the Blackfeet Tribe. I have been a firm believer in the policy of self-government and I feel that we have all been extremely indulgent of honest mistakes. . . . We had hoped that you would heed the admonitions of the Secretary of the Interior, and Officers of the Indian Service and begin to function in a businesslike and proper manner." The age of admonitions ended when Fickinger told the council it was "guilty of deliberate mismanagement and maladministration."[70]

Fickinger's criticisms of the council certainly were not captious. However, the timing of their distribution, and the manner in which he wrote them, raised legitimate concerns that BIA officials intended to meddle in tribal politics; the release of the letters just before the June elections was tantamount to Fickinger campaigning against the incumbent council and its termination amendments. Indeed, critics of Fickinger's actions complained about the distribution of his charges rather than the charges themselves. The BIA's interference in Blackfeet political affairs angered tribal attorney Cohen and his associates at the Association on American Indian Affairs (AAIA), where he served as general counsel. AAIA president Oliver La Farge telegraphed Oscar Chapman after the election and requested an explanation of Fickinger's "calculated" efforts to "influence" voters, asking whether the action constituted a new departmental policy. Chapman responded that "it was the feeling of the Commissioner that the members of the Blackfeet Tribe should know how the Tribl [*sic*] Council in years past had discharged its obligation with respect to the husbanding of tribal funds and property." Despite encouraging the council's effort to assume greater responsibility for the Nation's affairs, Chapman argued that until such termination occurred Interior officials "are obligated to act prudently where tribal property is involved."[71]

It is difficult to classify Fickinger's behavior—and by extension Myer's—as "prudent." His barrage of inflammatory letters—eight in all, totaling thirty-four pages—guaranteed that the incumbent council would have no chance to respond to the charges or make appropriate changes. As a result, no incumbent retained his or her seat. The dissemination of information angered council members, who argued with considerable justification that the letters damaged their candidacies, even though the reports also documented abuses that occurred during previous administrations. The incumbents were equally troubled by Fickinger's invasion of the Blackfeet political domain, a sensitive issue for all Blackfeet since Frank Campbell's electioneering campaigns of the late 1920s. Fickinger's letters also affected voters' perception of the termination measures, though the final tallies suggest that the Blackfeet did not need Fickinger or his information to help them decide how to cast their vote. Fickinger simply reinforced voters' own perceptions of the council's "mismanagement and maladministration," as well as their prejudices against expanding its authority.

Fickinger's epistolary encroachment on tribal sovereignty prompted countercharges from tribal attorney Felix Cohen and new BTBC chairman George Pambrun, which set the stage for this new relationship between the BTBC and the OIA. The BTBC as an institution had faced an intrusive campaign from a high-level BIA employee, whose criticisms—some spurious and some substantive—had been designed to destabilize an incumbent administration. Cohen bluntly told outgoing council members that Fickinger's charges were neither new nor true: "Some are false because Mr. Fickinger is mistaken as to the facts. Others are false because Mr. Fickinger is mistaken [as] to the law. In several cases Mr. Fickinger is apparently trying to evade responsibility for his own mistakes by trying to shift the blame to the Blackfeet Indians."[72] Cohen rejected Fickinger's right to call for either the reform of tribal administration or the right to approve council expenditures, saying that "[t]his is a matter for the people of the Tribe to decide. The Tribal Council is responsible for these decisions to the Blackfeet Indians." Cohen's attack on Fickinger took on an ad hominem flavor. Cohen concluded that Fickinger very well might be "a well-meaning, hard-working individual" who suffered from "a sort of delirium, in which the delirious official imagines that he is God and that all he needs to do is to give orders and his Indian world will obey. . . . Sometimes it is necessary for courts or Indians to explain to the patient that he really is not God. Some patients have been known to recover. Let's all be charitable and give Mr. Fickinger our best help if he shows any signs of returning sanity." Cohen charged that Fickinger "is deeply engaged in sabotaging the progressive Indian policy of the administration."[73]

Fickinger showed signs of courage but not sanity by returning to the reservation in July to address the new council that he had helped elect, somewhat chastened by Cohen's aggressive defense of the council's rights, which served notice that Cohen would monitor carefully Fickinger's words and actions. Fickinger gave a frank and yet conciliatory talk, promising both to hold the new council to the provisions of the Blackfeet constitution and charter and to help it regain the confidence of tribal members through the reform of its business practices. He explained that financial conditions impelled him to distribute the letters. "I had to do it in protection of the people of the Blackfeet Tribe and still may have to do it," Fickinger said. But he admitted, as Cohen had argued, that the BIA and himself were partly to blame. "It is a reflection on me that we allowed the Blackfeet to get into this kind of a mess," he said. "We make mistakes, too, but let's get together and hash it out."[74] Fickinger pledged to provide the necessary assistance to "vest more and more control" in the BTBC because the federal government was not ready to withdraw its supervision. To further self-termination of federal control, Fickinger first advised council members to restore the council's fiscal integrity and the tribe's credit rating, recommending that council members consider constitutional amendments being devised by BIA attorneys to clarify the council's fiduciary responsibilities. Council members listened patiently to Fickinger's long lecture about the need for fidelity to the constitution and charter and for fiscal and moral integrity. They said little about his letters and his charges. But several acknowledged his call for better cooperation. Walter Wetzel bluntly stated that the BTBC had "more or less failed because [it] failed to cooperate with the U.S. Government."[75]

Cohen's and Pambrun's arguments addressed Fickinger's attitude toward tribal government as much as they did the content of his letters. Fickinger had asked new council members to read the letters before judging him. Pambrun answered for the council in an August letter in which he pledged cooperation with Fickinger and the BIA while defending the idea of tribal government and its right to make decisions for the Nation; the council would "insist on respect for the existing legal powers of the Blackfeet Tribe and its council as the very foundation of any such cooperation." Pambrun acknowledged the advisability of certain of Fickinger's recommendations and agreed to study his other demands for improving the Nation's credit operation and the council's standing with the Blackfeet citizenry; the council had already passed an ordinance prohibiting loan guarantees to tribal members as Fickinger had "ordered." But Pambrun qualified each of the fourteen points of contention outlined in the letter with an admonition to Fickinger that neither he nor the BIA had a legal authority to demand changes in tribal administration. The council would make certain changes and provide certain information "as a matter of courtesy and in the interests of cooperation and not with a view of conceding that federal officials have a [legal] right" to demand audits, council minutes, or copies of council budgets. Pambrun, like Cohen, also challenged Fickinger's right to demand changes in the administration of the BRCE: "The Council is not aware of any law or contract by which the Indian Bureau has acquired authority to decide when or how repayment cattle shall be returned by individuals to the Blackfeet Tribe or to determine what individuals shall receive loans of cattle from the Blackfeet Tribe."[76] Fickinger was indeed on less stable ground when he criticized the BRCE and tribal loan fund because the tribe was operating using its accrued surpluses in livestock and credit monies, having repaid its initial investment to the government.

Pambrun's pragmatic sanction prompted OIA officials to examine Fickinger's original charges. They determined that Fickinger had made "innocent" mistakes about the council's recordkeeping but supported his assessment of the tribe's lending operation as wasteful, ill-advised, and unstable.[77] OIA officials, including Myer, subsequently accused Cohen of writing Pambrun's letter, charging him with his own manipulation of the council. By doing so they refused to acknowledge the Blackfeet Nation's own political voice. Cohen, according to BTBC transcripts, did *help* the council write the letter that addressed Fickinger's demands, but only after telling council members, "I shall not advise on this question of general policy except to the extent that you may ask my advice."[78]

Cohen worked hard to avoid becoming anything but an adviser to Blackfeet politicians. In a letter to Sister Providencia, an "informant" and champion of Indian rights in Great Falls, he explained that he did not want the Blackfeet to "look upon me as a tribal leader—which would be the worst thing I could do to them, for such an attitude is fatal to independence. . . . I must refuse to be a tribal leader . . . just to make sure they don't come to rely on me for decisions they ought to make themselves."[79] More important, Pambrun did not need Cohen's animus against BIA coercion to assert the Blackfeet's right to make decisions independent of Interior and BIA officials. He had been publicly critical of BIA programs since joining the council in 1942 and had called on the BIA to give the tribe the right to select its own superintendent, arguing that a Blackfeet superintendent "would display a more active interest in Tribal affairs" than would a white superintendent.[80] Pambrun also had little interest in protecting his predecessors from scrutiny or investigation. He had attacked the Magee council before the election by contending that the Blackfeet needed to "get some intelligent men to do their business for them properly." And after he took office he supported Fickinger's call for an FBI investigation into his predecessors' lending practices.[81] But he and his fellow council members were not willing to concede to the BIA any moral or legal authority to administer tribal affairs not codified in the Nation's constitution or charter. Pambrun's letter served as a reaffirmation of Blackfeet sovereignty and formalized the division between the BIA and the BTBC.

Fickinger's treatment of the council was heavy-handed and ill-advised. He took the brunt of the criticism for Myer, under whose orders he had acted, partly out of loyalty and partly out of fear; his letters to Myer betray a certain obsequious quality that probably characterized other interagency correspondence during Myer's regime. Fickinger also raised substantive issues about the nature of Indian-white relations. In October 1950, he told Myer that he felt "up in the air" about the Blackfeet situation and again asked "just what my responsibilities are with reference to the Blackfeet Tribe or any Tribe so far as its affairs are concerned."[82] Fickinger asked for guidance from the Washington office, as to the degree to which he should pressure councils for reform as well as the degree to which he had legal authority to apply such pressure. Fickinger's confusion stemmed largely from Myer's sole public comment on the Blackfeet election controversy. Myer had told Pambrun after the BTBC election that "this Department generally adheres to the position that determinations of tribal governing bodies, in accordance with the principles of self-government, are entitled to great weight." He added that an "assumption of power by the Department is contrary to the very purpose of the Constitution, namely, that of Indian self-rule."[83] Myer referred to the council's request for OIA adjudication of a postelection controversy concerning the eligibility of two candidates who, their opponents charged, did not live on the reservation; Myer told the council to decide the issue for itself. His general statement articulated no real commitment to self-government, only that his department "generally adheres" to the idea of it. But his letter created the impression, for Felix Cohen in particular, that Myer was a defender of tribal sovereignty. Myer indeed left Fickinger "up in the air." It was part of Myer's strategy to appear progressive, as Cohen originally termed his administration, while organizing regressive actions through private channels and subordinates like Fickinger.

Fickinger, Zimmerman, and other BIA staff had been patient with the BTBC for a decade. Given the Blackfeet Nation's embrace of the IRA in 1934, its rapid adoption of a constitution and charter, and its general success in building a civic infrastructure, it is not surprising that BIA officials like Zimmerman and Fickinger, invested in tribal development with years of work and the counsel of disgruntled minority groups, would be extremely disappointed with the council's failings. The Blackfeet Nation—with its active political culture, oil revenues, and established livestock industry—could have managed its assets better. In 1950 a new BIA formed that heralded not only impatience but a new paternalistic politics of intimidation. The clash between the BTBC's Pambrun and the BIA's Fickinger, on the front lines of the struggle over Indian sovereignty, also amounted to a struggle between their respective intellectual patrons, Felix Cohen and Dillon Myer. Cohen and Myer, to understate it, had competing attitudes about Indian administration. Their struggle for the hearts and minds of the Blackfeet, and other Indians, would dominate Indian-white relations in the early 1950s. Fickinger had his own reasons to attack the BTBC, and he had been increasingly open in his criticism beginning in late 1949. However, Cohen misunderstood Fickinger's methods and his motives. As Chapman explained to Oliver La Farge, Fickinger wrote his letters on orders from Myer, who wanted to "educate" Blackfeet voters about the council's history before they elected to expand its powers and terminate those of the federal government; much of Fickinger's information came from his meeting with McNickle, Zimmerman, and other BIA staff. Fickinger was not playing god. He was simply a disciple delivering a message from Washington. Cohen had argued that Fickinger was "sabotaging the progressive Indian policy of the administration." It soon became clear to Cohen that the administration of Dillon Seymour Myer was far from progressive.

Besides serving as general counsel of the AAIA, Felix Cohen had used his knowledge of Indian law and BIA operations to secure attorney contracts with several tribes, including the Blackfeet. He had worked with Blackfeet leaders in the mid-1930s to fashion the Nation's constitution and charter and thus had an intimate familiarity with its political system. When he began advising the council in the fall of 1949, he came armed with a refined sense of belief in Indian self-government. In a 1949 essay entitled "Indian Self-Government," Cohen defended the internal sovereignty of Indian governments and the political expression of it in IRA constitutions and charters. Like other New Dealers, Cohen believed that Indians needed to make their own way toward sustainable government; he decried government experts dictating how Indian government should function, stressing the need for whites to let Indians "try out ideas of self-government, of economics, of social relations, that we consider to be wrong." Cohen discerned that a coercive element in the BIA had become intent on delaying or blocking Indians' hard-won rights to voluntarily terminate federal supervision, rights that were codified in IRA charters and constitutions; facing withdrawal, the bureau fought to ensure that it did not "work itself out of a job." Cohen contended that "[t]ribes without independent legal guidance frequently acquiesce in such infringements upon their constitutional and corporate powers. Thus many of the gains of the Roosevelt era are being chipped away."[84] He intended to guide the BTBC's efforts to maintain its rights in the face of rising pressure to strip them. Fickinger's infringements during the Blackfeet's 1950 termination election exemplified what Cohen considered to be the reemergence of BIA "colonialism."

Myer and Cohen would have several skirmishes in the early 1950s, particularly over the issue of attorney contracts, and these skirmishes evolved into a showdown between two distinct ideologies: Cohen the defender of tribal sovereignty against the neocolonial dictatorship of Myer the "terminator." In attacking Cohen, Myer took on perhaps the last active vestige of the Indian New Deal. Harold Ickes and John Collier waged their attacks against Myer in the press; Myer, Ickes wrote in his last *New Republic* column, was a "blundering and dictatorial tin-Hitler" who "intended to transform the Bureau of Indian Affairs into a puppet show with him pulling the strings."[85] Cohen and his supporters used words like "Gestapo" and "dictatorship" to describe the BIA's administration of

Blackfeet affairs; Myer in turn accused Cohen of picking a fight with the Bureau and of "abetting" tribal councils. This war of words turned into physical confrontation in April 1951 when the BTBC seized control of several agency buildings, contending that the tribe owned them because the government had deducted their construction costs from the Big Claim. Tribal police, with Cohen and council members watching, padlocked the buildings and posted eviction notices on them. After threatening an FBI investigation, Myer backed down on Chapman's insistence, giving tribal leaders what turned out to be a temporary victory.[86]

The conflict brought an immediate end to intergovernmental cooperation; détente devolved to a cold war. Fickinger and the BTBC would make efforts to work together during the early 1950s, as when Myer began to push his withdrawal program. But Myer's confrontational regime, especially once Guy Robertson assumed the superintendency, engendered ill-feeling among Blackfeet politicians that hardened their terminationist and nationalist views. The fight for tribal sovereignty transcended parochial concerns or sentimentalism, Cohen believed, and represented more than a war of words. The American Indian, he wrote, "is to America what the Jew was to the Russian czars and Hitler's Germany. For us the Indian tribe is the miners' canary and when it flutters and droops we know that the poison gasses [sic] of intolerance threaten all other minorities in our land. And who of us is not a member of some minority."[87] The Indian New Deal began to decline after Collier resigned; it began to "flutter and droop" when Myer took office.

Not surprisingly, Myer and Cohen also held different views on termination. Even as Myer pursued terminationist legislation in an unusually friendly fashion with Congress and greatly enlarged BIA appropriations rather than reducing them, his BIA subordinates, many of whom came from the War Relocation Authority (WRA), asserted a new paternalism on Indian reservations; the paradox of Myer's regime was that he nearly doubled the BIA's budget during his tenure while pursuing the most terminationist and repressive policies of any commissioner since the nineteenth century.[88] As Cohen, George Pambrun, and Joe Brown strove to expand the council's powers and to eliminate BIA jobs, Myer and his colleagues tried to circumscribe these powers and the council's plans for expanding self-government. Pambrun and Brown should have appealed to Fickinger and Myer and presented themselves as tribal leaders with whom the two government officials could do business. Pambrun was a moderate terminationist, a rancher, and an effective politician, though his record of taking advantage of political office to secure loans did not endear him to many Blackfeet; in fact he did not make it to the end of his term, having been forced out after he again borrowed large sums of tribal money to fund his livestock operations. But Myer's pathological distrust of Indian leaders, whom he called "wily Indians," prevented him from securing much cooperation with Blackfeet leaders. Myer objected to a piecemeal approach to termination. There was no middle ground, in Myer's mind, between Indian and white conceptions of tribal self-government.

While Pambrun and Brown continued to sponsor a limited termination program in Congress and fight BIA coercion on the reservation, the Blackfeet dissident group revived its agenda of curtailing the council's spending habits, increasing its share of tribal assets, and campaigning for expanded Interior Department control. As the BIA's confidence in the BTBC eroded, the Indian Office turned to this group and its agenda for political change. The 1950s, after all, saw the federal government attempt to destabilize "nonaligned" nations that had failed to demonstrate the proper respect for America's constitutional democracy and the needs of its freedom-loving corporations; the Blackfeet Nation and Guatemala lay roughly equidistant from Washington DC. Given the nationalistic flavor of the BTBC, it is not surprising that the BIA, especially under Myer's direction, could adopt in the early 1950s a position similar to the nation's stance toward countries that refused to choose sides in the Cold War. Although not surprising, the BIA's attitude toward Indian governments it considered recalcitrant was ironic, given that officials were ostensibly trying to help those Indians assume more responsibility for their welfare. Fickinger, already an advocate of full-blood interests after monitoring tribal conflicts for several years, accepted a directive from Myer to help or strengthen the Blackfeet minority group in an effort to create a countervailing source of indigenous political pressure.

The Magee council had attempted greater cooperation with its detractors by paying for a delegation's visit to Washington in January 1949, though it did so "only in an attempt to appease the minority group." It also insisted that the BIA give it a chance to respond to any of the delegation's complaints.[89] The protests of the older people stemmed in part from the age of the council. Zimmerman told the delegation that "we must accept the fact that there is a great difference in the world today from what it was 15 or 25 years ago. Because of the changed conditions, the younger generation cannot be expected to follow the pattern which was followed at that time."[90] More important than solicitude, Zimmerman and his colleagues provided the delegates, at their request, with drafts of possible amendments to the constitution. Both the BTBC and the Blackfeet electorate had the right to request a referendum on constitutional amendments. The secretary of the interior also had the authority to call for such an election if he or she deemed it in the best interests of the tribe. But the OIA decided that it would not force the issue if council leaders or an oppositional faction did not demonstrate the requisite effort and desire to do it themselves.

The OIA submitted to full-blood leaders drafts of several amendments that would have affected BTBC fiscal practices by providing greater public accountability for budgets and expenses and giving to the secretary of the interior *expanded* supervisory powers over those budgets and expenses; a separate amendment would have given the tribe the right to recall from office a council member deemed corrupt or incompetent. Zimmerman informed dissidents that they could force the council to submit their economic proposals to a vote if they got signatures from one-third of the electorate, a daunting task given the tribe's demographic makeup and the reservation's expanse.[91] It is difficult to predict whether the amendments as written would have passed in 1949. Zimmerman believed that "even though the amendments may not carry, the full-blood people may be better satisfied knowing that they were put to a vote."[92] Zimmerman, having spent a decade and a half trying to convince full-bloods that the constitution was the only cure for their voiceless condition, understood that their efforts might not succeed because of their demographic disadvantages. However, he wanted them to at least exercise their only political option rather than rely upon white bureaucrats like himself to manage their insurgency.

Full-bloods apparently did little to secure signatures or promote the proposed amendments and continued their campaign to get the OIA to make the changes for them. Just eight months after what appeared to be a productive meeting with top OIA officials, the full-blood group requested public funds to travel to Washington to protest the council's proposed termination election. Assistant Commissioner John Provinse informed Superintendent Kildow that OIA officials understood the issues "troubling the full blood group, but as yet we have not arrived at a solution. . . . Will you please advise the group that the Secretary's supervisory powers will not be terminated without a vote of the Tribe. If the members are opposed to termination they should vote against it when the matter is submitted to a vote."[93] Some full-bloods threatened to boycott the election. White Calf and Last Star explained to Chapman that the "full-blood Indian people are not in favor of voting to have all the powers of the Secretary of the Interior taken away. It is our desire to remain as we are. . . . We will not vote."[94]

Whether White Calf, Last Star, or like-minded full-bloods did vote in June 1950 is hard to determine. But the tribe's rejection of the termination amendments and their BTBC sponsors did embolden the minority group to become more assertive in its calls for political reform. Full-blood leaders like White Calf and Charles Reevis discovered more aggressive partners in Myer and in Fickinger, who finally acted on their complaints by giving the council his eight-letter shot across its bow. Zimmerman's regime had given full-bloods every opportunity to initiate a campaign for constitutional amendments. The Myer regime seized on the opportunity to expedite the reform process and help full-bloods—and thus the BIA—achieve a measure of control over the council.

Besides their mutual distrust of the BTBC, the minority group and the BIA shared a dislike of Felix Cohen. In July 1949, Reevis had joined with other tribal members in their unanimous support of the BTBC's selection of Cohen as tribal attorney.[95] In May 1951 Reevis contended that Cohen had few supporters among full-bloods and mixed-bloods because he sanctioned the withdrawal of federal supervision. He blamed Cohen for the tribe's financial troubles and the council's termination campaign, complaining to Chapman that "ever since the tribal council has hired Felix Cohen, he makes everything up side down. I can see very clearly that Mr. Felix Cohen does not want the tribe to have any kind of protection, so he can do as he pleases." Louis Plenty Treaty held Cohen responsible for the council "stirring up this trouble" against the federal government.[96] Full-bloods resented Cohen in part because in 1950 the tribe allocated more than $3,500 per annum for legal services that full-bloods believed ran counter to their interests. Cohen's services cost the tribe $4,600 in FY 1951–52, or 1.25 percent of the total budget of $367,600, a large increase that reflected the council's assessment of his value to the tribe and the increased work brought about by Myer's attacks on Indians' rights. In addition to Cohen's fees, the council spent another $1,000 on local legal advice and nearly $10,000 on audit fees and delegation expenses.[97] To the council's opponents, the sums spent on lawyers, accountants, and delegations produced no benefit to the tribe while reducing the available pool of per capita money.

The full-bloods' insurgency precipitated an OIA review of what it should do to assist factions dissatisfied with constitutional governments. Paul Fickinger again requested assistance from the OIA to help him deal with the "general question of the responsibility of the Secretary within the framework of tribal constitutions, bylaws, and charters" after getting complaints about the council's distribution of bank loans and loan guarantees to its members. In December 1950, the council had guaranteed nearly forty thousand dollars in bank loans made to council members, much of the sum going to Pambrun.[98] D'Arcy McNickle agreed that "events taking place on the Blackfeet Reservation are forcing this question for early resolution."[99]

McNickle proposed three "democratic remedies": the public should submit the council's loans to a binding popular referendum by securing a petition signed by one-third of the electorate, protest during council meetings to put the council "on notice that its actions were not approved," and create a constitutional amendment to codify a recall provision to prevent future abuses. The agency superintendent, McNickle argued, should educate dissatisfied members about these options. He advised Fickinger to discuss the council's history with new superintendent Guy Robertson, one of Dillon Myer's former WRA subordinates, and encourage him to initiate an "educational campaign directed at mobilizing public opinion against irresponsibility in tribal office."[100] This strategy became the department's official policy. Dillon Myer explained to Rep. Mike Mansfield that Blackfeet dissidents needed to resort "to the political power of the people to remove unfaithful public servants. There are provisions in the constitution for referendum and amendment, and it is the proper use of these tools of democracy which must be acquired by the members of the tribe. . . . Once the tribal members fully understand this and understand that they have the authority in their own hands to insist on responsibility in their tribal representatives, we may hope to see conditions improve."[101] Myer's advice was reasonable and appropriate, given the BTBC's continued transgressions. At the same time, the Blackfeet superintendency was devolving from that of an advisory role to Robertson's advocacy of one faction's interests.

A petition signed by roughly five hundred voters in March 1951 fell short of the number required to put a referendum to a vote, but it illustrated the depth of voter discontent and the evolving nature of Blackfeet political protest. The petitions of protest in the late 1930s had come from full-bloods only, but in the early 1940s they began to include the term "half-bloods" as well as "full-bloods." The March 1951 petition came from "Members of the Blackfeet Tribe of Indians."[102] As noted earlier, government officials and social scientists had dissolved the traditional dichotomy of full-blood and mixed-blood that was based solely on blood quantum in favor of new conceptions of *cultural* or *social* full-bloods. Felix Cohen, as assistant solicitor, had argued that the "lines of division are social and not simply biological." John Ewers wrote, "When I look back on those times I recognize that there were endless dual differences that are submerged in any effort to classify tribal members as full bloods or mixed." Blackfeet were either "Indian-oriented" or "White-oriented," to repeat Malcolm McFee's terms.[103] A full-blood thus came to signify in the 1940s a Blackfeet with (typically) one-half or more blood quantum who identified with the politics of the "minority group." Indeed, Charles Reevis, the leader of that group, was a half-blood, though he had attempted to pass as a full-blood to further his claim to power. The signatures on late 1940s and early 1950s petitions also began to reflect a wider spectrum of Blackfeet blood quantum and economic standing. A 1949 petition, for example, included the signatures of mixed-bloods like Archie St. Goddard, a quarter-blood rancher and former council member.[104] In addition, the March 1951 petition articulated in a legal manner the council's alleged abuses of its constitutional authority rather than simply reciting general complaints. The style of the writing suggests that someone other than White Calf, Reevis, or Plenty Treaty wrote the petition—most likely Superintendent Robertson.

The elderly leadership of the "minority group" finally adopted the BIA's advice and helped to form, under Robertson's guidance, a legitimate political opposition that crossed boundaries of race, ethnicity, and class. After June 1950 full-blood leaders became less apt to demand the end of the IRA, calling instead for constitutional reforms of the council, a strategy that dovetailed with that of politically dissatisfied mixed-bloods who protested corrupt BTBC members rather than the IRA itself. The "segregationists," as Reevis's group called itself, suspended their calls for the end of the IRA when it became clear that neither the BIA nor a majority of the Blackfeet people supported this agenda.[105] Full-bloods entered the political mainstream to attract the support of mixed-bloods and thus broaden the base of their dissenting coalition. In May 1951, Reevis asked Interior officials to help his group devise a constitutional amendment that would reduce the council's control of tribal income and alter income distribution patterns that favored enterprising mixed-bloods. His plan allocated tribal revenue along the following lines: 60 percent for per capita distribution, 20 percent for tribal welfare and social work, and 20 percent for council expenses and the sickness and funeral funds. In general, the minority faction believed that the council should cut administrative expenses in favor of increased per capita payments. The 1951–52 budget allocated 24 percent of revenues for administration—half of which went to council salaries and per diem expenses, totaling $44,600—and another 6 percent for the sickness and funeral funds, a full 10 percent above the level in Reevis's plan.[106]

The OIA's muted answer to Reevis's request for advice angered Fickinger, who argued that Reevis's "general idea may not be too far wrong." The OIA's second response, sent at Fickinger's urging, simply advised Reevis that his group should secure signatures from one-third of the tribe's eligible voters to put his plan to a vote. Fickinger had become convinced not only that the full-bloods' protests and proposals for remedy made sense but that they had the numbers to effect such political change.[107] By September 1951, Robertson stood firmly behind the full-blood faction as well and helped it to craft a new amendment. "I believe you feel as I do about the proposed amendment," he wrote Fickinger. "I believe that they are correct in trying to prevent unnecessary extravagances, and that they are entitled to full consideration in any attempt they make to try to correct a bad situation." The revised amendment altered Reevis's original proposal somewhat, setting the per capita amount at 50 percent of net tribal revenues rather than 60 and allocating 20 percent for health, welfare, sickness, and funeral programs; the remaining 30 percent was slated for administration, education, taxes, and other costs associated with corporate management. All of these monies would be distributed by a special disbursing agent—namely the agency superintendent—upon resolution by the BTBC. Any balances would go directly to the Nation's Class A treasury account without passing through the BTBC or the Blackfeet citizenry, which could only access the money through a popular referendum. Finally, to prevent further abuse, the proposal banned lending and guaranteeing bank loans to council members and their families.[108]

The amendment, as with other full-blood proposals, would have made it more difficult for Blackfeet politicians to extract money from the Nation's Class A account (which would remain subject to congressional control) than under the existing system. It also would have created an inflexible budget that could handcuff a council during legitimate emergencies such as winter storms, and it expanded the superintendent's role by making that person the special disbursing agent. Dillon Myer, at least privately, did not favor the transfer of the tribe's financial responsibilities to the superintendent or to the secretary of the interior, particularly in the area of per capita distributions. Such a change, he warned Fickinger, would add political pressures to an already complicated local situation by handicapping both the petitioners' primary goal of regularized per capita payments and the BTBC's administration of reservation resources. Myer concluded that "this amendment would probably insure the failure of any governing body and thus would discredit the Blackfeet people as being incapable of administering their own affairs."[109] Yet, despite what a thinking person might call serious reservations, he told sponsors Reevis and Louis Plenty Treaty that he was "unable to conclude that [proposed] changes will be adverse to the tribe's interest." He sanctioned their efforts to secure the amendment's passage because a large segment of the tribal membership supported the amendment's proposals.[110] Myer also backed the proposal because one of his lieutenants, Superintendent Robertson, helped to write it. But his support of the measure serves as a good example of what one might call Myer's agonistes. One side of Myer wanted to see the amendment "discredit the Blackfeet people as being incapable of administering their own affairs" and remain subject to government control. Another Myer wanted the Blackfeet to disappear as a political entity and fade into the landscape of rugged individualism. Myer respected the individual's wish to secure change, but not the right of an organized political body to foster it, demonstrating in the process a pathological distrust of Indian leaders.

The self-styled "People's Committee"—which enjoyed an increasingly higher number of mixed-blood supporters—secured enough signatures to warrant a referendum election the following January. Robertson warned Fickinger that because the BTBC opposed the proposal the government should "staff and supervise" the election.[111] Council members and Cohen naturally opposed such a measure. Control of tribal revenues had always been an important foundation of self-government. Past efforts by superintendents to limit the amount of per capita payments to the percentage of net tribal revenues, though heavy-handed, were initiated to keep the council operating according to the terms of the corporate charter. The full-bloods' amendment would have codified such limitations. Although the council's fiscal performance disappointed most observers, the proposal was in most respects a regressive measure. As Myer himself put it to Chapman, the amendment "would be a step backward."[112]

The constant public pressure for constitutional change had prompted the council to form a constitution amendment committee, but it had done little since forming in June 1951; previous councils had discussed the idea of regularizing per capita payments, but, as with many proposals, it never found its way to the referendum stage.[113] It took the threat of a BIA-sponsored amendment to force the council to address citizens' complaints, the result of the opposition's first exercise in democratic IRA politics after a decade of extralegal maneuvering outside the parameters of the Nation's constitutional government. During a February 27 public hearing to address the "processes of Indian democracy," council members and Cedor Aronow, Cohen's local associate attorney, calmly explained to members of the People's Committee that their amendment would grant the BTBC a greater percentage of tribal revenues, give the superintendent the power of approval over per capita payments and health benefits, and limit tribal officials' access to Class A monies. In addition, bureau officials could use the Nation's money to pay costs associated with health programs and law and judicial programs.

Council members viewed Robertson's role in the amendment campaign as particularly disturbing. When a council member asked Plenty Treaty who wrote the amendment, he answered, "Mr. Robertson wrote it." Joe Brown, in the background on most political issues by this time, delivered a stinging indictment of Robertson and the proposal: "The Superintendent is appointed to protect the interests of the Tribe. I can see from this petition that he has pulled the wool over your eyes and he has not only done that but he wants to perpetuate the power that the Indian Bureau has on the Indian. All it is is to protect their own power so they will always be [here]."[114] Brown in particular was unwilling to take that "step backward." Council leaders like Walter Wetzel acknowledged that the council could pare its expenses and operate more efficiently; he and several other council members, including Brown and Cora Irgens, had been pressing for a reduction of council expenses since June 1951. Wetzel asked for a delay of the election so that the two groups could "iron this thing out." Surprisingly, the full-blood representatives agreed. Theodore Last Star complained that he and other petitioners were not happy with some of the wording of the amendment and that they now expressed

"doubt about voting for it." The motion to postpone the original amendment and fashion a compromise passed unanimously. The tribe's most
influential full-bloods, including cosponsor Louis Plenty Treaty, signed
a telegram to Myer asking him to "disregard petition and vacate any election ordered. . . . People getting together to work out [new] language."[115]
The transcript of the meeting suggests that BTBC representatives were
respectful of the concerns expressed by petitioners, who, for their part,
seemed surprised by the logical arguments presented against their
amendment. Despite their criticism of the BTBC, full-blood leaders became concerned that new powers vested in the superintendent might
jeopardize their primary goal of regular per capita payments.

The February 27 meeting created for the first time a viable bipartisan
coalition committed to the goal of fiscal reform. Given the increasing
size and evolving social composition of the dissenting coalition, and its
consequent ability to force referenda, it would have been in the council's
interests to preclude a similar attempt by agreeing to adopt a compromise amendment. Shortly after the meeting, the BTBC's constitution
committee drafted and distributed to tribal members several amendments that proposed reducing the size of the council, prohibiting lending to council members, and extending the term of office from two years
to four years. One council member admitted, "We knew that important
changes would have to be made in order to streamline the Blackfeet
Tribal Corporation in its functions."[116] New chairman Walter Wetzel
had demonstrated a willingness to listen to full-bloods' complaints and
to consider fiscal reform; he had challenged Pambrun's "inefficient" corporate management skills, recommended hiring an experienced business
administrator to improve tribal finances, and initiated a series of public
meetings to address tribal dissension.[117] Pambrun and Brown had concentrated their efforts on the national level in campaigning for reductions in BIA services and asserting the Blackfeet Nation's sovereignty
while the local situation deteriorated. Under Wetzel's leadership, the
council appeared to be making a concerted effort to address local issues.
But Myer refused to seize this opportunity to facilitate bipartisan reform
by deciding against postponement. He explained to Plenty Treaty a
month after the meeting that he did not feel justified in withdrawing
from the Interior Department his request for authorization "on the recommendation of only 29 tribal members." Plenty Treaty and other
Blackfeet voters, he wrote, should express themselves at the pending May
9 election instead.[118]

Myer's decision, while defensible in the sense that it protected a seemingly legal act of Blackfeet voters, sabotaged this bipartisan effort to create structural reform and calm the factional dissension that continued to polarize the reservation. It exemplified Myer's contempt of Indian leaders; the "29 tribal members" he cited simply represented the most respected political figures of the Blackfeet Nation. BIA officials thus began the process of organizing an election that neither the duly elected government officials nor the amendment's original sponsors supported. Fickinger even questioned the legitimacy of the election itself, telling Myer that "some question might be raised as to the legality of the Secretary's election call" because the Blackfeet constitution considered absentee voters "qualified voters"; the number of petitioners, therefore, would fail to meet criteria for holding an election.[119]

Myer's decision to stage the election precipitated a crisis on the reservation by forcing the BTBC to find means other than diplomacy to prevent what it rightly considered to be an infringement of the Blackfeet Nation's sovereignty. The BIA's aggressive organization of the election exacerbated the conflict between the two governments. Robertson threatened to use tribal funds to pay for the election, occupy tribal buildings to stage it, and have federal employees supervise it, all of which violated the terms of the Blackfeet constitution and charter governing tribal elections; the BIA even failed to inform the BTBC in writing of its intent to hold an election. The BIA's staging of the election was characteristic of the Myer regime; Indian consent was always a bonus. It also represented a dramatic change in behavior. Fickinger's interference in the 1950 election had devolved to Robertson's appropriation of tribal property and privileges to control the 1952 election. Wetzel responded with an angry letter to Oscar Chapman protesting Robertson's authorship of the amendment and the BIA's disregard of the Blackfeet constitution. "It appears to us that your hired men are using the same tactics that Mr. Myer and Mr. Robertson learned while operating Japanese concentration camps during World War II. We Blackfeet are a proud people. . . . Our sense of propriety, our knowledge of the principles of our Government, and our love of freedom is as great as that of any other citizen of the United States. We have proven our loyalty to the Government of the United States time and time again and we refuse to permit your employees to treat us so shamefully as to attempt to hold and run our elections for us."[120] Wetzel's missive to Chapman was accompanied by Cedor Aronow's cover letter, which explained that he had helped Wetzel "prepare and dictate" the letter. He too protested the BIA's "usurpation of power."[121] Cohen likely influenced Wetzel's and Aronow's choice of words during an April 24 council meeting. Cohen had been publicizing Myer's "concentration-camp methods and thinking" since Myer took office; because his differences with Myer and Fickinger had taken on a life of their own, he chose to keep a low profile. But, as with full-blood petitioners, Wetzel needed little persuasion from others to respond in the manner that he did. Wetzel objected in such a visceral fashion because Robertson wrote proposed amendments that would serve to "increase the control of the Superintendent and the Indian Bureau over monies of the Blackfeet Tribe."[122]

The BIA, as Wetzel charged, intended to stage an "unlawful and unconstitutional" election by usurping the council's authority to control the process, using regular polling places, and appointing government employees as judges and clerks rather than using tribal employees. It did not intend to supervise the election but to manage every aspect of it. As Felix Cohen put it to a Senate appropriations subcommittee two days before the May 9 election, "The Blackfeet Reservation has been flooded with circulars, printed at Government expense, on Government paper, and distributed by Government employees on Government time, designed to influence Indian voting. . . . As I speak, Federal employees are racing all over the Blackfeet Reservation campaigning for a constitutional amendment that would turn millions of dollars of Indian income into the hands of these bureau employees."[123] In addition to writing all or part of the proposed amendment, Robertson distributed in each district a pamphlet, printed at agency expense, that warned voters about "false and misleading information." Robertson outlined the amendments clearly, but he offered a simplistic view of the choice voters had to make. "You should demand the truth," he told voters. "If you are in favor of restricting the tribal council in spending tribal money vote for the amendment. If you are not in favor of restricting the tribal council in the spending of tribal money vote against the amendment."[124] As he described it, most voters would choose the former option without realizing that Robertson and the Congress could control tribal funds as a result.

Cohen called the BIA's interference "a terribly serious attack on not only the rights of Indians as citizens, but on the integrity of our democratic process."[125] The BTBC, with Cohen's support, organized a "counterelection" for May 9, giving voters a chance to vote on the BIA-sponsored amendment and on its own proposal for organizational change. One of the weaknesses of the full-bloods' proposal was that it left little if any income for tribal investment; the BTBC's record of investment of tribal funds, as indicated above, became a factor in the full-bloods' decisions to seek an amendment in the first place. The council's version also allocated 50 percent of tribal income for per capita payments, but it limited social service expenditures to 15 percent and earmarked 15 percent for investment and tribal enterprises, which included the making of "productive loans on adequate security at a reasonable rate of interest and the purchase of land." The balance paid for taxes, accounting fees, law and order, and other forms of public service. Rather than send unspent funds to the Class A account, the council simply proposed to roll over the amount to the next year's budget, a more sensible idea than imprisoning it in the federal treasury.[126]

Voter turnout for the May 9 parallel elections was light, in part because of the general confusion created by dueling elections and the unfounded fears of violence; in addition, several hundred voters were off-reservation on seasonal labor assignments at farms in Oregon and Washington or at work on the Hungry Horse dam. Of the 606 Blackfeet who voted at the "peoples' election," as Robertson called it, 460 supported the measure. Of the 467 Blackfeet who participated in the council-sponsored election, only 133 voted for the full-bloods' amendment. The BTBC's version of fiscal reform attracted 300 votes, while 167 rejected it; the BTBC's separate referendum, which mirrored its amendment proposal, passed by a vote of 335 to 193. Full-bloods clearly supported the BIA-sponsored amendment, but the voting totals from mixed-blood communities indicate that the measure had solid support from mixed-blood voters as well, reinforcing the notion that the insurgency had gained broad support.[127]

It is impossible to determine with any degree of accuracy the combined total of voters in the two elections because participating Blackfeet could vote at both elections. Yet Robertson attempted to perform just such mathematical and intellectual gymnastics in a postelection letter to Fickinger. After acknowledging the duplication of voting, Robertson argued that the unofficial 593-to-480 total vote in favor of the amendment "shows clearly that the Blackfeet people are in favor of the amendment. I do not think that anyone should decide against this democratic expression of the people." Robertson's letter seems to indicate that he needed to convince not only Fickinger of the election's legitimacy but himself. It also demonstrates that Robertson lacked an understanding of and respect for election procedures. "Regardless of what the requirements are for the

Secretary to call an election," he contended, "the fact remains that the election was called. Democratic procedures suggest to me that after an election is called the will of the majority should govern."[128]

Robertson's statement gave credence to the council's original charge that he had manipulated voting lists to ensure that the election would be held. Opponents of the amendment now charged that the 606 voters did not constitute a 30 percent vote of the electorate. The issue hinged upon whether the official voting list should include nonresident adult members. Most Blackfeet disapproved of absentee voting, and the BTBC had passed an ordinance prohibiting it in 1950. It was natural, therefore, for federal officials to assume that nonresident voters were not qualified voters and thus assume that the government had the right to call the election. But the Blackfeet constitution did not prohibit absentee voting. The decision lay with Oscar Chapman, who marshaled his forces to help him determine whether the BIA's amendment should stand; his staff went so far as to poll other agencies to determine their policies on nonresident voters. Chapman, it should be noted, employed a double standard by disallowing the BTBC's election on the grounds that his office had not authorized it, while defending the BIA's infringement of the council's constitutional right to stage tribal elections.[129]

Two factors complicated Chapman's decision. One was the criticism leveled at him by former New Deal colleagues Harold Ickes and John Collier, who publicly complained that Chapman had let Myer run roughshod over the protections contained in New Deal reforms; he thus had an opportunity to send a message that their criticism was invalid. The other factor came in the form of a new petition from 707 Blackfeet voters asking him to approve the amendment. The petition's signers included a solid mixture of mixed-bloods and full-bloods, as had other recent petitions; the predominantly Scotch-Irish and French names of Kipp, Guardipee, La Breche, and St. Goddard joined the distinctly Indian names of Old Person, Longtime Sleeping, Still Smoking, and Calfrobe. Chapman rested his decision on the opinion of solicitor Mastin White, who ruled that because the Blackfeet constitution did not prohibit nonresidents from voting, the Department of the Interior "ought not, through the process of interpretation, to read into the constitution a limitation on voting which was omitted by the framers of the constitution."[130]

Myer made one final attempt to change Chapman's mind, arguing that the amendment's supporters should not be "thwarted either by the illegal interference of the Business Council or a ruling on a purely technical matter." Myer conveniently included the draft of a letter adopting the amendment in the event Chapman saw the wisdom of accepting his argument that the combined total of the two elections represented more than 30 percent of the eligible voters.[131] Chapman waited nearly four weeks to notify Robertson, Cohen, and other interested parties that 606 voters did not constitute 30 percent of the recalculated electorate of 2,884 voters. Chapman, unhappy with the decision, told Sen. James Murray that his department "has now *been forced* [emphasis added] to the conclusion . . . that the proposed amendment has not been adopted by the requisite number of voters."[132] While he was disappointed with the solicitor's opinion, Chapman was not so disappointed as to embrace Myer's specious reasoning and contempt for the Blackfeet constitution to undermine further the sovereignty of the Blackfeet Nation.

Levi Burd, the patrician half-blood who profited handsomely from Blackfeet oil leases throughout the 1940s, telegraphed William Zimmerman in January 1949 to plead for the BIA's continued recognition of full-blood interests. "[U]nless you have authority to protect the interest of the minority group the case of the Blackfeet is hopeless," he wrote. "An election to do away [with] the powers of the council will never work. The full blood is helpless. [They] have no conception of what is going on and it's the duty of the government to make equal distribution of all tribal funds and provision should be made to care for the old Indian and children."[133] Blackfeet full-bloods, and other tribal members who had come to identify with their fight for social and economic justice, were neither hopeless nor helpless, as Levi Burd claimed. They were misguided—by BIA officials—and led to believe that the federal government would be a better steward of their money than the BTBC, and they disregarded the counsel of BIA Indians such as D'Arcy McNickle, who warned them that the Blackfeet would become "beggars" if Congress and the BIA controlled tribal funds. But Blackfeet full-bloods had little interest in aligning with Indians like McNickle, whom they called a "white man," or with intertribal groups like the National Congress of American Indians, which had held its second annual meeting on the Blackfeet Reservation in 1945. Plenty Treaty told Harry Truman in May 1952, "We feel as if we were convicts trying to find protection and our only view is to go back to the United States Government for that protection where the Tribe would be benefited by the Interior Department's rules and regulations. We have no grudge against any of our Tribal members, half breeds, three quarters or one sixteenth, but it looks to me as though they want to get out from under the Interior blanket and emancipate themselves so they can get away from the Blackfeet Tribe."¹³⁴ For most mixed-bloods, that blanket represented the possible suffocation of the Nation's sovereignty and the advent of a neocolonial administration of Blackfeet affairs. For most full-bloods, it represented a return to their chrysalis. The minority faction's desire to retain the overriding protection of the secretary of the interior reflected not so much a helplessness as a choice between guardians. Caught between paternalistic whites and enterprising mixed-blood Indians, many full-bloods chose the former over the latter in part because their sense of history suggested that they would be in better hands with the federal government than with the tribal government. Members of the minority group would have achieved both a psychological and a Pyrrhic victory had its reforms been adopted. Reclaiming a prominent role in the leadership of the tribe may have resulted, though the intended benefits of greater per capita distributions may not have.

John Collier once argued before Congress that the strongest resistance to the IRA came from "groups of full-blood Indians—Indians who are the most old-fashioned and archaic in their customs." Blackfeet full-bloods, Collier said, protested the IRA "because they said it Americanizes them too fast. The old warriors were asserting their stand against Americanization through resisting the reorganization act." "Resistance," Michael Walzer argues, "is itself an exercise of power, and politics is the sphere through which all the others are regulated"; Blackfeet full-bloods were forced by demographic circumstances and attendant political changes to "assert themselves . . . and to defend their own sense of meaning." Full-blood leaders ultimately accepted the BIA's argument that the IRA constitution could be used to cure their faction's voiceless condition; they used its provisions for establishing referenda to reassert their political voice and thus restore an element of social status. They maintained a vigil for the preservation of the *idea* of Tribe and for their own Indianness. As Chewing Blackbones simply but poignantly declared during one particularly heated debate on the prospect of becoming full-fledged American citizens, "I am going to stay an Indian."¹³⁵

Full-bloods "stayed Indian" while becoming acculturated to democratic political life and exercising their rights as democratic citizens of an empowered Blackfeet Nation. Through the crucible of class conflict, full-bloods also helped to engender among a diverse group of Blackfeet reconstituted or syncretic conceptions of tribal and Indian identity that were based more on the common ground of economic dislocation and invidious class distinction than on shared blood quantum; by speaking for a heterogeneous group of Blackfeet, elders enlarged their constituency of "real Indians who constitute the real Tribe." Full-bloods sought to preserve the tribe as a mechanism for social control, to restore the idea of the tribe as a "family," as Wades in the Water put it, rather than as a corporate body; according to BTBC leader Walter Wetzel, "the main thing [full-bloods] asked me to [do was] keep the reservation—the tribe—together."[136] Elders like White Calf, Plenty Treaty, Blackbones, and Reevis served as the conscience of the Blackfeet Corporation while striving to preserve the cultural core of the Blackfeet Tribe. Per capita distributions of tribally owned assets represented both a form of economic justice and a symbol of the Blackfeet Nation "taking care of its own," an institutional form of the give-away custom that governed traditional Blackfeet social relations. Although these dissidents did not succeed in amending the constitution, their grass-roots campaign politicized the electorate, reoriented income distribution patterns, and ensured that the full-blood ethos of the past remained a constituent of the Blackfeet future. They also ensured that the balance of power between the BTBC and the people remained steady, helping to maintain accountability for the council's corporate behavior and prevent further downsizing of its commitment to Blackfeet citizens and the democratic process that regulated their political and economic lives.

The 1950 referendum on terminating the supervisory powers of the federal government concluded nearly forty years of Blackfeet citizens' efforts to expand the sovereign powers of the Blackfeet Nation's government. The 1952 amendment election was the culmination of nearly fifteen years of political activity on the part of Blackfeet opposed to that expansion. The first measure would have limited Interior's supervisory powers; the second would have expanded them. The two elections represent the high points of political engagement between those Blackfeet who asserted their right to manage their own affairs and those who wanted to stay under the "Interior blanket." The middle ground between these worldviews proved to be elusive.

The BIA failed to help the Blackfeet Nation reach that middle ground. In March 1951, Dillon Myer had told the chairman of the House Subcommittee on Indian Affairs that, although he knew little about Indian factionalism, he could say that "tribal programs are hampered and even defeated by failure of agreement between contending parties."[137] Myer's decision to hold the 1952 election in the face of a possible compromise defeated the possibility of factional peace on the Blackfeet Reservation. The two amendment proposals were similar enough to warrant the conclusion that this compromise may have been reached; the differences that existed between the contending parties were ingrained by cultural and historical divergence, yet the compromise would have been codified. The Indian New Deal, for the Blackfeet, ended when the BIA interfered with the Nation's constitutional rights during the 1952 election, for what was the Indian New Deal but the codification of sovereign rights and an institutional articulation of the belief that Indians should take more responsibility for their affairs while adapting to new political conditions of liberal capitalism and its attendant welfare state? The council's shortcomings were serious and endemic, and they rightfully drove Blackfeet citizens to campaign for reform. Yet the BTBC seemed to be making progress under Wetzel's leadership and seemed to be willing to reach some kind of agreement. Thus, ironically, the sharpened polarization came at a time when tribal leaders were even more focused on quelling factional disturbances than previous councils had been. None of this mattered to Dillon Myer, Guy Robertson, and Paul Fickinger, all of whom arrogated power to determine what the Blackfeet needed; no longer was it "a matter for the Indians."

The alignment in the 1950s between Myer's BIA and the Blackfeet's People's Committee highlights the inherent contradiction of post-IRA Indian affairs administration: the BIA's resistance to working itself out of a job through the embrace of Indian self-determination. Myer's regime called for and received increasingly larger budgets in its buildup to the final resolution to the "Indian question," a manifestation of bureaucracies' internal logic of self-preservation, characterized by the bureaucrat's aggrandizement of political power and the consequent inclination toward protecting it. Congress, too, embraced the group least likely to support itself. Sen. Burton Wheeler's persistent refusal to support Blackfeet like Joe Brown reflected the schizophrenic mindset of conservative politicians, who had difficulty providing enough support to make Indians not only citizens but productive citizens. Wheeler, like Myer, seemed to distrust "wily Indians," those mixed-blooded council leaders who had their own ideas about how to construct native political and economic communities. The Blackfeet Nation's efforts at self-termination and thus self-determination were stymied by a mixture of such bureaucratic self-preservation and institutionalized racism, as well as by climatological instability, its own political and economic shortcomings, and a divided mind about expanded sovereignty of the tribal political body.

Neither faction succeeded in winning its respective election; the electorate rejected the council's termination election in 1950, and the Interior Department deemed the constitutional amendment vote of 1952 illegitimate. Yet the tribe as a whole benefited from the election campaigns. The public discussions, the factional dissension, and the anger over government interference perforce pushed the factions closer together even as BIA officials and contentious issues pulled them apart. Although the BTBC did not secure expanded powers of supervision, it did retain control of tribal revenues. Equally important, the issue of per capita distributions assumed a prominent place in budget considerations because the minority group secured a prominent role in tribal politics; the BIA had supported the group's amendment beyond its legal authority, but the group retained ownership of the amendment and what it represented in political and cultural terms. It became obvious to council leaders that they had to regularize per capita distributions. The BTBC's referendum of May 9, 1952, patterned after its amendment proposal, had passed by a vote of 335 to 193. Although the referendum also failed to satisfy election requirements, the vote nonetheless served as an unofficial symbol of compromise between the two groups. During the July 1952 BTBC budget meeting, the "per capita payment" was the top item on the agenda, reflecting its political importance. The council chairman announced that "the people should be informed that in accordance with their wishes, approximately 50% of the anticipated income has been set aside for the item and the rest of the budget was cut accordingly."[138]

The council also agreed to budget $800 for per diem payments to members of the honorary council committee, indicating its newfound influence. The BTBC subsequently approved per capita payments in late 1952, 1953, 1954, and 1955. The council's actions reflected the importance of the consensus forged during the spring of 1952, as well as the reduction of tribal loans and the dramatic increase in oil revenues. The 1955 payment amounted to $225, the largest amount ever released, the result of oil lease bonuses totaling nearly $2.5 million.[139] Per capita distributions failed to solve the Nation's political problems; dissidents, full-bloods in particular, continued to protest the actions of the council, push for constitutional amendments, and pressure Interior officials to monitor tribal finances. The distributions did, however, serve as reminders that the Blackfeet electorate had demanded an equitable distribution of tribal resources and that political action could produce change if properly organized. Since 1934, most of the tribe's financial resources had gone to fund the expansion of the livestock industry; the council allocated funds for cattle and land purchases, credit committee and cattle board expenses, cattle and hay loans, and the reservation's irrigation infrastructure. These expenditures were mostly legitimate and had resulted in the creation of what could be called a Blackfeet middle class. As noted, however, cattle had not become the "second buffalo" for many Blackfeet citizens. Oil had. And the people accordingly and rightly demanded distributive justice. "There are always some people, and after a time there are a great many, who think the seizure [of wealth and power] is not justice but usurpation," Walzer writes. "Social conflict is intermittent, or it is endemic; at some point, counterclaims are put forward."[140]

The minority group's counterclaim reoriented distribution patterns and redefined the group's role in the Blackfeet political community. There would be more battles between the advocates of the assimilated ideal and those of the tribal ideal, but this is the nature of life in a democratic community; interest groups continually negotiate for resources and the power to distribute them.

CONCLUSION

The Roots of Blackfeet Self-Determination

Close the Rolls. Sell the heriship [heirship] land. Issue certificates of ownership to each individual for their proportionate share of tribal assets. Help to prepare necessary
legislation. Insist that such legislation be mandatory and
not subject to approval of local and state authorities or of
Indian council and Tribes. – BIA Withdrawal Programming Directive, 1952

The first breakthrough came with the Indian Reorganization Act of 1934. This permitted a Government policy
of organization by allowing tribes to adopt constitutions
which provided terms for managing their own affairs. But
the Indian Bureau became impatient with the progress of
Indians under this system. – Earl Old Person, BTBC chairman, at NCAI conference, 1966

By the 1940s the Blackfeet Nation had become a mirror of American society: patriotic during wartime, community oriented, racially and ethni-
cally segregated, economically stratified, and democratically organized.[1]
Its conservative elites opposed both an excessive federal bureaucracy and
the maintenance of a tribal welfare state, while its poorer citizens campaigned for enhanced political status and the redistribution of economic
resources. The Blackfeet Nation was a municipality, a corporation, and a
cultural entity, and it faced the problems inherent in each. If political institutions and leaders were perfect beasts, then the Blackfeet would have
enjoyed a degree of success greater than they did during the first two decades of life under the IRA. But they are not, and the Blackfeet did not.
The Blackfeet Tribal Business Council, like other political bodies in Indian America and America at large, squandered money on ill-advised

projects and investments, distributed part of the proceeds of the tribal estate to those who deserved it less than others, violated certain provisions of the Nation's constitution and charter, and failed to live up to the ethical standards of both white administrators and Blackfeet citizens. But the BTBC also served its constituents by providing supplementary welfare and per capita payments, burial and sickness funds, credit for individual and cooperative livestock enterprises, support for job training and tribal enterprises like the arts and crafts cooperative, and grants to full-blood groups to help maintain cultural traditions. The Blackfeet Indians defended the IRA by using its provisions for economic development and political organization mostly to good effect. Blackfeet constitutional democracy under the IRA was flawed, but it provided mechanisms for change. Members of the minority group, who used the IRA as a scapegoat for social and economic problems created more by cultural, demographic, and generational differences than by ethnic or racial discrimination, ultimately benefited from its provisions for political action.

Political theorist Robert Dahl outlined four measures for "protecting fundamental rights and interests in a democratic order": the expansion or the reduction of the demos, alternative voting schemes, assertive public opinion, and the assumption of control by a quasi-guardian. First, members of the Blackfeet minority group declined the opportunity given them during the 1945 constitutional convention to reduce the demos by qualifying tribal membership, and though the council passed ordinances prohibiting nonresident voting, it failed to amend the constitution, thus creating the 1952 election controversy. Second, the Blackfeet adopted the popular vote in a 1945 amendment election, which gave all voters the right to support each council candidate; full-bloods declined the opportunity provided by Oscar Chapman during their January 1946 meeting to effectively veto the majority's vote. Third, the BIA's manipulation of public opinion during the 1950 and 1952 elections emboldened council members to disregard the legitimate efforts of dissidents to reform financial practices and distribution patterns; Dillon Myer's use of public opinion to pressure the council may have led to short-term turnover among officeholders, but it failed to facilitate productive reform of the political culture. Dahl writes that the fourth alternative, quasi-guardianship, is the only "nondemocratic solution" because quasi-guardians (like an agency superintendent) entrusted with the power of financial distribution are "so insulated from prevailing public opinion and can mobilize such great resources for coercion that they can impose their own views despite opposition from . . . electoral majorities."[2] The result would be a restricted democratic process because the quasi-guardian would presume to have the "superior knowledge and virtue" necessary to ensure a "good political order." Dahl concludes,

> If however the best political order is one in which the members individually and collectively gain maturity and responsibility by confronting moral choices, then they must have the opportunity to act autonomously. Just as individual autonomy necessarily includes the opportunity to err as well as to act rightly, so too with a people. To the extent that a people is deprived of the opportunity to act autonomously and is governed by guardians, it is less likely to develop a sense of responsibility for its collective actions. To the extent that it is autonomous, then it may sometimes err and act unjustly. The democratic process is a gamble on the possibilities that a people, in acting autonomously, will learn how to act rightly.[3]

Felix Cohen had studiously avoided becoming a leader of the Blackfeet for this reason. He understood that the democratic process meant giving a people the right to make decisions without an outside influence insinuating itself into the political process like a virus that weakens the host's immune system. The Blackfeet had worked too hard to prevent a reversion to the old system that, for many, "was no success."

The quasi-guardianship of the BIA, whose authority diminished with the passage of the IRA, would have been harder to contend with had it reasserted its control over tribal finances and income distribution. The new system at least offered the promise of political change. Although some council members abused their office for personal gain or used it to help relatives and friends, Blackfeet voters had a way to get rid of them at the end of their two-year term. This they did on a regular basis, creating the kind of turnover common to that in the U.S. House of Representatives. A case in point is the June 1954 BTBC election, in which nearly every council member failed to secure reelection. The principal reason was the BTBC's latest proposal to assign the tribe's oil rights to a single operator, which would have stifled the emerging interest of national oil companies. Voters again asserted themselves to restrict the council's economic agenda and protect what they perceived to be the integrity of the oil leasing system and thus their tribal loans and per capita payments; by a vote of 882 to 281, the Cullen deal died at the polls. Whether such an economic decision was shortsighted is impossible to determine because the Cullen deal never took effect. What is important is that Blackfeet citizens had a medium in which to participate in tribal decision-making that affected each of them. As the *Glacier Reporter* opined, the referendum was "the result of an intelligent understanding of what [the voters] believe to be the best interests of all the tribal members and the community as a whole."[4]

The IRA was as much about process as it was about progress. By this I mean that members of the Blackfeet political community had to learn anew what it meant to be responsible for their future; the IRA gave tribal groups both a sense of political efficacy and the means to produce change. Joe Jennings, perhaps the OIA's most eloquent advocate of Indian self-government, spoke of the IRA's "intangible accomplishments." Acknowledging the flaws of IRA councils, Jennings argued that "Indians have made surprisingly few mistakes in the management of their affairs when we consider how little experience they have had in self-government. In any event, the mistakes Indians make in managing their resources are no more serious than mistakes Indian Service employees have made for them in the past. People usually are more willing to accept the consequences of their own mistakes and to try to correct them than they are to endure the results of the mistakes of others. Initiative, self-reliance and independence can be developed only by people who make decisions."[5]

American Indians have continually adapted to changing political and environmental conditions that rarely favored them. Their ability to adapt to democratic life should not be underestimated. The Blackfeet had participated in democratic decision-making before 1934 by electing, every two years, representatives from the reservation's four districts. The IRA reconstituted the tribe's political community by giving its government greater supervisory powers, in particular the right to distribute tribal income, which created new levels of social stress and thus a new impetus for adaptation. The IRA was not "magical," as D'Arcy McNickle argued in 1945, but it did allow the Blackfeet to again "think for themselves" and act for themselves.[6] The Blackfeet Tribe of Indians survived, held together in one sense by its version of American democracy.

Although the IRA by itself failed to create the conditions in which the Blackfeet Nation could establish a self-supporting economy for all its members, it quite possibly prevented federal termination as experienced by the Klamaths and Menominees. After extensive examination of all things Blackfeet, BIA officials classified tribal members as "qualified to handle their own affairs immediately," noting, "except for a minority."[7] Congress elected not to pass legislation terminating the tribe's wardship status, perhaps because the 1950 and 1952 elections had both revealed intense political factionalism and demonstrated the Blackfeet's spirited and organized opposition to federal encroachment of tribal sovereignty. Thus, in comparison to the Klamaths and the Menominees, two non-IRA tribes that were terminated in the 1950s, the Blackfeet electorate was politically active, largely as the result of two decades of maneuvering through the provisions of the IRA. Although the three tribes had different socioeconomic dynamics, the IRA had politicized Blackfeet citizens more than the Klamaths and Menominees, making it harder for federal officials to justify wholesale termination.

What was wrong about termination was not so much the idea as the implementation of it. The ideas behind the termination movement dominated and animated Blackfeet political life for forty years. Several years before Congress and a coercive BIA began peddling a radical brand of termination, the Blackfeet political leadership, anticipating such a campaign, tried to find a middle road between an aggressive withdrawal policy that would have revoked the tribe's trust status and the expansion of federal powers under the minority group's reform proposals; in the process, the BTBC served the interests of full-blood allottees especially vulnerable to the revocation of federal trust protection. Blackfeet politicians and Felix Cohen held a series of conferences with BIA officials between 1951 and 1953 to discuss the transfer of BIA functions in order to preclude coercive action.[8] Just as tribal elders resisted "Americanization," as John Collier put it, so too did acculturated and pragmatic political leaders resist the BIA's attempt to force the tribe to adopt Americanization through wholesale withdrawal of federal services. Earl Old Person, the great full-blood Blackfeet leader, discussed this problem of BIA coercion in his speech at the NCAI convention in 1966. He told the audience, "The first breakthrough came with the Indian Reorganization Act of 1934. This permitted a Government policy of organization by allowing tribes to adopt constitutions which provided terms for managing their own affairs. But the Indian Bureau became impatient with the progress of Indians under this system."[9] According to Old Person, the BIA failed to provide the BTBC and the Blackfeet people with adequate information to manage the reservation's economic development. The Blackfeet received "no encouragement" from bureau officials to facilitate their administration of the Nation's financial, human, and natural resources. When he joined the council in June 1954, "we didn't have the knowledge to deal with these things," he said.[10]

During the 1940s the OIA *had* made a concerted effort to provide the Blackfeet with an administrative infrastructure, offering guidelines for effective management of tribal government. OIA leaders like Joe Jennings and William Zimmerman were committed to fostering Indian self-government, in part by embracing the notion that Indians had to "learn how to act rightly." As Howard Gaare noted, BTBC leaders resisted certain aspects of this postcolonial administrative training. By 1954, however, the opportunity for such intergovernmental cooperation had essentially disappeared, largely because of the friction created by Dillon Myer, his associates, and their conceptions of the democratic process. The termination campaign of the 1950s accelerated trends in self-government initiated in 1934 to the point where the Blackfeet were not prepared to assume *complete* responsibility for their affairs. BTBC treasurer Iliff McKay, an assiduous defender of tribal sovereignty, asserted in 1954 that if the BIA had not "threatened the Indians with liquidation of their reservations and would show a willingness to allow normal growth and development to take its course, the Indians would not be grasping at every straw to maintain their existence."[11]

The coercive nature of BIA withdrawal programming during the Myer years is startling. The BIA's recommended procedure to "overcome obstacles" to termination on the Blackfeet Reservation read in part, "Close the Rolls. Sell the heriship [heirship] land. Issue certificates of ownership to each individual for their proportionate share of tribal assets. Help to prepare necessary legislation. Insist that such legislation be mandatory and not subject to approval of local and state authorities or of Indian council and Tribes."[12] Is it surprising that BIA termination failed to appeal to a cross section of Blackfeet citizens?

Such endemic mistrust between Blackfeet leaders and federal officials continually surfaced, hampering the Nation's efforts to become self-supporting and self-governing. In 1938, the OIA had argued that the "attainment of the goal of self-support by the Indians is, to a large degree, dependent upon a successful extension program."[13] In January 1954, Superintendent Guy Robertson complained to Milton Johnson, area supervisor of extension and credit, that after reviewing the 1953 extension report he was "at a loss to know what to suggest to improve our extension service. . . . I hope that something can be done to take the extension program out of the fairy land implication that I think is threatening it and get down to a realistic something that will do a lot of good." Robertson, by this time, had been superintendent for more than three years and was just now addressing the problem. He suggested to Johnson, "Maybe if we quit shooting at the bunch every time and pick a few good singles out of the bunch for our targets we would have a bigger bag of accomplishments."[14] Robertson's disturbing metaphor reveals as much about his attitude toward Indians as it symbolizes the failure of the BIA organization to devise a realistic agricultural program for the tribe after twenty-five years of operation. Johnson defended his staff's efforts, but he echoed some of Robertson's complaints. His response to Robertson is printed here at length because it summarizes neatly the heart of the problem: the disjunction between ideational conceptions of Indian self-support and self-government posited by OIA leaders and their implementation by BIA agents in the field.

> Much of the Extension worker's effectiveness depends on his ability to interest, develop and train local community and group leaders to assist with local phases of the Extension program. This is where our greatest weakness in Extension work with Indians lies. We have not yet sold the program to the people. In many instances, we have been too involved with the management of Credit and other non-Extension activities. We have often times been trying to do too much of the work ourselves and consequently the Indians do not regard the Extension program developed by the Agency staff as their program. We must build a base of popular support for Extension work among the Indian people if there are to be any substantial accomplishments. . . . [O]ur staff at Blackfeet ought to give special attention this year to ways and means of obtaining more active participation by the men of the communities in planning for their own social and economic improvement. The development of constructive community leadership will be an important by-product of this process, once it gets under way.[15]

Twenty years after the passage of the IRA, a workable program engendering Indian control of agricultural production had yet to get under way. Johnson's consideration of community leadership as a by-product illustrates the problem white administrators had with creating the conditions for community control and the BIA's failure to listen to Indians themselves about what would work in their part of America. The Blackfeet had been calling for the *gradual* withdrawal of federal services for more than two decades. Superintendent Forrest Stone had argued in 1930 that the Blackfeet would respond better to a state extension agent than a federal agent.[16] George Fox had noted in 1942 that Blackfeet stockowners complained that the cooperative ventures proposed by the Extension Service did not involve "Indian understanding, support, and participation"; they asserted that Blackfeet were "distinctly individualistic in their make-up" and did not want help from either the tribal or the federal government. Fox attributed dissension to the imprint of the BIA's past failures on "Indian memory and Indian consciousness."[17] The Blackfeet would have attributed such dissension to the BIA's persistent failure to accept their voices as authentic and authoritative, a problem of intergovernmental relations that dominated the political sphere as well.

Even as Johnson and Robertson debated the failed partnership between the Blackfeet and extension staff, by 1954 the extension service's influence on the reservation had been reduced considerably by the increasing presence of state and county agents. The support given to Blackfeet 4-H clubs by county extension agents and the tribal cattle board paid dividends when they began winning awards in county and reservation fairs in 1952, fifteen years after extension agent John Krall called them the backbone of the extension program; nearly two hundred Blackfeet were enrolled in roughly twenty clubs by 1953, a 450 percent increase from 1939. A home management program initiated in 1951 to develop leadership among the Indian women and a "cooperative spirit in solving [i]ndividual and community problems" helped to raise living standards of both mixed-blood and full-blood families by offering instruction in home decoration, upholstery repair, "time efficiency," bookkeeping and budgeting, "buying problems," and nutrition. County and state extension agents assisted in the program, giving federal extension workers more time to deal with conservation and livestock programs.[18] Thus, as BIA officials began pushing their rapid withdrawal program in 1952, the kind of gradual transfer of federal responsibilities initiated by Blackfeet leaders was already under way. As Joe Brown suggested to Congress in 1951, the Blackfeet did not need help from eleven irrigation workers and six soil conservation specialists. Brown articulately proposed measured but deep cutbacks of BIA personnel, an attendant increase in Indian personnel, and expanded county and state operations. Any savings, he told a congressional subcommittee, could be channeled into improving health and education programs, the most important federal contribution to the general welfare and advancement of Blackfeet citizens.[19]

The BIA provided services to Indians in the areas of education, health, welfare, law and order, and management of Indian lands and resources.

According to the BIA's initial withdrawal programming report of September 1952, the Blackfeet Nation had fulfilled its credit and cattle obligations to the government as of June 1952, assumed responsibility for welfare payments in conjunction with county agencies, reached an agreement with county agents to conduct soil conservation studies, and maintained a law and order program for dealing with Indian offenses exclusive of the so-called "Ten Major Crimes" adjudicated by the federal government; in addition, the Montana state government had assumed responsibility for all reservation day schools, thus reducing the federal presence in education.[20] Not all of these programs functioned efficiently, but most importantly, the Blackfeet had taken the initiative to foster contact with county agencies and had an opportunity to learn by doing. Health and education expenditures amounted to 59 percent of the BIA's 1954 budget for Blackfeet agency administration. The bulk of the federal government's commitment to the Blackfeet people, therefore, lay in the area of human services, which had expanded greatly under the New Deal for all American citizens or had been transferred from federal control through Johnson-O'Malley contracts; of the $235,124 allocated for education in the 1954 budget, nearly half was channeled through such contracts.[21] The Blackfeet thus achieved a modified form of self-termination, securing both the preservation of federal trust protection and the withdrawal of federal workers and programs that had reached a point of diminishing returns to their community.

The Blackfeet Nation was one of fifty-four Indian communities to have adopted a law and order code by the end of the Indian New Deal. Blackfeet business councils generally were ambivalent about maintaining the tribal law and order program. "Corporative" council members like Brian Connolly tried to abolish the program, claiming that it was the federal government's responsibility to pay for law and order. As noted in chapter 6, the BTBC stopped paying for welfare and law and order programs in 1948. Superintendent Warren O'Hara stepped in to preserve the programs and run them using fines collected for liquor distribution, disorderly conduct, domestic abuse, and other violations of the Tribal Law and Order Code adopted in May 1937.[22] O'Hara told BTBC members that their decision was "a shameful act and that any self-respecting community goes as far as possible to maintain a good law and order program."[23] It was ironic that even as the BTBC was sanctioning the termination of Interior's supervisory powers, it was abandoning control of the tribe's welfare and law and order programs, the cornerstones, as Michael Walzer argues, of any political community. An evolving problem for the Blackfeet, then, was the varying degree to which council members defined self-determination by the interests of the community. Even when supportive of the law and order program, councils continued to petition the BIA to assume greater financial responsibility for the program's costs than it was willing to spend; the BIA on occasion would supplement tribal funds but typically told council members that it was the Nation's responsibility, in part because many tribes had less tribal money than the Blackfeet or because they had no formal law and order program.[24]

The Blackfeet were not alone in demonstrating this ambivalence. The BIA's chief of Indian law and order programs noted that while Indian courts "have operated reasonably well," they also were "permeated with tribal politics and are subject to the possibility of abolishment by the tribal councils."[25] During the 1940s and 1950s, BTBC members and official delegations, with one exception, put little effort into expanding tribal jurisdiction, focusing instead on securing federal funds for maintaining a tribal law and order program that varied in quality from "miserable" to "excellent."[26] Yet tribal officials, with the exception of the Connolly faction, were loath to cede complete control of law and order functions. In 1956, the BTBC asked the BIA to either assume the entire responsibility for maintaining law and order or let the tribe handle it. Council members rejected the BIA's offer of supplementary aid because they did not want to "surrender supervisory powers if they were to furnish the major portion of funds to finance the program."[27] The abnegation of jurisdiction over tribal offenses would have been a step backward for any self-respecting and self-sustaining community.

While the BTBC neglected to support local law and order with great enthusiasm, it did continue to press legal claims and pursue an expansion of tribal powers. The council's use of more than 1 percent of the tribal budget to fund the filing of a suit with the Indian Claims Commission and Felix Cohen's legislative activities in Washington divided the tribe in the 1950s.[28] While most tribal members approved of the legal claim, an extension of the 1935 Big Claim, many viewed the council's legislative agenda as terminationist. As the 1950 and 1952 elections demonstrated, the Blackfeet demos did not have great confidence in the council's abilities to expand its control of reservation functions and resources to the benefit of the community as a whole; the heterogeneous composition of the Reevis coalition belied the notion that it was just elderly "ward Indians" who resisted the council's expansion of tribal sovereignty. Tribal members also were divided over citizens' and council members' participation in pan-Indian groups such as the Montana Indian Organization, the Montana Inter-Tribal Policy Board, and the National Congress of American Indians. Full-bloods in particular did not want the Blackfeet Nation linked to other tribes for fear that its already limited pool of money would be stretched even thinner with the support of tribes less well off than the Blackfeet. The BTBC's campaign for self-determination on both a national and regional level, therefore, had reached a point of diminishing returns for many tribal members, who demonstrated that tribal politics should be, first and foremost, local. Blackfeet elites' pursuit of sovereignty outpaced the electorate's interest in it along the lines fashioned by the BTBC.[29]

This disjunction between the Blackfeet Nation's foreign and domestic policy, as it were, does not necessarily mean that council leaders were wasting time in Washington. Indeed, Blackfeet leaders employed a good understanding of how their objectives fit within the national political environment and with American values. The BTBC had fought for nearly two decades to win the right to select the agency superintendent. Felix Cohen asked Dillon Myer to grant the tribe this right, partly because they were "entitled" to it, but also to provide "a further step in educating these Indians in the ways of American democracy"; at the same time Cohen added, reflecting the nationalistic attitude of Blackfeet leaders, that "it is quite customary . . . in the selection of important diplomatic officials to consult in advance with the officials of the state to whom our representative is to be sent."[30] The BTBC's articulation of the $2 million Blackfeet Rehabilitation Bill in 1950 represented the Blackfeet version of the Marshall Plan, which the council had been calling for since the Marshall Plan was born; council members asked for "no charity . . . only a chance to build our own future to free ourselves from economic subordination . . . and the right to expend our own funds."[31] A 1953 council delegation, with Cohen's assistance, worked to ensure that tribal members had the same right to Social Security funds as other American citizens. And the BTBC's suggestions for federal withdrawal from the reservation were in large measure reasoned and reasonable.[32]

These efforts by the BTBC were, on one level, part of a burgeoning but diffuse campaign for equal civil rights that would become in the 1960s and 1970s a core element of the national movement of self-determination. Indians, as Rides at the Door had said in 1933, continued to call for a "'new deal' as we want to be treated the same as the white people."[33] The BIA under Dillon Myer was not ready to accord Indians such a right. As Blackfeet political leaders gradually pushed these issues of equal rights and sovereign powers, so too did a new constituency representing "the real Indians, who constitute the real Tribe" demand a fair and new deal within the Blackfeet political community. The battles over the tribal estate during the Blackfeet New Deal reflected the Blackfeet Nation's divisions over wardship, sovereignty, and its continuing efforts to "develop a self-supporting condition."

As the Blackfeet New Deal ended in the early 1950s, a new phase of self-determination began. The Blackfeet New Deal, encompassing IRA political reforms, government livestock and credit programs, and tribal economic enterprises, was the formative stage of Blackfeet self-government, especially for a new generation of political leaders that included Walter Wetzel and Earl Old Person. These new council leaders came to understand that the BTBC had to both protect the Nation from BIA job protectionism and federal encroachment on its sovereignty and provide to its citizens an equitable distribution of community-owned resources. The threat of termination interrupted Blackfeet self-determination but also accelerated it. Old Person, who won a council seat in that June 1954 BTBC election, believed that the national and local termination debates forced tribal leaders to "start asking some questions about BIA agencies and questioning who was running tribal affairs."[34] People had begun to "lose faith in the council and the bureau." Beginning with the June 1954 election, the Nation "started to get people with knowledge on the council . . . [who] began to participate in the decision-making," he said. The council understood that Blackfeet citizens "didn't feel the council was doing anything to protect them." As a result, "the councils realized we have to do more than we're doing to help the people out with the resources we have." Old Person attributed this change in attitude partly to the insistence of elders and other concerned citizens who demanded "access to address the councils" and forced them to "take leadership."[35]

Old Person and Walter Wetzel would assume the leadership of not only the BTBC but of the National Congress of American Indians; both served as NCAI president in the 1960s. Their service on the national level speaks to their role as defenders of both tribal sovereignty and social peace, as well as to the Blackfeet Nation's prominent place in postcolonial Indian-white relations. The Blackfeet had contributed to the national debate on the IRA in 1934 and subsequently helped to initiate a series of debates among OIA personnel about its administration; BTBC policies and resolutions precipitated discussions on blood rule, gratis services, political representation, constitutional amendments, and self-termination. The IRA was what an Indian community made of it, and Blackfeet interest groups assiduously pursued their right to make it conform to their respective goals and to use its tools to construct their version of an Indian-American community. By 1954, through the crucible of termination, citizens of the Blackfeet Nation could renew their collective efforts to fulfill John Collier's mandate to "take the responsibility of thinking out their own problems and arriving at their own conclusions, and determining their own future."

NOTES

Abbreviations

AAIAA Association on American Indian Affairs Archives, Seeley G. Mudd Manuscript Library, Princeton University Library, Princeton NJ

BF Blackfeet Agency records, National Archives, Record Group 75, Washington DC

CCF-1 Central Classified Files, 1907–39, Record Group 75, National Archives, Washington DC

CCF-2 Central Classified Files, 1940–56, Record Group 75, National Archives, Washington DC

CIA Commissioner of Indian Affairs

FCP Felix S. Cohen Papers, Yale Collection of Western Americana, Beinecke Rare Book and Manuscript Library, New Haven CT

GPO Government Printing Office

GRCIO General Records Concerning Indian Organization, Record Group 75, National Archives, Washington DC

NA National Archives and Records Administration, Washington DC

RCWHA Records Concerning the Wheeler-Howard Act, 1933–37, Record Group 75, National Archives, Washington DC

RG Record Group, National Archives, Washington DC

Introduction

1. Quoted in Philp, comp., *Indian Self-Rule*, p. 130.

2. "Statement of Earl Old Person, Chairman of the Blackfeet Tribe, Montana, Against the Omnibus Bill (1966)," in Deloria, ed., *Of Utmost Good Faith*, p. 219. Old Person later served as president of the NCAI from 1969 to 1971 and vice president in 1990.

3. John Collier to Superintendents, Tribal Councils and Individual Indians, Circular Letter, Jan. 20, 1934, p. 11, NA RG 75, Central Classified Files (CCF), Records Concerning the Wheeler-Howard Act, 1933–37, Box 1, pt. 1-A, File 4894-34-066.

4. *Statutes at Large of the United States*, 48 (1934): 984. Congress passed the act as the Wheeler-Howard Bill in June 1934.

5. Parman, *Indians and the American West*, p. 106.

6. The best history of the Blackfeet focusing on the nineteenth century remains Ewers's *The Blackfeet*. The tribe commissioned a number of historical treatments for a 1975 Court of Claims case—*The Blackfeet Tribe of Indians v. United States of America* (see in particular U.S. Indian Claims Commission, "Historical Report," by Thomas R. Wessel, and U.S. Indian Claims Commission, "An Historical Analysis," by Michael F. Foley). For an insightful tribal history and compelling photographs of tribal members, see Farr, *Reservation Blackfeet*. McFee offers an anthropological study of Blackfeet of the 1960s in *Modern Blackfeet*. For an excellent study of Montana's contemporary tribal governments, including the Blackfeet's, see Lopach, Brown, and Clow, *Tribal Government Today*. Confusion about the name of the tribe lingers. Some historians have confused the Blackfeet with the Blackfoots of the Blackfoot Reserve in Alberta, Canada, a legacy of the original Blackfoot Confederacy, which comprised the Blackfeet, Piegan, and Blackfoot Tribes. The Blackfeet themselves debated their official name. In December 1943, John Ewers asked the council by what name he should call tribal members in the tribal history he was writing. The council considered Blackfeet, Pecunys, Bloods, Blackfoots, and Piegans before authorizing the name Blackfeet as the official designation. The tribe's name, according to councilman Joseph Brown, came from a French explorer of the 1700s who named the Blackfeet on the basis of their dark moccasins. For the debate, see "Minutes of the Meeting of the BTBC, Dec. 2, 1943," NA RG 75, GRCIO, File 9522-E-1935-BF-054.

7. See, for example, Fowler, *Arapahoe Politics*; Stern, *Klamath Tribe*; Peroff, *Menominee Drums*; Parman, *Navajos and the New Deal*; and Hoxie, *Parading through History*.

8. Biolsi, *Organizing the Lakota*, p. 83; Taylor, *New Deal and American Indian Tribalism*, p. xiii; Olson and Wilson, *Native Americans in the Twentieth Century*, p. 123.

9. U.S. Congress, House Committee on Indian Affairs, *Investigate Indian Affairs*, 78th Cong., 2d sess., p. 445.

10. See Fowler's *Arapahoe Politics*.

11. See Kelly, "Indian Reorganization Act."

12. Meriam et al., *Problem of Indian Administration*. For Blackfeet statistics, see pp. 449–59 and 544–46.

13. The reservation's allotting agent reported that only a "small proportion of the reservation [is] arable, most being stony and much of it very rough. This is not an agricultural country on account of the lack of rainfall and because of the very short seasons." See "Report of Edgar A. Allen, Special Indian Agent," Feb. 23, 1910, NA RG 75, File 17107-1910-BF-150. The Montana state weather bureau estimated that the growing season in northwestern Montana lasted roughly

seventy-two days, and even during that period crops were vulnerable to killing frosts.

14. U.S. Congress, House, *Compilation of Material Relating to Indians of the United States and Alaska*, Serial No. 30, 1950, p. 736; "Ten-Year Program for the Blackfeet Indian Agency," March 1944, section by Freal McBride, p. 24, NA RG 75, CCF-2, File 7056-1944-BF-071. When one takes into account postwar inflation the 1950 figure is less impressive, yet it reflects the general growth of the Blackfeet economy.

15. "Estimate of Self-Support Attained by Borrowers" and "Individual Loan Summary," in the "Annual Report of Revolving Fund Operations, Blackfeet Agency," 1950, NA RG 75, CCF-2 File 17592-1948-BF031.

16. House Committee on Indian Affairs, *Investigate Indian Affairs*, pp. 437–38.

17. Nagel, *American Indian Ethnic Renewal*, p. 12.

18. Anderson, *Sovereign Nations or Reservations*, pp. 4–7. See also Cornell and Kalt, "Culture and Institutions as Public Goods," p. 246; Champagne, "Economic Culture Institutional Order, and Sustained Market Enterprise"; and Jorgensen, "Century of Political Economic Effects." These works, for the most part, concentrate on Native American economic development of the 1960s, 1970s, and 1980s.

19. Walzer, *Spheres of Justice*, p. 16. My discussion of the Blackfeet political community draws upon Ackerman, *Social Justice in the Liberal State*; Barber, *Strong Democracy*; Berry, *Idea of a Democratic Community*; Dahl, *Democracy and Its Critics*; Held, *Models of Democracy*; Jones, "Political Equality and Majority Rule"; Miller, "Democracy and Social Justice"; Pateman, *Participation and Democratic Theory*; Rae, "Decision Rules and Individual Values"; and Westbrook, *John Dewey and American Democracy*.

20. Olson and Wilson, *Native Americans in the Twentieth Century*, p. 123.

21. Felix Cohen, "Memorandum for Mr. Collier," Oct. 1, 1938, FCP, MSS S-1325, Yale Collection of Western Americana, Beinecke Rare Book and Manuscript Library, Series 1, Box 5, Folder 64.

22. "Ten-Year Program for the Blackfeet Indian Agency," March 1944, section by John Ewers, p. 30.

23. McFee, *Modern Blackfeet*.

24. Michael Walzer emphasizes that "distributive justice" is achieved by providing goods to "needy members . . . in such a way as to sustain their membership" in the community (*Spheres of Justice*, p. 78).

25. For recent discussions on the writing of Native American history, see Mihesuah, ed., *Natives and Academics*; Fixico, ed., *Rethinking American Indian History*; and Edmunds, "Native Americans, New Voices."

26. I interviewed several individuals at the Blackfeet Reservation in September 1995. Among those I interviewed were Earl Old Person, chairman of the

BTBC; Vicky Santana, tribal attorney and Blackfeet historian; and Anna Bullshoe, tribal historian at the Blackfeet Community College. I subsequently did telephone interviews with James Welch; Earl Old Person; Walter Wetzel, former BTBC chairman; Lorraine Owens, daughter of Joseph Brown, the long-standing BTBC chairman of the 1930s and 1940s; and Elouise Cobell, community organizer and the winner of a 1997 MacArthur genius grant.

1. "The Old System Is No Success"

1. See "Ten-Year Program for the Blackfeet Reservation," Population and Trend, section by Freal McBride, p. 3. Of the two thousand Blackfeet, eleven hundred were females ("Report of Investigation of Affairs on the Blackfeet Indian Reservation, Montana," by E. B. Linnen and F. S. Cook, NA RG 75, CCF-1 File 30650-1915-BF-150).

2. For histories of the Dawes Act (General Allotment Act: *Statutes at Large of the United States*, 24 [1887]: 388) and the allotment period that followed, see Otis, *Dawes Act*; and Carlson, *Indians, Bureaucrats, and Land*.

3. *Statutes at Large of the United States*, 34 (1907): 1015, 1035. The physical survey of the reservation was completed in 1912. For Blackfeet census records, see Blackfeet Heritage Program, *Blackfeet Heritage, 1907–1908*.

4. Senate Committee on Indian Affairs, *Indian Appropriation Bill*, 63d Cong., 2d sess., pt. 1, Mar. 12, 1914, p. 249. The act stipulated that unsold land "shall be sold . . . at not less than one dollar and twenty-five cents per acre." For the valuation of the land by a BIA official, see Acting Secretary of the Interior Janus Adams to Gamble, 1913, NA RG 75, CCF-1 File 49760-1913-BF-308.1.

5. Wolf Tail, the chairman of the Blackfeet General Council, the tribe's de jure political body, complained that Blackfeet leader Robert Hamilton was "acting without proper authority from the tribe." See Wolf Tail to Sen. J. T. Robinson, Feb. 13, 1914, in Senate, *Blackfeet Indian Reservation: Serial One*, 63d Cong., 2d sess., pt. 6, Feb. 21, 1914, p. 567.

6. Senate, *Blackfeet Indian Reservation: Serial One*, p. 573. For an excellent biographical essay on Hamilton, see Wessel, "Political Assimilation on the Blackfoot Indian Reservation."

7. Senate, *Blackfeet Indian Reservation: Serial One*, pp. 610–11. The reservation was divided into four farm districts—Browning, Heart Butte, Old Agency, and Seville—that ultimately became the basis of electoral representation.

8. Senate, *Blackfeet Indian Reservation: Serial One*, p. 632.

9. For a short history of Blackfeet agriculture, see Wessel, "Agriculture on the Reservations." The Homestead Acts of 1909 and 1912 drew thousands of immigrants to Montana between 1909 and 1919. Roughly ninety thousand settlers, lured by railway companies promising inexpensive arable land, filed for land patents in Great Falls and Miles City MT during this period (see Farr, *Reservation Blackfeet*, p. 101). Representatives of the Great Northern Railway were "particu-

larly interested in the settlement of the Blackfeet Indian Reservation" and asked for a reservation map "showing the Indian allotments" and their "appraised values" (see W. R. Mills to CIA, Sept. 27, 1913, NA RG 75, CCF-1 File 115997-1913-BF-150).

10. For an example of the spirited debate on Indian irrigation, see Senate Committee on Indian Affairs, *Indian Appropriation Bill*, 63d Cong., 2d sess., pt. 1, 1913.

11. Senate, *Blackfeet Indian Reservation: Serial One*, p. 632.

12. Senate, *Blackfeet Indian Reservation: Serial One*, p. 632. Curley Bear, a full-blood councilman and a Hamilton ally, told Secretary of the Interior Franklin K. Lane that the "majority of the full blood Indians do not want to open the Blackfeet Reservation" (see Curley Bear to Secretary of the Interior Franklin K. Lane in NA RG 75, CCF-1 File 29068-1914-BF-308.1).

13. Senate, *Blackfeet Indian Reservation: Serial One*, p. 645. The executive committee of the association comprised seven mixed-bloods and three full-bloods. The association also appears to have been called the Blackfeet Stock Protective Association. The papers of half-blood tribal leader Joseph Brown contain some data on members owing dues during 1912 and 1913, as well as a "List of Outside Permittees Grazing Stock on the Blackfeet Reservation, 1914" (in author's files).

14. Senate, *Blackfeet Indian Reservation: Serial One*, pp. 587–88, and in the appendix files of that source see "Minutes of the Meeting Held at Blackfeet Agency ... on February 7, 1914."

15. McFatridge to CIA, Feb. 9, 1914, NA RG 75, File 15907-1914-BF-308-1. The file contains the full text of the council meeting. See also McFatridge to CIA, Mar. 2, 1914, File 29068-1914-BF-308-1.

16. Senate, *Blackfeet Indian Reservation: Serial One*, pp. 586–88.

17. Senate, *Blackfeet Indian Reservation: Serial One*, p. 592.

18. Senate, *Blackfeet Indian Reservation: Serial One*, p. 591. Clark—three-quarters Blackfeet—was the point man of the group, perhaps because he could be presented as a more legitimate representative of "the Indians." An OIA official described Clark as "a highly educated progressive Indian, and well fixed financially" ("Report of Investigation of Affairs on the Blackfeet Indian Reservation, Montana," by Linnen and Cook).

19. Senate, *Blackfeet Indian Reservation: Serial One*, pp. 610–11.

20. Senate, *Blackfeet Indian Reservation: Serial Two*, 63d Cong., 2d sess., pt. 6-A, Feb. 11, 1915, pp. 656–57.

21. Senate, *Blackfeet Indian Reservation: Serial Two*, p. 654.

22. Senate, *Blackfeet Indian Reservation: Serial Two*, p. 656. In 1914, there were 1,189 full-bloods, 1,117 Blackfeet of one-half-blood or more, and 335 Blackfeet of less than one-half-blood.

23. Senate, *Blackfeet Indian Reservation: Serial Two*, p. 656.

24. "Report of Investigation of Affairs on the Blackfeet Indian Reservation, Montana," by Linnen and Cook.

25. Senate, *Blackfeet Indian Reservation: Serial Two*, pp. 662, 663.

26. Senate, *Blackfeet Indian Reservation: Serial Two*, p. 663. The physician chose to remain anonymous for fear of reprisal.

27. Memorandum of the CIA, Jan. 13, 1916, NA RG 75, CCF-I File 3755-1916-BF-150.

28. Malcolm Clark indicated that "Hamilton has great influence with these Indians since Senator Harry Lane came here last winter and told the Indians they were badly mis-used" (NA RG 75, CCF-I File 451-1914-BF-056). Hamilton also petitioned Congress to improve Blackfeet education and, with Curley Bear, negotiated with agency personnel for permission to hold the sacred Medicine Dance. He was thus active on most of the issues that concerned full-bloods.

29. "Report of E. B. Linnen, Chief Inspector," Feb. 3, 1916, Exhibit C, NA RG 75, CCF-I File 35332-1916-BF-150.

30. Charles Ellis to CIA, Jan. 24, 1916, NA RG 75, CCF-I File 33924-1915-BF-047. Buck, a registered cattle and horse dealer, also served as the general manager of the Browning telephone company. I refer to the Buck faction as a mixed-blood group, though again each faction contained both full-bloods and mixed-bloods.

31. For a breakdown of stock ownership, see "Report of E. B. Linnen, Chief Inspector," Feb. 3, 1916, Exhibit D.

32. "Minutes of the BTBC meeting of Dec. 13, 1915," NA RG 75, CCF-I File 135860-1915-BF-054.

33. NA RG 75, CCF-I File 83797-1915-BF-150. Hamilton was first elected as a councilman-at-large by a wide majority of voters. Fifteen council members were elected from the four farm districts on the basis of proportional representation: five from Browning district, three from Old Agency district, three from Seville district, three from Heart Butte district, and one councilman-at-large.

34. Sanderville to Secretary of the Interior, Dec. 15, 1915, File 135860-1915-BF-054.

35. Ellis to Sclls, Feb. 15, 1916, File 135860-1915-BF-054. See also Ellis to Sells, Jan. 24, 1916 (same file).

36. Hamilton to Sells, Jan. 15, 1916, File 135860-1915-BF-054.

37. "Proceedings of Business Council, December 28, 1915," p. 24, File 35332-1916-BF-150 (Exhibit F, p. 158).

38. Quoted in Prucha, *Great Father*, p. 298. Sells was principally responsible for accelerating the number of patents sold between 1913 and 1920, the period during which Blackfeet land was actively allotted and sold.

39. "Meeting of Mixed Bloods," p. 7, NA RG 75, CCF-I File 5109-1916-BF-054.

40. Senate Committee on Indian Affairs, *Indian Appropriation Bill*, 64th Cong., 1st sess., Feb. 19, 1916, p. 151.

41. Charles Simon to Sen. T. J. Walsh, June 4, 1917, NA RG 75, CCF-1 File 58684-1917-BF-054.

42. Senate Committee on Indian Affairs, *Indian Appropriation Bill*, 64th Cong., 1st sess., Feb. 19, 1916, pp. 152, 154. Hamilton appeared during these hearings to argue in favor of additional appropriations for Blackfeet educational facilities. No other Blackfeet did.

43. Senate Committee on Indian Affairs, *Surplus Lands, Blackfeet Indian Reservation, Mont.*, 64th Cong., 1st sess., pt. 1, Apr. 11, 1916, pp. 11, 12.

44. Senate Committee on Indian Affairs, *Surplus Lands, Blackfeet Indian Reservation, Mont.*, p. 9.

45. Senate Committee on Indian Affairs, *Surplus Lands, Blackfeet Indian Reservation, Mont.* Clark's testimony can be found on pp. 13–23.

46. "Report of E. B. Linnen, Chief Inspector," p. 19.

47. Senate Committee on Indian Affairs, *Surplus Lands, Blackfeet Indian Reservation, Mont.*, p. 47. The Blackfeet were certainly capable of agricultural production. In September 1915 the tribe presented the First Annual Blackfeet Indian Fair, which inspired other Montana tribes to organize their own fairs. Full-bloods won most of the agriculture prizes, while mixed-bloods won most of the livestock prizes. See Ellis to CIA, Jan. 24, 1916, File 33924-1915-BF-047. See also Department of the Interior, *Report of the Commissioner of Indian Affairs to the Secretary of the Interior, FY 1916* (Washington DC: GPO, 1916), pp. 33–36.

48. Senate Committee on Indian Affairs, *Surplus Lands, Blackfeet Indian Reservation, Mont.*, p. 16.

49. Senate Committee on Indian Affairs, *Surplus Lands, Blackfeet Indian Reservation, Mont.*, p. 55.

50. Senate Committee on Indian Affairs, *Surplus Lands, Blackfeet Indian Reservation, Mont.*, p. 61.

51. See House Committee on Indian Affairs, *Disposition of Surplus Lands of Blackfeet Indian Reservation, Mont.*, 64th Cong., 1st sess., July 12, 1916.

52. *Statutes at Large of the United States*, 41 (1919): 3, 17. For details, see Cato Sells to Charles M. Roblin and Louis S. Irvin, Special Allotting Agents, July 29, 1919, NA RG 75, CCF-1 File 1630-1943-BF-175.2.

53. "Memorial and Petition to the Honorable Senate of the United States in Congress," attached to "Minutes of a Meeting of the Business Council of the Blackfeet Tribe Held at the Blackfeet Agency, Browning, Montana, on May 20, 1916," NA RG 75, CCF-1 File 61576-1916-BF-054.

54. Hamilton to Francis K. Lane, May 29, 1916, File 61576-1916-BF-054.

55. Hamilton to Indian Office, May 29, 1916; Meritt to Hamilton, May 31, 1916, both in NA RG 75, CCF-1 File 63114-1916-BF-322.

56. Simon to CIA, June 23, 1916, NA RG 75, CCF-1 File 70682-1916-BF-322.

57. Blackfeet petition to CIA, May 24, 1916, File 83797-1915-BF-056.

58. Clark to CIA, Sept. 28, 1916, File 83797-1915-BF-056.

59. Ellis to CIA, July 17, 1916, File 83797-1915-BF-056.

60. "Declaration of Policy in the Administration of Indian Affairs," Apr. 17, 1917, in Department of the Interior, *Report of the Commissioner of Indian Affairs to the Secretary of the Interior, FY 1917* (Washington DC: GPO, 1917), pp. 3–5.

61. Robert Hamilton, Curley Bear, and Joseph Grant to Cato Sells, Apr. 19, 1918, NA RG 75, CCF-I File 40150-1918-BF-054.

62. Meritt to Hamilton et al., August 1918, NA RG 75, CCF-I File 40150-1919-BF-54.

63. Baker to CIA, Feb. 14, 1912, NA RG 75, CCF-I File 16295-1912-BF-124.

64. Assistant Chief Sturelwarren to CIA, Apr. 8, 1912, NA RG 75, CCF-I File 16295-1912-BF-124.

65. Second Assistant Commissioner to Baker (n.d., 1912), NA RG 75, CCF-I File 16295-1912-BF-124. The first draft indicated that "there is no objection to the Indians of that locality inaugurating such a plan for their own benefit should they wish to do so," but that sentence was crossed off and did not appear in the final version.

66. James White Calf and Bird Rattler to CIA, Mar. 12, 1919, NA RG 75, CCF-I File 24001-1919-BF-054.

67. Meritt to James White Calf and Bird Rattler, Mar. 27, 1919, NA RG 75, CCF-I File 24001-1919-BF-054.

68. When Campbell assumed the superintendency in 1921, the Blackfeet tribal herd had shrunk from roughly two thousand head of cattle to about six hundred. For details, see Senate Committee on Indian Affairs, "Report of Walter W. Liggett," p. 12749.

69. "Report of the Commissioner of Indian Affairs," in Department of the Interior, *Annual Report of the Secretary of the Interior*, 1922, p. 12. The drought and the winter that followed put to an end the great migration into Montana. Between 1919 and 1925 roughly 20 percent (nearly eleven thousand) of Montana's farms were vacated. Wheat prices fell after World War I from $2.40 a bushel to $0.92, affecting a number of Blackfeet farmers who prospered during the war. See Spence, *Montana*, p. 138.

70. "Five Year Industrial Program from April 1, 1921 to April 1, 1926: A Ground Plan to Place the Indians of the Blackfeet Reservation on a Self-Respecting and 90% Self-Supporting Basis," NA RG 75, CCF-I File 81643-1924-BF-100.

71. "Five Year Industrial Program."

72. Burke, "The Progress of the Blackfeet Indians," Western Americana Collection, Beinecke Rare Book and Manuscript Library, Yale University Library. For a contemporary description of the FYIP, see "The Five-Year Program on the Blackfoot Indian Reservation" in the Mar. 16, 1923, issue of the *Indian Leader*, the Haskell Institute newspaper.

73. Burke to Campbell, Nov. 16, 1922, File 48633-1926-BF-150. Burke later

told Campbell, "The more I study the question, the more I realize that, in the last analysis, the Indians are much like other people and are very human" (Burke to Campbell, June 6, 1923, NA RG 75, CCF-1 File 61770-1918-BF-175.5).

74. Resolutions of Conference of Superintendents, Blackfeet Agency, Sept. 3–6, 1924, NA RG 75, CCF-1 File 27506-1923-BF-100.

75. Oscar Lipps to Chapter Officers and Members of the Nez Perce Home and Farm Association, Sept. 12, 1924, File 27506-1923-BF-100.

76. It would be misleading to represent this division as being purely between mixed-bloods and full-bloods. As with many other Indian factions, the two sides of this struggle comprised both full-blood and mixed-blood supporters. But given the preponderance of full-bloods in the Heart Butte and Old Agency districts, where most of Campbell's activities took place, the principal division ran along blood or ethnic lines.

77. "Minutes of Meeting: Resolutions Committee," Mar. 30, 1925, File 27506-1923-BF-100.

78. "Minutes of Conference of Chapter Officers—Five Year Program," Aug. 22, 23, 1925, p. 12, File 27506-1923-BF-100.

79. "Minutes of Meeting: Resolutions Committee," Aug. 22, 1925, File 27506-1923-BF-100.

80. Campbell to CIA, Jan. 20, 1926, File 27506-1923-BF-100.

81. "Meeting of the Tribal Business Council [BTBC]," Feb. 25, 1926, NA RG 75, CCF-1 File 13256-1926-BF-054.

82. "Meeting of the Tribal Business Council," Feb. 25, 1926.

83. "Meeting of the Tribal Business Council," Feb. 25, 1926. James White Calf and Rides at the Door lived in the Starr School community of the Browning district. Tribal factionalism thus had an urban-rural dimension as well as an ethnic or a racial dimension.

84. "Meeting of the Tribal Business Council," Feb. 25, 1926.

85. "Meeting of the Tribal Business Council," Feb. 25, 1926.

86. Richard Sanderville to Campbell (no date), File 13256-1926-BF-054. Sanderville, three-quarters-blood Blackfeet, served as Campbell's interpreter during his initial tour of the reservation and was one of his strongest supporters. For a short biographical sketch, see Ewers, "Richard Sanderville, Blackfoot Indian Interpreter."

87. Campbell to CIA, Apr. 12, 1926, File 27506-1923-BF-100.

88. See Campbell to CIA, Apr. 20, 1926, File 13256-1926-BF-054.

89. Hamilton to Walsh, Mar. 6, 1926, and Mar. 16, 1926, NA RG 75, CCF-1 File 11887-1926-BF-154.

90. Chief Inspector J. F. Gartland and E. K. Burlew, "Memorandum for the Secretary," Oct. 11, 1926, NA RG 75, CCF-1 File 4833-1926-BF-150. For an important contrasting opinion, see Samuel Blair, "Inspection Report," Mar. 19, 1926, and "Supplemental Report of Inspector Blair in the investigation of charges pre-

ferred against Superintendent Campbell of the Blackfeet Agency," Mar. 24, 1926, both in NA RG 75, CCF-1 File 11887-1926-BF-154).

91. Stone to CIA, Mar. 9, 1926, File 13256-1926-BF-054.

92. OIA Memorandum, Apr. 23, 1926, File 13256-1926-BF-054.

93. For Montana's history of oil production, see Douma, "History of Oil and Gas in Montana;" Rowe, *Geography and Natural Resources of Montana*; and U.S. Indian Claims Commission, "Management of Oil and Gas Resources on the Blackfeet Indian Reservation," by J. H. Ashford and K. M. Raymond.

94. "Minutes of a Blackfeet Tribal Council [BTBC] meeting," Jan. 8, 1921, NA RG 75, CCF-1 File 3434-1921-BF-322.

95. "Minutes of a Blackfeet Tribal Council [BTBC] meeting," Jan. 8, 1921.

96. "Minutes of a Blackfeet Executive Committee meeting," Jan. 8, 1921, File 3434-1921-BF-322.

97. "Minutes of a Blackfeet Executive Committee meeting," Jan. 8, 1921.

98. "Minutes of a Blackfeet Tribal Council meeting," Jan. 10, 1921, File 3434-1921-BF-322.

99. "Minutes of a Blackfeet Tribal Council meeting," Jan. 10, 1921, evening session.

100. Sells to Wilson, Jan. 12, 1921, File 3434-1921-BF-322.

101. Roblin to CIA, Jan. 16, 1921; see also Wilson to Indian Office, Jan. 11, 1921, both in File 3434-1921-BF-322.

102. Hamilton to Secretary of the Interior, Jan. 19, 1921; Payne to Hamilton, Feb. 4, 1921, both in File 3434-1921-BF-322.

103. Oscar Boy to Secretary of the Interior (no date), File 3434-1921-BF-322.

104. Louis Hill to Secretary of the Interior, Jan. 25, 1921, File 3434-1921-BF-322. Hill was the son of James J. Hill, the founder of the Great Northern Railroad.

105. "Blackfeet Tribal Council [BTBC] Proceedings," Feb. 23, 1921, File 3434-1921-BF-322. For a copy of the Hill lease and the OIA's regulations governing leasing on Blackfeet lands, see NA RG 75, CCF-1 File 11677-1921-BF-322.

106. Burke to Campbell, Apr. 18, 1921, File 3434-1921-BF-322.

107. Hamilton to Secretary of the Interior, Apr. 15, 1921, NA RG 75, CCF-1 File 32595-1922-BF-054.

108. Burke to the BTBC, May 5, 1921, File 32595-1922-BF-054.

109. Wilson, *Underground Reservation*, p. 122.

110. Burke to Campbell, Dec. 6, 1921, NA RG 75, CCF-1 File 78163-1921-BF-322.

111. Campbell to CIA, Apr. 6, 1921; see also Wilson to CIA, Feb. 10, 1921, both in File 11677-1921-BF-322.

112. See the Department of the Interior's "History of Oil Leasing on Black-

feet Reservation: 1921–1926 Inclusive," Sheet 2, NA RG 75, CCF-1 File 35135-1926-BF-324.

113. Louise Dogears to CIA, Jan. 4, 1922, NA RG 75, CCF-1 File 84814-1921-BF-322.

114. Louise Dogears to CIA, Jan. 4, 1922.

115. Meritt to Louise Dogears, Feb. 10, 1922, File 84814-1921-BF-322.

116. Campbell to CIA, Nov. 22, 1921, File 84814-1921-BF-322.

117. Meritt to Campbell, Dec. 22, 1921, File 84814-1921-BF-322.

118. J.J. Galbraith to Assistant Commissioner E. B. Meritt, May 12, 1922, NA RG 75, CCF-1 File 38331-1922-BF-322. Galbraith wrote to Meritt on Sherburne's behalf.

119. The USGS classified the entire reservation as "non-oil land" in 1912. Advances in petroleum geology provided a better picture of the reservation's potential after 1912. See Department of the Interior, U.S. Geological Survey, *Anticlines in the Blackfeet Indian Reservation, Montana.*

120. Joseph Brown et al. to CIA, Apr. 27, 1922, NA RG 75, CCF-1 File 36461-1922-BF-322.

121. Campbell to CIA, Jan. 12, 1923, NA RG 75, CCF-1 File 80619-1922-BF-322, pt. 1.

122. For the transcript of the hearing, see File 80619-1922-BF-322, pt. 1.

123. "Minutes of Blackfeet Council [BTBC] meeting," Mar. 1, 1924, NA RG 75, CCF-1 File 29017-1924-BF-054.

124. Meritt to Campbell, Apr. 26, 1924, File 29017-1924-BF-054.

125. Burke to Campbell, Apr. 12, 1927, NA RG 75, CCF-1 File 16642-1927-BF-322; Burke to Sen. Thomas Walsh, July 28, 1926, File 35135-1926-BF-324.

126. "History of Oil Leasing on Blackfeet Reservation," Sheets 1 and 2. The Interior Department issued the report at the request of Senator Walsh, who had received complaints from Blackfeet about the slow progress of oil leasing.

127. "Blackfeet Tribal Council [BTBC] Proceedings," Feb. 24, 1927, NA RG 75, CCF-1 File 16072-1927-BF-054. The quotation does not appear to be verbatim but paraphrased by the council stenographer.

128. "Blackfeet Tribal Council Proceedings," Feb. 24, 1927.

129. George Arnoux, William Brown, et al., to Campbell, Aug. 4, 1927, NA RG 75, CCF-1 File 41869-1927-BF-322.

130. Wright to Campbell, Sept. 24, 1927, File 41869-1927-BF-322.

131. "Minutes of the BTBC," Apr. 30, 1929, NA RG 75, CCF-1 File 22496-1929-BF-054.

132. BTBC telegram to President of the United States, Apr. 30, 1929, File 22496-1929-BF-054.

133. The company's principals included Levi Burd, Joe Sherburne, and two other white businessmen. For a debate on the lease, see the "BTBC Proceedings," Mar. 3, 1928, File 60543-1929-BF-322.

134. Hamilton lost his seat on the council. Joseph Brown, a Campbell supporter, became the new chairman. A Senate investigator charged in 1927 that Campbell was guilty of improper electioneering, or influence peddling, putting Campbell's prediction of a political "boomerang" in a new light (see File 27506-1923-BF-100).

135. "Senator Wheeler Informs Indians at Browning of Measures for Their Good," *Great Falls Tribune*, Oct. 9, 1928 (clipping), NA RG 75, CCF-1 File 53578-1928-BF-150.

136. Stone to CIA, Oct. 10, 1928, File 53578-1928-BF-150.

137. Campbell to CIA, Feb. 27, 1924, NA RG 75, CCF-1 File 17576-1924-BF-013.

2. "Give Us a Fair and New Deal"

1. Meriam et al., *Problem of Indian Administration*, p. 455. The report differentiated between earned income and total income, which included unearned income from such sources as annuities, rations, and rent.

2. Meriam et al., *Problem of Indian Administration*, p. 42.

3. Meriam et al., *Problem of Indian Administration*, pp. 14, 42.

4. Meriam et al., *Problem of Indian Administration*, p. 462.

5. For Collier's testimony, see U.S. Congress, Senate, *Hearings on S.R. 341*, Subcommittee of the Committee on Indian Affairs, 69th Cong., 2d sess., 1927, pp. 37–53.

6. "Minutes of the BTBC," July 16, 1929, p. 7, NA RG 75, CCF-1 File 40274-1929-BF-054.

7. "Minutes of the BTBC," July 16, 1929, pp. 8–9.

8. "Speeches of a General Tribal Council Held July 20, 1929," p. 2, File 40274-1929-BF-054. Reevis thought the $1 million credit fund "wasn't a good thing" because "the full bloods would get to use it."

9. "Speeches of a General Tribal Council Held July 20, 1929," p. 7.

10. "Speeches of a General Tribal Council Held July 20, 1929," p. 4.

11. "Speeches of a General Tribal Council Held July 20, 1929," pp. 2–3.

12. See Senate Committee on Indian Affairs, *Survey of Conditions of Indians of the United States*, 72d Cong., 1st sess., pt. 23, 1930, pp. 12671–85, for Hamilton's testimony.

13. Senate Committee on Indian Affairs, "Report of Walter W. Liggett," p. 12768.

14. Senate Committee on Indian Affairs, "Report of Walter W. Liggett," p. 12747. The BIA fired Hazlett in 1919.

15. Senate Committee on Indian Affairs, "Report of Walter W. Liggett," pp. 12747–48. Liggett cited the case of Peter Tail Feathers, a young "mentally defective" full-blood with epilepsy and tuberculosis, who lost his land under suspi-

cious circumstances in 1920. His land was appraised at thirty-two hundred dollars and sold for eleven hundred, of which he received three hundred.

16. Senate Committee on Indian Affairs, "Report of Walter W. Liggett," p. 12751.

17. Senate Committee on Indian Affairs, "Report of Walter W. Liggett," p. 12748.

18. Senate Committee on Indian Affairs, *Survey of Conditions of Indians of the United States*, 72d Cong., 1st sess., pt. 23, 1930, p. 12699. Three superintendents were fired, one went to prison, and another left Browning fearing indictment.

19. Senate Committee on Indian Affairs, "Report of Walter W. Liggett," pp. 12751, 12775.

20. Senate Committee on Indian Affairs, "Report of Walter W. Liggett," p. 12767.

21. See Senate Committee on Indian Affairs, *Survey of Conditions of Indians of the United States*, pp. 12652–64, for the committee's discussion of leasing.

22. Senate Committee on Indian Affairs, *Survey of Conditions of Indians of the United States*, pp. 12665, 12666–67.

23. Stone to Campbell, Jan. 2, 1929, NA RG 75, CCF-1 File 1525-1929-BF-054. Congress declined to support the plan.

24. Stone to "Lessees of Grazing Lands on the Blackfeet Reservation," Mar. 1, 1929, NA RG 75, CCF-1 File 11714-1929-BF-054.

25. Petition from members of the Blackfeet Tribe of Indians to CIA, Apr. 12, 1929, File 11714-1929-BF-054.

26. C. R. Trowbridge to CIA, Oct. 1, 1929, NA RG 75, CCF-1 File 50541-1929-BF-150. The Blackfeet earned $105,814.10 in grazing fees during 1928, most of which came from lands leased at $0.10 per acre. See Stone to Acting Commissioner J. Henry Scattergood, fiscal report, NA RG 75, CCF-1 File 46850-1929-BF-150.

27. Trowbridge Inspection Report, Exhibit G, p. 11, CCF-1 File 50541-1929-BF-150; Trowbridge to CIA, Oct. 1, 1929 (see pp. 14–20 for the complete report on "leasing matters").

28. Montana stockowners managed to prevent the implementation of certain grazing regulations promulgated in June 1931 during a conference on Indian grazing lands held in Washington DC in January 1932 that was attended by Montana politicians and representatives of large stock companies that used Indian lands. The opinions of the landowners did not matter. For a conference summary, see Charles J. Rhoads to Stone, Feb. 12, 1932, NA RG 75, CCF-1 File 5507-1930-BF-321. Also see "Montana Stockmen Have Satisfactory Session with Indian Bureau Heads on Grazing Matter," *Cut Bank Pioneer Press*, Jan. 29, 1932.

29. Stone to J. Henry Scattergood, fiscal report, File 46850-1929-BF-150.

30. Stone to CIA, Jan. 14, 1930, NA RG 75, CCF-1 File 3284-1930-BF-165.

31. For 1914 figures, refer to "Report of Investigation of Affairs on the Black-

feet Indian Reservation, Montana," by Linnen and Cook. For 1929 figures, see 1930 reservation census, NA RG 75, CCF-1 File 00-1930-BF-034.

32. "Minutes of the Meeting held at Heart Butte," May 7 and 8, 1931, p. 2, NA RG 75, CCF-1 File 30804-1931-BF-057.

33. "Minutes of the Meeting held at Heart Butte," May 7 and 8, 1931, p. 2.

34. The Blackfeet, in conjunction with the Gros Ventres and Fort Belknap Indians, initiated the claim in 1911. In 1913, the tribe retained the law firm of Serven and Joyce of Washington DC. The Blackfeet were prevented from entering their claim until the passage of the Jurisdictional Act of March 13, 1924 (*Statutes at Large of the United States*, 43 [1924]: 21).

35. Stone told John Collier that the "failure in crops last year [1929] was unprecedented. . . . Public works, such as road building and other summer work, did not offer a great deal of employment . . . and our Indians went into the winter poor" (Stone to Collier, Apr. 5, 1930, NA RG 75, CCF-1 File 5830-1930-BF-059).

36. "Minutes of the Meeting of the BTBC," July 12, 1932, NA RG 75, CCF-1 File 1592-1926-BF-059.

37. "Minutes of the Meeting of the BTBC," July 12, 1932.

38. Department of the Interior, U.S. Geological Survey, *Geological Report, Milk River Anticlines*, Blackfoot Indian Reservation, Glacier County–Northwestern Montana, by E. B. Emrick, Feb. 23, 1929, NA RG 75, CCF-1 File 60543-1928-BF-322 (also published by the USGS in 1929).

39. Stone to CIA, Apr. 19, 1930; Rhoads to Stone, May 7, 1930, both in NA RG 75, CCF-1 File 22126-1930-BF-322. Stone's letter to officials of the Texas Production Company, and their response, also are in this file.

40. Stone to CIA, May 14, 1930, File 22126-1930-BF-322.

41. Rhoads to the Secretary of the Interior, July 1, 1930, File 22126-1930-BF-322.

42. "Minutes of the BTBC," Aug. 12, 1932, NA RG 75, CCF-1 File 39873-1932-BF-331.

43. Stone to CIA, Aug. 13, 1932; Acting Commissioner of Indian Affairs B. S. Garber to Stone, Aug. 27, 1932, both in File 39873-1932-BF-331.

44. "Notice of Oil and Gas Lease Sale," Sept. 1, 1932, NA RG 75, CCF-1 File 42577-1934-BF-322.

45. "Minutes of the Meeting of the BTBC," Oct. 19, 1932, File 42577-1934-BF-322.

46. Stone to CIA, Nov. 4, 1932, File 42577-1934-BF-322.

47. "Was Joyful Week for the Blackfeet," *Cut Bank Pioneer Press*, Dec. 23, 1932.

48. "Blackfeet Members Cut 'Melon,'" *Cut Bank Pioneer Press*, Feb. 23, 1933.

49. "First Reservation Producer," *Cut Bank Pioneer Press*, Apr. 28, 1933.

50. "Minutes of the BTBC," Mar. 1, 1926, File 13256-1926-BF-054.

51. For a brief sketch of Collier's career, see Philp's "John Collier, 1933–1945."

52. "Report on talks made at a special meeting called by Mountainchief," Oct. 1, 1933, in Senate Committee on Indian Affairs, *Survey of Conditions of the Indians in the United States*, 73d Cong., 1st sess., pt. 31, pp. 16772, 16773.

53. Senate Committee on Indian Affairs, *Survey of Conditions of the Indians in the United States*, pt. 31, p. 16696. Of the 107,000 acres selected for irrigation districts in 1907, only 21,000 were being irrigated and only 10,000 acres were being cultivated in 1933.

54. Senate Committee on Indian Affairs, *Survey of Conditions of the Indians in the United States*, pt. 31, p. 16698. The BTBC held district meetings prior to Oct. 19 to decide which issues Brown should present to the committee.

55. Senate Committee on Indian Affairs, *Survey of Conditions of the Indians in the United States*, pt. 31, pp. 16728, 16741.

56. Senate Committee on Indian Affairs, *Survey of Conditions of the Indians in the United States*, pt. 31, pp. 16699, 16716.

57. Senate Committee on Indian Affairs, *Survey of Conditions of the Indians in the United States*, pt. 31, p. 16743. See also the statement of Forrest Stone on pp. 16743–54.

58. Senate Committee on Indian Affairs, *Survey of Conditions of the Indians in the United States*, pt. 31, p. 16769.

59. Senate Committee on Indian Affairs, "Report of Walter W. Liggett," p. 12765.

60. Quoted in Prucha, *Great Father*, p. 311.

61. Quoted in Philp, "John Collier and the American Indian," p. 81.

62. Quoted in Deloria and Lytle, *Nations Within*, p. 57.

63. Quoted in Philp, "John Collier and the American Indian," p. 88.

64. Quoted in Prucha, *Great Father*, p. 317.

65. John Collier to Superintendents, Tribal Councils, and Individual Indians, Jan. 20, 1934, Circular Letter, p. 2, NA RG 75, Entry 1011, RCWHA, Box 1, pt. 1-A (hereafter cited as Collier, Circular Letter); see also Felix Cohen to CIA, Jan. 17, 1934, Box 9, pt. 11-C, both in File 4894-34-066.

66. Collier, Circular Letter, pp. 4, 11.

67. "Minutes of the BTBC," Feb. 5, 1934, pp. 2–3, NA RG 75, CCF-1 File 9522-E-1936-BF-054, pt. 1.

68. "Minutes of the BTBC," Feb. 5, 1934, p. 9.

69. "Minutes of the BTBC," Feb. 5, 1934, pp. 13, 14.

70. "Minutes of the BTBC," Feb. 5, 1934, p. 5.

71. "Minutes of the BTBC," Feb. 5, 1934, p. 25.

72. Charles Reevis to CIA, Feb. 7, 1934, RCWHA, Box 1, pt. 1-A, File 4894-34-066. The delegation included Brown; councilmen Oscar Boy, Wright Hagerty, Richard Grant, and James Fisher; oil booster John Galbraith; and community

leader Mae Aubrey Coburn. For the initial Senate debate on the Collier Bill, see Senate Committee on Indian Affairs, *To Grant to Indians Living under Federal Tutelage the Freedom to Organize*.

73. Stone to CIA, Feb. 9, 1934; Collier to Stone, Mar. 1, 1934, both in RCWHA, Box 1, pt. 1-A, File 4894-34-066.

74. The Wheeler-Howard Bill—S. 2755 and H.R. 7902—had four main sections: Title I—Indian Self-Government; Title II—Special Education for Indians; Title III—Indian Lands; and Title IV—Court of Indian Affairs.

75. The Blackfeet delegation included all thirteen council members, Stone, and delegates-at-large Levi Burd, Charles Reevis, Running Weasel, Mae Coburn, and Little Blaze. All told there were 198 official delegates from forty tribes. Collier was supported by Walter Woehlke, a BIA field representative; Ward Shepard, a land policy specialist; and Felix Cohen. For a good review of the congresses and the evolution of the IRA, see Deloria and Lytle, *Nations Within*.

76. "Minutes of the Plains Congress, Rapid City Indian School, Rapid City, South Dakota, March 2–5, 1934," pp. 2, 7, RCWHA, Box 3, pt. 2-AA, File 4894-1934-066. See Box 7, pt. 9, for media coverage of the conferences.

77. "Minutes of the Plains Congress," Mar. 5, 1934, p. 14.

78. "Minutes of the Plains Congress," pp. 15, 16, 17.

79. "Minutes of the Plains Congress," Mar. 4, 1934, p. 8.

80. Flathead full-bloods opposed the bill for fear that mixed-bloods would take control of reservation affairs. The principal objection was that many mixed-bloods had sold their allotments and squandered the proceeds, while the tribe's full-bloods had dutifully tended to their land as the Dawes Act intended, as many Blackfeet full-bloods had done. See Superintendent Charles E. Roe to CIA, May 1, 1934, RCWHA, Box 4, pt. 3-A, File 4894-1934-066. For a notable anecdote on a related issue by Felix Cohen, see "Attitude toward Government," November 1935, FCP, MSS S-1325, Series 1, Box 1, Folder 7.

81. "Minutes of the Plains Congress," p. 18. Collier argued that "[w]hite people all over the United States own land in partnerships and companies and corporations. It is not communism to allow Indians to do the same if they want to" (see "Minutes of the Plains Congress," Mar. 5, 1934, afternoon session, pp. 8–9).

82. "Minutes of the Plains Congress," Mar. 4, 1934, p. 19.

83. "Minutes of the Plains Congress," Mar. 5, 1934, afternoon session, p. 1. The delegation was very pleased with its performance and its role in the proceedings. Oscar Boy said later, "This is a tough tribe to deal with, we are too smart. I wanted to say that at Rapid City, those 18 different tribes represented there, ex-Haskell and Carlisle men, they would all stop to see what the Blackfeet were doing. They watched and just as soon as the Blackfeet were called on, there was the biggest applause you ever heard at a meeting" (see "Minutes of the BTBC Meeting," June 4, 1934, NA RG 75, CCF-I File 42654-1934-BF-054).

84. "Minutes of the Plains Congress," Mar. 5, 1934, p. 9.

85. "Minutes of the Plains Congress," Mar. 5, 1934, p. 21.

86. The Montana Crow delegation, in contrast, indicated that it believed the Crow people were not ready for the kind of self-government proposed in Collier's legislation. The Crows rejected the IRA when it came to a referendum, despite the support of a Crow superintendent, Robert Yellowtail; only 112 of 801 voters supported it, virtually the opposite result of the Blackfeet vote. For a good discussion of Crow tribal politics, see Hoxie, *Parading through History*, pp. 295–343.

87. "Minutes of the Meeting of the BTBC," Mar. 31, 1934, p. 2, RCWHA, File 4894-34-066 pt. 2-A. All the meetings drew hundreds of Blackfeet, representing some of the largest gatherings ever held on the reservation.

88. "Minutes of the Meeting of the BTBC," Mar. 31, 1934, p. 2.

89. "Minutes of the Meeting of the BTBC," Mar. 31, 1934, p. 4.

90. "Minutes of the Meeting of the BTBC," Mar. 31, 1934, pp. 6–7.

91. "Minutes of the Meeting of the BTBC," Mar. 31, 1934, p. 3.

92. "Minutes of the Meeting of the BTBC," Mar. 31, 1934, p. 11.

93. "Minutes of the Meeting of the BTBC," Mar. 31, 1934, p. 14.

94. U.S. Congress, Senate, *Hearings on S. 2755*, 73d Cong., 2d sess., pt. 2, p. 62.

95. In his autobiography, Wheeler wrote that the IRA was the "one bill I was not proud of having enacted" and claimed that he sponsored it "without even having read the bill" (Wheeler with Healy, *Yankee from the West*).

96. Senate, *Hearings on S. 2755*, pp. 66–68.

97. Senate, *Hearings on S. 2755*, p. 167. When asked by Sen. Elmer Thomas of Oklahoma why the chapter organizations had presidents and secretaries but no treasurers, Brown answered, "Well, we never had any money to handle" (p. 167).

98. Senate, *Hearings on S. 2755*, p. 168. Joe Brown replaced Robert Hamilton as the Blackfeet's most influential leader in the late 1920s. One-half Blackfeet, like Hamilton, Brown engendered better support among full-bloods and with the agency administration; he also served the government in various capacities, including supervisor of livestock.

99. Senate, *Hearings on S. 2755*, p. 170. Judging from the press accounts of the IRA debate in the *Glacier County Chief*, the white-owned newspaper published in Browning, Wheeler did not speak for all the county's citizens. The Browning Lions Club, the whites' main civic organization, approved of the BTBC's endorsement of the Wheeler-Howard Bill and the council's amendments. This approval was "a recognition of the close bond which binds the interests of red and white blood alike in all that affects the reservation." The "white people of the reservation . . . are in hearty sympathy with them and their welfare." Whites endorsed the council's actions, however, only after it pledged to "preserve their rights" (see "Civic Club Endorse Action of Tribal Council Which Approved Amended Bill Now before Congress," *Glacier County Chief*, Apr. 13, 1934).

100. Senate, *Hearings on S. 2755*, p. 171.

101. U.S. Congress, House Committee on Indian Affairs, *Readjustment of Indian Affairs*, 73d Cong., 2d sess., pt. 5, p. 244.

102. House Committee on Indian Affairs, *Readjustment of Indian Affairs*, pp. 245, 246.

103. House Committee on Indian Affairs, *Readjustment of Indian Affairs*, p. 247.

104. House Committee on Indian Affairs, *Readjustment of Indian Affairs*, pp. 248, 249.

105. House Committee on Indian Affairs, *Readjustment of Indian Affairs*, pp. 249, 250.

106. Brown and Kennerly to CIA, June 5, 1934, RCWHA, File 4894-34-066 pt. 2-A; *Statutes at Large of the United States*, 48 (1934): 984.

107. "Excerpts from Speech on Senate Floor by Senator Burton K. Wheeler, June 6, 1934 (*Congressional Record*, pp. 11460–76)," RCWHA, Box 7, pt. 8, File 4893-34-066.

108. "Facts about the New Indian Reorganization Act: An Explanation and Interpretation of the Wheeler-Howard Bill as Modified, Amended, and Passed by Congress," by John Collier, RCWHA, Box 7, pt. 8, Memo 90027, p. 1.

109. "Facts about the New Indian Reorganization Act," p. 2.

110. S. 3645: "A Bill to conserve and develop Indian lands and resources; to extend to Indians the right to form business and other organizations; to establish a credit system for Indians; to grant certain rights of home rule to Indians; to provide for vocational education for Indians; and for other purposes" (RCWHA, Box 7, pt. 11-B).

111. "Memo for the Organization Committee," July 31, 1934, FCP, Box 8, Folder 117.

112. "Analysis of Indian Reorganization Act," by H. C. Hall, RCWHA, Box 8, pt. 11-C, File 37045.

113. Collier to Stone, Aug. 30, 1934, RCWHA, Box 8, pt. 11-C, File 37045. For the OIA's analysis of the act, see "Analysis and Explanation of the Wheeler-Howard Indian Act," by John Collier, RCWHA, Box 9, pt. 11-C.

114. "Minutes of the Meeting of the BTBC," Sept. 11, 1934, NA RG 75, CCF-1 File 46597-1934-BF-054; "Members of the BTBC to Secretary of the Interior," Sept. 11, 1934, GRCIO, Box 2, File 9522-1936-BF-066.

115. Stone to CIA, Sept. 13, 1934, GRCIO, Box 2, File 9522-1936-BF-066.

116. Stone to Indian Office, Oct. 28, 1934 (telegram), GRCIO, Box 2, File 9522-1936-BF-066.

117. Collier to "the Indians of the Blackfeet Reservation," Nov. 5, 1934, GRCIO, Box 2, File 9522-1936-BF-066. Collier sent a similar letter to all tribes that adopted the act.

118. For a breakdown of voter participation in IRA referenda, see Taylor, *New Deal and American Indian Tribalism*, pp. 157–58.

119. Barber, *Strong Democracy*, p. 121.

3. On the Road to Self-Government

1. Senate Committee on Indian Affairs, *Survey of Conditions of the Indians in the United States*, pt. 31, p. 16743.

2. "Comment on Blackfeet Reservation Chapter Organizations," by Forrest R. Stone, Apr. 7, 1934, p. 1, NA RG 75, E 1012, GRCIO, File 9522-1936-BF-068.

3. "Comment on Blackfeet Reservation Chapter Organizations," p. 2. Stone's bitter criticism of the FYIP supported the contention of critics who had charged that it had become oriented to public relations rather than long-term economic rehabilitation.

4. "Comment on Blackfeet Reservation Chapter Organizations," pp. 3, 4.

5. "Comment on Blackfeet Reservation Chapter Organizations," p. 6.

6. "Questionnaire on Tribal Organization," in Stone to CIA, Aug. 8, 1934, p. 5, File 9522-1936-BF-068.

7. "Questionnaire on Tribal Organization," pp. 6, 7.

8. "Questionnaire on Tribal Organization," p. 9. For a brief view of the role of women in Blackfeet history, see Kehoe, "Blackfoot Persons."

9. "Questionnaire on Tribal Organization," p. 10.

10. *Glacier County Chief*, Feb. 8, 1935. Stone left in early March 1935.

11. Section 12 of the IRA provided that "qualified Indians shall hereafter have the preference to appointments," but it did not specify that a tribe had the right to select its own superintendent (*Statutes at Large of the United States*, 48 [1934]: 984).

12. "Minutes of the Meeting of the BTBC, Feb. 18, 1935," NA RG 75, CCF-I File 25146-1935-BF-054.

13. "Minutes of the Meeting of the BTBC, Feb. 18, 1935."

14. "Minutes of the Meeting of the BTBC, Feb. 18, 1935."

15. See Stone to CIA, Apr. 3, 1931, NA RG 75, CCF-I File 16072-1927-BF-054. Stone believed the amendment would "stabilize the work of the Council" and strengthen its "feeling of responsibility."

16. Lorraine Owens, interview by author, Aug. 28, 1996 (author's files). Brown had been blind in one eye since boyhood; his brother accidentally shot him as they pretended to hunt grizzly bears. He was educated at a school near Fort Benton in the 1880s. Ms. Owens, Brown's youngest daughter, lives on the reservation.

17. "Minutes of the BTBC Meeting, Apr. 4, 1935," pp. 11–16, NA RG 75, CCF-I File 20858-1935-BF-054.

18. "Minutes of the BTBC Meeting, Apr. 4, 1935," pp. 1–3.

19. "Memorandum to the Director of NPS and CIA" (Exhibit C), in "Minutes

of the BTBC Meeting Held at the Community Hall, May 2, 1935." See also Brott to CIA, Apr. 25, 1935 (Exhibit D), all in File 29288-1935-BF-054.

20. "Minutes of the BTBC Meeting Held at the Community Hall, May 2, 1935," p. 6. Brown was referring to Baker's Massacre, the tribe's Sand Creek. Blackfeet writer James Welch examines the massacre in his novel *Fools Crow*.

21. "Minutes of the BTBC Meeting Held at the Community Hall, May 2, 1935," pp. 7, 8. For Collier's response and reprimand to Brown, see Collier to Brown, Jan. 31, 1936; Collier to Brown, May 14, 1935; and Brown to Collier, June 5, 1935 (author's files).

22. "Minutes of the BTBC Meeting Held at the Community Hall, May 2, 1935," pp. 8–10.

23. "Minutes of the BTBC Meeting Held at the Community Hall, May 2, 1935," pp. 13–14.

24. The OIA issued an "Outline of Tribal Constitutions and Bylaws" on Mar. 9, 1935, to help field agents write individual constitutions.

25. Jennings et al. to CIA, July 18, 1935, File 9522-A-1936-BF-068.

26. O'Hara to CIA, Aug. 4, 1935. See also O'Hara to Jennings, Aug. 4, 1935, both in File 9522-A-1936-BF-068.

27. "Meeting of the BTBC, Aug. 12, 1935," File 9522-A-1936-BF-068.

28. O'Hara to CIA, Nov. 14, 1935, File 9522-A-1936-BF-068.

29. Daiker to Woehlke (no date); Woehlke to Daiker (handwritten reply on same document), File 9522-A-1936-BF-068.

30. U.S. Department of the Interior, Office of Indian Affairs, *Constitution and By-Laws for the Blackfeet Tribe*.

31. William Zimmerman Jr. to Secretary of the Interior, Sept. 19, 1935, File 9522-A-1936-BF-068.

32. "Memorandum for the Assistant Secretary," Acting Solicitor Frederick Bernays Wiener to Charles West, Sept. 26, 1935, FCP, Box 8, Folder 106.

33. "Memorandum for the Acting Secretary," Nathan Margold to Acting Secretary of the Interior Charles West, Oct. 14, 1935, FCP, Box 8, Folder 106.

34. West to O'Hara, Oct. 19, 1935, NA RG 75, GRCIO, File 9522-A-1936-BF-068.

35. O'Hara to CIA, Nov. 14, 1935, File 9522-A-1936-BF-068. The vote by district was as follows: Browning, 509 to 94; Old Agency, 113 to 26; Heart Butte, 109 to 32; Little Badger, 77 to 1; Seville, 41 to 2; and Babb, 35 to 2. The Blackfeet's rate of participation was just above the national average for tribes holding constitution elections. For figures, see Taylor, *New Deal and American Indian Tribalism*, pp. 157–58.

36. O'Hara to CIA, Nov. 14, 1935, File 9522-A-1936-BF-068.

37. For details see NA RG 75, CCF-1 File 46597-1934-BF-054.

38. O'Hara to CIA, Nov. 14, 1935.

39. Collier to Brown, Dec. 23, 1935, File 9522-A-1936-BF-068. Interior approved the constitution on Dec. 11, 1935.

40. "Petition of Protest" to Honorable Franklin D. Roosevelt, President; Honorable Roy E. Ayers; and Honorable B. K. Wheeler (no date, but probably late 1935), File 9522-A-1936-BF-068.

41. Zimmerman to James White Calf, Jan. 11, 1936, File 9522-A-1936-BF-068.

42. See John G. Carter to CIA, Feb. 20, 1936; and Zimmerman to Carter, Feb. 24, 1936, both in NA RG 75, CCF-1 File 7509-1936-BF-308.

43. "Results of Election, Jan. 4, 1936," File 9522-C-1936-BF-057.

44. On this important subject, see Lurie, "Contemporary American Indian Scene"; Anderson, *Sovereign Nations or Reservations*, chapter 1; Cornell, *Return of the Native*, chapter 6; and Taylor, *New Deal and American Indian Tribalism*, chapter 5.

45. "Results of Election, Jan. 4, 1936."

46. "Report of Mr. David Rodnick from Browning, Montana. Week ending March 21," NA RG 75, CCF-1 File 46768-1936-BF-150.

47. Department of the Interior, Office of Indian Affairs, *Constitution and By-Laws for the Blackfeet Tribe*, Article III, sec. 3.

48. See "Blackfeet Tribal Council Says Nay to General Election," *Glacier County Chief*, Sept. 10, 1937.

49. See "Minutes of the BTBC, Jan. 4, 1934," NA RG 75, CCF-1 File 3599-1934-BF-054.

50. "Minutes of the Meeting of the BTBC, March 14, 1934," NA RG 75, CCF-1 File 27648-1934-BF-054.

51. See Department of the Interior, Office of Indian Affairs, *Constitution and By-Laws for the Blackfeet Tribe*, Article II, sec. 1.

52. "Report of Mr. David Rodnick from Browning, Montana. Week ending April 4," File 46768-1936-BF-150.

53. John Collier, in Department of the Interior, *Annual Report of the Secretary of the Interior*, FY 1938, p. 258.

54. Collier to Hon. B. K. Wheeler, Feb. 12, 1937, NA RG 75, CCF-1 File 8306-1937-BF-051. Wheeler was, by this time, actively trying to repeal the act that bore his name, which partly explains Collier's terse style. See also Daiker to Fish Wolf Robe, Mar. 5, 1937, File 8306-1937-BF-051.

55. Walter Woehlke, Memorandum to Mr. Collier, Sept. 29, 1938, FCP, Box 5, Folder 64; see also "Membership in Indian Tribes" in Circular No. 3125, Nov. 18, 1935, in which Collier outlined OIA policy.

56. Felix S. Cohen, Memorandum for Mr. Collier, Oct. 1, 1938, FCP, Box 5, Folder 64.

57. Joe Jennings, Memorandum to Mr. Collier, Oct. 7, 1938, FCP, Box 5, Folder 64.

58. F. H. Daiker, Memorandum to Mr. Collier, Oct. 10, 1938, FCP, Box 5, Folder 64.

59. "Senator Wheeler and the Indian Reorganization Act," p. 5, RCWHA, pt. 8, Box 7, File 4894-1934-066. For congressional debates on repeal, see U.S. Congress, Senate, *Repeal of the So-Called Wheeler-Howard Act*, S. Rept. 1047, Aug. 2, 1939; and U.S. Congress, Senate Committee on Indian Affairs, *Survey of Conditions of the Indians in the United States*, 76th Cong., 1st sess., pt. 37, 1940.

60. Collier to Murray, Feb. 6, 1939, NA RG 75, CCF-1 File 4904-1939-BF-056; Zimmerman to Murray, Feb. 4, 1937, NA RG 75, CCF-1 File 5800-1937-BF-056.

61. Joe Jennings et al., Memorandum for the CIA, Dec. 22, 1935, FCP, Box 104, Folder 7.

62. Joe Jennings et al., Memorandum for the CIA, Dec. 22, 1935.

63. "Comments on Blackfeet Charter," Mar. 30, 1936, File 9522B-1936-BF-061.

64. H. M. Critchfield, Memorandum for Indian Organization, Apr. 2, 1936, File 9522B-1936-BF-061.

65. Robert Marshall, Memorandum on Blackfeet and Fort Belknap Charters, Mar. 30, 1936, File 9522B-1936-BF-061. Marshall was concerned about the vulnerability of full-bloods to mixed-blood control of tribal assets. See also "Mountain Chief," by Robert Marshall, Chief of Forestry, in Department of the Interior, *Indians at Work*, Apr. 15, 1935, vol. 2, no. 17.

66. Memorandum to the Organization Committee, from James E. Curry, Attorney, Indian Organization, Apr. 2, 1936, File 9522B-1936-BF-061.

67. Department of the Interior, Bureau of Indian Affairs, *Corporate Charter of the Blackfeet Tribe*. Sec. 6 pertained only to provisions 5 and 8.

68. Bureau of Indian Affairs, *Corporate Charter of the Blackfeet Tribe*. See sec. 6, "Termination of Supervisory Powers."

69. Jennings to Zimmerman, Apr. 9, 1936, File 9522B-1936-BF-061.

70. Zimmerman informed Joe Brown on Apr. 15 that the Indian Office had approved the charter.

71. Zimmerman to Field Agent Don W. Hagerty, Aug. 27, 1936, File 9522B-1936-BF-061.

72. "Results of Charter Election Aug. 15, 1936," File 9522B-1936-BF-061. The Starr School numbers are from the *Glacier County Chief*, Aug. 21, 1936.

73. The number of voters participating in the various elections ranged from 994 in the IRA election to 1,041 in the constitution election to 1,038 in the charter election.

74. No Coat to Honorable Harold Ickes, Feb. 20, 1937, NA RG 75, CCF-1 File 11582-1937-BF-050.

75. Charles West to No Coat, Mar. 3, 1937, File 11582-1937-BF-050.

4. Feeding the "Second Buffalo"

1. "Annual Report of Extension Workers, Jan. 1, 1936, to Dec. 31, 1936," p. 10, NA RG 75, CCF-1 File 4634-1937-BF-031.

2. "Annual Report of Extension Workers, Jan. 1, 1936, to Dec. 31, 1936," p. 5 of statistical report. In 1934 762 families received relief, and nearly all Blackfeet received aid of one kind in 1935. See the 1934 and 1935 "Annual Report of Extension Workers." Some families also received money from the Old Age Assistance and Aid to Dependent Children programs. Family incomes ranged between four hundred and seven hundred dollars.

3. "Indian Homes—Blackfeet Reservation," in Department of the Interior, *Indians at Work*, vol. 2, no. 3 (Sept. 15, 1934). For short narrative accounts of the Blackfeet experience, see the following articles in *Indians at Work*: "From Flathead to Blackfeet," by Mary Heaton Vorse, vol. 2, no. 21 (June 15, 1935); "Heavy Runner Indian Women's Club," by Margaret Smith Stinson, vol. 3, no. 12 (Feb. 1, 1936); " '40 Mile' I.E.C.W. Camp," by George C. Walters, vol. 3, no. 17 (Apr. 15, 1936); "The Blackfeet Medicine Lodge Ceremony," by Kathleen Higgins, vol. 3, no. 23 (July 15, 1936).

4. See Department of the Interior, *Indians at Work*, "Indians in Supervisory Positions," vol. 1, no. 7 (Oct. 15, 1933), and "Buffalo Coats at Blackfeet," vol. 1, no. 13 (Feb. 15, 1934).

5. *Statutes at Large of the United States*, 49 (1936): 1568. The resolution authorized the distribution of $455,644.80 to the Blackfeet; the tribe's attorneys earned $48,118. The tribe retained $71,776.19 for "future disposition." See NA RG 75, CCF-1 File 12112-1936-BF-013 and File 14505-1950-BF-170.

6. "Blackfeet 'Big Claim' Money," pp. 10–12, in "Annual Report of Extension Workers," 1936.

7. *Glacier County Chief*, Nov. 20, 1936.

8. "Annual Report of Extension Workers," 1936, p. 11.

9. O. H. Lipps, Supervisor, to CIA, Nov. 19, 1935, File 12112-1936-BF-013.

10. "Annual Report of Extension Workers," 1936, p. 2 of statistical report.

11. See "Minutes of the Meeting of the BTBC, Mar. 14, 1934," pp. 3–4, NA RG 75, CCF-1 File 27648-1934-BF-054. Rides at the Door told the council, "Get the white man to do it rather than listen to oil talk. The main thing is to watch the white man so that they don't get the best of us as we have a proven area now."

12. Acting Solicitor Frederic L. Kirgis to CIA, May 22, 1937, FCP, Box 5, Folder 73.

13. Assistant Solicitor Felix Cohen to Acting Solicitor [Frederic L. Kirgis], May 18, 1937, FCP, Box 5, Folder 73.

14. "Minutes of a Meeting of the BTBC, June 3, 1937," p. 6, NA RG 75, CCF-1 File 10809-1936-BF-322.6.

15. "What Remains to Be Done in the Field of Tribal Organization," Felix Cohen to Organization Division, July 15, 1937, FCP, Box 8, Folder 119.

16. John Herrick to Collier, Apr. 7, 1937, NA RG 75, CCF-1 File 30654-1937-BF-054.

17. Cohen, "Memorandum: Blackfeet Oil and Gas Leases" (no date), File 30654-1937-BF-054.

18. Zimmerman to Superintendent Charles Graves, May 15, 1937, File 30654-1937-BF-054.

19. On several occasions, OIA officials recommended to the attorney general's office the prosecution of oil operators. The council was mainly concerned with warning operators that it would not tolerate speculation. For examples, see NA RG 75, CCF-1 File 11716-1936-BF-322 and File 11708-1936-BF-322.

20. "Sum-Up of Glacier County's Major Industry—Its Future," *Glacier County Chief*, Jan. 8, 1936; for an overview of Montana oil production in the 1930s and beyond see Douma, "History of Oil and Gas in Montana."

21. For two discussions of these problems, see "Minutes of the Meeting of the BTBC, June 4, 1934," pp. 9–13; and "Minutes of the Meeting of the BTBC, Sept. 11, 1934," both in File 46597-1934-BF-054.

22. Narrative section of "Annual Report of Extension Workers," 1935, NA RG 75, CCF-1 File 00-1935-BF-031. See sec. III, "Narrative Report, Forestry and I.E.C.W."

23. These statistics were compiled from the tables of the "Annual Report of Extension Workers," 1936.

24. These numbers were compiled from the list titled "Grazing Leases as of June 30, 1936," in "Annual Forestry and Grazing Report," 1936, NA RG 75, CCF-1 File 13002-1936-BF-031.

25. Senate Committee on Indian Affairs, *Survey of Conditions of the Indians in the United States*, pt. 31, pp. 16716–43.

26. Oscar Chapman to Burton K. Wheeler, June 16, 1934, NA RG 75, CCF-1 File 21729-1934-BF-013. According to Chapman, the Blackfeet needed roughly three hundred to five hundred head of sheep or thirty to fifty head of cattle to provide a "comfortable living for the average family."

27. "Mountain Chief," by Robert Marshall, Chief of Forestry, Indian Service, in Department of the Interior, *Indians at Work*, vol. 2, no. 17 (Apr. 15, 1935).

28. "Minutes of the BTBC Meeting, April 4, 1935," NA RG 75, CCF-1 File 20858-1935-BF-054.

29. Full-bloods were split on the buffalo question. Elders like Mountain Chief and Louis Champagne maintained little interest in buffalo. Champagne told the council during the initial debate, "I practically was raised on buffalo, but I am grown up now, and I have forgotten the buffalo entirely. I don't care about having the buffalo at all." He was more concerned with developing the tribe's oil resources. Other full-bloods supported the buffalo plan, but for economic rather

than cultural reasons. See "Minutes of the BTBC, Jan. 4, 1934," pp. 14–19; see also "Minutes of the Meeting of the BTBC, Mar. 14, 1934," both in File 27648-1934-BF-054.

30. "Annual Extension Report," 1934, File 00-1935-BF-031.

31. "Indian Cattle Purchase Program," by A. C. Cooley, director of Extension and Industry, in Department of the Interior, *Indians at Work*, vol. 2, no. 4 (Oct. 1, 1934).

32. "Annual Extension Report," 1935, NA RG 75, CCF-1 File 6663-1936-BF-031. See the Animal Industry section of the report.

33. Collier's letter is quoted in "Minutes of the BTBC Meeting, Apr. 4, 1935," p. 7, File 20858-1935-BF-054.

34. Councilman James Fisher was concerned that the cattle "are going to those best equipped to handle them, but there will be people who are not equipped to handle them, what of their interests?" See "Minutes of the Meeting of the BTBC, June 4, 1934," File 42654-1934-BF-054.

35. The percentages were determined from figures in "Annual Extension Report," 1935. For details, see Individual Cattle Repayment Records, Seattle Federal Archives and Records Center, RG 75.

36. "Report on the Blackfeet Indians of Montana," by David Rodnick, Apr. 1936, p. 3, NA RG 75, CCF-2 File 9004-1943-BF-042.

37. "Report on the Blackfeet Indians of Montana," p. 9.

38. "Annual Report of Extension Workers, January 1, 1937, to December 31, 1937," p. 8, NA RG 75, CCF-1 File 1712-1938-BF-031.

39. "Annual Report of Extension Workers, Jan. 1, 1937, to Dec. 31, 1937," pp. 8–9.

40. "Annual Report of Extension Workers, Jan. 1, 1937, to Dec. 31, 1937," pp. 14–16.

41. "Annual Report of Extension Workers," 1936, p. 6. The employment of three Blackfeet farm aides in the Old Agency, Little Badger, and Starr School communities helped to secure their cooperation, Krall wrote, though full-blood "agitators" in Heart Butte resented the white farm agent posted there.

42. See "Annual Report of Extension Workers" for the years 1934–37. In 1936, 482 families received relief.

43. See "Annual Forestry and Grazing Report," 1936 and 1937.

44. "Annual Report of Extension Workers," 1937, p. 3.

45. Superintendent C. L. Graves to "Farmers and Stockmen of the Blackfeet Reservation," October 1937, File 1712-1938-BF-031.

46. "Annual Report of Extension Workers," 1937, pp. 7–11.

47. Collier told Wheeler in December 1937, "We are all agreed, I think, that if the Blackfeet are to approach anything like a self-sustaining economy they must base that economy upon the livestock industry" (see Collier to Wheeler, Dec. 10, 1937, NA RG 75, CCF-1 File 69848-1937-BF-021.5).

48. "Minutes of a Meeting of the BTBC, March 6, 1937," NA RG 75, GRCIO, File 9522-E-1936-BF-054.

49. Members of the BTBC to Commissioner of Indian Affairs and Others Concerned, Apr. 9, 1937, File 9522-E-1936-BF-054.

50. "Blackfeet Indian Reservation," by C. L. Graves, November 1937, File 9522-A-1936-BF-068.

51. Department of the Interior, Office of Indian Affairs, *Constitution and By-Laws for the Blackfeet Tribe*, Article VI (Powers of the Council), sec. 1, Enumerated Powers, k, m, and p. See also "Tribal budget, Mar. 1 to June 30, 1937," NA RG 75, CCF-1 File 15708-1937-BF-050.

52. See "Minutes of a Meeting of the BTBC, June 3, 1937," File 9522-E-1936-BF-054. For a complete description of the Blackfeet Tribe's regulations, laws, and administrative requirements, see "Code of Laws of the Blackfeet Tribe of the Blackfeet Indian Reservation, Montana," NA RG 75, CCF-2 BF-1, Box 1.

53. Congress had approved Collier's request for a $10 million credit fund but appropriated only $2.5 million in 1936.

54. "Loan Application of the Blackfeet Tribe of the Blackfeet Indian Reservation for a Loan from the Revolving Fund for Loans to Indian Corporations," Sept. 3, 1936, NA RG 75, CCF-1 File 19522-1936-BF-259, pt. I-A.

55. H. D. McCullough to CIA, Sept. 22, 1936, File 19522-1936-BF-259, General.

56. "Loan Application of the Blackfeet Tribe," Sept. 3, 1936, Exhibit E, p. 26.

57. "Commitment Order for a Loan of Revolving Credit Funds from the United States to the Blackfeet Tribe of the Blackfeet Reservation, an Indian Chartered Corporation," File 19522-1936-BF-259, pt. I-A. The tribe issued its first promissory note on Apr. 26, 1937.

58. Credit agent H. D. McCullough to field representative C. E. Faris, Nov. 3, 1937, File 9522-A-1936-BF-068.

59. "Minutes of a Meeting of the BTBC, April 8, 1937," File 9522-E-1936-BF-054. Credit committee members were elected by the council to serve five-year terms.

60. Figures are from Renne, *Montana County Organizations, Services and Costs*, as cited in "Some Observations on the Blackfeet Reservation," by George Fox, June 1942, File 9004-1943-BF-042.

61. "Annual Report of Extension Workers," 1937, pp. 10–11 of the supplementary report.

62. "Annual Report of Extension Workers," 1937, p. 20.

63. See "Blackfeet Reservation," by Faris and Mekeel, Nov. 17, 1937, File 9522-A-1936-BF-068.

64. *Glacier County Chief*, Oct. 22, 1937.

65. The cooperative, which initially comprised eight craft clubs totaling about 160 workers, appears to have been organized along the lines of the PFLA,

another predominantly full-blood organization. Each club selected a representative to serve on the craft council, which in turn elected its officers. Craft workers created "articles true to Blackfeet tradition and artistic standards" and sold them to tourists at the reservation craft shop or in Glacier National Park souvenir stores. Workers were taught by two Blackfeet women who interviewed elderly full-bloods "to learn exactly how things were done in the old days, and to recover techniques now almost lost" (see "Narrative Report of Jesse Donaldson Schultz," May 5, 1937, NA RG 75, CCF-1 File 30124-1937-BF-032). The BTBC authorized a small loan from credit funds to assist the craft cooperative's operation in June 1937. After only six months, the cooperative had sold roughly thirty-five hundred dollars' worth of goods, providing supplemental income and meaningful work to Blackfeet women.

66. See "Blackfeet Indian Reservation," by C. L. Graves, November 1937; see also Graves to Collier, Oct. 5, 1936, File 19522-1936-BF-259, General; "Annual Report of Extension Workers," 1937, pp. 20–21; "Blackfeet Reservation," by Faris and Mekeel; and Collier to Wheeler, Dec. 10, 1937, File 69848-1937-BF-021.5.

67. The secretary's ruling was pursuant to the Act of February 26, 1923 (*Statutes at Large of the United States*, 42 [1923]: 1289). For a comprehensive report on all four Blackfeet irrigation projects, see A. L. Walthen, director of irrigation, to CIA, Nov. 13, 1937, File 69848-1937-BF-021.5.

68. "Minutes of the BTBC, Nov. 5, 1937," p. 2, File 9522-E-1936-BF-O54.

69. "Minutes of the BTBC, Nov. 5, 1937," p. 9.

70. "Minutes of the BTBC, Nov. 5, 1937," p. 5.

71. Department of the Interior, "Memorandum for the Press," Dec. 27, 1937, GRCIO, File 3633-1934-BF-054. See also "Blackfeet Irrigation Project Is Approved," *Glacier County Chief*, Jan. 7, 1938.

72. "Official Figures in the Blackfeet Election for Tribal Councilmen," *Glacier County Chief*, Jan. 21, 1938. See also "Blackfeet Tribe Elect Almost Entirely New Business Council at Election Tuesday," *Glacier County Chief*, Jan. 14, 1938.

73. Leo Kennerly, William Spanish, and Frank Vielle received loans averaging $1,250. See "Status of Loans: The Blackfeet Tribe . . . May 1, 1938," NA RG 75, CCF-1 File 19522-1936-BF-259, General, pt. 2.

74. "Minutes of Meeting of the BTBC, July 20, 1937," File 9522-E-1936-BF-054.

75. Liggett covers Hazlett's controversial stint with the Indian Service in Senate Committee on Indian Affairs, "Report of Walter W. Liggett," pp. 12747–48. According to Hazlett's résumé, he graduated from Carlisle in 1899 and from Wilson's Modern Business College of Seattle in 1908. After "getting out of the [Indian] Service," he edited the *Browning Review*, then served as superintendent of garbage collection in Great Falls before moving to Seattle, where he worked for the Metropolitan Building Company. See "Resume [*sic*] of the training and

experience of tribal officers," in "Loan Application . . . April 9, 1938," p. 33, NA RG 75, CCF-1 File 19522-1936-BF-259, pt. 1-B.

76. The balance amounted to $67,273.80 in June 1937. See "Blackfeet Indian Resolution, July 20, 1937," File 9522-E-1936-BF-054. For financial data, see "Statement of Trust Fund Balances . . ." in File 9522-A-1936-BF-068.

77. See "Minutes of a Second Meeting of the BTBC, January 11, 1933," NA RG 75, CCF-1 File 4011-1933-BF-054.

78. See, for example, "Xmas at Starr School," *Glacier County Chief*, Dec. 31, 1937; see also the Jan. 7, 1938, issue of the newspaper.

79. "'Mistakes' Made in Leases," *Glacier County Chief*, Sept. 3, 1937.

80. *Glacier County Chief*, Oct. 8, 1937.

81. "Blackfeet Water Question," *Glacier County Chief*, Oct. 15, 1937; "Work Needed by Indians through Reservation Irrigation," Oct. 22, 1937.

82. "Indian Department Opposes per Capita Payments," *Glacier County Chief*, Oct. 29, 1937.

83. "Tribal Business Council Election," *Glacier County Chief*, Dec. 3, 1937.

84. "New Blood Wanted," *Glacier County Chief*, Jan. 7, 1938. Most candidates simply announced that they were running for office.

85. "Letter to the Public," *Glacier County Chief*, Jan. 28, 1938.

86. Assistant Chief, Fiscal Division, to Daiker, Mar. 8, 1938, File 19522-1936-BF-259, pt. 1-A.

87. Hazlett et al. to CIA, Mar. 12, 1938, File 19522-1936-BF-259, pt. 1-A.

88. Hazlett to Zimmerman, Mar. 18, 1938, NA RG 75, GRCIO, File 9522-C-1936-057.

89. R. S. Bristol, Memorandum to the Commissioner, Mar. 30, 1938; Collier to Tribal Council of the Blackfeet Reservation, Apr. 5, 1938, both in File 19522-1936-BF-259, pt. 1-A.

90. Donald Hagerty, organization field agent, to CIA, Mar. 8, 1938, File 14592-1938-BF-050.

91. "Tribal Council Meets," *Glacier County Chief*, Apr. 22, 1938; "Meeting of the BTBC, April 7, 1938," both in File 9522-E-1936-BF-054.

92. "Meeting of the BTBC, Apr. 20, 1938," File 9522-E-1936-BF-054. See also minutes of the May 17 and June 2 sessions.

93. "Minutes of Meeting Held by the BTBC, July 7, 1938," NA RG 75, CCF-1 File 46374-1938-BF-054.

94. Herrick to Graves, Apr. 4, 1938, File 19522-1936-BF-259, pt. 1-A.

95. Herrick to Hazlett, Apr. 21, 1938, File 14592-1938-BF-050.

96. Herrick to Graves, Apr. 1, 1938; Hazlett to CIA, Apr. 14, 1938, both in NA RG 75, CCF-1 File 29267-1937-BF-054.

97. Graves to CIA, Apr. 15, 1938; Acting Commissioner E. J. Armstrong to Graves, Apr. 27, 1938, both in File 29267-1937-BF-054.

98. Special agent Martin Overgaard conducted a review of the Blackfeet Cor-

poration's finances for the Interior Department's Division of Investigations. See Overgaard to CIA, June 6, 1938, File 29267-1937-BF-054.

99. Hazlett to Herrick, July 9, 1938; Herrick to Hazlett, July 16, 1938, both in File 9522-C-1936-BF-057.

100. John Pohland, principal accountant auditor, to CIA, File 19522-1936-BF-259, General, pt. 2.

101. Herrick to Hazlett, Dec. 1, 1938, File 29267-1937-BF-054.

102. Herrick to all Superintendents, Circular Letter 33859, Aug. 15, 1938, NA RG 75, CCF-1 File 64640-1938-BF-054.

103. Department of the Interior, Office of Indian Affairs, *Constitution and By-Laws for the Blackfeet Tribe*. According to Article VI, sec. 1(c), the tribe's "enumerated powers" include the right "to prevent the sale, disposition, lease, or incumbrance [*sic*] of tribal lands, interests in lands or other assets, without the consent of the tribe."

104. "Resolution Adopted by the BTBC, Sept. 8, 1938," File 64640-1938-BF-054. See also Hazlett, "That Reimburseable Fund," *Glacier County Chief*, Sept. 16, 1938, and "Minutes of the Meeting Held by the BTBC, September 23, 1938," File 9522-E-1936-BF-054.

105. Zimmerman to Hazlett, Mar. 27, 1939, File 64640-1938-BF-054.

106. Joe Jennings, Memorandum to the Commissioner, Jan. 25, 1939, File 3633-1934-BF-054, pt. 1. The Appropriations Act stipulated that Indians could be charged for medical, hospital, and dental services and the fees deposited in the U.S. Treasury.

107. Daiker, Memorandum to Commissioner Collier, Feb. 3, 1939, File 3633-1934-BF-054, pt. 1.

108. U.S. Congress, House Committee on Appropriations, *Interior Department Appropriation Bill, 1939*, 75th Cong., 3d sess., pt. 2, pp. 7–8.

109. The council discovered in October 1939 that the OIA had resolved the USGS subsidy issue by impounding the fee from tribal funds, though it charged the Blackfeet 5 percent rather than 10. See "Blackfeet Tribal Council Hold Special Meeting," *Glacier County Chief*, Oct. 13, 1939.

110. See James White Calf et al. to Wheeler, Mar. 19, 1939, File 9522-1936-BF-066.

111. Collier to Charles E. Heacock, Jan. 27, 1940, File 9522-1936-BF-066. The letter to Heacock apparently was drafted by John Herrick.

112. Collier to the Chairman and Members of the BTBC, Oct. 31, 1939, File 9522-C-1936-BF-057. Clark was a special agent of the Department of the Interior's Division of Investigations. Mae (nee Coburn) Williamson and her husband were well off, earning more than ten thousand dollars per year in oil revenues.

113. "Hazlett Makes Scathing Reply to Audit Letter," *Glacier County Chief*, Nov. 17, 1939.

114. "An Open Letter by Stuart Hazlett," *Glacier County Chief*, Nov. 24, 1939.

115. "Indian Reorganization," by Joe Jennings, in Department of the Interior, *Indians at Work*, vol. 6, no. 10 (June 1939), p. 14.

116. "Our Reservation Problem," *Glacier County Chief*, Dec. 8, 1939.

117. "Hugh Jackson Writes Regarding Coming Tribal Council Election," *Glacier County Chief*, Nov. 10, 1939; "Hugh Jackson's Letter," *Glacier County Chief*, Dec. 1, 1939.

118. Heacock to Jennings, Dec. 22, 1939, File 9522-1936-BF-066.

119. White Calf et al. to Wheeler, Mar. 19, 1939, File 9522-1936-BF-066. White Calf quoted his colleague in the letter to Wheeler.

120. "Blackfeet Tribe Elect Business Council for Next 2-Year Term," *Glacier County Chief*, Jan. 19, 1940.

121. Collier to Heacock, Jan. 27, 1940, File 9522-1936-BF-066.

122. See Deloria and Lytle, *Nations Within*, p. 258; and Biolsi, *Organizing the Lakota*, chapter 5.

123. "Blackfeet Reservation" by Faris and Mekeel, Nov. 17, 1937.

124. John Herrick, "Memorandum," Feb. 1, 1938, File 9522-C-1936-057.

125. Zimmerman to Wheeler, Dec. 3, 1937, File 69848-1937-BF-021.5.

126. "Annual Extension Report, Narrative Section, January 1, 1938, to December 31, 1938," NA RG 75, CCF-1 File 4776-1939-BF-031.

127. "Annual Report of Extension Workers, Narrative Section, Jan. 1, 1939, to Dec. 31, 1939," NA RG 75, CCF-2 File 1173-1940-BF-031.

128. "Stuart Hazlett Writes," *Glacier County Chief*, Mar. 4, 1938.

129. "Table of Resident Blackfeet Indian Net Income, 1943," NA RG 75, CCF-2 File 7056-1944-BF-071.

5. "Reconciling the Old Men"

1. Walzer, *Spheres of Justice*, p. 283.

2. "Minutes of Meeting of BTBC, Feb. 1, 1940," pp. 2, 4, NA RG 75, CCF-2 GRCIO File 9522-E-1936-BF-054. See also Heacock to CIA, Feb. 14, 1940, File 9522-C-1936-BF-057.

3. "Minutes of Meeting of BTBC, Feb. 1, 1940," pp. 6, 10.

4. "Minutes of Meeting of BTBC, Feb. 1, 1940," pp. 6, 8.

5. "Minutes of Meeting of BTBC, Feb. 1, 1940," p. 11.

6. "Minutes of Meeting Held by the BTBC, Feb. 5, 1940," File 9522-E-1936-BF-054.

7. Heacock to CIA, Feb. 14, 1940.

8. Department of the Interior, *Annual Report of the Secretary of the Interior, FY 1941*, pp. 409–19.

9. Pateman, *Participation and Democratic Theory*, p. 105.

10. "Minutes of Meeting Held by the BTBC, Mar. 6, 1940," File 9522-E-1936-BF-054.

11. Louis Plenty Treaty protested White Calf's resistance to economic rehabilitation, arguing that his own group in Starr School "unanimously favors the restock [of cattle] to exist in perpetuation" (Plenty Treaty to Wheeler, Mar. 11, 1940, NA RG 75, CCF-2 File 17863-1940-BF-910).

12. Earl Old Person, interview by author, Dec. 5, 1997 (author's files).

13. "Blackfeet Delegation Conference with Organization Division," by George Fox, Mar. 20, 1940, NA RG 75, CCF-2 File 00-1940-BF-056.

14. U.S. Congress, House Committee on Indian Affairs, *Relief of Needy Indians*, 76th Cong., 3d sess., 1940, H.R. 8937, p. 13. The bill would have allocated $10 million for Indian relief.

15. House Committee on Indian Affairs, *Relief of Needy Indians*, p. 13.

16. House Committee on Indian Affairs, *Relief of Needy Indians*, p. 33. The Johnson-O'Malley Act of Apr. 16, 1934, gave the secretary of the interior the authority to appropriate money for states' management of Indians in the areas of health, education, agriculture, and relief.

17. "Annual Extension Report, Narrative Section," 1939.

18. "Annual Extension Report, Narrative Section," 1938. Roughly 370 families earned an average of $372 from livestock and crop sales in 1938.

19. "Annual Extension Report, Narrative Section," 1939.

20. See Department of the Interior, *Annual Report of the Secretary of the Interior*, 1941, p. 425.

21. Burd to Collier, July 12, 1940, File 9522-C-1936-BF-057.

22. A. C. Cooley to D'Arcy McNickle, Aug. 27, 1940, File 9522-C-1936-BF-057.

23. Connolly issued a "report" for the self-styled "loan investigation committee," which had no official standing. See "Report," by Brian Connolly, NA RG 75, CCF-2 File 241-1941-BF-155.

24. For the council discussion of Burd's alleged transgressions, see the minutes of the Feb. 1, 1941, BTBC meeting, File 9522-E-1936-BF-054. For the OIA investigation, see File 241-1941-BF-155.

25. Allan G. Harper to Hon. James O'Connor, Oct. 6, 1941; C. L. Graves to CIA, July 21, 1941, both in File 241-1941-BF-155.

26. "Credit Committee [of the BTBC] Report," by George Pambrun, March 1942, File 9004-1943-BF-042.

27. "Some Observations on the Blackfeet Reservation," by George Fox, June 26, 1942, pp. 4–6.

28. Fox to Joe McCaskill, Oct. 22, 1942, NA RG 75, CCF-2 File 37123-1942-BF-054.

29. "Minutes of the BTBC in Special Session, December 20, 1941," File 9522-

E-1936-BF-054. The BTBC usually tried to release per capita payments in December.

30. Walzer, *Spheres of Justice*, p. 11.

31. Champagne, "Economic Culture, Institutional Order, and Sustained Market Enterprise," p. 209.

32. "Relief," by Kate W. Smith, Nov. 30, 1942, NA RG 75, CCF-2 File 00-1942-BF-056.

33. Daiker to Freal McBride, Aug. 8, 1942, NA RG 75, CCF-2 File 50403-1941-BF-720.

34. "Advance Estimate of Direct Relief Funds Required for Fiscal Year 1944," File 50403-1941-BF-720. Class A funds derived mainly from the balance of the 1935 Big Claim judgment and from oil revenues earned prior to the adoption of the charter in 1935.

35. Daiker to McBride, Aug. 5, 1944, File 50403-1941-BF-720.

36. McBride to Daiker, Aug. 14, 1944, File 50403-1941-BF-720. The tribe voted overwhelmingly on Jan. 18, 1944, to provide $150 for "funeral insurance" for each Blackfeet. See "Tribal Council Certifies Vote Cast at Election," *Browning Chief*, Jan. 28, 1944.

37. Pambrun to CIA, Sept. 4, 1945, File 50403-1941-BF-720.

38. "Project—Assisting in the Nation's War Effort," in "Annual Report of Extension Work," 1942, p. 11, NA RG 75, CCF-2 File 1332-1943-BF-031.

39. "Ten-Year Program for the Blackfeet Indian Agency," March 1944, p. 27, NA RG 75, CCF-2 File 7056-1944-BF-071.

40. "Minutes of Meeting Held by the BTBC in Special Session, Feb. 1, 1941," File 9522-E-1936-BF-054.

41. An August 1944 Boeing advertisement offered free transportation to Seattle and full pay during a training period. See "BOEING NEEDS YOU!" *Browning Chief*, Aug. 11, 1944, and ". . . Jobs in Hop Fields," same issue.

42. FY 1943 Budget, "Council Expense Administration," File 9522-E-1936-BF-054.

43. "Minutes of Meeting Held by the BTBC in Special Session, Dec. 20, 1941," File 9522-E-1936-BF-054.

44. Statistics calculated from figures in "Total Individual Income (Resident Population)," 1942, 1944, File 50403-1941-BF-720.

45. "Distribution of Families by Estimated Income," 1942, 1944, File 50403-1941-BF-720.

46. "Ten-Year Program for the Blackfeet Indian Agency," March 1944, p. 24.

47. "Annual Report of Extension Work," 1944, pp. 13–14, File 5506-1945-BF-031; "Annual Report of Extension Work," 1945, p. 27. For Sioux numbers, see Biolsi, *Organizing the Lakota*, p. 120.

48. Extension Division "Program of Work," 1945, pp. 9–10, NA RG 75,

CCF-2 File 16326-1945-BF-919.1. The BTBC approved each "Program of Work" after consulting with Extension staff.

49. "Status of Credit Loan Accounts: Blackfeet Tribe of the Blackfeet Indian Reservation," NA RG 75, CCF-1 File 19522-1936-BF-259, General, pt. 3; A. C. Cooley to Jennings, Nov. 12, 1943, File 9522-1936-BF-066.

50. "Annual Extension Report, Narrative Section," 1939.

51. Extension Division "Program of Work," 1945, pp. 4–5, File 16326-1945-BF-919.1.

52. "Relief," by Kate W. Smith, Nov. 30, 1942.

53. "Ten-Year Program for the Blackfeet Indian Agency," March 1944, p. 28.

54. "Ten-Year Program for the Blackfeet Indian Agency," March 1944, pp. 29–30 (see the section "Cultural Conditions"). Ewers also edited the report.

55. Hugh W. Jackson to Collier, Nov. 26, 1941, File 9522-C-1936-BF-057.

56. Zimmerman to Jackson, Dec. 12, 1941, File 9522-C-1936-BF-057.

57. Zimmerman to John Yellow Kidney, Dec. 30, 1942, File 9522-C-1936-BF-057. See also in the same file Yellow Kidney's letters of Sept. 16, 1942, and Nov. 28, 1942.

58. "A Summary of Statements Expressing the Views and Wishes of the Older Indians of Blackfeet (Predominately [sic] full blood) since Passage of the So Called Wheeler Howard Act," 1942, File 9522-C-1936-BF-057. Either James White Calf or Charles Reevis penned the resolution.

59. Zimmerman to Grant, BTBC chairman, Jan. 9, 1943, NA RG 75, CCF-2 File 174-1943-BF-056.

60. "Full-bloods Meet," *Glacier County Chief*, May 24, 1940.

61. Charles Reevis to CIA, Nov. 6, 1943, File 9522-1936-BF-066.

62. Zimmerman to Reevis, Nov. 25, 1943, File 9522-1936-BF-066.

63. John Ewers, interviews by author, June 15, 1996, and Feb. 17, 1997 (author's files).

64. "To the Honorable Commissioner of Indian Affairs: Also to Members of the Blackfeet Indians It May Concern," July 1945, File 00-1940-BF-056.

65. "Ten-Year Program for the Blackfeet Indian Agency," March 1944, pp. 30–31.

66. *Congressional Record*, 78th Cong., 1st sess., Mar. 16, 1943, pp. 2098–2103; U.S. Congress, Senate, Partial Report 310, Pursuant to S.R. 17 extending S.R. 79 in the 70th Cong., in Senate Committee on Indian Affairs, *Survey of Conditions among the Indians of the United States*, 78th Cong., 1st sess., 1943.

67. U.S. Congress, House Committee on Indian Affairs, *Investigate Indian Affairs*, 78th Cong., 2d sess., 1944, p. 400.

68. House Committee on Indian Affairs, *Investigate Indian Affairs*, pp. 437–38.

69. House Committee on Indian Affairs, *Investigate Indian Affairs*, pp. 437–

38. Brown's testimony appears on pp. 399–409, Buffalohide's is on pp. 412–16, and Ironpipe's is on pp. 416–20.

70. House Committee on Indian Affairs, *Investigate Indian Affairs*, p. 442.

71. House Committee on Indian Affairs, *Investigate Indian Affairs*, pp. 365, 478.

72. House Committee on Indian Affairs, *Investigate Indian Affairs*, p. 445.

73. House Committee on Indian Affairs, *Investigate Indian Affairs*, pp. 432–34.

74. House Committee on Indian Affairs, *Investigate Indian Affairs*, pp. 444, 445.

75. U.S. Congress, House, *An Investigation to Determine Whether the Changed Status of the Indian Requires a Revision of the Laws and Regulations Affecting the American Indian*, 78th Cong., 2d sess., 1944, H. Rept. 2091.

76. "Minutes of the Blackfeet Tribal Constitutional Convention under Sponsorship of the BTBC," Apr. 23, 1945, NA RG 75, CCF-2 File 36128-1945-BF-054 (hereafter cited as "Constitutional Convention Minutes").

77. "Constitutional Convention Minutes," Apr. 24, 1945, pp. 7–9.

78. "Constitutional Convention Minutes," pp. 9, 12.

79. "Constitutional Convention Minutes," Apr. 26, 1945, pp. 3–4.

80. "Constitutional Convention Minutes," pp. 4, 5, 6.

81. "Constitutional Convention Minutes," p. 10. For FY 1946 (July 1, 1945, to June 30, 1946), council expenses—which included per diem for committee meetings, council salaries, and Washington delegations—represented about 8.4 percent of the total budget. See "Monthly Financial Statement: Blackfeet Tribe of the Blackfeet Indian Reservation. For Month Ending September 30, 1945," File 36128-1945-BF-054.

82. See "Constitutional Convention Minutes," May 1, 1945, for the debate on the IRA and p. 16 for Juniper Old Person's comment. His son Earl would later become BTBC chairman and the president of the National Congress of American Indians.

83. "Constitutional Convention Minutes," Apr. 25, 1945, pp. 2–12.

84. "Constitutional Convention Minutes," Apr. 26, 1945, p. 17. Reevis explained that "it is easier to buy off five than thirteen members."

85. "Constitutional Convention Minutes," Apr. 25, 1945, p. 13.

86. Mary Salois, "Blackfeet Favor Changes at Long Conference," *Browning Chief*, May 4, 1945. Accounts of the convention appeared in the Mar. 30, Apr. 27, and May 4 issues of the *Browning Chief*.

87. "Memo: List of Complaints against Tribal Self-Government by the Blackfeet Full-Blood Minority" (no date, ca. March 1945), File 174-1943-BF-056.

88. William Brophy to Joseph Brown, May 24, 1945, File 174-1943-BF-056. FYIP chapters remained a Blackfeet version of the 4-H program, emphasizing

farming and good citizenship rather than politics. See, for example, *Browning Chief* issues for Mar. 6, 1942, and Mar. 19, 1943.

89. "Meeting of BTBC and D'Arcy McNickle on the Wheeler-Howard Act" (hereafter cited as "Meeting of BTBC and McNickle"), Nov. 5, 1945, p. 1; see also Nov. 6 session, p. 34, both in File 36128-1945-BF-054.

90. "Meeting of BTBC and McNickle," Nov. 5, 1945, pp. 4–5.

91. "Meeting of BTBC and McNickle," Nov. 6, 1945, p. 33.

92. "Meeting of BTBC and McNickle," Nov. 5, 1945, p. 3.

93. "Meeting of BTBC and McNickle," Nov. 3, 1945, p. 1.

94. "Meeting of BTBC and McNickle," Nov. 6, 1945, p. 17.

95. McNickle to Zimmerman, Nov. 13, 1945, File 174-1943-BF-056.

96. McNickle to Brown, Nov. 20, 1945, File 9522-1936-BF-066.

97. Thomas Biolsi found that the Rosebud Sioux Tribal Council's promulgation of ordinances regulating traditional dances and the use of peyote in healing ceremonies angered both the OIA and many of the Sioux people. The regulations ultimately contributed to a "disempowerment" of the tribal government. See Biolsi, *Organizing the Lakota*, chapters 6 and 7.

98. Full-bloods got 379 loans from tribal funds totaling about $47,500, compared with $86,500 for half-bloods, and $85,000 for those with between one-thirty-second and one-half blood. Full-bloods repaid the loans quicker than the other groups. See "Meeting of BTBC and McNickle," Nov. 6, 1945, pp. 25–26. Between 1937 and 1950, full-bloods got 488 of the 1,311 individual RCF loans, compared with 467 for those with "half or over but less than full" blood, and 356 for those with less than half blood. Those Blackfeet with less than half blood got 46 percent of the $1,325,304 lent to the tribe during the period. Those with "half or over but less than full" blood got 38 percent, and full-bloods got just 16 percent. Of the 603 total individual borrowers, 428 got just 1 or 2 loans during the thirteen-year period, while 60 Blackfeet got 5 or more loans. See "Annual Report of RCF Operations," Aug. 30, 1950, NA RG 75, CCF-2 File 17592-1948-BF-031. See Table C (Individual Loan Summary) and sec. 2A9.6(f) (Distribution of Loans).

99. See Grant and Kennerly to CIA, Jan. 26, 1944; McBride to Zimmerman, Jan. 28, 1944, both in NA RG 75, CCF-1 File 5422-1938-BF-055. See also Brown and Pambrun to CIA, Mar. 7, 1944, File 174-1943-BF-056.

100. "Resolution No. 13 of the BTBC, Jan. 4, 1945"; and "To the Members of the Blackfeet Tribe," Sept. 17, 1945, a mimeographed handout that explained to voters the "relative risks and advantages" of the amendment, both in NA RG 75, GRCIO File 9522-B-1936-BF-067.

101. "Indian Voters Reject Change of Charter," *Browning Chief*, Oct. 5, 1945; see also McBride to Secretary of the Interior, Oct. 9, 1945, File 9522-B-1936-BF-067.

102. Voters had rejected a similar proposal by a count of 241 to 199 in a referendum held in October 1944. For the Nov. 30, 1945, vote, see "Tribal Election

Returns" and "Blackfeet Indian Voters Balloting on Sale of Oil Royalty Proposals," both in *Browning Chief*, Nov. 30, 1945, and Nov. 16, 1945, respectively.

103. John Herrick argued this point to Stuart Hazlett in 1938: "I fail to see wherein the amendment would help the full-blood people. As a matter of fact, in my opinion it works out very definitely to their disadvantage." Mixed-bloods, he said, could thus "control the situation completely" (Herrick to Hazlett, July 22, 1938, File 9522-A-1936-BF-068).

104. Browning voters supported it by a two-to-one ratio, while Starr School voters rejected it by a two-to-one ratio. Heart Butte residents, who had the most to lose, rejected it by a three-to-one ratio. The other voting districts voted nearly unanimously in favor of it. See "Excerpts of Minutes of a Regular Session of the BTBC, Dec. 1, 1945," File 1141-1946-BF-068. The Walker River Paiute Tribe, the Southern Utes, and the Gila River–Maricopa Indian Community also passed amendments in 1945.

105. Chapman to McBride, Jan. 9, 1946, NA RG 75, CCF-2 File 1141-1946-BF-068.

106. For a transcript, see File 1141-1946-BF-068.

107. McBride to CIA, Jan. 24, 1946, File 1141-1946-BF-068.

108. For a breakdown of voting by community and by district see "Election Results: Tribal Election of Jan. 22, 1946," File 5422-1938-BF-055.

109. John C. Ewers to author, Mar. 22, 1997 (author's files).

110. Jones, "Political Equality and Majority Rule," p. 209.

111. Held, *Models of Democracy*, p. 4. For other recent works on democratic community, see Barber, *Strong Democracy*, and Berry, *Idea of a Democratic Community*.

112. Department of the Interior, *Annual Report of the Secretary of the Interior*, FY 1941. See pp. 409–19.

113. "Constitutional Convention Minutes," Apr. 23, 1945, p. 13, File 36128-1945-BF-054.

114. "Constitutional Convention Minutes," Apr. 26, 1945, p. 17.

115. Miller, "Democracy and Social Justice," pp. 95–96.

116. Barber, *Strong Democracy*, p. 197.

117. Pateman writes that participatory democracy provides an "educative" function, "including both the psychological aspect and the gaining of practice in democratic skills and procedures" (Pateman, *Participation and Democratic Theory*, pp. 42–43).

118. McBride to CIA, Dec. 5, 1945, File 9522-A-1936-BF-068.

119. "Minutes of Meeting of [BTBC], Feb. 1, 1940," p. 11, File 9522-E-1936-BF-054.

120. Heacock, statistician, to Tribal Relations, Dec. 19, 1945, File 9522-A-1936-BF-054.

6. "We Have a Way"

1. See Deloria and Lytle's assessment of Collier's legacy in *Nations Within*, especially pp. 168–70 and 180–89.

2. For recent assessments of the termination era, see Philp, *Termination Revisited*, and Fixico, *Termination and Relocation*.

3. U.S. Congress, House Committee on Public Lands, *Emancipation of Indians*, 80th Cong., 1st sess., 1947, H.R. 2958, H.R. 2165, and H.R. 1113.

4. House Committee on Public Lands, *Emancipation of Indians*, p. 42.

5. House Committee on Public Lands, *Emancipation of Indians*, Apr. 11, 1947, pp. 131, 132. Brown traveled to Washington for the congressional hearings with five other Blackfeet delegates, but only he spoke.

6. House Committee on Public Lands, *Emancipation of Indians*, Apr. 11, 1947, pp. 137–39.

7. George Fox to Joe Jennings, June 27, 1942; Charles Heacock, field agent, to CIA, June 22, 1942, both in File 9522-1936-BF-066.

8. "A Resolution of the BTBC Relating to a Proposed Investigation by Congressional Authority of the United States Indian Department and Its Officers and Employees," Dec. 7, 1945, File 9522-1936-BF-066.

9. Brophy to Hon. James Murray, Jan. 3, 1946, File 9522-1936-BF-066 (see also the unsigned draft copy of this letter).

10. U.S. Congress, Senate Committee on Post Office and Civil Service, *Hearings on S. Res. 41*, 80th Cong., 1st sess., 1947, p. 547.

11. For information about the Blackfeet Repayment Cattle Enterprise, see "Narrative Summary: Activities of the Blackfeet Repayment Cattle Enterprise," in "Annual Report of Extension Workers," FY 1946, NA RG 75, CCF-2 File 3636-1947-BF-031.

12. "Annual Report of Extension Workers," CY 1945, NA RG 75, CCF-2 File 3350-1946-BF-031. For information about Blackfeet sheep ranching, see "Annual Report of Extension Workers," CY 1945–47. For income figures, see "Distribution of Families by Estimated Net Agricultural Income" in "Annual Report of Extension Workers," CY 1945–50.

13. "Annual Report of Revolving Fund Operations, Blackfeet Agency," CY 1950. See also "Estimate of Self-Support Attained by Borrowers," File 17592-1948-BF-031.

14. See Table C, "Individual Loan Summary," in "Annual Report of Revolving Fund Operations, Blackfeet Agency," CY 1950.

15. Richard Grant Sr. et al. to CIA, June 22, 1942, File 3633-1934-BF-054, pt. 1.

16. See Brian Connolly, Phil Aubrey, and Louis Momberg to the Secretary of the Interior, Jan. 12, 1948, NA RG 75, CCF-2 File 25145-1946-BF-067.

17. In a 1958 letter to Commissioner Glenn Emmons, Connolly wrote, "It is true that I myself am far better off than many of my Indian brothers. There are a

few of us who do have fairly decent ranches and livings. We are in less than ten percent of the entire population of this reservation however, unfortunately" (Connolly to Emmons, July 8, 1958, NA RG 75, CCF-2 File 17260-1954-120). Biolsi examines what he calls the OIA's "technology of power" in *Organizing the Lakota*.

18. "Tribal Secretary Points Out Purpose of Corporate Group," *Browning Chief*, Mar. 1, 1946.

19. Walzer, *Spheres of Justice*, p. 64.

20. See Zimmerman to McBride, Mar. 19, 1946, NA RG 75, CCF-2 File 50403-1941-BF-720.

21. See O'Hara's letters to Zimmerman of Jan. 13, 1949, and Jan. 11, 1949, File 25145-1946-BF-067. The council no longer wanted to fund the positions of tribal police officer and tribal judge.

22. For reports from county officials, see File 50403-1941-BF-720. For a good comparison of Indian and non-Indian relief loads in Glacier and Pondera Counties, see O'Hara to CIA, Jan. 23, 1948, File 50403-1941-BF-720.

23. Peter Vielle, BTBC secretary, to CIA, Nov. 25, 1947, File 50403-1941-BF-720.

24. Henry Magee et al. to Zimmerman, Apr. 11, 1949, NA RG 75, CCF-1 File 7056-1944-BF-071.

25. See "Minutes of a Meeting Held by BTBC in Special Session, January 16, 1947," File 50403-1941-BF-720.

26. Fickinger, telegram to CIA, Apr. 8, 1949, File 50403-1941-BF-720.

27. Lawson, *Tradition versus Democracy in the South Pacific*, p. 167.

28. See McFee, *Modern Blackfeet*. In addition, see his excellent essay, "The 150% Man, a Product of Blackfeet Acculturation."

29. Spindler and Spindler, *Dreamers without Power*.

30. See Stern, *Klamath Tribe*.

31. "Resolution No. 20 of the BTBC, December 8, 1947," File 25145-1946-BF-067.

32. See "Corporate Powers" and "Corporate Dividends" in Bureau of Indian Affairs, *Corporate Charter of the Blackfeet Tribe*.

33. See "Termination of Supervisory Powers," in Bureau of Indian Affairs, *Corporate Charter of the Blackfeet Tribe*.

34. Zimmerman to Vernon Northrup, director of Division of Budget and Administrative Management, Jan. 5, 1947 [1948], File 25145-1946-BF-067.

35. O'Hara to the Secretary of the Interior, Feb. 27, 1948, File 25145-1946-BF-067.

36. O'Hara to Acting Commissioner William Zimmerman Jr., Dec. 5, 1948, File 25145-1946-BF-067.

37. O'Hara to Zimmerman, Dec. 5, 1948.

38. Zimmerman to Warne, Mar. 29, 1948, File 25145-1946-BF-067.

39. Howard Gaare (Wilson Ferris accountant), interview by author, Mar. 6, 1996 (author's files). McKay reassumed the position after Wright Hagerty lent him the money to make up the shortfall.

40. Paul L. Fickinger to CIA, Oct. 13, 1949, File 25145-1946-BF-067.

41. Chapman to Magee, Feb. 28, 1950, File 25145-1946-BF-067.

42. Chapman to Magee, Mar. 16, 1950, File 25145-1946-BF-067.

43. "Meeting of the BTBC, March 2, 1950," File 25145-1946-BF-067. See also Fickinger to Zimmerman, Mar. 8, 1950, and "Confidential," Kildow to Fickinger, Apr. 5, 1950, both in File 25145-1946-BF-067.

44. "Introduction," BTBC termination election voter handout (no date), File 25145-1946-BF-067.

45. "Referendum No. 5," voter handout (no date), File 25145-1946-BF-067.

46. Melzner to Fickinger, June 9, 1950, File 1141-1946-BF-068.

47. "CERTIFICATE OF ELECTION," June 23, 1950, File 1141-1946-BF-068.

48. "Present Indian Council Ousted by Recent Election," *Cut Bank Pioneer Press*, June 23, 1950. See also "All Old Members of Tribal Council Ousted Tuesday," and "Exactly Like the Whiteman Does," both in *Browning Chief*, June 23, 1950.

49. Kildow to Fickinger, July 7, 1950, File 1141-1946-BF-068.

50. Quoted in "Indians Voice Plaints, Protests to the Second District Congressman," *Cut Bank Pioneer Press*, Dec. 16, 1949.

51. Bureau of Indian Affairs, *Corporate Charter of the Blackfeet Tribe*, pp. 3–4.

52. "BTBC Res. No. 15-48, October 20, 1948"; Contract between Blackfeet Tribe and John Loewen, both in File 25145-1946-BF-067. The contract also stipulated that Loewen should employ "competent" tribal members if possible, but it did not require the employment of Blackfeet workers.

53. O'Hara to Zimmerman, Jan. 13, 1949, File 25145-1946-BF-067. Full-bloods objected to the investment in part because the store was in Browning; Heart Butte full-bloods had been calling for a commissary in their community for years to no avail.

54. Gaare interview, Mar. 6, 1996. John Ewers wrote of the council's "repeated failures in seeking to operate their own business enterprises," mentioning in particular the "tribal store" (John C. Ewers to author, Mar. 8, 1997 [author's files]).

55. For Wilson Ferris's audit report of the store and other features of Blackfeet administration, see "Minutes of the BTBC, December 2, 1949," NA RG 75, CCF-2 File 44997-1945-BF-224.

56. "Report Issued on Tribal Store at Browning," *Cut Bank Pioneer Press*, Aug. 18, 1950.

57. O'Hara to Zimmerman, Jan. 31, 1949, File 25145-1946-BF-067.

58. "Meeting of the BTBC, March 11, 1948," File 44997-1945-BF-224.

59. Fickinger to Lucille A. Hastings, Chief, Welfare Section, Feb. 1, 1950; Hastings to Zimmerman, Feb. 2, 1950, both in File 50403-1941-BF-720.

60. Gaare interview, Mar. 6, 1996.

61. Gaare interview, Mar. 6, 1996.

62. Gaare interview, Mar. 6, 1996. Gaare indicated that other tribes also had difficulty investing money in worthy programs.

63. William Fenton, interview by author, Feb. 15, 1997. Fenton spent only a week on the reservation investigating Blackfeet self-government, staying on Wright Hagerty's ranch many miles from Browning. He said he did not get a chance to "bore in on the situation."

64. Cohen to BTBC, June 16, 1950, NA RG 75, CCF-2 File 16112-1950-BF-154.

65. See Lawson, *Tradition versus Democracy in the South Pacific*, p. 35.

66. Bureau of Indian Affairs, *Corporate Charter of the Blackfeet Tribe*, sec. 8. For a review of the proceedings, see McNickle to the Commissioner, May 24, 1950, NA RG 75, CCF-2 File 4915-1949-BF-057.

67. McNickle to the Commissioner, May 24, 1950, p. 1. Myer assumed office on May 5, 1950.

68. D. S. Myer to Fickinger, May 25, 1950, File 4915-1949-BF-057.

69. Fickinger to the Blackfeet Tribe of the Blackfeet Indian Reservation, June 12, 1950; Fickinger to the BTBC, June 12, 1950, both in File 1141-1946-BF-068.

70. Fickinger to BTBC, June 9, 1950, p. 8, File 1141-1946-BF-068.

71. Oliver La Farge to Oscar Chapman, June 16, 1950, Association of American Indian Affairs Archives (AAIAA) Series 2, Subseries 2, Box 250, Folder 8, Seeley G. Mudd Manuscript Library, Princeton University Library; Chapman to La Farge, July 11, 1950, AAIAA Series 1, Subseries 3, Box 44, Folder 1.

72. Felix S. Cohen, Tribal Attorney, Memorandum for the BTBC, June 16, 1950, AAIAA Series 2, Subseries 2, Box 250, Folder 8.

73. Cohen memorandum to the BTBC, June 16, 1950, p. 4. See the subsection titled "Occupational Disease."

74. "Minutes, Blackfeet Tribal Council [BTBC]," July 6, 1950, pp. 3, 6, File 4915-1949-BF-057.

75. "Minutes, Blackfeet Tribal Council," July 6, 1950, p. 6.

76. Pambrun to Fickinger, Aug. 21, 1950, File 16112-1950-BF-154.

77. Fickinger's charges were not so much false as they were based on old information. Cohen had tried to reform the council's sloppy recordkeeping system since becoming the Blackfeet's attorney in late 1949. For details of the controversy, see McNickle to Provinse, July 27, 1950, File 1141-1946-BF-068. See also Melzner to Fickinger, Aug. 29, 1950, File 1141-1946-BF-068; M. A. Johnson, supervisor of extension and credit, to Fickinger, Aug. 28, 1950; Office Memoran-

dum, Shirley N. McKinsey to Fickinger, Aug. 28, 1950; and Fickinger to Pambrun, Sept. 8, 1950, all in File 16112-1950-BF-154.

78. Cohen to BTBC, June 30, 1950, AAIAA Series 2, Subseries 2, Box 250, Folder 8.

79. Cohen to Sister Providencia, June 10, 1950, FCP, Box 88, Folder 1410.

80. Pambrun to CIA, March 1949, File 19024-1950-BF-150.

81. Pambrun to Zimmerman, Apr. 7, 1950, File 1141-1946-BF-068. See also "Pambrun Flays Record of Tribal Council in Letter to Blackfeet," *Cut Bank Pioneer Press*, Dec. 23, 1949.

82. Fickinger to Myer, Oct. 11, 1950; Fickinger to Myer, Oct. 23, 1950, both in File 1141-1946-BF-068.

83. Myer to Pambrun, Aug. 7, 1950, File 1141-1946-BF-068.

84. Felix S. Cohen, "Indian Self-Government," pp. 24, 25. The article appeared originally in *The American Indian*, the journal of the AAIA.

85. Ickes, "The Indian Loses Again," p. 16.

86. See the following *Cut Bank Pioneer Press* articles: "Blackfeet Will Press Claim for Agency Buildings and Properties," Feb. 23, 1951; and "Blackfeet Post Eviction Notices Saturday," Apr. 20, 1951. See also "Tribal Council Begins Battle against Bureau," *Browning Chief*, Apr. 20, 1951; and "Blackfeet Indians Padlock Buildings against Palefaces," *Great Falls Tribune*, Apr. 14, 1951. The construction cost deductions are detailed in *The Blackfeet Nation v. United States*, 81 Ct. Cl. 101 (1935). See also Cohen, "Erosion of Human Rights," p. 368.

87. Cohen, "Indian Self-Government," p. 28. See also Cohen to Sister Providencia, Jan. 4, 1951, FCP, Box 88, Folder 1410.

88. The BIA budget grew from $44 million in FY 1949 to $85 million in FY 1953. Myer had requested $122,350,000 for FY 1953. The figures are from Drinnon, *Keeper of Concentration Camps*, p. 233.

89. Henry Magee, telegram to CIA, Jan. 17, 1949, File 174-1943-BF-056.

90. Zimmerman to Iron Pipe, Old Chief, and Whitecalf, Mar. 7, 1949, File 174-1943-BF-056.

91. For an example of his recommendations to tribal dissidents, see Zimmerman to Fish Wolf Robe, Mar. 7, 1949, File 174-1943-BF-056.

92. Zimmerman to Levi Burd, Mar. 7, 1949, File 174-1943-BF-056. For copies of the proposed amendments, see Zimmerman to Iron Pipe, Old Chief, and Whitecalf, Mar. 7, 1949 (same file). A successful recall would have required a majority vote of participating voters rather than a majority vote of council members.

93. Provinse to Kildow, Sept. 28, 1949, File 174-1943-BF-056.

94. See Theodore Last Star and James White Calf to Chapman, Mar. 16, 1950, File 25145-1946-BF-067.

95. A group of roughly three hundred interested Blackfeet "voted unani-

mously to hire Mr. Cohen." Reevis spoke for the minority group, voting to "re-tain Mr. Cohen to protest against [proposed acts of] vicious legislation," and he noted that Cohen wanted to accept thirty-six hundred dollars per year rather than the five thousand dollars offered by a council member. See "BTBC in Special Session," July 16, 1949, NA RG 75, CCF-2 File 19220-1949-BF-174.1

96. Reevis to Secretary of the Interior, May 28, 1951, File 1141-1946-BF-068; see also Reevis to CIA John Nichols, Mar. 27, 1950, File 25145-1946-BF-067; and Plenty Treaty to Hon. Mike Mansfield, File 1141-1946-BF-068.

97. Cohen earned $4,762.91 from the Blackfeet between late 1949 and June 1951. His contract for FY 1951–52 called for a thirty-six-hundred-dollar retainer fee and up to one thousand dollars in expenses. See "Tribal Budget—Approved by Blackfeet Tribal Council, June 29, 1951," in "Minutes of the BTBC in Special Session, June 29, 1951," File 4499-1945-BF-224.

98. "Minutes of a Meeting of the BTBC, December 15, 1950," File 1141-1946-BF-068.

99. McNickle to Eric Hagberg, Mar. 7, 1951, File 1141-1946-BF-068.

100. McNickle to Fickinger, Mar. 20, 1951, File 1141-1946-BF-068.

101. Myer to Hon. Mike Mansfield, Mar. 22, 1951, File 1141-1946-BF-068.

102. See Louis Plenty Treaty to James E. Murry [sic], Mar. 15, 1951, and the accompanying two-page "Petition of Members of the Blackfeet Tribe of Indians," File 1141-1946-BF-068.

103. Felix S. Cohen, Memorandum for Mr. Collier, Oct. 1, 1938; John C. Ewers to author, Mar. 22, 1997 (author's files); McFee, *Modern Blackfeet*.

104. "A Petition to the Government," Sept. 6, 1949, File 4915-1949-BF-057.

105. The council held three meetings to allow the segregationists to voice their complaints and discuss their plan to "pull away from the Blackfeet Corporation." Council members warned them that they would no longer get emergency loans, medical and educational assistance, or relief. See "Segregationists to Express Opinions," *Cut Bank Pioneer Press*, Mar. 23, 1951.

106. "Tribal Budget—Approved by Blackfeet Tribal Council, June 29, 1951."

107. Fickinger to Gifford, July 5, 1951; Gifford to Reevis, July 19, 1951, both in File 1141-1946-BF-068.

108. Guy Robertson to Fickinger, Sept. 25, 1951, File 1141-1946-BF-068.

109. See Myer to Fickinger, draft (no date), File 1141-1946-BF-068 pt. 2. The letter, like much of the commissioner's correspondence, was drafted by Interior and OIA staff.

110. Myer to Charles Reevis and Louis Plenty Treaty, Nov. 21, 1951, File 1141-1946-BF-068.

111. Robertson to Fickinger, Jan. 24, 1952, File 1141-1946-BF-068 pt. 2.

112. Myer to Secretary of the Interior, Feb. 27, 1952, File 1141-1946-BF-068 pt. 2.

113. See "Minutes of a Meeting Held by the BTBC, December 21, 1949"; and "Minutes of a Meeting Held by the BTBC, January 13, 1950," both in File 25145-1946-BF-067.

114. "Public Hearing," Feb. 27, 1952, pp. 3, 4, File 1141-1946-BF-068 pt. 2.

115. "Public Hearing," Feb. 27, 1952, pp. 6, 7.

116. "Tribal Constitution Needs Amendments to Serve Purpose," *Browning Chief*, Mar. 21, 1952. See also "Constitutional Amendments Being Studied," *Browning Chief*, Mar. 28, 1952.

117. For a discussion of the budget and the role of the council, see "Minutes of the BTBC in Special Session, June 29, 1951." For Wetzel's public statement on the full-bloods' agenda, see "Segregationists to Express Opinions," *Cut Bank Pioneer Press*, Mar. 23, 1951. See also "Finance, Cattle Repayment Up for Discussion," *Browning Chief*, Apr. 4, 1952.

118. Myer to Plenty Treaty, Mar. 25, 1952, File 1141-1946-BF-068 pt. 2.

119. Fickinger to CIA, Apr. 10, 1952, File 1141-1946-BF-068 pt. 2.

120. Walter Wetzel to Secretary of the Interior, May 1, 1952, File 1141-1946-BF-068 pt. 2.

121. Cedor Aronow to Honorable Oscar L. Chapman, May 1, 1952, File 1141-1946-BF-068 pt. 2. See also Aronow's May 3 and May 7 letters to Chapman.

122. Wetzel to Secretary of the Interior, May 1, 1952.

123. U.S. Congress, Senate Committee on Appropriations, *Interior Department Appropriations for 1953*, 82d Cong., 2d sess., 1952, p. 847.

124. Robertson to Qualified Voters in Browning Voting Precinct (no date), File 1141-1946-BF-068 pt. 2.

125. Senate Committee on Appropriations, *Interior Department Appropriations for 1953*, p. 854. See also "Blackfeet to Decide May 9 on Amendment," *Browning Chief*, May 2, 1952.

126. See "Blackfeet Tribe of the Blackfeet Indian Reservation: REFERENDUM" (no date), File 1141-1946-BF-068 pt. 2. For newspaper coverage of the "parallel" elections, see "Blackfeet Voters Puzzled Over Contention of 'Who's Boss?'" *Browning Chief*, May 9, 1952; "Tribal Amendment Election May 9," *Browning Chief*, Apr. 18, 1952; "Two Elections Same Day Slated on Reservation," *Great Falls Tribune*, May 1, 1952; and "Blackfeet Council Appeals for 'Protection' against 'Bureau Interference' in Election," *Great Falls Tribune*, May 3, 1952.

127. For a breakdown by voting district, see "Tribal Election" (no date) and "Secretary's Election Returns" (no date), File 1141-1946-BF-068 pt. 2.

128. Robertson to Fickinger, May 13, 1952, File 1141-1946-BF-068 pt. 2.

129. Chapman to Wetzel, June 26, 1952, File 1141-1946-BF-068 pt. 3. The Blackfeet constitution stipulated that any election required the approval of the secretary of the interior and necessitated a twenty-day waiting period between the time of the secretary's approval and the election itself.

130. Solicitor Mastin G. White to the Secretary, July 18, 1952, File 1141-1946-BF-068 pt. 3.

131. Myer to the Secretary, Aug. 7, 1952, File 1141-1946-BF-068 pt. 3.

132. Chapman to Sen. James Murray, Aug. 13, 1952, File 1141-1946-BF-068 pt. 3. For a copy of Chapman's letter to Robertson, see "Chapman Rules May 9 Election Is Invalid," *Browning Chief*, Aug. 29, 1952. See also Alexander Lesser, Confidential Memorandum to Oliver La Farge, Sept. 23, 1952, FCP, Box 64, Folder 1021.

133. Levi Burd to Zimmerman, Jan. 23, 1949, File 174-1943-BF-056.

134. Louis Plenty Treaty to Harry S. Truman, May 9, 1952, File 1141-1946-BF-068 pt. 2.

135. See House Committee on Appropriations, *Interior Department Appropriation Bill, 1939*, p. 114; Walzer, *Spheres of Justice*, pp. 310, 318; "Meeting of BTBC and McNickle," Nov. 5, 1945, p. 4.

136. Walter Wetzel, interview by author, Aug. 15, 1997.

137. Myer to Toby Morris, chairman of the House Subcommittee on Indian Affairs, Mar. 16, 1951, NA RG 75 CCF-2 File 2669-1951-BF-066.

138. "Meeting of the BTBC, July 11, 1952," NA RG 75, CCF-2 File 44997-1945-BF-224.

139. "Blackfeet to Receive per Capita Payment," *Browning Chief*, Nov. 28, 1952.

140. Walzer, *Spheres of Justice*, p. 12.

Conclusion

1. For a well-developed argument on how another Indian tribe came to reflect the structure of mainstream America, see Young, "Cherokee Nation."

2. Dahl, *Democracy and Its Critics*, pp. 184–90.

3. Dahl, *Democracy and Its Critics*, p. 192.

4. "Cullen's Proposal Is Rejected: Blackfeet Tribal Members Select New Council Members and Vote Overwhelmingly to Reject Further Consideration of Proposal to Delegate Tribal Authority," *Glacier Reporter*, June 18, 1954. For information about the Cullen deal, see correspondence and meeting transcripts in NA RG 75, CCF-2 File 19868-1953-BF-220.

5. "Indian Reorganization," by Joe Jennings, field administrator in charge, in Department of the Interior, *Indians at Work*, vol. 6 (June 1939), p. 14.

6. "Meeting of BTBC and McNickle," Nov. 5, 1945, p. 1.

7. See U.S. Congress, House, *Report with Respect to the House Resolution Authorizing the Committee on Interior and Insular Affairs to Conduct an Investigation of the Bureau of Indian Affairs*, 83d Cong., 2d sess., 1954, H. Rept. 2680.

8. For examples, see File 4915-1949-BF-057.

9. "Statement of Earl Old Person, Chairman of the Blackfeet Tribe, Mon-

tana, against the Omnibus Bill (1966)," in Deloria and Lytle, *Of Utmost Good Faith*, p. 220.

10. Earl Old Person, interview by author, Browning MT, Sept. 28, 1995. At twenty-five, Old Person was the youngest Blackfeet to join the council. As of January 1998, he continued to serve as chairman of the BTBC.

11. "Iliff McKay Explains Stand on the Cullen Proposal," *Glacier Reporter*, June 11, 1954.

12. "Listing and Description of Tasks Remaining to Be Done to Effect Complete Withdrawal of Bureau Services by Termination or Transfer to Other Auspices," in "Withdrawal Programming, Schedule C, Blackfeet Agency," pp. 16–17, NA RG 75, CCF-2 File 17091-1952-BF-077, pt. 1. For a brief review of withdrawal programming, see U.S. Congress, House, *Report with Respect to the House Resolution Authorizing the Committee on Interior and Insular Affairs to Conduct an Investigation of the Bureau of Indian Affairs*, 82d Cong., 2d sess., 1953, H. Rept. 2503.

13. "Importance of Extension Work," in House Committee on Appropriations, *Interior Department Appropriation Bill, 1939*, pt. 2 (BIA), p. 160.

14. Guy Robertson to M. A. Johnson, Jan. 6, 1954, NA RG 75, CCF-2 File 1522-1954-BF-919.1.

15. M. A. Johnson to Guy Robertson, Jan. 25, 1954, File 1522-1954-BF-919.1.

16. Stone to CIA, Jan. 14, 1930, File 3284-1930-BF-165.

17. "Some Observations on the Blackfeet Reservation," by George Fox, June 26, 1942, File 9004-1943-BF-042.

18. "Program of Work," 1952, NA RG 75, CCF-2 File 6999-1952-BF-919.1.

19. For Brown's plan to reduce BIA services on the Blackfeet Reservation, see "Economies in Indian Bureau Program," in U.S. Congress, House Committee on Appropriations, *Interior Department Appropriations for 1952*, 82d Cong., 1st sess., 1951, pt. 1, pp. 1127–1243.

20. "Summary of Accomplishment in Withdrawal by Termination or Transfer of Bureau Services to Other Auspices," in "Withdrawal Programming, Schedule B, Blackfeet Agency," File 17091-1952-BF-077, pt. 1.

21. "Background Data on Indians at the Blackfeet Reservation Relating to Termination of Federal Supervision, October 1, 1953," p. 5, File 17091-1952-BF-077, pt. 1-A.

22. See "Law and Order Code of the Blackfeet Indian Tribe," NA RG 75, CCF-2 File 86457-BF-170.

23. O'Hara to Zimmerman, Jan. 11, 1949, NA RG 75, CCF-2 File 27057-1950-BF-170.

24. The Pambrun council of 1950–52 asked the BIA to "pay a fair share of the expenses incurred in maintain[ing] law and order" and welfare programs. The BIA responded that it had no available monies for Blackfeet law and order. See

"Memorandum to Commissioner of Indian Affairs," 1950; and Chief Special Officer to Mr. Provinse, Dec. 5, 1950, both in File 174-1943-BF-056.

25. William Benge, chief, Branch of Law and Order to Acting Chief, Coordinating Staff, Sept. 2, 1954, NA RG 75, General Service File 13146-1954-170. The council would on occasion collect more money from the tribal court than it gave back to the law and order program. See also Mueller to Superintendent Roy Nash, Feb. 19, 1942, File 86457-BF-170.

26. The one exception was in 1942, when a BTBC delegation asked the BIA to focus on livestock thefts rather than on liquor violations and sought approval to establish jurisdiction over additional cases in order to make the law and order program "self-sustaining." Zimmerman argued that the tribal court's lenient sentences handed down for major crimes convinced him that the federal court should maintain jurisdiction to ensure that stiffer penalties deterred repeat offenders (Zimmerman to Richard Grant Sr. et al., Dec. 19, 1942, File 00-1942-BF-056).

27. Superintendent Spencer to Area Director, June 12, 1956, NA RG 75, CCF-2 File 14505-1950-BF-170.

28. The Blackfeet Nation filed a claim with the Indian Claims Commission (ICC) in 1951, arguing that the government used faulty survey data to determine the value of the 1935 "Big Claim" (*Blackfeet et al. Nations v. United States*, 81 Ct. Cl. 101). The suit called for compensation for additional land and for the interest on any judgment. See "Petition," in *The Blackfeet and Gros Ventre Tribe of Indians v. the United States of America*, Aug. 9, 1951, Indian Claims Commission, NA RG 279, Entry 11UD, Box 2419, Docket 279A; and "Report of Findings in Resurvey of Boundary Blackfoot [*sic*] Indian Reservation and Glacier National Park," July 19, 1957, Indian Claims Commission, NA RG 279, Entry 11UD, Box 2437, Docket 279B.

29. The pursuit of national policy objectives can come at the expense of local policy initiatives and thus community interests. See Powers, *Oglala Women*.

30. Cohen to Myer, Sept. 13, 1950, AAIAA Series 2, Subseries 2, Box 250, Folder 8.

31. Henry Magee et al. to Zimmerman, Apr. 11, 1949, File 7056-1944-BF-071.

32. See in particular, "Statement of George Pambrun, delegate of Blackfeet Tribe, before a Special Senate Committee on Blackfeet Affairs," Apr. 15, 1952, AAIAA Series 2, Subseries 3, Box 301, Folder 4; and "Blackfeet Program for Indian Bureau Withdrawal," February 1953, AAIAA Series 2, Subseries 2, Box 250, Folder 9.

33. "Report on talks made at a special meeting called by Mountainchief," Oct. 1, 1933, p. 16672.

34. Old Person interview, Dec. 5, 1997.

35. Old Person interview, Sept. 28, 1995.

BIBLIOGRAPHY

Archival and Manuscript Collections

Archives of the Association on American Indian Affairs. Seeley G. Mudd Manuscript Library, Princeton University, Princeton NJ.

Blackfeet Indian Agency. Bureau of Indian Affairs, Record Group 75, National Archives, Washington DC.

Blackfeet Tribal Archives. Blackfeet Community College, Browning MT.

Felix S. Cohen Papers. Beinecke Rare Book and Manuscript Library, Yale University, New Haven CT.

General Records Concerning Indian Organization, 1934–56. Blackfeet Indian Agency, Record Group 75, National Archives, Washington DC.

Government Documents. Philadelphia Free Library, Philadelphia PA.

Indian Claims Commission. Record Group 279, National Archives, Washington DC.

Records Concerning Wheeler-Howard Act, 1933–37. Record Group 75, National Archives, Washington DC.

Western Americana Collection. Beinecke Rare Book and Manuscript Library, Yale University, New Haven CT.

Interviews

Bullshoe, Anna. Interview by author. Browning MT, September 26, 1995.

Cobell, Elouise. Telephone interview by author. August 22, 1997.

Ewers, John. Telephone interviews by author. June 15, 1996, February 17, 1997.

Fenton, William. Telephone interview by author. February 15, 1997.

Gaare, Howard. Telephone interviews by author. March 6, 1996, August 13, 1997.

Old Person, Earl. Interview by author. Browning MT, September 28, 1995.

———. Telephone interview by author. December 5, 1997.

Owens, Lorraine. Telephone interviews by author. August 27, 1996, June 10, 1999.

Santana, Vicky. Interview by author. Browning MT, September 26, 1995.

———. Telephone interview by author. December 21, 1998.

Walzer, Michael. Interview by author. Princeton NJ, December 4, 1998.
Welch, James. Telephone interview by author. February 6, 1997.
Wetzel, Walter. Telephone interviews by author. February 8, 1997, August 15, 1997.

Newspapers

Browning Chief (previously *Glacier County Chief*), Browning MT, 1944–52.
Cut Bank Pioneer Press, Cut Bank MT, 1932–54.
Glacier County Chief, Browning MT, 1934–44.
Glacier Reporter (previously *Browning Chief*), Browning MT, 1952–55.
Great Falls Tribune, Great Falls MT, 1934–52.
New York Times, 1934–54.

Books, Articles, Dissertations

Ackerman, Bruce. *Social Justice in the Liberal State*. New Haven: Yale University Press, 1980.

Anderson, Terry L. *Sovereign Nations or Reservations: An Economic History of American Indians*. San Francisco: Pacific Research Institute for Public Policy, 1995.

Barber, Benjamin R. *Strong Democracy: Participatory Politics for a New Age*. Berkeley: University of California Press, 1984.

Berry, Christopher J. *The Idea of a Democratic Community*. New York: St. Martin's, 1989.

Biolsi, Thomas. *Organizing the Lakota: The Political Economy of the New Deal on the Pine Ridge and the Rosebud Reservations*. Tucson: University of Arizona Press, 1992.

Blackfeet Heritage Program. *Blackfeet Heritage, 1907–1908: Blackfeet Indian Reservation, Browning, Montana*. Browning MT: The Program, 1980.

Burke, Charles H. Commissioner of Indian Affairs. "The Progress of the Blackfeet Indians." OIA *Bulletin* 18. Washington DC: GPO, 1922.

Carlson, Leonard A. *Indians, Bureaucrats, and Land: The Dawes Act and the Decline of Indian Farming*. Westport CT: Greenwood Press, 1981.

Champagne, Duane. "Economic Culture, Institutional Order, and Sustained Market Enterprise: Comparisons of Historical and Contemporary American Indian Cases." In Terry L. Anderson, ed., *Property Rights and Indian Economies*. Lanham MD: Rowman & Littlefield, 1992.

Cohen, Felix S. "The Erosion of Indian Rights, 1950–1953: A Case Study in Bureaucracy." *Yale Law Journal* 62, no. 3 (February 1953): 348–90.

———. "Indian Self-Government." In Alvin M. Josephy Jr., *Red Power: The American Indians' Fight for Freedom*. Lincoln: University of Nebraska Press, 1971.

Cornell, Stephen. *The Return of the Native: American Indian Political Resurgence*. New York: Oxford University Press, 1988.

Cornell, Stephen, and Joseph P. Kalt. "Culture and Institutions as Public Goods: American Indian Economic Development as a Problem of Collective Action." In Terry L. Anderson, ed., *Property Rights and Indian Economies*. Lanham MD: Rowman & Littlefield, 1992.

Dahl, Robert A. *Democracy and Its Critics*. New Haven: Yale University Press, 1989.

Deloria, Vine, Jr., ed. *Of Utmost Good Faith*. San Francisco: Straight Arrow Books, 1971.

Deloria, Vine, Jr., and Clifford Lytle. *The Nations Within: The Past and Future of American Indian Sovereignty*. New York: Pantheon Books, 1984.

Douma, Don. "The History of Oil and Gas in Montana." In Merrill G. Burlingame and K. Ross Toole, *A History of Montana*. New York: Lewis Historical Publishing, 1957.

Drinnon, Richard. *Keeper of Concentration Camps: Dillon S. Myer and American Racism*. Berkeley: University of California Press, 1987.

Edmunds, R. David. "Native Americans, New Voices: American Indian History, 1895–1995." *American Historical Review* 100 (June 1995): 717–40.

Ewers, John C. *The Blackfeet: Raiders on the Northwestern Plains*. Norman: University of Oklahoma Press, 1958.

———. "Richard Sanderville, Blackfoot Indian Interpreter." In Margot Liberty, ed., *American Indian Intellectuals*. St. Paul: West Publishing, 1978.

Farr, William E. *The Reservation Blackfeet, 1882–1945: A Photographic History of Cultural Survival*. Seattle: University of Washington Press, 1984.

Fixico, Donald. *Termination and Relocation: Federal Indian Policy, 1945–1960*. Albuquerque: University of New Mexico Press, 1986.

———, ed. *Rethinking American Indian History*. Albuquerque: University of New Mexico Press, 1997.

Fowler, Loretta. *Arapahoe Politics, 1851–1978: Symbols in Crises of Authority*. Lincoln: University of Nebraska Press, 1982.

Held, David. *Models of Democracy*. Stanford: Stanford University Press, 1987.

Hoxie, Frederick E. *Parading through History: The Making of the Crow Nation in America, 1805–1935*. Cambridge: Cambridge University Press, 1995.

Ickes, Harold. "The Indian Loses Again." *New Republic*, September 24, 1951.

Jones, Peter. "Political Equality and Majority Rule." In John Arthur, ed., *Democracy: Theory and Practice*. Belmont CA: Wadsworth Publishing, 1992.

Jorgensen, Joseph G. "A Century of Political Economic Effects on American Indian Society, 1880–1980." *Journal of Ethnic Studies* 6 (fall 1978): 1–82.

Kappler, Charles J., comp. *Indian Affairs: Laws and Treaties*. 5 vols. Washington DC: GPO, 1904–41.

Kehoe, Alice B. "Blackfoot Persons." In Laura F. Klein and Lillian A. Ackerman, eds., *Women and Power in Native North America*. Norman: University of Oklahoma Press, 1995.

Kelly, Lawrence C. "The Indian Reorganization Act: The Dream and the Reality." *Pacific Historical Review* 46 (January 1975): 291–312.

Lawson, Stephanie. *Tradition versus Democracy in the South Pacific: Fiji, Tonga, and Western Samoa.* Cambridge: Cambridge University Press, 1996.

Lopach, James J., Margery Hunter Brown, and Richmond L. Clow. *Tribal Government Today: Politics on Montana Indian Reservations.* Boulder CO: Westview Press, 1990.

Lurie, Nancy Oestreich. "The Contemporary American Indian Scene." In Eleanor Burke Leacock and Nancy Oestreich Lurie, eds., *North American Indians in Historical Perspective.* New York: Random House, 1971.

McFee, Malcolm. *Modern Blackfeet: Montanans on a Reservation.* New York: Holt, Rinehart, and Winston, 1972.

———. "The 150% Man, a Product of Blackfeet Acculturation." *American Anthropologist* 7 (December 1968): 1096–1103.

Meriam, Lewis, et al. *The Problem of Indian Administration: Report of a Survey Made at the Request of Honorable Hubert Work, Secretary of the Interior, and Submitted to Him, February 21, 1928.* Baltimore: Johns Hopkins University Press, 1928.

Mihesuah, Devon A., ed. *Natives and Academics: Researching and Writing about American Indians.* Lincoln: University of Nebraska Press, 1998.

Miller, David. "Democracy and Social Justice." In Pierre Birnbaum, Jack Lively, and Geraint Parry, eds., *Democracy, Consensus, and Social Contract.* London: Sage, 1978.

Nagel, Joane. *American Indian Ethnic Renewal: Red Power and the Resurgence of Identity and Culture.* Oxford: Oxford University Press, 1996.

Olson, James, and Raymond Wilson. *Native Americans in the Twentieth Century.* Provo UT: Brigham Young University Press, 1984.

Otis, D. S. *The Dawes Act and the Allotment of Indian Land.* Norman: University of Oklahoma Press, 1973.

Ourada, Patricia K. "Dillon Seymour Myer, 1950–1953." In Robert M. Kvasnicka and Herman J. Viola, eds., *The Commissioners of Indian Affairs, 1824–1977.* Lincoln: University of Nebraska Press, 1979.

Parman, Donald L. *Indians and the American West in the Twentieth Century.* Bloomington: Indiana University Press, 1994.

———. *The Navajos and the New Deal.* New Haven: Yale University Press, 1976.

Pateman, Carole. *Participation and Democratic Theory.* Cambridge: Cambridge University Press, 1970.

Peroff, Nicholas. *Menominee Drums: Tribal Termination and Restoration, 1954–1974.* Norman: University of Oklahoma Press, 1982.

Philp, Kenneth R. "John Collier and the American Indian, 1920–1945." Ph.D. diss., Michigan State University, 1968.

———. "John Collier, 1933–1945." In Robert M. Kvasnicka and Herman J. Viola, eds., *The Commissioners of Indian Affairs, 1824–1977*. Lincoln: University of Nebraska Press, 1979.

————, comp. *Indian Self-Rule: First-Hand Accounts of Indian-White Relations from Roosevelt to Reagan*. Chicago: Howe Brothers, 1986.

Powers, Marla N. *Oglala Women: Myth, Ritual, and Reality*. Chicago: University of Chicago Press, 1986.

Prucha, Francis Paul. *The Great Father: The United States Government and the American Indians*. Lincoln: University of Nebraska Press, 1986.

Rae, Douglas. "Decision Rules and Individual Values in Constitutional Choice." *American Political Science Review* 63, no. 1 (March 1969): 40–56.

Rowe, J. P. *Geography and Natural Resources of Montana*. Missoula: Montana State University, 1941.

Spence, Clark C. *Montana: A Bicentennial History*. New York: Norton, 1978.

Spindler, George, and Louise Spindler. *Dreamers without Power: The Menomini Indians*. New York: Holt, Rinehart, and Winston, 1971.

Stern, Theodore. *The Klamath Tribe: A People and Their Reservation*. Seattle: University of Washington Press, 1965.

Taylor, Graham D. *The New Deal and American Indian Tribalism: The Administration of the Indian Reorganization Act, 1934–45*. Lincoln: University of Nebraska Press, 1980.

Walzer, Michael. *Spheres of Justice: A Defense of Pluralism and Equality*. New York: Basic Books, 1983.

Welch, James. *Fools Crow*. New York: Penguin Books, 1987.

Wessel, Thomas R. "Agriculture on the Reservations: The Case of the Blackfeet, 1885–1935." *Journal of the West* 18 (October 1979): 17–24.

————. "Political Assimilation on the Blackfoot Indian Reservation, 1887–1934: A Study in Survival." In Douglas Ubelaker and Herman Viola, eds., *Plains Indian Studies: A Collection of Essays in Honor of John C. Ewers and Waldo R. Wedel*. Washington DC: Smithsonian Institution Press, 1982.

Westbrook, Robert B. *John Dewey and American Democracy*. Ithaca: Cornell University Press, 1991.

Wheeler, Burton K., with Paul F. Healy. *Yankee from the West: The Candid, Turbulent Life Story of the Yankee-born U.S. Senator from Montana*. New York: Doubleday, 1962.

Wilson, Terry P. *The Underground Reservation: Osage Oil*. Lincoln: University of Nebraska Press, 1985.

Young, Mary E. "The Cherokee Nation: Mirror of the Republic." *American Quarterly* 33 (winter 1981): 503–24.

Government Documents

Annual Report of the Board of Indian Commissioners, Fiscal Year 1923. Washington DC: GPO, 1923.

Annual Report of the Board of Indian Commissioners, Fiscal Year 1926. Washington DC: GPO, 1926.

Annual Report of the Board of Indian Commissioners, Fiscal Year 1929. Washington DC: GPO, 1929.

Statutes at Large of the United States. Washington DC: GPO.

U.S. Department of the Interior. *Annual Report of the Secretary of the Interior*. Washington DC: GPO, 1912–56.

——— . *Decisions of the Department of the Interior*. Vol. 55. Washington DC: GPO, 1938.

——— . *Indians at Work*. Washington DC: GPO, 1933–45.

——— . *Indians in the War, 1945*. Chicago: Bureau of Indian Affairs, 1945.

——— . "Reports of the Commissioner of Indian Affairs." In *Annual Report[s] of the Secretary of the Interior*. Washington DC: GPO, 1912–56.

——— . Office of Indian Affairs. *Constitution and By-Laws for the Blackfeet Tribe of the Blackfeet Indian Reservation, Montana*. Washington DC: GPO, 1957.

——— . Office of Indian Affairs. *Corporate Charter of the Blackfeet Tribe of the Blackfeet Indian Reservation, Montana*. Washington DC: GPO, 1957.

——— . U.S. Geological Survey. *Anticlines in the Blackfeet Indian Reservation, Montana (January 2, 1917)*, by Eugene Stebinger. Bulletin 641-J. Washington DC: GPO, 1917.

——— . *Geological Report, Milk River Anticlines, Blackfoot Indian Reservation, Glacier County–Northwestern Montana (February 23, 1929)*, by E. B. Emrick. Washington DC: GPO, 1929.

U.S. Indian Claims Commission. "An Historical Analysis of the Administration of the Blackfeet Indian Reservation by the United States, 1855–1950s," by Michael F. Foley. In *The Blackfeet Tribe of Indians v. United States of America*. Washington DC: Indian Claims Commission, Docket No. 279-D, 1975.

——— . "Historical Report on the Blackfeet Reservation of Northern Montana," by Thomas R. Wessel. In *The Blackfeet Tribe of Indians v. United States of America*. Washington DC: Indian Claims Commission, Docket No. 279-D, 1975.

——— . "Management of Oil and Gas Resources on the Blackfeet Indian Reservation, 1873–1946," by J. H. Ashford and K. M. Raymond. In *The Blackfeet Tribe of Indians v. United States of America*. Washington DC: Indian Claims Commission, Docket No. 279-D, 1975.

Congressional Hearings and Reports

Congressional Record. 78th Cong., 1st sess., March 16, 1943, pp. 2098–2103.

U.S. Congress. House. *Compilation of Material relating to Indians of the United States and Alaska*. 1950. Serial No. 30.

——— . *Disposition of Surplus Lands of Blackfeet Indian Reservation, Mont.: Hear-*

ings before a Subcommittee of the Committee on Indian Affairs. 64th Cong., 1st sess., July 12, 1916.

———. *Emancipation of Indians: Hearings before the Subcommittee on Indian Affairs of the Committee on Public Lands.* 80th Cong., 1st sess., 1947. H.R. 2958, H.R. 2165, and H.R. 1113.

———. *Interior Department Appropriation Bill, 1939: Hearings before a Subcommittee of the Committee on Appropriations.* 75th Cong., 3d sess., pt. 2, 1938.

———. *Interior Department Appropriation Bill, 1939: Hearings before a Subcommittee of the Committee on Appropriations.* 75th Cong., 3d sess., pt. 2, Bureau of Indian Affairs, 1939.

———. *Interior Department Appropriations for 1952: Hearings before the Subcommittee of the Committee on Appropriations.* 82d Cong., 1st sess., pt. 1, 1951.

———. *Investigate Indian Affairs: Hearings before a Subcommittee of the Committee on Indian Affairs, Part 3, Hearings in the Field.* 78th Cong., 2d sess., 1944.

———. *An Investigation to Determine Whether the Changed Status of the Indian Requires a Revision of the Laws and Regulations affecting the American Indian.* 78th Cong., 2d sess., 1944. H. Rept. 2091.

———. *Readjustment of Indian Affairs: Hearings before the Committee on Indian Affairs.* 73d Cong., 2d sess., pt. 5, 1934.

———. *Relief of Needy Indians: Hearings before the House of Representatives Committee on Indian Affairs.* 76th Cong., 3d sess., 1940. H.R. 8937,

———. *Report with Respect to the House Resolution Authorizing the Committee on Interior and Insular Affairs to Conduct an Investigation of the Bureau of Indian Affairs.* 82d Cong., 2d sess., 1953. H. Rept. 2503.

———. *Report with Respect to the House Resolution Authorizing the Committee on Interior and Insular Affairs to Conduct an Investigation of the Bureau of Indian Affairs.* 83d Cong., 2d sess., 1954. H. Rept. 2680.

U.S. Congress. Senate. *Blackfeet Indian Reservation: Serial One, Hearings before the Joint Commission of the Congress of the United States to Investigate Indian Affairs.* 63d Cong., 2d sess., pt. 6, February 21, 1914.

———. *Blackfeet Indian Reservation: Serial Two, Hearings before the Joint Commission of the Congress of the United States to Investigate Indian Affairs.* 63d Cong., 2d sess., pt. 6-A, February 11, 1915.

———. *Hearings on S. 2755, to Grant to Indians Living under Federal Tutelage the Freedom to Organize for Purposes of Local Self-Government and Economic Enterprise.* 73d Cong., 2d sess., pt. 2, 1934.

———. *Partial Report 310,* Pursuant to S. Res. 17 extending S. Res. 79 in the 70th Cong.

———. Committee on Appropriations. *Interior Department Appropriations for 1953: Hearings before a Subcommittee of the Committee on Appropriations.* 82d Cong. 2d sess., 1952.

———. Committee on Indian Affairs. *Indian Appropriation Bill: Hearings before the Committee on Indian Affairs.* 63d Cong., 1st sess., 1913.

———. *Indian Appropriation Bill: Hearings before the Committee on Indian Affairs.* 63d Cong., 2d sess., pt. 1, March 12, 1914.

———. *Indian Appropriation Bill: Hearings before the Committee on Indian Affairs.* 64th Cong., 1st sess., February 19, 1916.

———. *Repeal of the So-Called Wheeler-Howard Act.* 75th Cong., 3d sess., August 2, 1939. S. Rept. 1047.

———. "Report of Advisors on Irrigation on Indian Reservations," by Porter J. Preston and Charles A. Engle. In *Survey of Conditions of the Indians of the United States.* 71st Cong., 2d sess., pt. 6, 1930.

———. "Report of Walter W. Liggett on Blackfeet Indian Reservation." In *Survey of Conditions of Indians of the United States: Hearings before a Subcommittee of the Committee on Indian Affairs.* 72d Cong., 1st sess., pt. 23, 1930.

———. *Surplus Lands, Blackfeet Indian Reservation, Mont.: Hearings before the Committee on Indian Affairs.* 64th Cong., 1st sess., pt. 1, April 11, 1916.

———. *Survey of Conditions among the Indians of the United States.* 78th Cong., 1st sess., 1943.

———. *Survey of Conditions of Indians of the United States: Hearings before a Subcommittee of the Committee on Indian Affairs.* 72d Cong., 1st sess., pt. 23, 1930.

———. *Survey of Conditions of the Indians in the United States: Hearings before a Subcommittee of the Committee on Indian Affairs.* 73d Cong., 1st sess., pt. 31, 1933.

———. *Survey of Conditions of the Indians in the United States: Hearings before a Subcommittee of the Committee on Indian Affairs.* 76th Cong., 1st sess., pt. 37, 1940.

———. *To Grant to Indians Living under Federal Tutelage the Freedom to Organize for Purposes of Local Self-Government and Economic Enterprise: Hearing before the Committee on Indian Affairs.* 73d Cong., 2d sess., pt. 1, 1934.

———. Committee on Labor. *Migratory Labor: Hearings before the Subcommittee on Labor and Labor-Management Relations.* 82d Cong., 2d scss., pt. 1, 1952.

———. Committee on Post Office and Civil Service. *Hearings on S. R. 41, Post Office and Civil Service Officers and Employees of the Federal Government: Hearings before the Committee on Post Office and Civil Service.* 80th Cong., 1st sess., 1947.

———. Special Committee to Study Problems of American Small Business. *Problems of Small Business: Oil Subcommittee of the Special Committee to Study Problems of American Small Business.* 80th Cong., 2d sess., pt. 36, 1948.

INDEX

Blackfeet Reservation (*cont.*)
8; and Browning District (Agency),
116–17, 139, 151–52, 159; and Heart
Butte District, 16, 35, 65, 114, 116,
124, 139, 149, 174, 186, 192, 211–12;
and Old Agency District, 16, 35,
114, 116, 128, 139, 174, 186, 211;
and Seville District, 16, 117, 128,
136, 211, 225; and Starr School community, 38, 116–18, 124, 128, 147,
152, 158, 174, 211–12

Blackfeet Strip. *See* Blackfeet Reservation

Blackfeet Tribal Business Council
(BTBC), 3, 6, 21, 28, 38, 41–42, 48,
63–64, 68–69, 71, 75, 84–85, 94–
95, 98, 103–6, 110–11, 114, 117,
119, 122, 125, 127–28, 133–36, 138–
39, 142–44, 146–47, 149–50, 152–
57, 160–61, 164, 169, 175, 177–78,
180–81, 183, 186–87, 191–93, 196,
198–99, 202, 204–8, 210, 219, 221–
48, 250, 252–53, 256–57, 259–60,
263–64, 266–68, 270–72, 274, 279–
82; audits of finances of, 159, 161–
62, 171, 231–33, 239–40; budgets
of, 143, 156, 158, 162, 171, 173, 185,
253, 256, 268, 279; elections to, 64,
116–17, 150–52, 154, 158, 161, 164–
65, 169, 172–73, 177, 191, 211, 225,
237–38, 243–44, 272, 281; founding
of, 21; meetings of, 55, 66, 79, 85,
105, 108, 137, 148, 158, 170–74,
235, 237, 261, 268; reports on, 103,
147; and termination, 87–88, 127–
28; and termination agenda, 197,
218, 224–25, 229–31, 233, 237, 251,
274, 278–79; and termination referendum, 231, 234–37, 241, 250, 252–
53, 266–68, 274, 279

Blackweasel, 109

blood quantum, 8, 88, 115, 119–23,
182, 202–3, 211–12, 255, 266; and
"blood rule," 121–22

Boeing Aircraft, 186

Bristol, R. S., 156

Brophy, William, 204–5, 215, 221–22,
227

Brott, J. H., 108, 110

Brown, James, 164

Brown, Joseph, 55, 58, 65, 73–74, 77,
83, 85–92, 96, 105–12, 114–16, 118–
19, 126, 134, 136–37, 139, 148–49,
151–52, 154, 158, 165, 186, 189,
193, 196–202, 205–8, 211, 213,
218–21, 224–25, 229, 237, 240,
250–51, 258–59, 267, 277

Browning Development Company, 69

Browning-Fertig Oil Company, 51

Browning MT, 16, 35, 132, 147, 149–
50

Browning Stock Growers' Assocation,
17

Browning War Mothers Club, 187

Bruner, Joseph, 114

BTBC. *See* Blackfeet Tribal Business
Council

Buck, Charles, 17–8, 21–23, 29, 32,
68–69

budget-investigation committee,
BTBC, 173, 179

Buffalohide, William, 162, 165, 196,
212

buffalo question, 137

Bullcalf, 57

Burd, Levi, 43, 68–70, 114–16, 119,
136, 156–57, 159, 165, 175–77, 179,
182, 208, 264

Bureau of Indian Affairs (BIA), 3, 54,
60, 62, 72, 76, 116, 138, 157, 160,
171, 176–77, 181, 183, 195, 197,
199, 205–6, 218, 221–22, 225, 233–
34, 237, 239, 241–43, 245–51, 253,
255, 260–61, 264, 266–68, 271–72,

Milton Keynes UK
Ingram Content Group UK Ltd.
UKHW011906020524
442038UK00015B/203